Opera for a New Republic
The *Zeitopern* of Krenek, Weill, and Hindemith

Studies in Musicology, No. 96

George J. Buelow, Series Editor

Professor of Music
Indiana University

Other Titles in This Series

Opera for a New Republic
The *Zeitopern* of Krenek, Weill, and Hindemith

by
Susan C. Cook

U·M·I Research Press

Ann Arbor / London

Produced and distributed by
UMI Research Press
an imprint of
University Microfilms Inc.
Ann Arbor, Michigan 48106

Library of Congress Cataloging in Publication Data

Cook, Susan C.
 Opera for a New Republic : the *Zeitopern* of Krenek, Weill, and
Hindemith / by Susan C. Cook.
  p. cm.—(Studies in musicology ; no. 96)
  Bibliography: p.
  Includes index.
  ISBN 0-8357-1811-5 (alk. paper)
  1. Opera—Germany—20th century. I. Title. II. Series.
ML1729.C66 1988
782.1'0943—dc19
                                                              87-30113
                                                                  CIP
                                                                  MN

British Library CIP data is available.

For the boys

Contents

Figures

Acknowledgments

Many individuals and institutions deserve recognition for their support of my work. Professor Glenn E. Watkins, at The University of Michigan, encouraged me from the earliest inception of this project as a paper for his seminar on the year 1927 to its present expanded form. Special thanks go to H. H. Stuckenschmidt, music critic and historian, and composer Ernst Krenek. Both allowed me to interview them concerning various aspects of my research, Professor Krenek by telephone and Mr. Stuckenschmidt during my stay in Berlin.

Other individuals who gave me access to special collections or archival holdings were Lawrence Schoenberg; Dieter Rexroth and Giselher Schubert of the Paul-Hindemith-Institut of Frankfurt am Main; Stefan Stompor, director of the East Berlin Komische Oper; Michael Richter, head of the Leipzig theater and opera houses; Brigitte Richter of the Leipzig City Museum, Alfred Schlee and Eva Smirzitz of Universal Edition in Vienna; and Kim H. Kowalke, president of The Kurt Weill Foundation for Music. European American Distributors Corporation graciously granted me permission to reproduce many musical examples, and the Interlibrary Loan Department of Middlebury College was particularly helpful in tracking down my many, and often obscure, requests.

Initial research in Germany and Austria was funded in part by a grant from The University of Michigan, Rackham School of Graduate Studies. More recently, faculty research grants from Middlebury College expedited the completion of this book.

Friends, colleagues, and students gave aid throughout the project. Elisabeth Strekalovsky deserves recognition above others. She gave up her summer to check footnotes and proofread copy, and she buoyed my spirits throughout. Finally, my husband, Timothy S. Mazur, while establishing his own career and taking primary responsibility for our son Andrew, never failed to take an active interest in my work and encourage me at every turn. And Andy, who with the wisdom of a four-year-old, always knew when I needed a break and made me take it. So it is to the both of them that I dedicate this work.

1

Introduction:
The Weimar Republic and Musical Life

The Weimar Republic: the words conjure up images of a reckless age, Berlin nightlife, decadence, artistic experimentation, economic instability, a failed democracy, and the rise of fascism. Germany in the twenties is a fascinating time; its rich cultural life has become synonymous with the modern spirit of our century. The Weimar era possessed a singularly isolated position in history, framed on one side by the First World War and on the other by a depression and a second world war. National Socialism was a by-product of the Republic and proof of its essential fragility. With all its artistic vitality, the Republic could never reconcile the pre- and postwar worlds; much of the country opposed the very spirit cultural historians now celebrate.

Sparked by the reestablishment of international contacts, the influence of new artistic and theatrical experiments, and increased public funding, Weimar musical life thrived. Composers who had begun careers before the war returned to their work, and young composers were encouraged to make their way in an age which promised new technology, new forums for experimentation, and new governmental support. Yet of all aspects of Weimar cultural life, music is perhaps the least known. Whereas the Bauhaus and the theater of Brecht are cultural household words, composers from this time—with the exception perhaps of Kurt Weill because of his collaboration with Brecht—enjoy little widespread recognition for their work in the 1920s.

Two institutions, in particular, represent the best Weimar musical life had to offer: the Krolloper and the Donaueschingen/Baden-Baden Chamber Music Festivals. The yearly summer festivals, begun in 1921 under the patronage of Prince Max Egon von Fürstenberg, provided a new forum for modern German music, especially the works of young composers. The directors, notably Paul Hindemith, chose different themes each year and these now provide a kind of encyclopedia of Weimar musical experimentation: new kinds of chamber music; chamber opera; music for mechanical instruments, for film, for radio, and for young people. The original festivals lasted until 1929, when they moved to

Berlin as the *Neue Musik Berlin* festivals. In their first nine seasons, the festivals were enormously influential and stimulated the creation of new music in keeping with the modern spirit of the age.

The establishment in 1927 of the Berlin Krolloper represented the Republic's particular support of postwar operatic life. Most historical accounts of the Weimar age single out Berlin as the innovative center of German cultural life, rivaled only by Paris as the cosmopolitan center of all Europe. Such is not the case for Berlin operatic life prior to the Krolloper. Berlin's two original opera houses, the Staatsoper unter den Linden located on the main street of Berlin (still standing today in East Berlin) and the Städtische Oper in the western suburb of Charlottenburg (destroyed during World War II, now the site of the West Berlin Deutsche Oper) provided standard operatic repertory and rarely produced modern works. The Staatsoper am Platz der Republik, or Krolloper as it was commonly called due to its location in the old Kroll theater building, was to become the "mid-wife to a new operatic age."[1] Its innovative spirit contrasted markedly with its two other competitors, and the resulting tension is symbolic of the Republic itself: governmental support for innovation tempered by widespread distrust for it in other circles.

Leo Kestenberg, the influential head of the Prussian Ministry of Culture, suggested that Otto Klemperer become the Krolloper's first director. Klemperer was offered a ten-year contract and accepted it with the stipulations that he be allowed to conduct symphonic concerts in the hall, and that he could retain Ewald Dulberg as a set designer and Hans Curjel as a separate dramatic specialist [*Dramaturg*]. The Krolloper, hailed at the time as a monumental example of the Weimar Republic's concern for culture, opened on 18 November 1927 with a production not of a twentieth-century work, but of Beethoven's *Fidelio*. But it was a Weimar *Fidelio* with stark cubist sets designed by Dulberg which led one reviewer to call the production "Fidelio on Ice."[2]

Klemperer regarded his tenure at the Krolloper as an opportunity to put new ideas of operatic reform and renewal into practice through well-rehearsed performances which combined the talents of separate set designers and dramatic advisers. The Krolloper's repertory was remarkably similar to its two Berlin competitors. What differed significantly was the treatment of its chosen works. Klemperer produced such standards of the repertory as *Le Nozze di Figaro, Der Freischütz,* and *Der fliegende Holländer*. He resurrected unknown works by Cimarosa, Gluck, Auber, and Charpentier, premiered one new opera, and staged the first Berlin performance of a handful of other modern works. Much of the negative reaction to the Krolloper had more to do with its unconventional treatment of standard repertory than with its support of modern music.

The Krolloper closed in July of 1931. Economic reasons were cited for the closure, even though the Krolloper cost much less to run than either of the other two houses. Certainly by 1931 the financial situation was severe, and most opera houses had been forced to make sizable budget cuts the year before.[3] Many critics who supported Klemperer's attempted operatic renewal maintained along with Klemperer that the closing was due to political pressure. Conservative critics and government officials claimed Klemperer's productions were leftist, if not Communist-inspired, and thus smacked of *Kulturbolschewismus,* the term coined to describe any artistic work not acceptable to the National Socialist party. Economic exigencies provided an easy excuse. The Krolloper, or *Republikoper* as its detractors called it, had become too controversial by the end of the decade, and there was no longer support for an institution which fostered republican ideals.

The Krolloper was part of an increased interest in opera during this time. Opera, throughout its history, has been marked by continuing debate over its nature, future, and need for reform. After World War I, German writers and composers were especially concerned about opera and its future. Virtually every music journal and periodical published essays by critics and composers which debated various issues—musical, historical, and social—of what was called the "opera crisis."

Even with all the concern for its future, an unprecedented number of new operas were performed in the state-supported opera houses during the twenties. Berlin music critic Alfred Einstein, surveying the accomplishments of the Republic from the vantage point of National Socialist control, designated the 1927–28 season as the climax of operatic activity.[4] That season the state and municipal opera houses premiered 60 new works. Germany then had 101 separate opera companies, and the Weimar government as a whole subsidized productions at the record amount of $15,000,000—a huge sum for the 1920s.[5] As Hans Heinsheimer, director of the Opera Department at Universal Edition, noted, "The citizens pay taxes not only for street cars . . . but for the maintenance of a cultural consciousness."[6] With financial support no longer a primary concern, smaller opera houses—notably Leipzig and Frankfurt am Main—competed with one another to obtain premieres of new works which might provide the houses with prestige.

The opera which proved to be the unexpected success of the decade was *Jonny spielt auf,* which appeared in 1927 just as the Krolloper opened and the Republic was enjoying its longest time of financial stability. Its Austrian-born composer, Ernst Krenek, was not yet 27, but he was already a recognized leader among the generation of postwar composers. His greatest rivals were Paul Hindemith and Kurt Weill, who had made names for themselves through the Donaueschingen Festivals and with their own early operas. Together all three would come to speak for Weimar musical life and operatic renewal.

Coming out of this ferment of operatic discussion and activity, *Jonny spielt auf* was recognized as something altogether new, the first of its kind: the *Zeitoper.* The English translation as "topical opera" loses much of the German essence, the genre's relationship to its age, of the *Zeitgeist,* the spirit of the time. The term probably originated as a variation of another topical creation, the *Zeitstück.*[7] *Zeitstücke* were typically literary or theatrical works set in the present, whose themes and characters were representative of the time. Music critics applied variants of the term—*Zeitopernrevue* and *Gegenwartsoper*—to *Jonny spielt auf* after its premiere, as they attempted to define its new, modern spirit.

The term was in common enough usage by 1928 that Kurt Weill, in an article for *Melos,* condemned its "transformation from concept to slogan" and its overuse through application to any work remotely influenced by modern culture.[8] Further expressions used by critics to define these operas were *Spiegel der Zeit* [mirror of the time], *Tempo der Zeit,* and *Alltäglichkeit* [everyday-ness]. Critics hailed the *Zeitoper* as an attempt to mirror or depict the age, to infuse opera with the tempo of modern culture, and to bring to the fore aspects of everyday life, all of which came about through the conscious effort by composers to find inspiration from the time in order to create a new relationship with their audience.

Today, *Zeitoper* is a term used casually and with little care for its historical or aesthetic context.[9] Writers typically mention the genre in passing, stress its topicality, its reliance on jazz idioms, and single out *Jonny spielt auf* as the epitomizing work. Based on the works and composers I have studied, I would like to put forth a more complete definition. The *Zeitoper* was firstly a comic genre and typically relied on parody, social satire, and burlesque as dramatic tools. As most writers acknowledge, *Zeitopern* were obvious expressions, even celebrations, of modern life. Composers tried to incorporate as many attributes of contemporary life into all facets of the operatic production as possible. The libretti were set in the present; characters were typically everyday people or were presented as recognizable modern stereotypes. The action takes place in locales considered either modern or everyday: office buildings, elevators, train stations, cabarets, and private family dining rooms. Along with the modern setting, composers also relied on theatrical properties of the age: characters talk on the phone, play gramophones, take pictures, and shoot movies. The staging relied on up-to-date theatrical and cinematic techniques as composers tried to depict modern life on the stage.

Although the musical component of *Zeitopern* took a variety of styles, these scores shared one important feature: the incorporation of idioms borrowed from American dance music and jazz. Composers of *Zeitopern,* many of whom were influenced by French composers and explored the use of popular music in earlier compositions, were naturally drawn, in a genre generally obsessed with modern life, to make use of musical sources which typified that era. However, jazz was also a potent political and cultural symbol. And these composers shared with the French an infatuation with America, a country which represented both political democracy and cultural modernity. The use of jazz, which was discussed in music journals of the time, also helped fulfill these composers' desire to remove distinctions between popular and art music.

The universally acknowledged *Zeitoper, Jonny spielt auf*, puts this definition into practice. The opera takes place in Europe of the 1920s, with Paris as the most important location. The characters are five modern stereotypes: a black jazz band leader (Jonny), a coquettish French maid, a withdrawn modern composer, an opera singer, and a classical violinist. Krenek makes use of parody and satire, pokes fun at the two classical musicians and the composer, and makes a central statement on current artistic life. Jonny, the purveyor of entertainment music, triumphs. The action takes place in a hotel lobby, a modern living room, a police car, and a train station. Slide projections or an animated film was required to make the police car appear to move, and special staging allowed the depiction of the train's arrival. Krenek's score utilized banjos and saxophones—instruments associated with jazz—and jazz-influenced sections of the score include a blues, tango, and shimmy.

Kurt Weill and Paul Hindemith, the other leading contributors to modern German opera before *Jonny spielt auf*, wrote *Zeitopern* too—*Der Zar lässt sich photographieren* (1928) and *Neues vom Tage* (1929) respectively. Their works, along with Krenek's, form the basis of this present study. All three composers attained notable successes early in their careers, and critics carefully watched and documented their continued development. Premieres of their works were cause for special discussion.

Of the three, Kurt Weill is perhaps the best known today because of *Die Dreigroschenoper*. He has been the subject of a major collection of essays and most recently an exhaustive catalog of his works appeared.[10] However, most studies of Weill, perhaps in order to bring him out from under Brecht's powerful shadow, treat him as a special case, as an isolated individual possessing a profound sense of the theater and the desire to create new kinds of opera and musical theater. This study provides the opportunity to view Weill in a wider context and to identify similarities of aesthetic perceptions shared by a number of young composers.

Paul Hindemith came last to *Zeitoper* with *Neues vom Tage*, although he provided an early stimulus for the genre with his *Kammermusik No. 1*, the first major German work to use jazz dance idioms. Hindemith is best known today for having taught generations of American composers while on the composition faculty of Yale from 1940 to 1953. His importance as an innovative, even iconoclastic teacher and leader was already recognized during the Weimar age through his organization of the Chamber Music Festivals and then his appointment to the Berlin Hochschule faculty in 1927 at the age of 32.

The political and economic realities which brought about the demise of the Krolloper affected Krenek, Weill, Hindemith, and the *Zeitoper*. The stable years of 1924 to 1929 brought with them a general feeling of prosperity, a renewed hope for the future of the Republic, an optimism about modern life, and the *Zeitoper*. As the economy worsened, such positive feelings towards modern life and the Republic vanished. The stock market crash of October 1929, which had greater repercussions in Germany than in the United States, brought an end to any hope of true economic recovery. Unemployment increased and exacerbated the growing discontentment with the government, a discontentment that resulted in the National Socialists' rise to power in 1933. The new leaders withdrew their financial support and then actively censored performances of modern works.

All three composers were eventually forced to leave Germany, and with them went countless other artists, writers, performers, conductors, critics, and publishers—virtually everyone who had influenced or supported *Zeitoper*. Weill and Krenek both left in 1933 soon after the formation of the National Socialist state. Weill went to Paris before settling in the United States, while Krenek returned to his native Austria and then emigrated to the United States in 1938. Hindemith remained in Berlin until 1935, but then the controversy surrounding his opera *Mathis der Maler* created an intolerable situation. Hindemith went to Switzerland and then came to the United States in 1940.

Hindemith and Krenek obtained teaching posts in American universities, while Weill composed for the Broadway stage. All three did well in the United States, although they never realized their full potential as opera composers in the way they might have—as the critics predicted in the twenties—had they been able to continue to live, work, and develop in a stable, native environment.

It has been 60 years since the premiere of *Jonny spielt auf*, yet only its remarkable popularity has been remembered. The *Zeitoper* was shortlived, and Krenek himself turned his back on it before the end of the Weimar era. To dismiss the *Zeitoper*, however, as a series of single aberrations produced by otherwise serious composers or, as some critics at the time charged, as attempts to pander to mass taste, is to ignore much of the artistic life at the time and the aims and intentions of the composers themselves. Likewise, a judgment of *Zeitoper* based solely on whether it had a lasting influence further ignores the social and political realities of the age.

Zeitoper deserves a reappraisal, if for no other reason than to account for Krenek's success. If the arts are part of intellectual and social history, then we need to at least ask *why* about such a popular success. Why did *Jonny spielt auf* succeed with both the general audience and many critics? I argue for returning to the age and exploring its surrounding social and cultural context, providing its "thick description," to use Clifford Geertz's concept. Such an exploration, I believe, will show that the *Zeitoper* was a logical manifestation of Weimar artistic life. These composers questioned the role of art and the artist in society and proposed some striking new answers. In this regard they shared ideals with concurrent artistic and dramatic trends and show how much the cultural avant-garde held in common.

What follows in the next seven chapters is a reexamination of the *Zeitoper*, or rather an excavation of its contextual layers: the surrounding discussion of an opera crisis, the aesthetics of the *Zeitoper*'s creators, the influences of concurrent artistic trends—particularly *Neue Sachlichkeit*—theatrical media, American popular culture, and the critical reception of the works involved. The *Zeitoper* emerges as a serious musical product of a divided and fragile age.

2

New Opera for a New Republic

It was a time when everything had to be questioned, everything condemned, everything conquered anew.
Hans Heinsheimer, "Youth Leaves the Vanguard"

So Hans Heinsheimer of Universal Edition described the years following the German defeat in World War I, a time first of chaos, then national self-examination and rebuilding, and always political and artistic tension. The Treaty of Versailles ended Wilhelmine rule, and for many Germans it signaled a subsequent liberation from nineteenth-century values. The establishment of the Weimar Republic provided the opportunity then, even the necessity, to search for new directions and to uncover innovative solutions to age-old problems about the nature and purpose of art.

While one segment of German society enthusiastically and often idealistically embraced anything seen as modern or republican, another faction defended and upheld its nineteenth-century heritage. These Germans gloried in the past and regarded the new republic as symbolic of an embarrassing defeat and national betrayal. Such radically opposing views, while stimulating artistic recovery and activity, also insured a crucial lack of political, social, and artistic consensus. They bred a continuing clash between republican and Wilhelmine, progressive and conservative, young and old.

In the musical world, young and old alike searched for signs of postwar renewal and rejuvenation. Young composers and critics, in particular, indulged in painstaking analyses of genres or works and produced numerous articles which sought to define the chaotic state of music and prophesy its future in the republican age. Opera received its fair share of critical dissection. Writers in music and literary journals reviewed and critiqued aspects of current opera composition and production. Titles such as "Krisis der Oper," "Die Krise im deutschen Opernschaffen" and "Gibt es eine Krise der Oper?" further demonstrate the prevailing belief that the postwar state of opera was one of uncertainty and chaos.[1]

Opernkrise became a catch-phrase used throughout the 1920s to describe a variety of problems plaguing modern opera. Writers discussed the economic condition of the Republic and its specific effect on opera, the rise of "absolute" music at the expense of dramatic, entertainment media and public sporting events which competed with opera for audiences, the impact of radio and recording technology, and technical issues of operatic production. They also suggested specific formal, stylistic, and spiritual directions that opera should take in order to survive in the postwar age.

Although most writers accepted the precarious nature of postwar opera, the causal perception of the crisis and the proffered solutions differed tremendously, again depending on the writer's age and political stance. Progressive and conservative writers on music disagreed, naturally, on their views of the nineteenth century, with young composers renouncing or denigrating romanticism. With regard to opera specifically, Richard Wagner, whose works and aesthetic had been attacked before the war as symbolic of fin-de-siècle decadence, acted as the watershed.[2] Composer Alfred Casella described the feelings of young composers after the war as "boredom with Wagner."[3] Hans Pfitzner, however, along with Erich Wolfgang Korngold and other older composers, continued to create operas in the Wagnerian mold, and Pfitzner was particularly outspoken in his condemnation of modern trends. Both the positive and negative views concerning Wagner are often naive, highly subjective, and anachronistic, given the current state of scholarship on Wagner. Rather than representing reasoned critiques of Wagner, his work, and his place in history, they aptly reflect the overall tension between the rejection or affirmation of prewar artistic values. Wagner became a symbol for many young composers of a moribund, hyperemotional past which they wished to leave behind.

One of the first indications of new postwar operatic activity occurred in 1920 with a new production of Handel's *Rodelinda* and a subsequent interest in other pre-nineteenth-century operas. This so-called Handel revival, along with a later interest in Verdi's works begun with Franz Werfel's translation of *La Forza del destino* in 1925, reflected both a shift away from Wagnerian ideals as well as a nostalgia for pre-nineteenth-century German music.

Begun as student productions at the University of Göttingen under the direction of Oskar Hagen, the Handel performances, which included productions of *Rodelinda* in the summer of 1920, *Ottone* in 1921, and *Giulio Cesare* in 1922, combined abstract or symbolist sets, found in much contemporary theater of the time, with stylized acting based on the Baroque concept of *Affekt*. For young composers, the successful Handel revival presented the paradoxical solution of looking to the past for new compositional resources and ideas. Egon Wellesz, in particular, embraced Handel and maintained that through him the music drama had been replaced and the opera crisis resolved.[4] And to varying degrees, Krenek, Weill, and Hindemith adopted clear-cut sectional forms in keeping with Handel and in opposition to a Wagnerian formal approach.

Concurrent with the Handel revival, Ferruccio Busoni (1866–1924) came to the fore as a Wagnerian antagonist and a proponent of new, non-Wagnerian directions for opera. As early as 1907, Busoni published his *Entwurf einer neuen Aesthetik der Tonkunst,* which rejected nineteenth-century programmatic trends in general and attacked Wagner in particular.[5] The second expanded edition of the work appeared in 1919. To young composers espousing boredom with Wagner, Busoni became a mentor and model. As proof of his currency with the postwar generation, *Anbruch,* the in-house organ of the Viennese music publishing company Universal Edition and a journal known for its aggressively avant-garde position throughout the 1920s, devoted a double issue to Busoni in 1921.[6]

Busoni published further essays which clarified his position on opera and his theory of *junge Klassizität.* He supported the use of absolute musical forms in opera and vehemently objected to Wagner's use of *Leitmotiv,* which he felt gave music undue abstract, subjective, and emotional connotations. Throughout his writings, Busoni voiced his singular devotion to creating a new kind of opera in opposition to music drama. "I expect in the future the opera will be the chief, that is to say the universal and one form of musical expression and content."[7]

Busoni's two early operas, *Arlecchino* and *Turandot,* patterned on *commedia dell'arte* models and premiered in 1917, provided examples of his musical aesthetic in practice. His last opera, *Doktor Faust,* finished posthumously by his student Philipp Jarnach and first performed in Dresden in 1925, served as a further model. Lazare Saminsky called it "a relief from the stodgy and artificial continuity of the Wagnerian music drama."[8] These three works further embodied Busoni's recommendations for operatic subject matter: "The opera should take possession of the supernatural or unnatural as its only proper sphere . . . in such a way that life is reflected in either a magic or a comic mirror, presenting that which is not to be found in real life."[9]

Paul Bekker (1882–1937), influential music critic for the *Frankfurter Zeitung* and dubbed by Alfred Einstein as the "foremost champion of all 'new' music,"[10] was another older voice calling for postwar change. Busoni recognized Bekker as being in sympathy with his own beliefs and wrote an open letter to the *Frankfurter Zeitung* in which he clarified his position on *junge Klassizität* in support of Bekker's controversial article "Impotenz oder Potenz," which had attacked Hans Pfitzner.[11]

As early as 1911, in his biography of Beethoven, Bekker expressed a sociological understanding of music history which became a primary theme in his later writings. In *Das deutsche Musikleben* (1916) Bekker refined this sociological concern and expressed his belief in the engendering power of the musical community.[12] His postwar work, *Kritische Zeitbilder* (1921), was especially important for its populist assertions that art no longer belonged to a well-to-do elite, but should reflect all of society. He asserted that a new society, such as was created in the Weimar Republic, required correspondingly new forms of artistic expression which would be "the truly, productive, direct incarnation of the new state. The cultural life of the community is the justification and culmination of the economic life; both need, support, and supplement one another. The 'State of Social Rights' determines the state of social art."[13] With regard to opera's musical component, Bekker called for a return to the primacy of the human voice and the creation of a new, distinctly twentieth-century singing style.

In 1924 Bekker published a lengthy study of Wagner which was translated into English in 1931 as *Richard Wagner: His Life in His Work*. Although not anti-Wagnerian, Bekker starts from the position of ridding Wagner of his mythology. He defines Wagner's aesthetic as *expressionist*—music expressing something else—and he dwells on the highly emotional nature of Wagner's music. In his conclusion to the preface, Bekker defines Wagner's historical place; Wagner is an important composer who needs to be understood, but who is clearly of the past and not to be emulated in the present age.

> Thus we may learn to love and admire Wagner and his art for the very reason that he and it already belong as it were to another planet. The light which that planet sheds upon us will help us to see our own path, for the clearer and more reverent our knowledge of the past the better shall we understand the present.[14]

As *Intendant* at the opera houses of Cassel-Basel beginning in 1925 and later at Wiesbaden, Bekker had practical experience with postwar operatic life. Later writings, such as *Wandlungen der Oper* (1934), dealt specifically with opera and its future and show Bekker's reciprocal admiration for Busoni, calling him the only member of his generation "who proceeds from a realization of opera's need for thorough remodeling."[15] He applied his sociological view of music to opera and stressed that opera must be a product of its time. "The opera is not of court origin, and has always and everywhere adapted itself to the prevailing social order."[16]

Busoni and Bekker fostered the split between old and new which characterized postwar musical life. While Busoni advocated a break with the nineteenth century and a return to older formal and structural principles, Bekker preached a sociological understanding of one's own age and a sensitivity to the needs of the larger community. Bekker's contention that art must be a product of its community proved particularly influential for Krenek. But both viewpoints were critical to the development of *Zeitoper,* which was non-Wagnerian in form and especially in subject matter. Furthermore, the love both had for opera as a special genre requiring the utmost attention and care inspired Krenek and Weill, in particular, and galvanized their determination to prove the viability of opera in the new Weimar age.

The Aesthetic Aims of Krenek, Weill, and Hindemith

Krenek, Weill, and Hindemith all betrayed their early interest in opera and music theater with compositions which were critical if not popular successes. Hindemith composed his three one-act operas, *Mörder, Hoffnung der Frauen, Das Nusch-Nuschi*, and *Sancta Susanna* (1921–22) to largely expressionist libretti by painter Oskar Kokoschka, Franz Blei, and August Stramm, respectively. His *Cardillac* (1926), with its number-opera division and contrapuntal textures, shows his interest in neo-classicism and principles inspired by the Handel revival. Hindemith retained these two features in his later works of the 1920s while aspects of the instrumentation, musical style, and libretti came to reflect the influences peculiar to *Zeitoper*.

Krenek's *Zwingburg* (1924), a "scenic cantata" on a libretto by the poet Franz Werfel, and his third opera *Orpheus und Eurydike* (1926), on another libretto by expressionist painter Oskar Kokoschka, well demonstrate his early musical style distinguished by its high degree of dissonance and a tendency towards atonality. His second opera, *Der Sprung über den Schatten* (1924), while containing nascent features of the *Zeitoper*, is a number opera and suggests Krenek's affinity with aspects of the Handel revival.

Weill's one-act work *Der Protagonist* (1920) proved to be the most successful early work of any of the three composers and culminated Weill's highly chromatic first style period. Georg Kaiser, one of the foremost expressionist playwrights, supplied the libretto for *Der Protagonist* and was Weill's collaborator for *Der Zar lässt sich photographieren*. Weill wrote a second one-act work, *Royal Palace* (1926), on a surrealist text by Ivan Goll, and the *Mahagonny-Songspiel* (1927) in collaboration with Bertolt Brecht, both of which provide evidence of his changing direction in form and subject prior to the premiere of *Der Zar*.

During the later years of the 1920s, all three composers abandoned the expressionist musical and literary influences which characterized their early dramatic works and sought new musical and literary resources which surfaced in their *Zeitopern*. Krenek and Weill both published articles which articulated their understandings of the opera crisis and elaborated on their goals as composers.[17] Weill's activity as a writer, through his position as music and theater critic for *Der deutsche Rundfunk* from 1924 to 1929, has been shown to give evidence of his changing aesthetic concerns. Krenek's importance as a writer has not been recognized, perhaps because he had no regular forum although he was a frequent contributor to *Anbruch*. His writings are especially significant as they predict his move to the *Zeitoper*. Hindemith came to writing much later. Although a few articles appeared during the 1920s and 1930s, Hindemith rarely commented upon his work until the development of his theory of composition after the Second

World War. His activities in other musical realms clarify his aesthetic position and show him to be of a similar mind with Krenek and Weill.

Although Krenek, Weill, and Hindemith were frequently discussed together in articles as the foremost representatives of the young generation, their works appeared on the same forums, and they shared friends, they appear to have had little direct contact with each other. (Hindemith and Weill did work together on *Der Lindberghflug* with Brecht for the 1929 Baden-Baden Festival with some success.) Nor did they comment directly on each others' work. Hindemith, as the older of the three and with his prestigious positions at the Berlin Hochschule and the Donaueschingen/Baden-Baden Festivals, had less cause to be concerned about his reputation. Krenek and Weill were more often compared and as they shared the same publisher, they may have felt some competition with each other, although it was not expressed directly.

Bekker and Krenek met as early as 1922, and in 1925 Krenek became Bekker's assistant in Cassel-Basel.[18] More than Krenek's composition teacher Franz Schreker, Bekker became Krenek's mentor and provided the young composer with a sounding board for his ideas. Krenek's earliest article on the state of opera, "Zum Problem der Oper," appeared in 1925 as part of a collection of essays on modern music, *Von neuer Musik,* dedicated to Ferruccio Busoni.[19] Krenek's perception of opera is reminiscent of Busoni's ideas, as he favored the rule of music over drama.

In "Musik in der Gegenwart,"[20] a talk Krenek presented to the Congress on Music and Aesthetics in 1925 (translated in its entirety in appendix B), Krenek moved away from the theoretical tone of his first essay. Krenek assessed the state of music and now proposed specific changes to rectify the overall critical situation. The essay was later published in *25 Jahre neue Musik,* a collection of articles published in celebration of the twenty-fifth anniversary of Universal Edition, contributed by critics and composers, such as Weill, Wellesz, Schoenberg, Bekker, Weissmann, and Oskar Bie. "Musik in der Gegenwart" provides evidence of Krenek's new beliefs which would produce *Jonny spielt auf* within a year.

With a sociological view reminiscent of Bekker, Krenek maintains that throughout history composers have turned to the community they served for inspiration. And as composers could only sell what their community wanted or needed, the community exercised control over musical goods. In the nineteenth century Krenek identifies a major change in this relationship. New social factors produced a rift in the musical community between supplier and consumer which gave rise to a distinction between "light" [*heiter*] and "serious" [*ernst*] music.

This rift continued, worsened, and thus had created the then current unhealthy situation of postwar central European art music. This music served only an elite musical community, an intelligentsia who enjoyed its cerebral qualities. Krenek obliquely singled out Schoenberg and his followers as the leading perpetrators of this "head-in-hands" music.

The vast majority of musical consumers, in Krenek's estimation, wanted something other than this cerebral music. They desired functional music for entertainment; more precisely, they wanted dance music. Krenek cast this desire for functional music as corresponding historically to the needs of J. S. Bach's public for his Lutheran service music. Krenek further stressed that purveyors of modern entertainment music, as was true of their counterparts in earlier eras, do not seek to create timeless, eternal works. If their music fulfills its function, it is successful.

Krenek was quick to point out that the rift he perceived between "serious" and "light" music existed only in central Europe. It was not a part of contemporary French music, which had managed to maintain a healthy relationship with its community.

> In France, there is still a certain kind of rapport between the music maker and his public. There are fairly large circles in Paris who still have a real need to hear contemporary music now and then, chiefly in the theater to be sure. The reason for this state of affairs lies in the fact that France still retains the last vestige of a homogeneous public. . . . No matter what objection some may raise against it [modern French music], it has a certain vital charm that is generally lacking in the products of Central European studio intellectualization.[21]

Krenek's perception of French culture came from personal experience while in Paris for a visit in 1924–25, which he vividly related in letters to Bekker. Describing Paris as "an enchanting city" and "unbelievable," Krenek wrote that he felt as if he had been transported to another planet.[22]

Krenek was by no means alone in his perception of a difference between French and German musical culture and in his preference for the French model. In 1922, the young critic H. H. Stuckenschmidt wrote in *Kunstblatt*, a journal of contemporary art, that whereas in Germany music was a science, in France, it was an art.[23] Stuckenschmidt further described a synthesis and solidarity within French artistic movements which were nonexistent in Germany. Writers Kurt Tucholsky (1890–1935) and Heinrich Mann (1871–1950) were also acknowledged Francophiles. Tucholsky, who worked in Paris from 1923 to 1926 as a correspondent for *Die Weltbühne* and other German newspapers, found Paris without equal and frequently extolled in his letters, poems, and essays its beauty and humanity. His 1927 travelogue, *Ein Pyrenäenbuch*, ends with a "Dank an Frankreich": "Thank you, France for letting me live in you. . . . I stand on this bridge and am again in Paris, in the real home of us all."[24]

Krenek's Parisian sojourn had enormous compositional ramifications, as will be discussed in greater detail in the chapter on his *Jonny spielt auf*. After he returned, he discussed this split between Central European and French music cultures in a number of articles, and it became the central theme of *Jonny spielt auf* with the confrontation between the serious studio musician, Max, and the triumphant purveyor of entertainment music, Jonny.[25]

At the end of his essay "Musik in der Gegenwart," Krenek addressed the subject of German opera directly and made specific recommendations for its future development. Similar to Busoni's call for libretti reflecting life in magic or comic mirrors, Krenek stressed the need to find libretti which had a psychological impact and relied on common cultural denominators. Krenek likened such common denominators—"character types, facts, situations and data"—to the mythology which served as the basis for Greek drama.[26]

Krenek's conclusion summarized his new philosophical and aesthetic stance, which ultimately gave birth to the *Zeitoper:*

> We want to live, look life in the face and say yes to it with a passionate heart. Then we will suddenly have art and not know how it happened. Art should never serve to express our lack of this or that, but should always flow out of the abundance of life; then it will be right and out of the reach of all our muddlings.[27]

Thus with his emphasis on facing up to the realities of life, reliance on well-known character types, and rejecting timeless art, Krenek created *Jonny spielt auf* to heal the rift in the German musical community and provide a new direction for postwar opera.

Following the successful premiere of *Jonny spielt auf* in 1927, Krenek's "'Materialbestimmtheit' der Oper," appeared in a special opera issue of *Anbruch.*[28] Indicative of the general concern for opera, editor Paul Stefan stated that the issue represented his long held wish to deal with the problem or problems of modern opera. As would be expected in a journal with an avant-garde identity, most of the contributions reflected a post-Wagnerian stance as in Stefan's introduction, "Die Oper nach Wagner," or critic Paul Pisk's call for opera written for the proletariat.[29]

"'Materialbestimmtheit' der Oper" acts as an apology for and further explanation of the artistic reasoning behind *Jonny spielt auf*. Krenek expounds upon the logical necessity of turning to modern jazz dances for germinal material as he did in *Jonny spielt auf*. "It is completely clear, that this emphasis on the dance will lead the composer, if he wants to realize the given possibilities of a scene with the conventions of the day, to the use of models of contemporary dance. No one will question their society-engendering power which we experience every day."[30] In his conclusion, Krenek restated his personal commitment to modern opera even in the face of "the hindrance of countless non-musical factors."

Krenek published a second article in 1927 which further defined his aesthetic. In "Über Sinn und Zweck des Theaters" he passionately condemns a view of theater and opera as purely pedagogic or moral institutions and attacks the prevalent notion that a dramatic work which provided pleasure could not be "serious" or worthwhile.[31] In answer to critics who found *Jonny spielt auf* "too entertaining," Krenek countered: "Isn't pleasure a part of life and a necessity of life which we need as much as our daily bread?"[32]

Anbruch published a second opera issue in 1929, and Krenek provided the opening essay, "Opernerfahrung" [the operatic experience].[33] Even though it had been just two years since the premiere of *Jonny spielt auf,* significant changes had taken place in Weimar political and social life. And some of the optimism expressed by progressives had begun to wane in the face of continuing economic and political problems. Krenek's three one-act operas, of which *Das geheime Königreich* and *Schwergewicht* contain features of the *Zeitoper,* had received their premiere in 1928. And more importantly by this time, he had begun work on *Leben des Orest,* in which he moved away from the topicality of the *Zeitoper.* "Opernerfahrung" correspondingly shows Krenek's retreat to a more traditional conception of opera and a softening of his *Zeitoper* aesthetic. He states now that the *Aktualität* or topical relevance of the subject matter is not important as long as the plot has a passionate nature or *Leidenschaftlichkeit* and possesses attendant music which is direct and *aktuell.* Krenek does not state specifically whether this *relevant* music should rely on dance idioms, as he recommended in earlier essays.

Krenek's last essay on opera until after World War II, "Zur Situation der Oper," appeared in the Prague contemporary music journal *Auftakt* in 1932.[34] By this time Krenek was at work on *Karl V,* a self-described grand opera finished by 1935, whose premiere was delayed by political pressure until 1938 by which time Krenek had fled Germany. Krenek makes his only mention of Weill in this essay and then in reference to Brecht's theories, which he judged deficient along with Weill's music. In this final essay, Krenek called for opera to fulfill an identifiable spiritual [*geistige*] function, a radical departure from earlier essays which stressed entertainment and usefulness as primary functions.

Weill did not have Krenek's influential experience with French culture, but his affiliation with the *Novembergruppe* provided a similar stimulus for questioning presumptions about German art. The *Novembergruppe* began in December of 1918 and took its name from the month in which the German revolution took place. Initially the group consisted of artists dedicated to creating new art for the German citizenry. To this end they sought to revolutionize schooling, museum management, public exhibitions, and to redefine the nature of art, preaching "the art of the people and the people, through handicrafts, to art."[35]

Founding members of the *Novembergruppe* included architect Erich Mendelsohn and artists Max Pechstein and Wieland Schmied, who were also associated with *Neue Sachlichkeit,* a broader artistic trend discussed in the following chapter. Weill joined the loosely knit artistic collective in 1922, along with Stuckenschmidt and composers Heinz Tiessen and Max Butting, who led the collective's music division until 1926. Later composer members included Busoni's students Philipp Jarnach and Vladimir Vogel, Hanns Eisler, Felix Petyrek, Stefan Wolpe, and the American George Antheil, who joined after his Berlin piano debut in 1922. Stuckenschmidt noted that the composers who belonged did not share a common musical style, but rather held a common artistic ideology.[36]

As the visual artists held exhibitions, so the music division of the *Novembergruppe* sponsored regular concerts or *Abende* of modern music, as many as three or four a year between 1922 and 1931. The concerts typically featured compositions for chamber ensemble, voice and piano, and solo piano, by member composers as well as other young German, East European, American, and French composers. Krenek, Weill, and Hindemith all had works performed on *Novembergruppe Abende*.

Although Krenek was not an acknowledged member, other Schreker students were and Eduard Erdmann, his close friend, performed on events. Bekker was affiliated with the group as well, and their private press published his *Wesensform der Musik* in 1925. Krenek would certainly have known of their aims through Bekker, and their ideals may well have influenced his own thinking. Certainly there was a shared concern for creating new music for a new age. For Weill, the *Novembergruppe* gave him the opportunity to associate with others who shared his admiration for Busoni and who sought to change postwar music.

Weill's essays, which appeared as early as 1925 and in a wide variety of journals and newspapers, expressed his desire for new aesthetic bases for opera and show the influence of Busoni's thought. From 1927 on, as Weill explored *Zeitoper* and began to work with Bertolt Brecht, his essays take on a greater sociological emphasis in keeping with issues addressed by Bekker, Krenek, and the *Novembergruppe*.

Weill was represented in Universal Edition's *25 Jahre neue Musik,* in which Krenek published "Musik in der Gegenwart," with an article "Bekenntnis [commitment] zur Oper" which bespoke the dedication to the genre fostered by Busoni and Bekker.[37] Weill echoed Busoni further in claiming to have found inspiration not in Wagner but in Mozart, a composer whom they both revered. "Die neue Oper," a broader discussion of the state of the opera, appeared the following year. In it Weill described the postwar shift away from Wagner, which had had unforeseen disastrous results for opera as a genre. "People looked on opera somewhat scornfully as an inferior genre, for they thought only of music drama, from which they wanted to escape."[38] This scornful treatment of opera thus necessitated the declaration of renewed devotion on the part of Weill and other young composers.

Weill singled out two works as representing contrasting trends in postwar opera: Alban Berg's *Wozzeck* as a twentieth-century culmination of Wagner and

Busoni's *Doktor Faust* as "the starting point for the formation of a golden age of 'opera' (in contrast to 'music drama')."[39] Weill repeated such extravagant praise for his teacher and *Doktor Faust* in other essays.[40] Unlike Krenek, Weill declined to make any further recommendations about opera in the future and instead concluded that "we know little of what tomorrow will bring."

The very title of Weill's 1927 article, "Verschiebungen [shifts] in der musikalischen Produktion," reflects his change of orientation and willingness to make specific recommendations.[41] Weill called for musical theater to go in a new direction in order to attract a wider audience. The year for this shift of emphasis, 1927, corresponds to the overall change in the musical atmosphere expressed by other writers and witnessed in the birth of the *Zeitoper* with the premiere of *Jonny spielt auf*. By this time, Weill had finished *Royal Palace,* an opera with latent features of the *Zeitoper,* and was already at work on his *Zeitoper Der Zar lässt sich photographieren.*

In this essay Weill's perceptions about the current state of music echo those of Krenek. Weill, too, perceived a tension between modern composers, between those who remained apart from their audience—Krenek's head-in-hand composers—and those "who take up an association with any audience . . . [who believe] there is a general human consciousness that springs from a social feeling of some kind and that this must determine the formation of an art work."[42] Weill also credited the French with leading the search for a community-based art, although he felt that Germany had begun to lose its taste for *gesellschaftliche* or socially exclusive arts. Weill, as did Krenek, aligned himself with the French breed of composer. He also acknowledged the potent possibilities of film, which he used in *Royal Palace,* and new mechanical instruments, which Hindemith later explored. To conclude, Weill discussed his own attempt to create a *gemeinschaftsbildende* or community-engendering art through his work with Brecht on epic opera.

Here, in 1927, Weill stated his belief in an art with direct connections to its engendering community, a belief shared by Krenek and which was at the heart of the *Zeitoper*. By 1928, Weill rebelled against the use of the term *Zeitoper* for his works, no doubt because he already saw his formulation of the epic opera with Brecht as something broader and more in keeping with the spirit of Busoni's *Doktor Faust*. Weill's 1928 open letter, "Zeitoper," written in answer to a request by the editors of *Melos,* shows his skepticism for a term which suffered from overuse.[43] Thus Weill distanced his work from an aesthetic which could embody topicality at any price without a true commitment to change, while restating his concern, shared by Krenek, for purging the arts of their exclusivity.

Weill's definition here of *Zeitoper* related it to *Zeitstücke,* works which brought "superficial manifestations of life in our time onto center stage." Even with the addition of a "rhythm of our time," Weill maintained that such works still occupied themselves with past ideas, no matter how up-to-date their outward trappings might be. Weill did not condemn *Zeitspiegel* [mirrors of the time], as found in the *Zeittheater* of Erwin Piscator. Piscator, with whom Weill worked, utilized new staging techniques to document the present situation, and his theatrical experiments influenced Krenek, Hindemith and other composers of *Zeitoper* as well. It is also possible that Weill meant this open letter as a response to Krenek's *Jonny,* which competed with *Royal Palace.* Weill could thus dismiss *Jonny spielt auf* as a *Zeitstück* in favor of his own works which were *Zeitspiegel.*

Weill, too, wrote about the influence of jazz and popular dance music on concert music. An early discussion of dance music appeared in 1926, and in 1929 *Anbruch* published his "Notiz zum Jazz," a lengthier endorsement of jazz and its positive influence.[44] Weill, showing evidence of his knowledge and appreciation, focused on the performance practice of jazz as well as the peculiar rhythms, harmonies, and instrumentation. Singling out the eagerness, devotion, ability to improvise, freedom to interpret, and overall talent of most jazz performers, Weill held them up as models for all musicians, not unlike Krenek did with his choice of the hero Jonny in *Jonny spielt auf.*

In the absence of published essays, Hindemith's activities prior to the composition of *Neues vom Tage* demonstrate a preoccupation with the direction of new music shared by Krenek and Weill. In 1924 Hindemith replaced Erdmann on the three-member jury of the Donaueschingen Chamber Music Festival. This annual festival, which moved to fashionable Baden-Baden in 1927, along with many similar events sponsored by other groups and even cities, attests to the lively and active musical life of the Weimar Republic. As a forum specifically for chamber music rather than the symphonic repertory associated with the nineteenth century, the festival further identified itself as a forum for the progressive, avant-garde, even republican, as its detractors would later maintain, music of Germany's young composers. Krenek, Weill, and Hindemith frequently contributed works to festival programs, along with other composers then establishing themselves.

Hindemith earned early notoriety with the premiere of his *Kammermusik No.1* on the 1922 festival. Although Hindemith never published an essay on jazz, his *Kammermusik No.1,* with its celebrated foxtrot finale, demonstrates his personal interest in using popular music idioms before either Krenek or Weill. After joining the jury, Hindemith became the "the God of Donaueschingen" and its guiding force and used it as a forum for his own particular interests—film music, music for mechanical instruments, chamber opera, *Lehrstücke* and other kinds of didactic works.[45]

In 1926, Hindemith met Fritz Jöde and subsequently became an active participant in Jöde's *Jugendmusikbewegung.* This movement preached a kind of music education and musical involvement for young people, and these interests showed up in later festivals as well as in Hindemith's *Sing- und Spielmusik.* In composing works for school groups or amateur performers, for mechanical instruments, or as accompaniments for film or radio broadcasts, Hindemith advocated a new practical approach to music which was generally referred to under the loose rubric of *Gebrauchsmusik,* or "music for use," although Hindemith preferred *Sing- und Spielmusik.* The term *Gebrauchsmusik,* coined in 1925 by Heinrich Bessler, carried with it the ideals of practicality, usefulness, relevance, didacticism and utilization of modern technology.[46] Writers also noted that models for such useful, functional music could be found prior to the nineteenth century.[47]

Krenek, Weill, and Hindemith all criticized the overuse of the term *Gebrauchsmusik* and the extremes to which some composers took the concept, but *Gebrauchsmusik* certainly partook of the same artistic aesthetic which spawned the *Zeitoper.*[48] In all its forms, *Gebrauchsmusik* reflects the optimistic view of modern life and technology shared by *Zeitoper.* Composers of *Gebrauchsmusik* further recognized the gulf between composer and community. Both the *Zeitoper* and *Gebrauchsmusik* sought to remedy this situation by creating music for the modern musical consumer.

Hindemith experimented first, in 1926, with works for mechanical instruments, player piano and organ, and film music. By 1927, he was teaching at the Berlin Hochschule für Musik and had established a radio technology department. His *Schulwerk des Instrumental-Zusammenspiels,* op. 44, published by Schott in 1927 as part of a series of *Gemeinschaftsmusik für Jugend und Haus,* represents the didactic side of *Gebrauchsmusik,* influenced by Hindemith's work with the *Jugendmusikbewegung.* Fritz Jöde served as editor of the Schott series and participated in a number of festivals. The years of these first experiments, 1926–27, correspond with Krenek and Weill's philosophical shifts as articulated in their essays and reproduced in their *Zeitopern.* And Schott's term—*Gemeinschaftsmusik*—echoes the audience-expanding sentiments of Krenek and Weill's essays from this time as well.

Hindemith's visible role with the festivals and self-proclaimed support for *Gemeinschaftsmusik* brought him recognition as the leading figure in a drive to reconcile modern music with the modern audience, to create music which fit the new demands of the time, and to coordinate life and art.[49] In one of his few essays from the time, "Über Musikkritik," Hindemith gave his view on community and public. "What concerns all of us is this: The old public is dying off. How and what must we write in order to get a larger, different, and new public; where is that public?"[50]

Between 1924 and 1926, Krenek, Weill, and Hindemith all demonstrated in either essays or compositions similar concerns for establishing new, useful relationships with a modern, larger audience. They also sought to put these ideas about music into practice through opera, a genre which needed to be reclaimed in the postwar age and a genre they already loved and for which they wanted to create a new audience. Such was the aesthetic basis for the *Zeitoper,* a new breed of opera for a new age.

Further Critical Commentary

Reviews of *Zeitopern,* both for and against, recognized the aim of the composers to bring opera into line with the realities of modern society and to close the gap between "serious" and "popular" music. These reviews also indicate the continuing debate concerning opera and postwar music in general. Distinguished Berlin critic Adolf Weissmann, known for his enthusiastic support of modern music, wrote just months after the premiere of *Jonny spielt auf* that in the opera Krenek revealed himself to be a "musician who understands his time," and concluded that such modern operatic experiments were "a definite reflection of the *Zeitgeist,* and for that reason of the greatest musical significance."[51]

Critic Hans Mersmann in "Probleme der gegenwärtigen Operndichtung," from *Anbruch*'s 1927 opera issue, compared Hindemith's *Cardillac* (1926) and *Jonny spielt auf* as operas which demonstrated contrasting compositional approaches.[52] Mersmann described *Jonny spielt auf* as "a drama throbbing throughout with the tempo of our time, employing all accompanying means of expression."[53] Mersmann pointed out that Krenek supplied up-to-date language for his libretto, thereby identifying himself with his society. In *Cardillac,* Hindemith, on the contrary, chose a libretto which in its old-fashioned story distanced itself from modern life. Hindemith would change in 1928 with *Hin und zurück.*

Other critics shared Mersmann's identification of the "tempo of our time" as a hallmark of *Jonny spielt auf* and the *Zeitoper* along with a related notion of *Zeitoper* as *Spiegel der Zeit,* a concept already described in Weill's essay "*Zeitoper.*" Leipzig critic Adolf Aber credited Krenek with introducing "das Tempo der Zeit" into opera and thus taking "a decisive step forward on the road to genuine opera of our time."[54] This catch-phrase, combining *Tempo* with its meaning of speed, fast-paced modern urban life, new jazz tempi and rhythms, and the multifarious connotations of *Zeit,* became a commonly applied description for not only *Zeitopern* but other choral and instrumental works identified as commenting on modern life.[55]

Kurt Westphal further defined the documentary nature of the *Zeitoper* as implied by the phrase *Spiegel der Zeit.*[56] Writing for an issue of the *Blätter der Staatsoper und der Städtischen Oper* in honor of the Berlin premiere of *Der Zar,* Westphal pointed out how Krenek, Weill, and Hindemith drew upon aspects of modern culture: film, the revue, and *Kabarett.* The composers further showed their understanding of the 1920s as a technical age, by relying on automobiles, trains, and radios as stage properties. Siegfried Günther in "Gegenwartsoper," published a year later, echoed Westphal's positive assessment.[57] He further noted that the works of Krenek, Weill, and Hindemith made use of jazz as an "utterance of life" in their aim to bring aspects of modern life into their operas.

Hans Curjel, Klemperer's *Chefdramaturg* at the Krolloper, in an article published in *Die Blätter der Staatsoper* for the premiere of *Neues vom Tage* in

1929, described another related feature of the *Zeitoper*, its grounding in *Alltäglichkeit*, or "everyday-ness."[58] He first described the postwar sobering-up process which occurred as a reaction to nineteenth-century excesses. *Zeitopern*, as part of the sobering up, not only dealt with modern society, but singled out the day-to-day common features of life as worthy of artistic treatment. Curjel underscored the communal nature inherent in *Alltäglichkeit*. "A work should fulfill a definite purpose for the listener or viewer. In a new sense, the work is created for the customer."[59] In closing, Curjel made it clear that while reveling in the everyday, the *Zeitoper* and other works infused with *Alltäglichkeit* possessed true artistic significance. "Matter-of-factness is the principle, *Alltäglichkeit* is the substance of their formal representation. The result is a highly complex, functional, polished art work, which with all its bright and alluring appearance, possesses all the profundity or even shallowness of pure art."[60]

Curjel's article summarizes many of the ideas already expressed concerning the opera crisis and the aims of *Zeitoper*. In subject matter, the glorification of the everyday and timeliness was in complete opposition to Wagnerian music drama, which purposefully chose timeless themes. *Alltäglichkeit* also incorporated the importance of the community and the direct and supposedly healthier relationship of the artist and public. The aesthetic of *Alltäglichkeit* was not peculiar to the *Zeitoper* or music, but was shared by many postwar artists, such as those belonging to *Novembergruppe* and *Die neue Sachlichkeit*. *Zeitoper* was thus a musical and operatic manifestation of a widely held artistic belief.

Zeitoper and its attendant cultural context had many bitter opponents within that segment of German society which upheld prewar cultural values. The controversial issue, aside from its general anti-Wagner ideology, was the *Zeitoper*'s topicality, its *Alltäglichkeit,* and how this topicality came to life on the stage. In the context of the opera crisis, these critics claimed that rather than providing a solution, *Zeitopern* were symptomatic of the continuing crisis and exacerbated opera's already precarious position.

Hermann von Waltershausen suggested in "Die Krise der zeitgenössichen deutschen Oper," published in the *Schweizerische Musikzeitung und Sängerblatt,* that much of the anti-Wagnerian rhetoric was politically rather than artistically motivated.[61] In contrast to *Jonny spielt auf,* whose turbulent Munich premiere prompted the article, Waltershausen called for opera to break away from a self-conscious interest in the everyday. Instead, modern opera should strive toward loftier goals in keeping with Waltershausen's perception of the Wagnerian spirit.

Julius Kapp, employed by the Staatsoper, the most conservative of Berlin's three opera houses, also wrote for the *Blätter der Staatsoper* and provided a conservative viewpoint in opposition to Hans Curjel and others associated with the Krolloper. In his 1929 article "Gibt es eine Krise der Oper?," Kapp flatly denied the existence of an opera crisis.[62] He claimed that the reduction in opera attendance, often used as evidence of a crisis, resulted from a variety of factors, none of which was serious. Kapp decried the attempts by modern composers associated with "the post-Wagnerian chaos" to fill opera houses through the use of cheap theatrical effects, a criticism clearly aimed at *Zeitopern*. He maintained that audiences did not want to see the problems of the day dealt with on the opera stage. Instead, most people attended opera as an escape from the realities of life.

Fritz Ohrmann also took issue with Curjel's point of view concerning *Zeitoper* and specifically *Neues vom Tage*.[63] In his rebuttal, "Triumph der Alltäglichkeit," Ohrmann attacked both the notion of *Alltäglichkeit* as a worthy artistic pursuit and Curjel's assumption that such an aesthetic position had triumphed at all. Reflecting the view of many opponents of *Zeitoper*, Ohrmann faulted Hindemith and others for catering to the present at the expense of creating eternal works of art.

In 1930, as the third article in a three-part series entitled "Zeitfragen des Operntheaters," published in the *Zeitschrift für Musik*, Hans Tessmer wrote "Die Oper am Scheidewege" [opera at the crossroads].[64] Tessmer, unlike Kapp, acknowledged the presence of an opera crisis and the uncertainty of opera's future. Tessmer divided the postwar group of successful opera composers into inferior imitators [*Epigonen*] and experimenters [*Experimentatoren*]. The imitators merely copied the models of Wagner, Italian *Verismo, Märchenoper* or Strauss. The experimenters, Tessmer claimed, though possessing much talent, searched for a renewal of operatic concepts while discrediting works in the Wagnerian mold. Tessmer recognized Busoni as their leader and found fault with most of the young experimenters, including Weill, Krenek, and Hindemith, either for their overly literary approach or for their excessive "up-to-date-ness" [*Zeitgemässheit*]. Neither approach provided a suitable basis for creating historically meaningful opera. Tessmer's solution to the crisis was to look for the arrival of a second Verdi who, in true Wagnerian fashion, would redeem contemporary opera.

Karl Lüthge's "Musik in der Gegenwart," from 1930, presents a balanced criticism of many postwar trends including *Zeitoper* and *Gebrauchsmusik*.[65] Although the article appeared in the conservative journal *Signale für die musikalische Welt*, it is devoid of the rancorous name-calling which characterized many essays and reviews from this and other periodicals. Lüthge presented his own prescription for contemporary music; it should be lively [*lebendig*] and have as its aims reality [*Wirklichkeit*], liveliness [*Lebendigkeit*], and soundness or *Gesundheit*.

Lüthge found much contemporary music to have been unduly influenced by the machine age, and he pointed to the "orgiastic-gymnastic" quality of jazz and virtuosic piano performances as evidence of this mentality. His ideal of *Lebendigkeit* did not incorporate *Aktualität* [relevance], which existed in the outward aspects of music without providing a vital inner spirit. Lüthge cited

Jonny spielt auf and *Neues vom Tage* as examples of works which sensational-
ized the concept of *Aktualität*. He acknowledged the legitimate concerns about
the future of modern music, and agreed that *Gebrauchsmusik* afforded a way out
of the perceived isolation of new music. But *Gebrauchsmusik*, in Lüthge's mind,
represented too great a compromise between art and entertainment music and
produced results of dubious quality. Lüthge proposed another solution: the
creation of a new music, a *Zusammenklang* [harmonization] of "down-to-earth"
and other-worldly qualities.

During 1930–33, as *Zeitoper* waned and the Weimar Republic struggled to
survive, the discussion of opera continued. But the changing political climate
polarized progressive and conservative opinion. Critics and composers who
formerly supported the *Zeitoper* now despaired over opera's worsening condition
caused by continued economic, social, and political upheaval. They lamented
that none of the experiments in the 1920s had proved to be viable or permanent
solutions to the crisis of postwar opera.[66]

At the same time, conservative critics, many of whom had already objected
to experiments on political grounds, became even more inflammatory in their
call to return to nineteenth-century traditions. Hans Tessmer, author of the 1930
article "Oper am Scheideweg," held an important position at the Berlin
Städtische Oper by 1933. His "Hat die deutsche Oper eine Zukunft?" demonstrates the anti-Semitic tone of these later reviews and articles.[67] Tessmer now
blamed the opera crisis on composers—aided by Jewish intellectuals, publishers
and critics—who sought to overintellectualize opera without regard for the
German people. In answer to his own question, Tessmer prophesied that in Adolf
Hitler's Germany, opera had a future.

Ultimately, only the demise of the Weimar Republic itself resolved the
crisis of postwar opera. The pro-Wagnerian position of the conservative musical
establishment triumphed to the detriment of Wagner, whose works became tools
of propaganda for the National Socialists. In 1933 many opera houses celebrated
the fiftieth anniversary of Wagner's death, and the National Socialists, who had
gained considerable strength with Hitler's appointment as chancellor in January
of that same year, seized these musical celebrations as a chance to characterize
Wagner as an artistic prophet of their movement and to discredit further any
remaining *republican* musical trends. After 1933, the National Socialists
effectively controlled the music press and the opera houses. And although critics
and composers spoke against this control, they were unsuccessful to say the
least.[68] Further musical experimentation came to a halt except within prescribed
guidelines.

These articles and the activities of Krenek, Weill, and Hindemith show the
broad spectrum of operatic discussion in the 1920s and early 1930s, produced in
a time of feverish activity. This activity was marked by divergent opinions

concerning the nature of opera, the existence of an opera crisis, and suggestions for opera's further development. Opera composers were required to justify their aims as progressives or conservatives, as Wagnerians or anti-Wagnerians.

This self-conscious desire to explore, renew, and create a place for opera in a modern republican age spawned the *Zeitoper,* the product of postwar composers "swollen with new hopes" for the future, to borrow from another one of Weill's essays.[69] All too painfully aware of what had happened to prewar German eternal values, these young composers chose not to write for the future, but instead sought to minister to the here and now. In order to bring their works into line with modern culture, these young composers turned to other arts of the time, and in doing so, they found much inspiration in literature, theater, popular entertainment, and especially in American jazz.

3

Neue Sachlichkeit and *Zeittheater:*
The *Zeitoper* and Concurrent Artistic Trends

Composers and critics justified the creation of the *Zeitoper* on aesthetic grounds as a solution to the perceived crisis of opera. Much of this new ground, in its negation of the past, concern for a new audience, and in partaking of the everyday, reflects larger concurrent artistic trends. Thus the *Zeitoper* emerges as a musical manifestation of a spirit which permeated German cultural life. In the visual arts and architecture, the number of new journals and public exhibitions well attest to a postwar resurgence of activity and to similar concerns, as in music, with finding new directions and solutions. As seen already in Weill's membership in *Die Novembergruppe,* artists and musicians could work together to realize shared goals.

Die *Novembergruppe* was just one of a number of postwar artistic collectives. Other groups, whose membership often overlapped depending on time and place, included the shortlived Utopian visionaries of *Die gläserne Kette* and the *Arbeitsrat für Kunst,* which had much in common with the goals of *Die Novembergruppe.* Most famous of all Weimar artistic institutions was the Bauhaus, which Walter Gropius opened in 1919. Architects associated with the New Architecture or *Neues Bauen* also partook of a similar vision. As H. H. Stuckenschmidt cautioned in his discussion of *Die Novembergruppe,* however, artists and architects often shared aims and visions without necessarily sharing, or even approving of, each other's individual means.[1]

One trend which developed during the 1920s and exercised a powerful influence on music as well as art was *Die Neue Sachlichkeit.*[2] Commonly translated as "the new objectivity," the term in German also carries notions of sobriety, detachment, and unemotional matter-of-factness, which were part of its artistic style, while a commitment to everyday life characterized its subject matter. Gustav Friedrich Hartlaub, director of the Mannheim Kunsthalle Museum, coined the term in 1923 in his announcement of an intended exhibition. He described the art in the exhibition as neither "impressionistically dissolved" nor "expressionistically abstract"; rather these works of *Neue Sachlichkeit* remained "loyal" or "rediscovered their loyalty to a positively tangible reality."[3] Hartlaub's Mannheim exhibition, *"Neue Sachlichkeit:* Deutsche Malerei seit dem Expressionismus," finally opened in 1925.

The artists presented in the show, Otto Dix, George Grosz, and Max Beckmann, and others who later were associated with *Neue Sachlichkeit* such as Christian Schad, Rudolf Schlichter, and Karl Hubbeck, had connections with the prewar expressionist movement. Some of these artists had experimented first with dada; others were also members of the *Novembergruppe* or had their works shown in exhibitions sponsored by the collective. *Neue Sachlichkeit* came to identify a change in their art works of the twenties, defining a new kind of realism which marked a dramatic "renunciation of Expressionism."[4]

While personal introspection and the subjective experience of the artist characterized expressionism, the spirit of *Neue Sachlichkeit* deemphasized artistic individuality and focused instead on a visible, objective reality.[5] The typical subject matter of *Neue Sachlichkeit* art demonstrates a "radical commitment to the modern environment and everyday life," as artists recorded activities and occurrences from their own experiences or those shared by their viewers.[6] Portraiture was especially popular. Subjects look out from the canvas in a detached, unemotional way, the everyday objects representative of their employment or lifestyle surrounding them. Christian Schad, who produced a great number of portraits, painted various Weimar celebrities with a sharply linear realism. But anonymous Weimar citizens—waiters, teachers, prostitutes—also figured prominently as portrait subjects, again reflecting an interest in recording the lives of ordinary people.

The style of *Neue Sachlichkeit* art was characterized by greater realism and a concern with replicating the visual experience. Many artists favored pen and ink or pencil, which allowed greater control and precision. This careful attention to detail produced a clarity or sobriety, again in marked contrast to the emotionalism of most expressionist art. Their works also lacked the heavy coloristic and emotional symbolism common to expressionism. H. Wieynck, writing in a photography journal in 1926, summed up the special quality of *Neue Sachlichkeit* art: "Photography, generally speaking, no longer imitates art, but rather art imitates photography."[7]

Left- and right-wing factions existed within the loosely connected movement. In general, right-wing artists, often referred to under the subcategory of *Magischer Realismus,* produced works with no overt political content. Artists associated with the left-wing or *Verist* faction created works directly influenced by their social or political beliefs. Through the choice of subject matter, *Verist* painters recorded their feelings about Weimar society, their concern for war veterans, and for the common and unknown victims of inflation, unemployment, and overindustrialization.

A corollary to the *Neue Sachlichkeit* in art was the simultaneous development of a "new vision" in photography. Advancements in camera design and technology, coupled with a greater use of photography in advertising and industry, created an interest in this medium during the 1920s, and photography came to be accepted as a legitimate art form. Some photographers, such as John Heartfield in his photomontages or Bauhaus teacher Laszlo Moholy-Nagy who experimented with light-sensitive paper to create *Photograms,* used the camera to produce fantastic and highly illusionary images less a part of *Neue Sachlichkeit.* But other photographers, especially Albert Renger-Patsch, created works in keeping with the style, subject matter, and philosophy of *Neue Sachlichkeit.*[8] While utilizing new camera techniques such as stop-action shooting, extreme close-ups, and unusual camera angles, photographers such as Renger-Patsch aimed their cameras at common subjects. *Neue Sachlichkeit* photographers chose images from everyday life—staircases, discarded toys, dishes—but captured them in such a way as to highlight the beauty or detail in otherwise unspectacular objects.

Photographic portraiture was popular as well, and portraitists, such as Berliner Lotte Jacobi, photographed famous and lesser known personalities of Weimar society with a starkness and lack of sentimentality in keeping with *Neue Sachlichkeit.* Gustav Stotz, director of the important "Film und Foto" exhibit of 1929 which chronicled many of the advancements in photography of the decade, summed up the new photographic vision:

> A new optic has developed. We see things differently now, without painterly intent in the impressionistic sense. Today things are important that earlier were hardly noticed: for example shoe lasts, gutters, spools of thread, fabrics, machines, etc. They interest us for their material substance, for the simple quality of the thing-in-itself.[9]

The term *Neue Sachlichkeit,* with its general meaning of commitment to the present and detached, matter-of-fact treatment, was borrowed by writers and critics and applied to literature and music. Young writers, many of whom were associated with the *Kabarett,* had their literary works of the 1920s described as in keeping with the spirit of the *Neue Sachlichkeit* vision. Erich Kästner (1899–1975), a novelist, poet, contributor to the famous Weimar literary journal *Die Weltbühne,* and a writer for many *Kabaretts,* was a leading figure in literary *Neue Sachlichkeit.* Other contributors to both *Die Weltbühne* and to Weimar *Kabaretts,* such as Kurt Tucholsky (1890–1935), Bertolt Brecht (1898–1956) and Walter Mehring (b. 1896), could likewise be numbered within the ranks of contributors to literary *Neue Sachlichkeit.*

As artists of the *Neue Sachlichkeit* changed their artistic approaches in the twenties, so Kästner and other similarly intentioned writers of the time chose different literary styles and techniques which better suited their new goals. Kästner's writing shows the influence of extraliterary sources, such as newspaper journalism, reportage, and the idiom of everyday speech. Kästner's style is straightforward, terse, and active, in comparison to other German prose of the age. Verbs outnumber nouns and the few descriptive adjectives are mostly derived from verbs.[10] Erich Kästner's writings demonstrate that *Neue Sachlichkeit,* as an artistic mentality and vision, permeated other areas of Weimar culture.

Kästner is best known today for his children's book *Emil und die Detektive* (1928), a straightforward story recounting the Berlin adventures of Emil, the son of a widowed hairdresser. Emil and his mother represent typical Weimar citizens. Emil's father was probably killed in the war, and the mother and son struggle to get along in the new republican age. Emil's mother is happy just to be able to earn a living. Kästner chose true-to-life characters, and his literary treatment of their situation is matter-of-fact and without sentimentality. The pride and courage of the characters speak for themselves.

Kästner articulated his interest in the everyday, so characteristic of the mentality of *Neue Sachlichkeit,* in the foreword to his second book of poetry, *Lärm im Spiegel* (1929). He described his poetry as *Gebrauchslyrik,* and the subject matter typically focused on the middle or lower class and their humble but honorable wishes and needs.[11] Kästner explained in *Lärm im Spiegel:*

> These are poems from which even the literarily innocent person gets palpitations or bursts out laughing in an empty room. There are poets who feel like normal human beings, and express these feelings (and views and desires) by proxy. And because they do not write just for their own benefit and to show off their two-penny originality, they get across to people. . . . Poets have their function again. Their occupation is once more a profession. They are probably not as indispensable as bakers and dentists; but only because rumbling stomachs and toothaches more obviously call for relief than non-physical ailments.[12]

Kästner's definition of his *Gebrauchslyrik*—a term obviously borrowed from *Gebrauchsmusik*—stressed the poetry's similar functional, practical, useful nature. The value of Kästner's work results, therefore, not from expressing the individuality of the poet, but in its ability to address, if not answer, the needs of a new middle-class audience.

The term *Neue Sachlichkeit* came into musical parlance around the time of the *Zeitoper.* In general, the term was used to describe aspects of the artistic and literary *Neue Sachlichkeit* which could be found in contemporary music: an unemotional or nonromantic approach both in form and subject matter, and an obvious interest in everyday life most clearly demonstrated in the choice of texts or the assimilation of popular music elements. The *Zeitoper* manifested *Neue Sachlichkeit.* It renounced the past in its topical, down-to-earth subject matter and in its musical style which further borrowed from popular music and returned to clearly articulated number-opera schemes.

Discussions of musical *Neue Sachlichkeit* were as polarized as the sentiments expressed on the crisis of opera. Many of the same opponents of anti-Wagnerian operatic trends similarly rejected a *Neue Sachlichkeit* in music, while supporters of operatic experimentation favored a trend in keeping with the culture of the time. As early as 1923, the influential critic and consistent supporter of new trends, H. H. Stuckenschmidt used a related term, *"objektive" Musik,* to describe the character of new works by Stravinsky and George Antheil.[13] Stuckenschmidt regularly wrote on music for the avant-garde art journal *Kunstblatt* and was probably aware of Hartlaub's use of *Neue Sachlichkeit* and its context. Stuckenschmidt adopted the concept of artistic "objectivity" to describe the unemotional and machinelike character of contemporary music. In a similar vein, Siegfried Kallenberg, writing a year later on new musical trends, used the expression *das kühle Sachliche* along with "topicality" and "irony," to characterize features of new works by Honegger, Stravinsky, Petyrek and Hindemith, features which accounted for the popularity of the music.[14] Although neither writer used Hartlaub's exact term, both defined an anti-nineteenth century, antiexpressionistic musical stance which acted as the starting point for artistic *Neue Sachlichkeit* as well as for postwar avant-garde music.

Heinrich Strobel, writing for a special issue of *Anbruch* entitled "Problems of New Music," formulated the first attempt to delineate *Neue Sachlichkeit* in a musical context.[15] Strobel's definition was two-sided. Musical *Neue Sachlichkeit* could possess a thorough grounding in modern culture or it could rely on pre-nineteenth-century or absolute forms, as in Busoni's *junge Klassizität.* Showing the correspondence between contemporary music and art in the common renunciation of expressionism, Strobel first defined a dedication to the everyday, present in much European music and demonstrated by the assimilation of popular dance elements and the rhythms of jazz, as evidence of a musical *Neue Sachlichkeit.* Strobel then singled out Max Reger, Busoni, and Stravinsky as important pioneers in a second kind of musical *Neue Sachlichkeit.* These composers embodied musical *Neue Sachlichkeit* through their use of objective, old-fashioned formal models. This second aspect of Strobel's definition suggests that the concept of neo-classicism, more commonly understood today, overlapped with the understanding of musical *Neue Sachlichkeit* in the 1920s. Strobel concluded his discussion of musical *Neue Sachlichkeit* on an optimistic note: "This new style is a consolidation after revolutionary fits of passion and the beginning of a period of calm maturity."[16]

In 1927, H. H. Stuckenschmidt tackled *Neue Sachlichkeit* in music more thoroughly with an article in the Berlin *Vossische Zeitung.*[17] Stuckenschmidt described the term as one of the most popular artistic catch phrases coined since the revolution and noted that in principle "objectivity" and romanticism are not necessarily mutually exclusive. He went on to write that the rise of *Neue Sachlichkeit* came as a direct result of postwar disintegration and the destruction of nineteenth-century artistic values; thus most music in this new vein was anti-Wagnerian. Stuckenschmidt further addressed the issue of where composers found musical inspiration for these objective works. He pointed to a new interest in American and French music and, like Strobel, discussed the reliance on jazz dances or marches, which he described as *Gebrauchsformen,* another play on *Gebrauchsmusik.*

Stuckenschmidt singled out Krenek as the most distinguished composer of this new music which demonstrated the turn away from nineteenth-century romanticism, but Hindemith, Toch, and Weill had gone similar ways as well. Stuckenschmidt concluded his discussion of musical *Neue Sachlichkeit* by acknowledging the opponents of the trend and by affirming his own belief that this musical objectivity, grounded in modern life and including neo-classicism, represented a major change of direction. However, he was less optimistic for its success than Strobel: "The public will, with horror, only be aware that we are at the beginning of a new musical culture arising from sociological restructuring, and that the inherited artistic ideology is dying, when it is too late."[18]

Ernst Krenek tackled the notion of *Neue Sachlichkeit* in music in two articles published in 1927. In *"Neue Sachlichkeit* in der Musik," published in the Dutch arts journal *i 10,* Krenek acknowledged *Neue Sachlichkeit* as an artistic conception now carried to music and drama.[19] Unlike Stuckenschmidt, Krenek did not see musical *Neue Sachlichkeit* as represented solely in the reliance on American dances or jazz rhythms, but rather in the more general attempt to reestablish clear and intelligible musical means after an era of abstraction and erudition. Echoing the sentiments expressed in his opera essays, Krenek noted that this return to clarity or objectivity was only taking place, and only needed to take place, in Germany and Austria, where the abstraction of Schoenberg and expressionism had been most influential and destructive.

In a second article, "Mechanisierung der Künste," published just months later in the same journal, Krenek pointed to the interest in machine music and mechanical instruments as a further consequence of modern musical culture's need and desire for clarity, conciseness [*Prägnanz*] and objectivity in reaction to nineteenth-century excesses.[20] Other writers also equated *Neue Sachlichkeit* with machine music, such as the experiments with mechanical organs at the Donaueschingen/Baden-Baden Festivals, or the fascination with rhythmic precision found in jazz.[21] Concurrent with his changing philosophy on opera after 1930, Krenek later spoke in favor of a "new humanity" in the place of the "old objectivity."[22]

Critics of avant-garde art, architecture, and design often charged artists with being too calculated in their aim to be modern and functional. And music critics likewise despaired over the loss of nineteenth-century humanity. Essays by Ernst Schliepe and Ludwig Misch represent typical conservative opinion regarding a musical *Neue Sachlichkeit.*[23] Misch recognized the basis of some new music which tried to be an *Es-Musik* [it-music] in opposition to the *Ich-Musik* [I-music] of nineteenth-century and early twentieth-century expressionism. But Misch also questioned the existence of a true objectivity which could rid itself entirely of all individuality. Schliepe also debated the notion of a musical *Neue Sachlichkeit* and maintained that music, as an invisible art form, cannot be defined as objective in the same way one can describe objective visual arts. Even the reliance on absolute musical forms, such as the fugue, did not guarantee objectivity. Agreeing with Misch, Schliepe stated that in the end, completely objective art or music is impossible. He concluded: "With any luck, the allegedly *sachlichen* composers of today who have any genius will not go against their nature. And it is pleasing and comforting to see how in their best moments they become highly *unsachlich,* thereby supplying the proof that in the long run, there is nothing to *Sachlichkeit* in music."[24]

Other artistic ideas from the time, while partaking less directly in *Neue Sachlichkeit,* maintain identifiable relations with the *Zeitoper*. Functionality was at the heart of the Bauhaus school, although the goal of the usefulness of art and good designs for objects of daily use was shared by many who believed that art could and should be useful and practical while still modern. The Bauhaus also preached a reconciliation with technology and an embracing of the time as a machine age which allowed the mass production and mass availability of items.

The Bauhaus concept of mass production and utilitarian art was shared by the Berlin-based *Neues Bauen*. Bruno Taut, Hans and Wassili Luckhardt, Erich Mendelsohn, and others connected with the architectural movement strove to supply architecture that was both functional and for large groups.[25] The postwar housing shortage necessitated the production of inexpensive public housing, and these Berlin-based architects took on projects in the Berlin suburbs which met utilitarian needs while simultaneously providing new architectural schemes in stark contrast to prewar concepts. Besides public housing projects, such as Taut and Martin Wagner's Horseshoe Development in Berlin-Britz (1925), *Neues Bauen* architects took on other mass building projects such as train stations, factories, hospitals, movie theaters, and department stores. Krenek, Weill, and Hindemith also sought to create purposeful, functional music for a mass audience. The overwhelming success of *Jonny spielt auf* indicates that Krenek did create a musical analog to Taut's mass housing projects—a work whose entertainment value had both a modern spirit and an identifiable utilitarian quality.

Entertainment and Media

Krenek, Weill, and Hindemith wanted their *Zeitopern* to revitalize German opera while fulfilling a community function, which meant their works had to compete with other kinds of popular entertainments, and what better way to compete and prove their interest in the present, than to incorporate features of these popular genres. From the postwar *Kabarett,* revue, and *Kabarettrevue,* they borrowed the lighthearted entertaining spirit as well as using these popular genres as settings within operas. *Zeitoper,* as a part of the Bauhaus machine age, also relied on the technical means concurrently used in the theater.

The German *Kabarett* and revue were popular forms of entertainment before World War I. Both took on new importance during the Weimar era as Berlin became the European capital of popular entertainment and theater. The revue was generally regarded as middle-class entertainment, and individual shows consisted of loosely connected dramatic sketches, musical and dance numbers assembled around a general theme. Music was an important component of a revue, whether freely borrowed from other sources or composed especially for a particular show. The success of a given revue often depended on a hit musical number or *Schlager,* and revue music typically reflected current popular music trends. With the growing interest in American jazz and popular dances discussed in the next chapter, the foxtrot, shimmy, Charleston, and other jazz dances became an increasingly important element of revues.[26]

Much has been written about the *Kabarett* of the Weimar era. A distinction must be made, though, between the *Amüsierkabarett* and the later *Kabarett* of the twenties. The *Amüsierkabarett,* most popular immediately following World War I, provided entertainment without any literary or political satire and tended to cater directly to public taste, often through the excessive use of nudity.[27] Plain *Kabarett* is what is typically thought of as the German pre-World War II cabaret: the small, intimate stage where the master of ceremonies engaged in a witty, satirical discussion of current events, and where separate musical numbers and sketches attacked the current political situation or made leftist political pronouncements before it became politically impossible to do so.

A primary feature of the *Kabarett* was its spirit of immediacy created by adapting sketches to daily changes in the social and political situation. Some of the best-known literary figures of the time—Bertolt Brecht, Kurt Tucholsky, Walter Mehring, Erich Kästner—wrote dramatic sketches and texts for the various *Kabarette* which came and went during the years of the Weimar Republic. Music was a less important feature of the *Kabarett* than it was in the revue, as few *Kabarette* had the financial resources or the stage space necessary for the five- to six-member revue band. Musical numbers, typically settings of strophic texts, were cast in a popular idiom and the accompaniment was simple, allowing the texts and performer to take center stage.

The *Kabarettrevue,* a third kind of popular entertainment which developed in the 1920s, combined features of both the middle-class revue, such as music and dance, with the satire, political commentary, and topicality of *Kabarett* material.[28] Writers and composers such as Rudolf Nelson, Friedrich Hollaender, and Marcellus Schiffer produced *Kabarettrevuen* which possessed a degree of sophistication akin to the *Kabarett,* but these *Kabarettrevuen* also provided the public with the spectacle, music, and entertaining good time it had come to associate with the revue.

Many of these *Kabarettrevuen* had more detailed story lines than the loosely connected sketches of the revue, and they often satirized or parodied modern life and aspects of contemporary culture, as was common in the *Kabarett*. Schiffer's *Fleissige Leserin* parodied modern newspapers and magazines, and Hollaender and Schiffer collaborated on a piece for Rudolf Nelson entitled *Quick* which took as its theme the newly invented automat.[29] A 1928 revue, written by Schiffer and Mischa Spoliansky, starring Marlene Dietrich and the black American tap dancer Louis Douglas, demonstrated in its title song, "Es liegt in der Luft eine Sachlichkeit" [*Sachlichkeit* is in the air], just how aware of modern trends such *Kabarettrevue* writers were.

In their topicality, many *Kabarettrevuen* used stage settings and properties which underscored the contemporary milieu. *Fleissige Leserin* did not merely take modern journalism as the subject matter, but each sketch came complete with a backdrop sporting a sensationalistic headline, advertisement, or some other journalistic trademark. An earlier satire of the print medium, *Die Nacht der Nächte,* used a large, mechanistic printing press as part of the set, and *Es kommt jeder dran,* a parody of modern cinema, used movie cameras as properties.[30] *Kabarettrevuen,* in keeping with their sophisticated theatrical nature, also employed advanced staging techniques. Rudolf Nelson experimented with multiple sets and a revolving stage, as was being done in contemporary serious theater.

Marcellus Schiffer, known for his *Kabarettrevuen,* supplied the libretti for Hindemith's *Hin und zurück* and *Neues vom Tage.* The contemporary subject matter of *Neues vom Tage,* a couple seeking a divorce, with its parody of modern mores, suggests the *Kabarettrevue.* The final scene of the opera, in which the couple is forced to relate their marital tribulations as part of a revue show, comes complete with a chorus line, a feature of many revues.

The popular topicality of all three forms of entertainment, especially the *Kabarett* and *Kabarettrevue,* provided inspiration for the *Zeitoper. Zeitopern* borrowed the entertaining spirit of these two genres, with comedy and lighthearted, tongue-in-cheek approaches predominating. And as Alfred Rosenzweig noted in his 1927 article "Die Revuetechnik in Operette und Oper," *Zeitopern* such as *Jonny spielt auf* also shared the aim of these popular entertainments: to provide direct links between modern life and the audience.[31] The revue and *Kabarettrevue* further relied on popular music, which would be important to *Zeitoper* as well.

Few *Zeitopern* incorporated the overt political tone of the *Kabarett.* Max Brand's *Maschinist Hopkins* (1929), with its story of modern factory life, perhaps came closest, and Weill's *Der Zar lässt sich photographieren,* with its central action of an attempted political assassination, incorporated some political satire as well. Certainly *Aufstieg und Fall der Stadt Mahagonny,* a work carrying some traces of *Zeitoper* in its new epic mold, betrays Brecht's work with the political *Kabarett*. Less overtly political pronouncements do find their way into *Zeitoper*, but they are more in keeping with the softer, charitable tone of the *Kabarettrevue*. *Zeitoper*'s irreverence for German operatic tradition—keenly perceived by critics of the genre—may show the broader influence of the *Kabarett*'s satirical nature, which poked fun at German institutions. *Zeitopern* often turned the tables on accepted operatic and cultural conventions, as when Jonny, the purveyor of popular music, triumphs in *Jonny spielt auf* or in Hindemith's parody of operatic arias in *Neues vom Tage*.

Composers of *Zeitopern* further demonstrated the influence of these popular entertainments through the incorporation of them as settings within their operas. As mentioned above, the hero and heroine of *Neues vom Tage,* in order to meet their legal expenses, agree to perform an autobiographical sketch in a revue show. D'Albert's *Die schwarze Orchidee* has a scene in the Mt. Everest Bar which includes a revue show number performed by the secondary heroine. The last act of Antheil's *Transatlantic* requires a "review [*sic*] dancer" who prances about the stage between scenes commenting on the actions of the characters and mocking their various predicaments. *Zeitoper* composers relied on the familiarity of these popular entertainments to provide their opera with the realism necessary to make them appealing to their audience.

The German Theater

Germany became a leader in theatrical innovation in the twentieth century. Before the war, expressionist playwrights dominated the German stage as expressionist writers dominated the literary scene. Prewar figures such as Ernst Toller (1893–1939), Georg Kaiser (1878–1945), and Oskar Kokoschka (1886–1980) continued to remain popular after the formation of the Weimar Republic, but they were eclipsed in the 1920s by postwar writers and new literary developments.

One major innovation in the theater world which began before the war but took on greater importance in the 1920s was in the role of the director. No longer anonymous or subservient to patrons and actors, the director became an important personality identified with an individual style or with specific techniques.

The young Berlin director who came to the fore during the Weimar decade and whose theatrical innovations most probably influenced the techniques of *Zeitoper* was Erwin Piscator (1893–1966). Piscator was one of the foremost representatives of *Zeittheater*—also referred to as political theater, topical theater, and epic theater—a genre which shared concerns of the *Zeitoper* in its interest in reaching a wider audience and addressing questions of the time.[32] The most productive years of Piscator's career, 1924–29, during which time he started his rise to fame at the Volksbühne and later opened his own

Piscatorbühne, overlap the years of *Zeitoper*.[33] Piscator's reliance on modern technology and documentation techniques can clearly be seen in the staging of *Zeitoper*.

Piscator's primary innovation as a director was to adapt aspects of postwar mass culture and entertainment to the theater. Both Piscator's *Revue Roter Rummel* (1924) and *Trotz Alledem* (1925) adapted the older revue format to overtly political themes and became models for other political theater genres. He further incorporated into his stage settings elaborate machines, radios, cars, and other trappings of modern life. But most importantly, he used film and photographic slide techniques as a means to document or verify the dramatic action. Piscator aimed "to convey the impression that [a dramatic work] was not fiction, but a piece of reality."[34] This new technology not only expanded the limits of the stage but provided a link between the audience and the drama as it underscored the technological, industrialized machine age of the Weimar Republic.[35]

Piscator was not the first to use such techniques. As early as 1920, poet and playwright Ivan Goll used slides and film clips in his *Die Unsterblichen*. Weill's opera *Royal Palace* (1927), a work with some features of the *Zeitoper* and with a libretto by Goll, also used a filmed sequence. Piscator, however, expanded the use of film and slide projections to where they replaced conventional dialogue and even entire scenes. In his 1924 production of Alfons Paquet's *Fahnen* for the Volksbühne, projections and placards provided scene titles in the manner of silent film captions. Slides of the actual events referred to in the play, as well as newspaper headlines, added a further dimension of reality to *Fahnen* and to later works as part of Piscator's aim to document stage events.

Piscator first used film in *Trotz Alledem* (1925) as a further means to verify events discussed on stage. Based on the last article published by Karl Liebknecht before his assassination in 1919, *Trotz Alledem* was written by Piscator and Felix Gasbarra as a "Historical Revue from the Years 1914–1919 in 24 Scenes with Interspersed Films." Piscator borrowed the film footage of historical events from the Berlin state archives. In Paquet's *Sturmflut* (1926) and in *Hoppla, wir leben* (1927), Piscator moved to a greater use of film. He shot special film sequences for each play which then became individual scenes.

For *Hoppla, wir leben,* Piscator's collaborator Traugott Müller constructed an elaborate four-tiered set which allowed smaller individual rooms to be lit for successive brief scenes or used simultaneously, while reserving the center stage for longer, more developed action. The set also contained a center screen for the newsreel and special filmed scenes. In his later productions—*Rasputin* (1927), *Die Abenteuer des braven Soldaten Schweik* (1928), and *Der Kaufmann von Berlin* (1929)—Piscator and his collaborators continued to explore the possibilities of slide projections, film, and new staging concepts.

Besides his use of these documentary techniques incorporating new kinds of set design, Piscator expanded the possibilities of the stage through the use of special machines and technological or industrial properties; any mechanical object associated with modern life became legitimate for stage use. *Sturmflut* utilized loudspeakers, and a radio appeared in *Hoppla, wir leben*. A specially built treadmill provided the stage innovation in *Schweik*. A car was driven on stage and left as a property for Leo Lania's *Konjunktur* (1928), and Bauhaus artist Moholy-Nagy designed hydraulic lifts and motorized bridges for *Der Kaufmann von Berlin*.

As in the revues he copied, music also played a part in Piscator's productions. Edmund Meisel (1874–1930), who supplied scores for such films as *Berlin, Symphonie einer Grossstadt* and *Battleship Potemkin,* conducted the Piscatorbühne band and provided most of the music for Piscator's productions. The music consisted of interludes or special numbers, such as a Charleston for *Hoppla, wir leben* choreographed by Mary Wigman, and settings of texts which acted as theme songs.

Hanns Eisler and Weill also collaborated with Piscator. Weill, who spoke so highly of Piscator's *Zeittheater* in his essays, contributed incidental music for *Konjunktur,* "a comedy of economics." Only individual numbers have survived, including the setting of a text by Gasbarra, "Die Muschel von Margate: Petroleum Song," which was performed by Tilla Durieux, one of Piscator's leading actresses.[36]

All *Zeitopern* demonstrate to some extent Piscator's interest in making use of all technical means at one's disposal both to modernize and to heighten the effect of the stage action. Whether composers of *Zeitoper* took their cue directly from Piscator is difficult to say. Piscator's work, although recognized in Berlin and throughout Germany for its theatrical innovation, reflects much of the fascination with technology and industry which was part of postwar society and cultural life. As *Zeitopern* demonstrated a clear, identifiable interest in modernizing operatic production as well as the libretti and relied on techniques similar to Piscator's documentary style, it is more than likely that Piscator acted as an important model.

On-stage machinery is a common feature of *Zeitopern,* such as the use in *Jonny spielt auf* of loudspeakers broadcasting radio programs and the depiction of an arriving train. The action of Weill's *Der Zar lässt sich photographieren* hinges on the photographic equipment in Angèle's studio and a seduction scene involving the use of a gramophone. Hindemith set scenes of *Neues vom Tage* in a business office complete with typewriters. Few *Zeitopern* incorporated actual filmed sequences, for which Piscator was known. However, Antheil's *Trans-atlantic* (1930) did include projected captions and headlines as well as a filmed segment in the third act which documents possible future actions between the hero and heroine. The final scene of *Transatlantic,* moreover, relies on a mammoth multilayered set which allowed a rapid shift between four different settings as well as the projection of the film in the middle, very much in keeping with Müller's simultaneous set for *Hoppla, wir leben.*

At times staging techniques in *Zeitopern* suggest filmed sequences, in the absence of actual footage. In *Jonny spielt auf,* stage directions indicate that one scene is to be performed as if taking place in a police car moving through the streets of Paris with lights flashed on a backdrop to suggest the movement. And the apotheosis, with its rapid changes, suggests the kind of time compression and cross-cutting more common to film than live theater. Likewise Hindemith's *Hin und zurück* spoofs the effect of running filmed sequences backwards, thereby reversing all previous stage action.

Zeitopern—with their aim to reach wider audiences and record modern life—were a musical expression of *Neue Sachlichkeit.* In order to prove their commitment to the present time, composers adopted the tone, attributes, and innovations of prevailing popular entertainment and theater. But libretti and stage settings aside, opera contains a central musical component lacking in theater. And composers of *Zeitoper* recognized that their works had to sound as up-to-date and post-Wagnerian as the libretti they chose to set, or the stage settings they employed. For musical modernity, they followed the down-to-earth spirit of the French and sought musical renewal in the rhythms and timbres of American jazz.

4

Jazz: The Sound of the New World

Americanism and American Performers in Europe

The Original Dixieland Jazz Band ushered in the recorded age of jazz in 1917 with their Victor release of "Livery Stable Blues" and "Dixie Jass [*sic*] Band One-Step." The musical antecedents of jazz—minstrel show music, ragtime, and blues—had existed, however, at least since the early part of the century. The advent of the social dance craze in 1912 and the subsequent abandonment of the waltz in favor of the one-step, foxtrot, and tango made popular a faster-paced, lively, syncopated music, and provided this precursor of early jazz with an audience outside the confines of black American culture. By 1917 a number of true jazz performers were already playing in Chicago and New Orleans, and jazz as a distinctly American musical genre was on its way to characterizing the age.

Although the purpose here is not to provide a history of jazz and its development, a distinction needs to be made between syncopated social dance music and ragtime, both precursors of jazz, and what is now considered to be or have been true jazz. The definition of jazz used here describes music relying on improvisation and possessing an identifiable rhythmic vitality produced through syncopation compounded by "swung" eighth-notes. Swung eighth-notes are a performance practice by which a quarter-note is subdivided into two notes of unequal length with the longer note played first. The actual mathematical relationship between the two eighth-notes varies depending on tempo, performer, style or style period.[1]

The year 1917 also marked the entry of the United States into World War I, and the American military provided a natural conduit for American music to reach foreign audiences. Jazz and its precursors soon became highly-prized exports. Because the largest number of American troops were stationed in France, it became the first European country to have contact with the new sound. French art music composers were thus among the first to use the new rhythmic and timbral qualities of jazz in their music, thereby providing models for German composers. Once the war was over and international contacts reestablished, jazz and its influence quickly spread to Germany and the rest of the Continent.

The European fascination with jazz was part of a larger obsession with America and things American. Bred in France during the war and then spreading elsewhere after the armistice, this Americanism was marked by a consuming interest in all aspects of American culture. European society, previously distinguished by its impressive cultural traditions, now looked to the United States. America was regarded as younger, fresher, more alive, and embodying modernity in all facets of life. Edmund Wilson, Jr., who decried France's postwar Americanization, tried to explain it:

> America since the war has almost a monopoly of life; now that the life of Europe is exhausted we are bound to command their attention if only by virtue of the energy and the money of which we dispose. Here at least, they feel, life is going on unencumbered by its burden of conventions. Our skyscrapers may be monstrous but they are at least manifestations of force; our entertainments may be vulgar but they are at least terrifically alive.[2]

This quest for a new culture "unencumbered by its burden of conventions" was even more pronounced in Germany, which had experienced a humiliating political defeat. H. H. Stuckenschmidt, who was not yet 20 years old at the time of the Treaty of Versailles, described how many young Germans felt:

> America, in many respects, was a great model, and we were eager to know all American art, American jazz, American dance, and so on. . . . Everything that came from America, except the business, interested us deeply. And we tried to have contact with young American people.[3]

American sports, such as boxing, were popular and terms such as "knock-out" and "k.o." became part of French and German slang.[4] German newspapers serialized novels by F. Scott Fitzgerald, Upton Sinclair, and John Dos Passos, and literary journals examined them in detail. The biography of Henry Ford, whose automobile factories were potent symbols of American modern industrialization, became a best-seller. By 1927, after his solo voyage across the Atlantic and his subsequent tour of Germany, Charles Lindbergh was hailed as an international hero and extolled in verse and song.[5]

The avant-garde, in particular, fell under the spell of *Amerikanismus,* as the German obsession came to be called. And much of German life and art in the 1920s was an attempt to emulate and surpass America in its love of sports, urban life, industry, fast-paced lifestyles, and popular culture. Architect Erich Mendelsohn, an original member of the *Novembergruppe,* celebrated the U. S. in a book of photographs, *Amerika: Bilderbuch eines Architekten.*[6] His book shows the interest in urban life as it was in the United States and is part of the *Neue Sachlichkeit.* In his photographs Mendelsohn sought to capture the essence of America, its gigantic, even grotesque nature, as well as the sense of rejuvenation. Photographs included the New York City harbor, Wall Street, and Macy's Department Store, Chicago's Michigan Avenue and Tribune Building, a factory in Buffalo, and Detroit billboards and city buses. Mendelsohn's foreword and captions saluted this postwar, energetic, American spirit. "Its people, a mass blown-together from all ends of the earth, forms the undercurrent of this Babylonian cauldron. . . . That this land carries with it all possibilities is without question."[7]

The interest in jazz was just part of this larger, consuming passion for America. And a number of performers during the late teens and early twenties helped spread the sound: James Reese Europe, Sidney Bechet, Josephine Baker, the Original Dixieland Jazz Band, Sam Wooding, and Paul Whiteman.[8] Much of the music brought by these performers was syncopated dance music, orchestrated ragtime, and other kinds of novelty music. Some of it, however, was New Orleans-style jazz and even early big band jazz. Josephine Baker was a dancer, and until World War II, most jazz was viewed largely as a utilitarian—if exciting—accompaniment to social dancing. There was little appreciation in Europe or the United States for jazz as an art music in its own right. Foreign audiences were fascinated with the dances introduced by Irene and Vernon Castle and then the new steps brought by Baker.

James Reese Europe (1881–1919) came to France as part of the 369th Infantry division, one of the all-black volunteer units. Europe directed the 369th Hell Fighters Band, which became popular with soldiers and French civilians alike. Through the Hell Fighters, Europe won international fame before his early death from stab wounds inflicted by his drummer. He was subsequently buried in Arlington National Cemetary with full military honors.

Before the war, Europe attained a national reputation as the leader of a number of bands in New York City, in particular the Clef Club Orchestra. Europe organized the Clef Club Union in 1910 to help protect the great number of black musicians then performing in the city. In May 1912, the 125-member Clef Club Orchestra received a thunderous reception at their Carnegie Hall performance with renditions of their own brand of orchestrated ragtime, marches, tangos, and waltzes. In 1914 Europe began his association with dancers Vernon and Irene Castle, and he continued to work for them until his enlistment.

Married in 1911, Irene Foote and Vernon Castle intended to make their living in the theater. A chance to perform in a revue took them to Paris, where they began their dancing career. Irene Castle describes their start:

> My mother had been sending us clippings describing the new dancing rage which was sweeping America, a syncopated ragtime rough and tumble called the "Grizzly Bear" or Texas Tommy. We decided as a finale for the show to introduce French audiences to the latest American dance fervor.[9]

Though neither Castle had actually seen this new American dance, they concocted their own version based on the newspaper descriptions. They chose as an accompaniment "Alexander's Ragtime Band," the hit tune of 1911 and one of a number of Tin Pan Alley ragtime songs. Their dancing, with its distinctive style and new ragtime influences apart from the waltz, proved popular with French audiences and they stayed in Paris as a dancing team.

In 1912 the Castles returned to the United States just in time to stimulate the American public dance craze which lasted until World War I and dramatically signalled the end of the Victorian era and the creation of twentieth-century nightlife.[10] The Castles' popularity grew, and Irene Castle soon came to be the most talked about woman of the age, a symbol of the New Woman. The Castles entertained at numerous private soirées and then founded their own dancing school, Castle House, where the offspring of New York high society "could go to learn the dances without being exposed to the discredited elements."[11] At their afternoon tea dances in Castle House, as well as at their other establishments such as Sans Souci, The Castle Club, and Castles in the Air, the couple introduced the tango and new variations of the waltz, and created their own dances such as the Castle Walk, the Half and Half, and most importantly, the foxtrot.

Not all of American society shared an enthusiasm for these new dances. Many critics, in particular, objected to the tango because of its slower tempo and suggestive hold, with the female partner tilted backwards and held slightly off-balance. The Castles, however, managed to make this new public dancing respectable for white America, particularly the upper class. Irene Castle explained: "We were clean-cut; we were married and when we danced there was nothing suggestive about it. We made dancing look like the fun it was."[12] As they stressed in their book *Modern Dancing* (1914), dancing was good exercise, a healthy recreation for American youth.[13] Their dancing had none of the overt sensual quality which later characterized the performances of Josephine Baker.

The Castles hired James Reese Europe and his band to accompany them in their first cabaret, Sans Souci. After it closed, Europe continued to provide music at various Castle institutions. He accompanied the Castles on their 1914 tour of 32 North American cities, during which they introduced the phenomenon of the American dance contest. In her autobiography, Irene Castle speaks little of Europe except to claim:

> It was we who made colored orchestras the vogue of Fifth Avenue. We booked Jim Europe's orchestra, the most famous of the colored bands. Jim Europe was a skilled musician and one of the first to take jazz out of the saloons and make it respectable. All of the men in his orchestra could read music, a rarity in those days.[14]

She also acknowledged that Europe provided all the new music required for their dance creations, such as the five-four meter music needed for the Half and Half. But other sources credit Europe with at least suggesting, if not entirely creating, the Castles' most famous dance, the foxtrot, which Irene Castle introduced in the

1914 Broadway show *Watch Your Step*.[15] Irene Castle's ambivalence towards Europe and his role is typical of the ingrained racism of the time. And such reluctance to acknowledge the influence of black Americans by name was true of later French and German composers as well.

Europe and his High Society Orchestra recorded a number of sides for Victor in 1913–14, including "Too Much Mustard," "Down Home Rag," "Castle Walk," and "Castle House Rag."[16] Europe's Society Orchestra, at its largest, consisted of clarinet, cornet, trombone, piano, guitar, mandolin, drums, several violins, cello, and string bass. On record the violins, cornet, and clarinet carry the melody in unison over a rhythmic accompaniment provided by the other instruments. These early recordings amply explain Europe's popularity. The music is fast, and the steady rhythmic accompaniment, particularly the furious drumming, lends both momentum and excitement. The cornet, with its more aggressive sound, typically overshadows the violins and suggests what would become characteristic of later jazz, a prominent brass timbre.

Vernon Castle and James Reese Europe both volunteered for World War I. Vernon Castle died while serving with the British air force, but Europe soon became part of the American military's musical war effort. Colonel William Hayward, who commanded the 369th Infantry division, recognized Europe's potential as a bandleader and raised the money on his own to recruit and outfit the musicians Europe deemed necessary for his army band.[17] Europe and his Hell Fighters Band played throughout France, appearing in some 25 cities for military and civilian audiences.[18]

Noble Sissle, a member of Europe's Clef Club and later an important composer for the black musical theater, was the Hell Fighters' drum major. He described the eclectic nature of their repertory with its combination of traditional martial numbers, modern orchestrated ragtime, and blues, and the tumultuous reception following one of their most popular tunes.

> Then came the fireworks, "The Memphis Blues." . . . He [Europe] turned to the trombone players, who sat impatiently waiting for their cue to have a "Jazz spasm," and they drew their slides out to the extremity and jerked them back with that characteristic crack.
>
> The audience could stand it no longer; the "Jazz germ" hit them, and it seemed to find the vital spot, loosening all muscles and causing what is known in America as an "Eagle Rocking Fit."[19]

Upon returning to New York City in 1919, Europe's Hell Fighters recorded 24 numbers on the Pathe label, one of which was a version of W. C. Handy's popular "Memphis Blues."[20] Its performance is tempestuous, with none of the langorous mood expected in blues today, and identifiable solo breaks make use of special timbral effects, such as a wailing clarinet melody and trombone glissandi. The 12-bar blues harmonic structure appears in two of the three strains.

Europe described how French army bands tried to copy his sound but were unable to as they were unfamiliar with the techniques and elementary improvisation.

> [A French band conductor] explained that he couldn't seem to get the effects I got and asked me to go to a rehearsal. I went with him. The great band played the compositions superbly—but he was right: the jazz effects were missing. I took an instrument and showed him how it could be done, and he told me that his own musicians felt sure that my band had used special instruments.[21]

James Reese Europe and his 369th Hell Fighters were not the only purveyors of the "Negro Music that Stirred France."[22] Other bands included the 350th Field Artillery Black Devils Band, under Lieutenant J. Tim Brymm, a member of the Clef Club, whose drum major was ragtime pianist Willie "The Lion" Smith.[23] A. Jack Thomas conducted the 368th Infantry Band, and the 370th Infantry Band was under the direction of George E. Dulf. Other black divisions with separate bands were the 349th and 350th Field Artillery and 365th, 366th, 367th and 807th Infantry regiments.[24] The 807th included in its ranks future band leader Sam Wooding, who introduced American jazz to Berlin.

France, with its enthusiastic reception of American popular music and lack of a color line, made an attractive place for black performers to stay after the war. And for black and white musicians residing in the United States, France became a popular place to tour. James Reese Europe returned to France in 1919 with a group of 65 musicians. Will Marion Cook, who shared Jim Europe's New York background, toured France and England with his 36-member Southern Syncopated Orchestra in 1918. As in Europe's group, the Southern Syncopated Orchestra played a variety of music from Brahms to blues and orchestrated ragtime. They also performed instrumental arrangements of spirituals already known through the original Fisk Jubilee Singers and other black choirs who toured Europe at the end of the nineteenth century.

Clarinetist Sidney Bechet played with Cook and attracted the attention of Ernst Ansermet. Ansermet, who conducted the first performance of Stravinsky's *L'Histoire du soldat,* would become an important transmitter of American popular music, purchasing sheet music during his tours of the United States and then sharing it with Igor Stravinsky and others. After a performance of the Southern Syncopated Orchestra Ansermet praised the whole group and singled out Bechet for special mention. "There is in the Southern Syncopated Orchestra an extraordinary clarinet virtuoso who is, so it seems, the first of his race to have composed perfectly formed blues on the clarinet. . . . I wish to set down the name of this artist of genius, as for myself, I shall never forget it—it is Sidney Bechet."[25] Bechet returned to Paris in 1925 as part of the Claude Hopkins's Band which accompanied Josephine Baker in *La Revue nègre.*

Example 4.1.   The Tango Rhythm

Black American groups were not the only ones to tour overseas. In 1919 the Original Dixieland Jazz Band played a one-and-a-half year engagement in London. Although extremely popular in their day—their "Livery Stable Blues" outsold recordings by Sousa and Caruso—the influence of the group, especially overseas, has been downplayed because they were white and used only rudimentary improvisation in their well-rehearsed arrangements. But the five-member ensemble, dominated by cornetist Nick LaRocca, and featuring trombonist Eddie Edwards, clarinetist Larry Shields, pianist Henry Ragas and drummer Tony Sbarbaro, took the preexisting formula of the early New Orleans sound and made it appealing to a predominantly white audience. Their music, with its rhythmic momentum, fast tempo, frenetic counterpoint, aggressive timbral colors, and novelty animal sounds, was as exciting to Europeans as it was to Americans. The group increased the European appetite for New Orleans jazz with its smaller, tighter ensemble.

The Jazz Dances

What appealed to composers, both French and German, who would look to jazz for inspiration, were the rhythms peculiar to the individual dances, the modal blues scale, and jazz's distinctive instrumental sonorities. The dances which served as the most common models were the foxtrot, Charleston, shimmy, tango, and occasionally the black bottom and Boston.

The foxtrot, introduced by the Castles, had its origin in the older two-step and one-step or Boston, both of which were variations on the waltz but were accompanied by faster music, thereby requiring fewer steps.[26] Central to the foxtrot, which appeared by the summer of 1914, was its accompanying music with four beats to the measure. Above a steady bass line, often an oom-pah oom-pah pattern, dance bands floated syncopated or swung melodies which gave the foxtrot its jazzy flavor. The foxtrot owed much of its popularity to the simplicity of its walking steps and its lively syncopated music. By the 1920s, the foxtrot had two distinctive styles: a slower, smoother "slowfox" version, and a faster style danced at a speed of 136–72 beats per minute with more heavily syncopated music.

The tango, with its South American heritage, predated the jazz dance craze, but came to be included in the catalogue of jazz dances. Characterized by a slow tempo, syncopated rhythm (see example 4.1), and distinctive position for the male and female partners, the tango gained notoriety as a dance of male

Example 4.2.   The Charleston Rhythm

domination and seduction. "To tango" became a double entendre for sexual intercourse, and the French even created new verbs such as *tanguarer*.[27] The prewar tango also subsumed the distinctive habanera rhythm which appeared in some examples of early blues.[28]

Both the shimmy and Charleston originated in the early 1920s. The shimmy was a faster, typically cut-time version of the four-four meter foxtrot. Its shaking dance steps lent the dance a racy, naughty connotation; Mae West even claimed to have invented it.[29] The Charleston was another fast dance generally believed to have been developed as a black social dance in Charleston, South Carolina around 1920 and introduced to the greater public via black revues.[30] Josephine Baker helped introduce to Europe this "cubist dance par excellence," with its angular kick steps, outstretched arms and distinctive rhythm (see example 4.2).[31]

European audiences also recognized the vocal tradition of the blues as a part of jazz. The early soldier bands played arrangements of blues numbers, made known in the teens by W. C. Handy, alongside their syncopated, faster tunes. Europeans understood both the modal aspect of blues, the reliance on the lowered third, fifth, and seventh, and the distinctive emotional quality, expressing melancholy, longing, and sadness. Generally, Europeans were less cognizant of the three-line aab textual/melodic form sung over a 12-bar harmonic pattern of I IV I V I.

Although the bands which introduced Europe to ragtime and jazz varied greatly in size, Europeans understood jazz to be a music of soloists and solo sound, and further recognized the peculiar timbral quality which came from the soloistic instrumentation. Audiences and critics attributed jazz's aggressive, exciting character to the rhythm and its percussion components, in particular the trap drum set and cymbals. Also part of the rhythm section was the piano, which provided harmonic and rhythmic support and an occasional solo. The banjo frequently rounded out the rhythm section and added its own peculiar color.

The melodic soloists—brasses and reeds—obtained special timbres through the use of mutes and unusual playing techniques such as glissandi, flutter-tonguing, harsh attacks, and an extension of the usual melodic range. Virtually all French and German writers on jazz in the early twenties regarded the saxophone as the premiere jazz solo instrument, a distinction earned through its flexible and immediately recognizable sound. Saxophone solos encompassed the melancholy blues, bright and virtuosic displays, and the especially popular dirty sax sound.

Jazz and Dance Music in France

Josephine Baker (1906–75) is often credited with inaugurating the Parisian jazz age when she arrived in September of 1925. But James Reese Europe, Will Marion Cook, and other black musicians had already stimulated the French appetite for ragtime, syncopated dance music, blues, and early New Orleans-style jazz. By 1917, Louis Mitchell, a former Clef Club member, and his Jazz Kings were accompanying dancers Gaby Deslys and Harry Pilcer at the Casino de Paris. Baker merely arrived at the right time. France was already taken with American popular music and dance, and in their love of the exotic, the French were further entranced by anything African or Afro-American.

The Parisian infatuation with the exotic had prewar roots. The World's Fair of 1889 brought Javanese gamelans and Balinese and Indian dancers to Paris, and these exotic sights and sounds soon found their way into the art, literature, and music of the time. As early as 1904–5, French artists such as Maurice Vlaminck, André Derain, Henri Matisse, along with Pablo Picasso, began collecting sculpture from Africa and Oceania. The primitivism of this sculpture soon found its way into their individual artworks. In December 1916 Paul Guillaume mounted the first European exhibit of African primitive art, which was celebrated by many important artists and writers.[32] The presence of Senegalese troops and black American soldiers in France during the war continued to stimulate their interest. And in 1925, before the arrival of *La Revue nègre*, the "Exhibition of Decorative Arts" opened in Paris and included another exhibit of African sculpture.

The central figure in the postwar enthusiasm for Africana in France and the first to recognize the importance of African language was the Swiss-born poet Blaise Cendrars (1887–1961).[33] With a fondness for the literature of exploration, Cendrars spent much of his life travelling. His 1913 collection, *La Prose du transiberian et de la petite Jeanne de France,* with illustrations by Sonia Delaunay-Terk, brought Cendrars acclaim and earned him the accolade from John Dos Passos as the "Homer of the Trans-Siberian."[34]

Cendrars earned his reputation as the leading figure of the postwar literary interest in Africa not with his poetry but with his *L'Anthologie nègre*.[35] Published in 1921 by Editions La Sirène, which Cendrars founded and directed with Jean Cocteau, *L'Anthologie nègre* is a compilation of African legends, stories, folklore, and humor, culled from a vast array of French-language sources. Cendrars organized his materials, which range in length from a paragraph to several pages, into 21 chapters. Beginning with "Cosmic Legends," Cendrars takes the reader on a tour of African literature and thought, with chapters on fetishism, totemism, historical legends, "Imaginary Science" and "Modern Tales." Although he spoke no African language, he revealed the seriousness of his interest by including an extensive bibliography.

The exoticism of Africa and black America was in the air, and Paris was primed for the entrance of Josephine Baker and her *La Revue nègre* at the Théâtre des Champs-Elysées. Baker was not yet 20 years old when she made her debut in Paris, but she was already a veteran performer. At the age of 14, she was touring the south on the Theatre Owners Booking Association (T. O. B. A.) circuit as part of the Dixie Steppers. She auditioned for a part in Noble Sissle and Eubie Blake's black revue *Shuffle Along* and eventually landed a role in the road company, where she was popular not for her dancing but for her comic antics. Her success in *Shuffle Along* earned her a place in another Sissle-Blake production, *Chocolate Dandies*. After the show closed in 1925, Baker moved on to Sam Slavin's Plantation Club, where she tried to launch a singing career and was discovered for *La Revue nègre* by entrepreneuse Caroline Dudley.

The troupe of actors and musicians chosen by Dudley for her revue, including clarinetist Sidney Bechet, set sail for France on 15 September 1925. Dudley had picked singer Maude de Forest to star, but it soon became clear that Baker possessed the quality of a leading lady. Baker opened the show with a Charleston danced to "Yes Sir, That's My Baby." The Charleston had already been introduced to Paris early in 1924 by Bricktop, another black American who was the popular hostess of a Montmartre nightclub. Many Parisians, however, found Baker's interpretation wilder and more exciting, and it was the first time the Charleston was danced on a public stage. But the success of the opening night show, whose audience included Cocteau, Francis Picabia, and Cendrars, came with the finale, "La Danse des sauvages," a French amalgamation of African dance and the Folies-Bergère, danced by Baker and Joe Alex.[36]

Janet Flanner, whose regular column "Letter from Paris" appeared in the *New Yorker,* reported dispassionately on the revue at the time. But later, in the foreword to a collection of her Paris essays Flanner recanted.

> I wrote about it [the revue] timidly, uncertainly, and like a dullard. As a matter of fact, it was so incomparably novel an element in French public pleasures that its star, hitherto unknown, named Josephine Baker, remains to me now like a still-fresh vision, sensual, exciting and isolated in my memory today. . . . She made her entry [in the finale] entirely nude except for a pink flamingo feather between her limbs; she was being carried upside-down and doing a split on the shoulder of a black giant. Midstage he paused, and with his long fingers holding her basket-wise around the waist, he swung her in a slow cartwheel to the stage floor, where she stood, like his magnificent discarded burden, in an instant of complete silence. She was an unforgettable female ebony statue. A scream of salutation spread through the theater. Whatever happened next was unimportant. The two specific elements had been established and were unforgettable—her magnificent dark body, a new model that to the French proved for the first time that black was beautiful, and the acute response of the white masculine public in the capital of hedonism of all Europe—Paris.[37]

After Paris, the revue went to Berlin, where it was equally successful. A reviewer for the *Berliner Tageblatt* described the "ebony Venus" at her Berlin premiere:

Long-legged and heavenly. . . . The combed-back, blue-black hair, the undulating hips, and the blazing white set of teeth from which the clear, merry, guttural French tumbles, expresses the entire meaning of a new word which sailed across the ocean from America to Berlin: sex-appeal.[38]

As Irene Castle was the modern American woman before the war, Baker became a symbol of the New Woman of the 1920s. Hans Heinsheimer of Universal Edition remarked that after Baker's performances, "Berlin's women were never the same again."[39] But in Germany, Baker also became a symbol for the nudist movement or *Freikörperkultur* and many conservatives labelled her an *Untermensch*.[40]

Before the Berlin tour, Baker had signed a lucrative contract with the Folies-Bergère and headlined their 1926 *La Folie du jour*. Baker opened her own club, *Chez Josephine*, where she taught dancing, and made a world tour in 1928–29 which included a second stop in Berlin at the Nelson Theater. Baker became a popular model for artists, including Pablo Picasso and Alexander Calder, and she also figured in literary works. F. Scott Fitzgerald mentions her in *Babylon Revisited* and Hemingway claimed to have spent an enchanted night dancing with her.[41]

During the years of Baker's success in France, "jazz orchestra" leader Paul Whiteman (1890–1967) earned a reputation in the United States and toured Europe in 1925–26, where he was both successful and influential in continuing the spread of American popular music. Whiteman was originally a viola player. After military service in World War I, he went to New York and organized a large ensemble which played at several well-known New York City establishments. The orchestra made use of some jazz techniques, and although he called his music jazz, it is not considered true jazz by today's standards.[42]

By 1923 the orchestra played in London, and in 1924 gave its most famous performance at New York City's Aeolian Hall, in which Whiteman introduced George Gershwin's *Rhapsody in Blue*. This performance, entitled "An Experiment in Modern Music," was meant to be educational. But as the program notes reveal, Whiteman had little knowledge of or true appreciation for authentic jazz or even orchestrated ragtime.

Mr. Whiteman intends to point out, with the assistance of his orchestra and associates, the tremendous strides which have been made in popular music from the day of the discordant Jazz, which sprang in to existence about ten years ago from nowhere in particular, to the really melodious music of today, which—for no good reason—is still called jazz.[43]

Whiteman favored a large ensemble which underscored his concept of jazz as concert rather than dance music. The melodious quality of Whiteman's music was distinctive, making abundant use of interesting timbral and instrumental effects, engineered by his master arranger Ferde Grofé. But the music possessed little rhythmic swing or improvisation. Darius Milhaud, who heard Whiteman in

New York City, described the refined sound as having "the precision of an elegant, well-oiled machine, a sort of Rolls-Royce of dance music."[44]

Whiteman's European tour took him to London, Paris, Berlin, and Vienna, where many critics proclaimed him the "King" and "Father" of jazz, titles which he encouraged. Gershwin's *Rhapsody in Blue* was as popular with European audiences as it was in the United States.

This synthesis of jazz and concert music, though, had begun in France long before Gershwin's popular model. As Stuckenschmidt claimed: "The artistic activity of street songs, of jazz, of variety music, in short, all suspect musical species were first prophesied by Cocteau."[45] Cocteau was less a prophet and more, as Milhaud declared, "our friend and our brilliant spokesman."[46] Stuckenschmidt's later assessment of Cocteau as a stimulator, supplier of texts, and cultural "pimp" [*Kuppler*] is more apt.

The popularity of Erik Satie's *Parade* (1917), with its aping of the French music hall and early interest in American popular music genres, as in the "Dance for the Little American Girl" and the "Ragtime du Paqueboat," demonstrated the viability of influences outside the traditional confines of classical music. Cocteau realized the potential for such stimuli, and in January 1918, he wrote to Albert Gleizes, then in New York, "I am working on a little book about music." And Cocteau further requested: "Bring me back as many Negro ragtimes and as much great Russian-Jewish-American music as you can."[47] The latter referred to the Tin Pan Alley music of Irving Berlin, who was often hailed as the father of ragtime on account of the popularity of "Alexander's Ragtime Band."[48]

Cocteau's "little book," the 74-page pamphlet *Le Coq et l'harlequin*, appeared in the spring of 1918.[49] The work consists of aphoristic statements supporting the creation of a new French music stripped of all German influences: a new astringent art of the cock in contrast to the foggy, impressionistic one of the harlequin. Cocteau suggested using new influences:

> The music-hall, the circus, and American negro bands, all these things fertilize an artist just as life does. To turn to one's own account the emotions aroused by this sort of entertainment is not to derive art from art. These entertainments are not art. They stimulate in the same way as machinery, animals, natural scenery, or danger.[50]

In 1918, Cocteau and Milhaud collaborated on *Le Boeuf sur la toit*, a work originally conceived by Milhaud as a celebration of South American carnivals, and thus showing little influence of jazz. The surrealist scenario, devised by Cocteau after Milhaud's score was completed, does demonstrate his Americanism. Set in prohibition-era America, the stage action takes place in a bar, and several participants are black. A feature of the premiere was its intermission entitled "American Bar" which consisted of no alcoholic beverages but a mandolin trio playing "jazz."[51] One can only guess what was meant by "jazz," but as mandolins were part of Europe's Clef Club Orchestra, the music may have been his brand of orchestrated ragtime or syncopated dance music.

Le Boeuf sur le toit proved to be popular, and Cocteau borrowed the title to rename the Bar Gaya which he adopted in 1921 as the meeting place for his circle of friends. He explained:

> It was the Bar Gaya, in the Rue Duphot, and was always empty. Jean Wiéner, a fellow student of Darius at the Conservatoire, was giving prodigious performances there of American music, and had asked Milhaud to get me to adopt this Bar as my headquarters. I did not hesitate a minute.[52]

Jean Wiéner did much to spread jazz dance music in Paris before Baker and Whiteman and to show how it could inspire composers. Trained as a concert pianist and composer, Wiéner began playing at the Bar Gaya after the war to support his family.[53] At the Bar Gaya, Wiéner's partner was the black American ex-soldier Vance Lowry, who played both saxophone and banjo. Wiéner also performed with Belgian pianist Clement Doucet. Their two-piano programs included standard repertory, works by Gershwin and Tin Pan Alley composers, "St. Louis Blues," and their own compositions, all of which they began recording in 1926.[54]

The bar became so popular that it moved to larger quarters in early 1922. And as young Germans came to Paris, it became an important place to soak up the new French atmosphere. In 1923, writer Count Harry Kessler lunched there with Cocteau, and Stuckenschmidt met members of *Les Six*.[55]

Although Wiéner's performances helped spread the new American sound, he performed an even greater service when he programmed Billy Arnold's American Novelty Jazz Band as his first *Concert-Wiéner* on 6 December 1921, thereby giving them legitimacy through a concert setting. Later *Concerts-Wiéners* featured *Le Sacre du printemps* performed on the mechanical Pleyela and Marya Freund in the French premiere of *Pierrot Lunaire* under the direction of Milhaud, with Wiéner at the piano. Billy Arnold's band had been Milhaud's first introduction to jazz when he and Cocteau were in London for a performance of *Le Boeuf sur le toit* in 1920. Arnold's band was an all-white group in the tradition of the Original Dixieland Jazz Band, with whom they played in London in 1919. Before the *Concert-Wiéner*, Arnold's band had performed at the Casino de Cannes and Casino de Deauville.[56]

Arnold and his "Novelty Band" recorded six works in London (1920), two of which were subsequently released on the British subsidiary of the Columbia label.[57] The recording group consisted of six: trumpet, trombone, clarinet, alto saxophone, piano, and drums, an ensemble identical in make-up to the Original Dixieland Jazz Band. The British recordings, such as "Stop It" and "Left All Alone Again Blues," were probably fast orchestrated ragtime and syncopated dance music which perhaps incorporated blues harmonies or rudimentary improvisation. Milhaud, however, claims that the group he heard in France consisted of four saxophones, violin, clarinet, trumpet, trombone, piano, and drums.[58] Reviews of the *Concert-Wiéner* performance describe yet another six-person ensemble of violin, saxophone, piano, clarinet, flute, and percussion, and yet a photograph of the group shows violin, saxophone, trombone, piano, banjo, and drum.[59] Arnold most likely changed the instrumental make-up of his group depending perhaps on availability of musicians or the nature of the audience, and individual musicians may have doubled on instruments depending on the repertory.

The *Concert-Wiéner* with Billy Arnold and his band was well attended and a success. Aaron Copland was in the audience as were members of *Les Six*. Milhaud reported that the presence of a jazz band in a concert setting offended some listeners but that they eventually "yielded to the lure—that is the languorous charm of the blues and the exciting clamor of ragtime and intoxicating freedom of the melodic lines."[60] The percussive and rhythmic qualities especially intrigued the reviewer for the avant-garde journal *L'Esprit nouveau*. "The percussion, clangorous or muffled, with the cymbal or bass drum, subdued by the wood drum, a calm with disturbing results. This percussion, an arsenal which entirely unlocks the rhythm. Synesthesia. The entrails are stimulated."[61]

Writers and critics frequently expressed such fascination with the rhythmic component of jazz. And André Coeuroy and André Schaeffner, who wrote the first French study of jazz, *Le Jazz* (1926), were likewise captivated by its rhythmic freedom and percussion section.[62] Throughout the book, the authors betray their fascination with jazz and its African roots as something primitive, exotic, and *other*.

The authors first cite a number of early ethnographic and anthropological studies of various African tribal rituals. They then draw correlations between these ancient rituals, accompanied by dance and drum music, and what could be seen and heard in contemporary Paris. For example, after quoting first from a 1667 study on the incessant, percussive nature of African drum music, they apply the description to the drums of American jazz, such as were used in the accompanying music for *La Revue nègre:*

> [The] same dryness, waves of the beat carried directly by the wood drum, the same alternation between this dryness and the lesser quality of the struck skin head, the same medium of distribution between two distinct timbres, the different periodicities of the measure and the rhythm.[63]

Many of the musicians polled in the final chapter, "Jazz before Judges," restate the authors' views. They applaud jazz's rhythmic drive, distinctive sonority, and brutality. Most commentators further admit to its great influence on French culture. The authors' final sentences sum up the general feeling shared by Cendrars, Cocteau, Wiéner, Milhaud, and later the Germans too: "In vain can you close your ears to jazz. It is life. It is art. It is the rapture of sounds and noises. It is the melancholy of suffering. It is us today."[64]

The Influence of Jazz on French Art Music

Coeuroy and Schaeffner's book, which explained the fascination with jazz as a new musical resource, postdated by almost nine years the assimilation of jazz idioms into French concert music. As early as 1908 Claude Debussy demon-strated his awareness of American minstrel show music and its cakewalk dance in "Golliwog's Cake-walk" from *The Children's Corner* and in the piano preludes "Minstrels" (volume I, 1910) and "General Lavine—eccentric" (volume II, 1913). For the sake of this study, music truly indebted to early jazz and jazz dances must postdate the convergence of the ballroom dance tradition and orchestrated ragtime.[65] Thus Satie's *Parade* of 1917 with its "Petite Fille Americaine" shows the first apparent assimilation of ragtime, followed by Stravinsky's syncopated *Ragtime for 11 Instruments* (1918), *Piano-Rag-Music* (1919) and the "Tango" and "Ragtime" sections in *L'Histoire du soldat*.

Various members of *Les Six* had passing flirtations with jazz. Francis Poulenc's *Rhapsodie nègre* (1917), dedicated to Satie, shows a fascination with, if some confusion about, black Americans, but contains no overt musical references to jazz or ragtime. Georges Auric composed a foxtrot, "Adieu, New York!" (1920) arranged for both solo piano and chamber ensemble and dedicated it to Cocteau. The cover depicts a ship sailing out of the New York City harbor, and the music captures the spirit of the dance with a four-beat per measure bass line and a dotted melody (see example 4.3). The dotted melodic line suggests an attempt to notate swung eighth-notes, and it may well have been conceived of and performed in a freer, less measured fashion. Auric's foxtrot was performed on the same concert with the premiere of *Le Boeuf sur le toit* in February 1920 and later at the opening of an exhibit of Francis Picabia's work in December 1920.[66]

The best-known exponent of jazz was Darius Milhaud. His *Caramel mou* for voice and jazz band dates from 1920, followed by the *Trois rag-caprices* in 1922, and his most famous work, *La Création du monde* in 1923. The *Caramel mou*, subtitled a "shimmy," was first performed in 1920 as part of a show staged by Pierre Bertin which included works by Poulenc, Auric, and Satie on texts by Cocteau, Raymond Radiguet and Max Jacobs. A black American, referred to only as "Gratton," danced to the work.[67] Scored for clarinet, saxophone, trumpet, trombone, percussion, and piano—a legitimate early New Orleans jazz

Example 4.3.   Georges Auric, *Adieu, New York!*

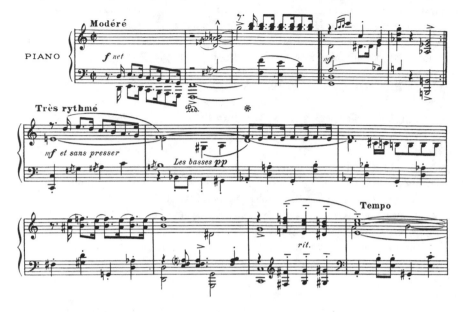

ensemble—the work has a text by Cocteau. The *Trois rag-caprices,* published in a piano solo arrangement as well, were dedicated to Jean Wiéner, who performed them at the sixth *Concert-Wiéner*. All three movements make use of pervasive syncopation.

   La Création du monde was by far the most celebrated work from the early 1920s which shows the direct influence of American jazz apart from ragtime. Milhaud wrote a great deal about his exposure to and fascination with jazz after his first introduction to it in London. He was intrigued by the new timbre, vitality of the rhythm section, syncopated melodic lines, and the possibilities these sounds suggested for his own compositions. Milhaud set out to write a work which did more than merely reinterpret dance rhythms, as he claimed had been done previously by Satie, Stravinsky, and Auric.

   After his first exposure in London and Paris, Milhaud learned more about jazz when he came to the United States in 1922. Singer Yvonne George took him to Harlem where he heard authentic performances of jazz and blues. "The music I heard was absolutely different from anything I had ever heard before and was a revelation to me. . . . Its effect on me was so overwhelming that I could not tear myself away."[68] During this visit, Milhaud flabbergasted the critics when he claimed that of all American music, jazz then had the most influence on contemporary European music. And Milhaud further claimed that American composers had yet to realize the importance of this native music.[69]

When Milhaud returned to France, bringing with him a number of Black Swan recordings, he began work on a ballet commissioned by Rolf de Maré for his Ballets Suédois. His collaborators were none other than Blaise Cendrars and Ferdinand Léger. Having already published his *L'Anthologie nègre,* Cendrars chose as the ballet's subject the creation of the world as described in African folklore. Léger followed Cendrars's lead and designed the curtain and scenery in a style reminiscent of African primitive art. The emphasis on Africana by his collaborators logically suggested to Milhaud his musical reliance on Afro-American musical idioms.

> At last in *La Création du Monde* I had the opportunity I had been waiting for to use those elements of jazz to which I had devoted so much study. I adopted the same orchestra as used in Harlem, seventeen solo instruments, and I made wholesale use of jazz style to convey a purely classical feeling.[70]

The instrumental ensemble Milhaud claimed to have heard in Harlem consisted of two flutes, two clarinets, oboe, bassoon, horn, two trumpets, trombone, piano, various percussion performed by one individual, a string quartet of two violins, cello, and bass viol, and saxophone. The ensemble is larger than the standard five- to seven-member New Orleans group, so he may have even heard an early version of a New York big band, which typically contained three brasses, three reeds, and a four-person rhythm section. The addition of the strings, with the exception of the bass, suggests a holdover from the prewar dance orchestra. Milhaud does not identify which specific group or groups he heard in New York, with the exception of a jazz violinist who conducted the dance band at the Hotel Brunswick.[71]

The music of *La Création du monde* shows the assimilation of numerous jazz techniques. Syncopation reigns supreme throughout the work. The score relies heavily on soloists, in particular the brasses, woodwinds and saxophone. The strings are not treated soloistically, but relegated to the rhythm section, perhaps in imitation of banjos. The piano doubles the rhythmic parts as in the standard jazz practice. Other jazz-influenced instrumental techniques include the use of mutes for the brass, flutter-tonguing, and glissandi.

Milhaud's clever adaptation of jazz idioms made him an overnight expert, and he wrote a number of articles on jazz history and technique.[72] In May of 1924 he lectured on jazz as part of the Groupe d'Etudes Philosophiques et Scientifiques. His musical examples included two Black Swan recordings, Bayou songs performed by Vera Janacopulos, works by Wiéner and Stravinsky, and a four-hands piano version of *La Création* performed by Milhaud and Wiéner.[73] But by the end of 1925 and early 1926, jazz had lost its fascination for

Example 4.4.   Jean Wiéner, *Sonatine syncopée*

him. His comments given during a second trip to the U.S. in 1926 indicate how quickly the jazz/art music interest had developed and spread, but then waned in France. Such would not be true in Germany.

Jean Wiéner composed a number of works showing his fascination with jazz as a compositional resource. The *Sonatine syncopée* (1923) for piano carried the important dedication: "Thank you dear negro orchestras of America. Thank you magnificent jazz bands for the charitable influence that you have had on the genuine music of my time."[74] As the title suggests, the work is marked by syncopated melodies which could be swung. The second movement, "Blues," a delicate, tender piece (see example 4.4), contains two illuminating performance instructions: firstly, in interpreting the second section "one should hear only the saxophone," and secondly, in the final section, the performer should aim to play "sweetly, like the trombones of the blacks."

Trois blues chantes (1924) for voice and piano, which was performed along with the *Sonatine* as part of Milhaud's lecture, contains a textless vocal part. Wiéner explained:

> The voice is treated here like an instrument, like a brass instrument. The author thought at first of composing these melodies for a negro saxophonist. One should thus sing supply and use a lot of breadth crescendi < > on the same note, and sing tenderly. One should also respect the duration and precede entirely in time, always striving to make each sound expressive, even the shortest note.[75]

The *Sept petites histoires extraites du grand alphabet instantané* (1924), also for voice and piano, has as its third movement an alliterative text on the letter "K" by René des Alyscamps, set to a "Rag-Time" with suitable syncopation. The 1929 collection *Album Wiéner-Doucet,* composed jointly with Clement Doucet, contains four works: a "Blues" and a "Haarlem-Tempo di blues" by Wiéner and the spunkier "Six-Cylinder Ragtime" and foxtrot "Chicken Pie" by Doucet. Wiéner's 1930 composition *Cadences pour deux pianos* has a syncopated first movement entitled "Jazz" dedicated to Paul Whiteman. The third movement, "Tango Argentin," uses both rhythms associated with the dance. This work, originally written for piano and orchestra and most likely performed by Wiéner and Doucet, appears to be Wiéner's last composition borrowing jazz or dance idioms.

Other Parisians who fell under the spell of American jazz were composer-conductor Gabriel Pierné (1863–1937) whose *Divertissement sur un thème pastoral* (1932) for orchestra contains a variation entitled "Cortège-Blues" which uses three muted trumpets and moves to a freely written alto saxophone solo, and Henri Cliquet-Pleyel (1894–1963), who wrote two early jazz-influenced piano works, *Deux blues* and *Cinq tangos.* Czech composer Bohuslav Martinů, who came to Paris in 1923 wrote a number of works showing his reliance on the jazz sound. His three-movement *Skizzy moderné tancǔ* (1927) contains "Blues," "Tango," and "Charleston" movements. The 1928 work for small orchestra *Jazz Suite* contains a "Prelude," "Blues," "Boston," and "Finale." "Blues" and "Foxtrot" movements appear in the later piano *Preludes* (1930).

Better known today are Maurice Ravel's several forays into the world of jazz. *L'Enfant et les sortilèges* (1925) contains a ragtime duet, suggested by Ravel to his librettist Colette, between the black Wedgwood teapot and chinoiserie cup. Colette enthusiastically supplied the two characters with suitable "American" dialogue—"I punch, I knock out you" and the especially telling phrase "Black, and strong, Black and chic."[76] The later *Violin Sonata* (1927), with its second movement "Blues," utilizes the lowered seventh, much syncopation and the violin imitating both the banjo, with pizzicato, and the saxophone, with glissandi. Ravel's *Concerto pour la main gauche* and the *Concerto for Piano and Orchestra* (both 1929–30) demonstrate his continued interest in jazz effects, especially blue notes and syncopation.

Jazz and Dance Music in Central and Eastern Europe

Central European composers came later than the French to the use of jazz idioms as a musical resource, but their enthusiasm for jazz and its possibilities was greater than that of the French. For many Central European composers, jazz was more than an infatuation; it provided a viable alternative to their worn-out nineteenth-century language. Jazz also reflected the modern age, and its widespread popularity with the mass audience made it philosophically attractive. And as French culture was to be emulated, the turn by its composers to jazz was to be followed as well.

A German source of exposure to jazz was the commercial radio system, which began broadcasting in October of 1923. The German radio aired symphonic music, programs of modern music often introduced by well-known critics, live concerts and operas, programs of light classics, dance music, and jazz. The Berlin stations, in particular, were famous for their fine jazz programming.[77] In 1924 *Funkstunde,* the weekly program guide for the Berlin Sende Stelle, shows *Tanzmusik* being broadcast most weeknights from 10:30 to 11:30 and on weekends until midnight. Featured groups on the dance music hour included violinist Robert Gaden and his ensemble performing such numbers as "Sahara" (foxtrot) "Dancing into Dreamland" (foxtrot), "Tabu" (blues), and "Ich liebe dich" (Boston).[78] Another radio ensemble was led by violinist Gerhard Hoffmann. His group, made up of three saxophones, two clarinets, two violins, trumpet, sousaphone, piano, banjo, and drums, appears to be a combination again of jazz's melodic and rhythmic sections and the violins of the older dance orchestra. In 1927–28, the Berlin radio broadcast 24 *Unterhaltungsmusik-Konzerte* by foreign salon ensembles and aired dance music on 221 evenings. Of these 221 dance shows, 46 were broadcast live from Berlin nightclubs and dance halls.[79] Also in 1927 the *Funkstunde* carried articles on self-instruction for the tango, Charleston, black bottom, blues and foxtrot.[80]

During the early 1920s, literally hundreds of native groups possessing some rudimentary knowledge of ragtime and dance music performed in Germany advertising themselves as jazz bands. Two particularly important German jazz pioneers were Eric Borchard and Fred Ross, popular between 1923 and 1925.[81] Borchard and his Yankee-Jazz-Band, consisting of Borchard on reeds and as vocalist, a trumpet, trombone doubling trumpet and banjo, a violin, piano, banjo, and drums, made a great number of recordings in Berlin. Many of these recordings have Americanized titles such as "Down on a Farm" and "Unfortunate Blues." Others show Borchard's knowledge of the Tin Pan Alley repertory.

German audiences could also obtain American records with little trouble. German recording companies, such as Lindström and Deutsche Grammophon, carried American labels such as Okeh, Odeon, Brunswick, Columbia, and others.[82] Thus interested composers and musicians would have had access to the top quality early recordings of King Oliver, Louis Armstrong and his Hot Five, Mamie Smith, and Bix Beiderbecke.

Sam Wooding and his band supplied the most important source of live American jazz for German audiences in the context of *The Chocolate Kiddies Revue.* The show, which never played in New York City although its name obviously borrows from the popular Sissle and Blake show *The Chocolate Dandies,* opened at the Berlin Admirals Palast in May of 1925 and ran intermittently for two years. With its cast of 40 singers, acrobatic dancers, and a chorus line of 10, *The Chocolate Kiddies* predates *La Revue nègre* and may have inspired André Daven of the Théâtre des Champs-Elysées to look for a black revue, thereby reversing the typical France-to-Germany flow of influence. Wooding was a veteran of a black army band and had played in New York City at The Club Alabam where he replaced Fletcher Henderson and his group. Wooding and his band continued to play throughout Europe apart from the revue and with greater success.

The actual revue depicted nightlife in a Harlem cafe and plantation life in the South and was not particularly successful, nor did it launch any star as did *La Revue nègre*. The music consisted of four numbers by Duke Ellington and Joe Trent, a number of other popular tunes by unspecified composers, several songs by Stephen Foster, and traditional spirituals. The revue concluded with "Swing Low, Sweet Chariot."[83]

The second act of the show was given over entirely to the revue band, and their solo music proved to be the most exciting and popular part of the revue. A photograph (see figure 4.1) probably dating from Wooding's New York City tenure shows him with an eight-piece group of two reeds, two brass (note doubling of horn), brass bass, banjo, piano and drums.[84] The original group Wooding took with him was slightly larger, as in an early New York big band, with brass players Bobby Martin, Maceo Edwards, and Tommy Ladnier (who had played with King Oliver); reeds Garvin Bushell, Willie Lewis, and Gene Sedric; Herb Fleming, trombone; John Warren, tuba; George Howe, drums; and Sam Wooding, piano and arranger. By October 1926, the probable date of the Hamburg photograph (figure 4.2), Tommy Ladnier is missing from the picture, King Edwards had replaced John Warren, and Percy Johnson had replaced George Howe.

The program for the second act jazz concert included a medley of American hit tunes, "Indian Love Call," "Shanghai Shuffle," "Some Other Day, Some Other Girl," and ended with the popular "St. Louis Blues." A later program from Stockholm included Negro spirituals, Tin Pan Alley standards, *Rhapsody in Blue,* "Memphis Blues," "Tiger Rag," and jazzed-up versions of the "1812 Overture," Sousa's "Stars and Stripes," and selections from Verdi's *Il Trovatore* and Gounod's *Faust.*[85]

Wooding and the band were so popular that within six weeks of the revue's opening the group recorded four sides for the German Vox label. The four tunes—"O Katharina," "Shanghai Shuffle," "Alabamy Bound," "By the Waters of the Minnetonka"—were taken from the revue and provide an idea of the exuberant, if not polished, quality of Wooding and his young group.[86] All four numbers are lively, with some decent solo work by Sedric and Ladnier, such as Ladnier's cornet solo in "Shanghai Shuffle." The arrangements are generally in the style of the "symphonic jazz" associated with Paul Whiteman and his larger ensemble, whom Wooding admired.[87] The banjo stands out prominently, and each work ends with a cymbal tag. "O Katharina" quotes snatches of "Ach, du lieber Augustin," "The Lorelei," and "O Tannenbaum" in obvious deference to

Figure 4.1. Sam Wooding and His Orchestra in New York, ca. 1925
(*Schomburg Center for Research in Black Culture, The New York Public Library, Astor, Lenox and Tilden Foundations*)

Figure 4.2. Sam Wooding and His Orchestra in Hamburg, ca. 1926 (*Schomburg Center for Research in Black Culture, The New York Public Library, Astor, Lenox and Tilden Foundations*)

the German audience.[88] Sound effects, popular with The Original Dixieland Jazz Band, appear in "Alabamy Bound," a tune which dated from the band's New York days. "By the Waters of Minnetonka," the slowest number of the four, features a sweet bassoon solo by Bushell and quotes the spiritual-like theme from Dvořák's *New World Symphony*. This number opened the revue as Wooding describes:

> When we finished, everything was still for about two seconds . . . then, like a clap of thunder the audience started banging their feet and shouting, "Bis, noch 'mal, Hoch, Bravo!" Well sir, the conglomeration of sound was so great that the word 'Bis'—a way of showing approval in German—sounded like 'beast' to us! Some of the boys—especially the saxophone section—had grabbed their horns and were all set to dash right out of the pit. But it went on for nearly five minutes, causing our fright to turn to confidence. . . . I knew we had made the grade and it would be smooth sailing from now on. "By the Waters of the Minnetonka" was not our best selection.[89]

Between 1925 and 1927 the group toured with the revue to Hamburg, then Stockholm, Copenhagen, back through Germany, parts of Eastern Europe, Switzerland, Spain, Russia (where they missed being the first jazz group there by days), France, and South America. They also broadcast live over the Berlin radio,[90] and recorded again in 1926 (Berlin), 1929 (Barcelona and Paris), and 1931 (Paris). They disbanded in Paris in 1931, although Willie Lewis stayed on and formed his own band.[91] The ten numbers recorded in Barcelona include such well-known songs as "Tiger-Rag," with a well-rehearsed clarinet solo and nascent scat singing, "I Can't Give You Anything but Love, Baby," and "Sweet Black Blues," which has a clarinet and dirty trumpet solos in imitation of blues singing.[92]

Although *The Chocolate Kiddies Revue* with Wooding's music was a foreign commodity, the native revue and *Kabarettrevue* also provided a forum for the increasingly popular music. Erik Charell is credited with being the first to use jazz bands in a revue; his *An Alle* of 1924 boasted two jazz bands, one on stage and one in the orchestra pit.[93] Charell's revue also featured the Tiller-Girls, a chorus line of 16 British dancers who starred in a number of revues and performed in Broadway musicals. Besides performing standard synchronized chorus line numbers, the Tiller-Girls also included jazz dances in their routines.

Charell's innovation caught on, and soon other revues advertised their jazz bands. A writer for the *Berliner Tageblatt* in 1925 claimed to have heard the London Corona Jazz Band with its saxophone quartet and Mr. Fuh's Jazz Band as part of two different *Kabarettrevue* shows.[94] Many of these new bands may simply have been revamped dance orchestras, but others appear to have been more in keeping with true early jazz ensembles. A photograph of composer Friedrich Hollaender with his *Kabarettrevue* band shows Hollaender seated at a piano surrounded by saxophone, banjo, trumpet, and trombone players.[95] With the inclusion of a drummer, this ensemble would fit New Orleans instrumentation.

As it was in the context of a Nelson Theater revue that Josephine Baker first appeared in Berlin, her back-up ensemble no doubt further stimulated the use of jazz bands in revues. Baker returned to Berlin in 1928 for a guest appearance in Hollaender's *Kabarettrevue Bitte Einsteigen*. She appeared with another popular black American dancer, Louis Douglas, who had also been in *La Revue nègre* and was billed as "the Best negro tap-dancer in the world."[96] As Baker did not bring a band with her to Berlin, and Douglas also appears to have been a guest star, the hosting theaters must have been able to supply the lively, syncopated music associated with these dancers.

Jazz permeated all areas of Austro-Germanic culture. With the proliferation of dance bands, many composers later claimed to have earned money in their student years playing in such ensembles. Even the Bauhaus had a jazz band. The Bauhaus five-member group supposedly lasted for some 10 years, 1923–33, and performed at many Bauhaus functions and toured.[97] Photographs by Bauhaus faculty member Lux Feininger, such as "X. Schawinsky Plays with Banjo" (1928) and "Johnny Plays" (1928) of a saxophonist, prove how jazz imagery could be borrowed by other areas of the avant-garde.[98]

Otto Dix's triptych *The Metropolis* (1928) includes a depiction of Berlin nightlife complete with the prominent saxophones of a jazz band. Karl Hofer's *Jazzband* (1927) shows a six-member ensemble dressed in tuxedos. The saxophonist is black; other instruments portrayed in the group are piano, violin, banjo, and drums.

The Influence of Jazz on Central and East European Art Music

With the presence of jazz through live performances by foreign and native groups, public radio broadcasts, and recordings, German composers soon followed the lead of the French in considering jazz idioms as suitable material for their compositions, particularly in their need to break with the past and write for the present. Unlike the French, young Germans and East Europeans exhibited an earnestness in their turn to jazz as a resource, and they tried to prove the logical necessity of their use. It did not take long before the discussion of the relative merits of jazz and its role in modern musical life filled the pages of German music journals. Jazz was widely discussed and much ink was spilled over its pros and cons. As with the opera crisis, those who favored anti- or post-Wagnerian operatic solutions generally supported jazz as a stimulus for composition.

Stuckenschmidt, always in support of new ideas and much influenced by the French, recognized jazz's potential early on and wrote in 1924: "This land

America has given the world new dance rhythms. They will provide the solution to the artistic struggle which binds Europe."[99] In the same year, Czech composer and jazz enthusiast Erwin Schulhoff published an essay, "Der Mondäne Tanz," which chronicled early attempts by composers to translate jazz dance idioms into classical compositions.[100] Schulhoff drew the correlation, as would many other writers, between modern composers producing suites of tangos, foxtrots, and shimmies, and J. S. Bach's reliance on the minuet or Chopin's use of the mazurka.

The editors of *Anbruch,* recognizing a new trend, devoted the April 1925 issue to jazz. Consisting of six articles, the issue included an essay by Milhaud on the history and development of the jazz band, along with other discussions of jazz performers and techniques.[101] American composer Louis Gruenberg, who was then living in Germany, gave his recommendations for using jazz idioms and techniques. Generally recognized as a jazz authority, Gruenberg had contributed another essay, "Vom Jazz und anderen Dingen," to the *25 Jahre neue Musik* publication, in which he described his own turn to jazz and gave predictions for its future use.[102]

In "Der Jazz als Ausgangspunkt," Gruenberg countered the prevalent European view already expressed by Schulhoff that dance forms represented the first "jumping-off place" for jazz usage. Claiming that no major works of art have had dance as their basis (e.g., Bach's *Passions* were greater than his keyboard *Suites*), Gruenberg stressed that composers must look to jazz's other attributes such as its reliance on soloists. Gruenberg concluded that the European jazz-inspired works he had heard confirmed his belief that only native Americans "whose blood, upbringing, and heart is from America" had the capacity to write this new music.[103] (Erwin Schulhoff later took exception to such American chauvinism in his "Eine Jazz-Affaire."[104]) Percy Grainger, whose article closed the *Anbruch* jazz issue, gave jazz a lukewarm reception. He maintained that all of jazz's supposedly new features, the rhythms, melody, and instrumentation, had already existed. At best, Grainger suggested, jazz would produce an impression on classical music without exerting a true influence.

Auftakt published a jazz issue as well.[105] Appearing a year later, the *Auftakt* issue was longer and more comprehensive than *Anbruch*'s. All the writers enjoyed jazz as entertainment music, supported its influence on classical music, and shared a common enthusiasm for its rhythmic character. Alicia Simon, of Washington, D. C., maintained that jazz provided rhythmic renewal. Artur Iger, in an article on the new jazz industry, mentioned that the percussion section in general had assumed a new role thanks to jazz's "glorification of rhythm." And Alfred Baresel, whose article was entitled "Jazz als Rettung [deliverance]," celebrated jazz's syncopation as a narcotic producing self-liberation. Baresel also praised jazz for demonstrating the possibilities of smaller ensembles and soloists, and for reintroducing the long-forgotten art of improvisation.

Alfred Baresel had earlier expounded the saving possibilities of jazz in a 1925 monograph, revised and expanded in 1929 as *Das neue Jazzbuch,* a "practical handbook for musicians, composers, arrangers, dancers and friends of jazz."[106] Baresel, who worked in Leipzig as a critic and taught at the conservatory, claimed he learned about jazz after the war from an American music student. And he published his first study of jazz, "Von Mozart bis Jazzband," in 1921.[107] In 1922, he had the opportunity to play piano in a jazz group and gained valuable practical experience.

His history of jazz, which opens the 1929 revised edition, is by far the most informed and objective treatment published in Europe during these early years. In his second chapter, entitled "The Elements of Jazz," Baresel provides a detailed analysis of different jazz rhythms and tempi, the mysteries of syncopation, harmonic and melodic aspects, and the particulars of different instruments. For example, he singles out the piano as the lead instrument which provided the entire group with direction through its twin role in the rhythm section and as a soloist. And he designates the saxophone as jazz's most important melodic instrument.

Baresel does identify the violin as a possible member of a jazz ensemble, which appears to have been the case in European ensembles and American dance orchestras, but was rare in actual American jazz bands. However, he does note that the second violin and viola of the salon orchestra are absent from true jazz ensembles, and that the violin, when used, doubles the melody with the woodwinds. He describes a typical jazz ensemble as composed of piano, drums, saxophone, trumpet, banjo, and violin.

A separate chapter deals with improvisation and provides advice on how to "jazz up" [*verjazzen*] preexisting melodies. He also discusses the use of jazz in art music or *Kunstjazz* as it came to be called, such as Gruenberg's *Jazzberries,* Milhaud's *Trois rag-caprices,* and Krenek's *Jonny spielt auf.* Baresel's extensive bibliography includes Coeuroy and Schaeffner's book, Paul Whiteman's questionable history of jazz, and W. C. Handy's *Blues.* Baresel published other pedagogical studies or *Schulen* for various jazz instruments and continued to write enthusiastically of jazz, "the most original kind of music of our time."[108]

Although not devoting an entire issue to the subject, the Berlin-based mainstream journal *Die Musik* published an early positive discussion by Hermann Schildberger-Gleiwitz.[109] He stressed jazz's rhythmic elements as well as the democratic nature of a jazz ensemble where everyone had an equal voice. Jazz and its joyful nature, he claimed, opened up a new musical world. Two later articles put jazz into a historical context, thereby providing it with some legitimacy. Alois Melichar in "Walzer und Jazz" claimed that dances are always the clearest indicators of an era, and therefore jazz, which he equated with dance music, was the Strauss waltz of the 1920s.[110] Rudolf Sonner put jazz in the context of nineteenth-century Viennese coffeehouse orchestras.[111]

Paul Bernhard's book *Jazz: Eine musikalische Zeitfrage* followed Baresel's study in 1927 and also tried to put jazz into a historical perspective.[112] Bernhard introduced his study by showing how European composers always sought new inspiration for their works. Jazz, then, was just the latest inspiration, which provided new and exciting rhythms. Bernhard gave as his typical jazz band: piano, and again violin, banjo, alto and tenor saxophones, double bass, and percussion. Related instruments which might be used included the trumpet, trombone, cello, swanee whistle and flexatone. (Krenek used the last two in *Jonny spielt auf.*) Other chapters described how syncopation and jazz harmonies function, gave a brief history of jazz, and provided further pointers on leading a jazz band and orchestrating works for one. Bernhard concluded with a discussion of Gruenberg's *Daniel Jazz*, which he felt best showed how jazz could be used in classical compositions, and he applauded Paul Whiteman for putting the jazz band on the European concert stage.

Not everyone shared Baresel or Bernhard's positive views on jazz. Critic Adolf Weissmann gave jazz and its influences on art music a mixed review in his *Die Entgötterung der Musik* (1926).[113] Although he did not entirely disapprove of music "coming to earth," as found both in *Gebrauchsmusik* and jazz-inspired works, Weissmann had some reservations about making music entirely conform to modern culture. Anti-jazz articles, which appeared in a variety of German musical journals, decried jazz's preoccupation with rhythm, its roots in primitive culture, its strident, aggressive, commercialized, erotic, un-German nature, and attacked any attempt to view jazz as art music.

Such negative responses were common in the American press too towards ragtime and jazz.[114] And Americans who supported jazz often harbored ambivalent feelings. J. A. Rodgers, in "Jazz at Home," published in the important anthology of the Harlem Renaissance *The New Negro*, celebrated jazz's popularity at home and abroad but concluded by saying that those who opposed it should work to "divert it into nobler channels."[115] Sam Wooding expressed similar mixed feelings about jazz's true worth. In a 1938 article relating his European experiences, he stressed his classical training, how he made his band members attend as many classical concerts as possible when they toured, and asserted that his tenure in Europe was just a means to "loftier" ends, such as the Wooding Southland Spiritual Choir he currently led.[116] His remarks were no doubt influenced by their inclusion in the cultivated mainstream journal *Etude* and his wish to put his choir in the best light.

In November of 1927, the actions of the Hoch Conservatory in Frankfurt am Main provided jazz antagonists with a major rallying point. Bernard Sekles, the conservatory's director, announced they would offer instruction in jazz, the first such institutional training offered anywhere in Europe or the United States.[117] Classes would begin in January of 1928 on drums, saxophone, banjo, trombone, and individual ensembles, and if there was enough interest, Sekles maintained, the conservatory planned to offer classes in jazz vocal performance. The teacher, unnamed at that point, was reputed to be a famous jazz drummer who had performed in the United States. Sekles tempted fate further by stating that the conservatory had both the right and duty to offer such training and that it now recognized jazz as an art music and hoped the new courses would prove to be a "transfusion of fresh [*unverbrauchten*] Negro blood."

When asked for his opinion by critic Karl Holl, Alfred Baresel pointed out that 80 percent of the conservatory's students ended up in entertainment fields, most without suitable preparatory training; thus he wholeheartedly approved of the plan. Holl himself took a more moderate stance. Unlike Sekles or Baresel, he viewed jazz not as a true art form but as a kind of musical arts and crafts; however, he welcomed the teaching of jazz instrumental techniques.

Mátyás Seiber (1905–60), a composer, former student of Kodály, and supposedly a jazz pianist and drummer, headed the Hoch jazz department. His American performing experience, however, seems to have been limited to playing the cello in an ocean liner orchestra on voyages to North and South America. Seiber taught the jazz piano and instrumentation classes, while five other musicians were responsible for instruction in saxophone, trumpet, trombone, percussion and banjo.[118] A typical weekly schedule for a student enrolled in the department included two hours of instrumental instruction, two hours of ensemble performance, and one hour of the instrumentation class. Seiber also organized the Hoch Conservatory jazz orchestra which gave concerts and broadcast over the Frankfurt radio. A 3 March 1929 concert by the ensemble included a performance of Gershwin's *Rhapsody in Blue* and the "Virginia Stomp." Seiber's ensemble also assisted in the Frankfurt premiere of *Die Dreigroschenoper* during the 1928–29 season. During the five seasons of its existence, the school enrolled from 12 to 19 students in its jazz program each year.[119]

While director of the program, Seiber published four essays on his work, enumerating the reasons for the serious study of jazz.[120] The first, "Jazz als Erziehungsmittel [educational means]," appeared in 1928 and justified teaching jazz techniques to any and all music students. Students would develop greater rhythmic precision, thereby increasing their facility with rhythmically complex modern scores. Even more importantly, jazz study encouraged students to reclaim lost improvisatory skills which had been an important aspect of musicianship prior to the twentieth century.[121] Schott Brothers later published Seiber's jazz percussion method in 1929.[122]

Seiber left Frankfurt in 1933 when the conservatory suspended the program in response to political pressure. He appears to have had little more to do with jazz or jazz instruction after 1945, when he published an article debunking jazz's supposed rhythmic complexity, calling it "childishly simplified clichés."[123] He emigrated to England and lived there until his death in 1960.

The Hoch Conservatory's announcement unleashed a storm of protest in the conservative music press, news of which even reached the United States; a *New York Times* story of 11 March 1928 carried the title "Jazz Bitterly Opposed in Germany." Many journals had already published articles decrying the influence of jazz on German music, but the Frankfurt decision provided a specific focus for their attacks. The *Zeitschrift für Musik,* a journal which became increasingly vitriolic towards modern trends during the later twenties, suggested that the Hoch Conservatory could bring about their wished for blood transfusion more easily by importing a number of young black men and women.[124] *Signale für die musikalische Welt* saw the proposed course as another manifestation of the dreaded *Gebrauchsmusik.*[125] The *Rheinische Musik- und Theater-Zeitung* described jazz as a kind of spiritual inflation, a reflection of a degenerate society which arose outside Germany, and the writer could not believe such barbarism would actually be taught in a German institution.[126] Paul Schwers, editor of the *Allgemeine Musikzeitung,* polled other directors of music schools about the Frankfurt venture.[127] While Franz Schreker of Berlin said the classes were premature, Hermann Abendroth of Cologne called for direct opposition to the influence of jazz. Hans Pfitzner's seething response cast jazz as not only anti-German but as a force in support of pacifism and internationalism, favored targets of the National Socialists.

The avant-garde press defended the Hoch. Heinrich Strobel, writing in *Anbruch,* claimed that jazz had a connection with life which was missing from nineteenth-century music.[128] He defended the training on the grounds that it improved instrumental virtuosity. He called to those who protested to live with the times, not against them.

Many Central and East European composers seeking artistic renewal in the postwar period turned to the rhythms and timbres of jazz for deliverance, to borrow from Alfred Baresel's 1926 article. One of the first to do so was the Czech composer and pianist Erwin Schulhoff (1894–1942). Schulhoff claimed to have worked in the 1920s as a jazz pianist in Prague. A prolific composer, Schulhoff found inspiration in Czech, Bohemian, and other folk sources as well as in jazz. And dances, both folk and jazz, provided models for many of his compositions.[129] Four of the five movements of his early *Fünf Pittoresken* for piano (1919), dedicated to painter George Grosz, have jazz dance tempi indications for titles, as in the first movement, "Zeitmass-Foxtrott." His *Ragmusic* (1922), dedicated to British composer Arthur Bliss, who also experimented with jazz idioms, has movements entitled "Tempo di Foxtrott," "Jazz-like" and "Tango-Rag." The 1922 piano work *Partita,* again dedicated to Bliss, contains "Boston" and "Tango" movements as well as a finale entitled "Jimmy-Jazz."

The *5 Etudes de jazz* (1927) opens with a chromatic "Charleston" dedicated to Zez Confrey, composer of the novelty piano piece "Kitten on the Keys" from

Example 4.5.   Erwin Schulhoff, *5 Etudes de Jazz*, "Blues"

1921. The second movement, "Blues," was dedicated to Paul Whiteman (see example 4.5). The right hand, dotted as in the accompaniment, spins a free chromatic melody which becomes more ornate and then returns to its original character. Again the dotted notation may have been meant to suggest swung eighth-notes. A highly syncopated "Chanson" follows. The rhythmically complex fourth movement, "Tango," shows evidence of the triplet bolero rhythm combined with the usual habanera rhythm (see example 4.6). A chromatic and highly syncopated "Tocatta sur le shimmy 'Kitten on the Keys'" dedicated to the great friend of jazz, Alfred Baresel, ends these piano studies.

Other jazz-inspired piano works by Schulhoff include the *Esquisses de jazz* (1928), written for student use, with "Rag," "Boston," "Tango," "Blues," "Charleston," and "Black Bottom" movements, the composition *Hot Music* (1928), subtitled "Ten Syncopated Studies," and a six-movement *Suite dansante en jazz* (1931). Further compositions using dance idioms were Schulhoff's incidental music for Molière's play *Le Bourgeois Gentilhomme*, the *Divertissement* (1927) for oboe, clarinet, and bassoon with its "Charleston" movement, and the jazz oratorio *H. M. S. Royal Oak*, on a text by Otto Rombach, for narrator, jazz singer, mixed chorus, and symphonic jazz orchestra. The latter work received its premiere in Frankfurt on 18 May 1931. Besides the large-scale oratorio, Schulhoff's opera *Flammen* (1932), on a libretto by Karl J. Benes which updated the familiar Don Juan story, used a jazz band and appropriate music to set scenes and provide dramatic irony.[130] Schulhoff also wrote a great number of works in the style of popular sheet music under several pseudonyms.

Example 4.6.   Erwin Schulhoff, *5 Etudes de Jazz*, "Tango"

And he left many works—a jazz concerto for two pianos and orchestra, "Rumba" for orchestra, and a jazz concertino for violin, saxophone and piano—unfinished at the time of his death in a German concentration camp.

Emil Burian (1904–59), another Czech composer, led what he called a jazz band in a Prague cabaret and likewise wrote a number of jazz-inspired works such as his song cycle *Koktarly* [cocktails] (1926) for voice and jazz band. Larger works include his jazz opera *Bubu vom Montparnasse* (1928) and his *Jazz-Requiem* (1928) for soprano and bass solo voices, voiceband, violino-saxophone, harmonium, piano and drums. Burian claimed that this religious work, which was premiered in a Prague church, had to incorporate jazz because jazz was "the music of our loves and dreams."[131] The activities of Burian and Schulhoff both show how far jazz spread and how important Prague was as a center of contemporary music prior to World War II.

Austrian composer Wilhelm Grosz (1894–1939) wrote a single-movement work for violin and piano entitled *Jazzband* (1924) which was performed alongside Gruenberg's *Daniel Jazz* at the 1925 I. S. C. M. meeting in Venice and probably provoked Gruenberg's American chauvinism. Grosz's *Jazzband* is a flashy work with some syncopation and prominent use of piano glissandi. While his first *Dance Suite* for piano (1922) had movements in the style of minuets, gavottes, waltzes, and polkas, his *II. Dance Suite* (1926) relied on jazz dances and included a syncopated cut-time "Foxtrot," a waltzlike "Boston," a habanera-based "Tango," a fast, energetic, and racy "Shimmy" (see example 4.7), and a five-four meter "Quasi-Fivestep." The work was performed over the

Example 4.7.   Wilhelm Grosz, *II. Dance Suite*, "Shimmy"

Berlin radio as part of an evening of contemporary music which included works by Poulenc, Milhaud, and Roussel.[132]

Grosz's best-known composition, and one which showed the full scope of his jazz knowledge, was the pantomime-ballet *Baby in der Bar*. The ballet, on a story by film writer Béla Balázs, tells the modern tale of an infant abandoned in a bar by its mother, a "young woman, like a proletarian film prostitute" [*proletarische Filmdirne*]. During the surrealistic course of the ballet, the baby grows up, learns to walk, gets drunk, flirts with bar patrons and the bartender, has a fight with the bartender, and is eventually thrown out on the street when its mother returns with a second infant.

Grosz cleverly adapted both jazz timbres and dance rhythms to his ballet score. The work relies on dance idioms throughout and is scored for solo violin, two alto saxophones, tenor saxophone, two trumpets, trombone, sousaphone, banjo doubling with cello, percussion and two pianos. The ensemble is large, in keeping with both Bernhard and Baresel's descriptions, and is also fairly true to the instrumentation of a twenties big band, which Grosz could have known from published arrangements. The *tragische Mutter* is characterized by a slow "Quasi Boston." The baby learns to walk to a "Shimmy-Blues," gets drunk and flirts

Example 4.8.   Wilhelm Grosz, *Baby in der Bar*, "Tango"

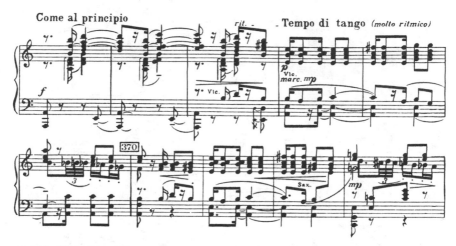

with the patrons during a "Tango," turns her affections towards the bartender with a "Shimmy" and has a fight accompanied by a "Charleston." Grosz reserves the tango, with its special rhythms and connotation, appropriately enough, for a scene of seduction (see example 4.8).

Later jazz-inspired works by Grosz include the *Afrika-Songs* (1930) and the *Zwölf kleine Negerlein* (1932), a setting of children's poems.[133] (His 1930 *Zeitoper, Achtung! Aufnahme!*, on a libretto by Balázs concerning the modern cinema industry, is discussed in the conclusion.) Grosz, like Schulhoff, also composed popular songs and revue numbers, such as the tango foxtrot "Isle of Capri" (1934) and "Red Sails in the Sunset" (1935). He emigrated to the United States in 1938, where he wrote for Tin Pan Alley.

Other Germans, Austrians, and Eastern Europeans wrote isolated examples of *Kunstjazz* (see appendix A). Jazz even invaded the closed circle of the Second Viennese School with Alban Berg's *Der Wein* (1928). The second theme of the opening movement, "Die Seele des Weines," is marked *Tempo di tango*. The trumpet and trombones are instructed to use jazz mutes, and the strings are to pizzicato "à la banjo." The standard rhythm appears in the piano, which Berg treated as a member of the rhythm section, and then moves to the drum. The alto saxophone enters four bars later with the melody. The text at this point, "Do you hear the echos of the songs of Sunday," refers to popular music. The *Tempo di tango* section returns during the last section, "Der Wein des Einsamen," as before, but with the addition of a muted trumpet solo. The textual allusion is even stronger here: "A tender kiss from the slender Adeline, the exciting and inviting sound of the violin." The tango mood captures the sense of longing in the poem.

The conservative view of jazz became a violent objection once the National Socialists came to power. Condemned for being a product of Jewish and black American elements, jazz was completely banned from the German radio in 1935.[134] In 1938, as part of the *Reichsmusiktage,* the town of Düsseldorf sponsored an exhibition of *Entartete Musik*—a variation on the "Degenerate Art" exhibit held a year earlier in Munich. Besides works of art which treated jazz themes, such as Hofer's painting, the exhibition featured recordings of the degenerate popular music "of the past era," along with scores by Stravinsky, Hindemith, Krenek, and Weill.[135] The pamphlet written in connection with the exhibition had as its cover illustration a black saxophonist striking the same pose as the one on the cover of the piano-vocal score of *Jonny spielt auf.* Here, however, the racial features are grotesquely exaggerated and on his lapel he wears a Star of David.[136] The amount of time spent by the government to degrade jazz not only indicates how popular it had been, but suggests that the National Socialists were not entirely successful in their efforts to suppress it.[137]

Jazz exerted such a pervasive influence on European culture during the 1920s that Krenek, Weill, and Hindemith could scarcely have escaped it. Espousing as they did the necessity for artists to maintain roots in popular culture, and with their interest in French artistic trends, their turn to jazz as a musical resource was only logical. All three composers explored the possibilities of the new sound before their *Zeitopern.* But their *Zeitopern* represent the first time the new sound broke into the world of German opera and in it jazz functioned as an important dramaturgical element composed not only of timbres and rhythms but bringing with it a cultural context and atmosphere. It was this German infatuation with both America and freer French culture that not only accounted for jazz's popularity but was at the heart of the first *Zeitoper,* Ernst Krenek's *Jonny spielt auf.*

Figure 5.1.   Ernst Krenek and Walther Brügmann before the Premiere of *Jonny spielt auf* in 1927
(Reproduced courtesy of Universal Edition, A.G., Wien)

Ernst Krenek: *Jonny spielt auf*

Berlin Years, 1920–1923

Krenek identified his trip to Paris in December of 1924 as having most influenced the creation of *Jonny spielt auf*, but his earlier works and association with other composers, performers, patrons, and critics paved the way for this first *Zeitoper*. Krenek came to Berlin in 1920 to continue composition studies with Franz Schreker, who had resigned his post in Vienna and taken a position at the Berlin Hochschule für Musik. At the Hochschule Krenek met pianist and composer Eduard Erdmann (1896–1958) and then pianist Artur Schnabel (1882–1951), both of whom would have a considerable effect on the course of Krenek's compositional development. Erdmann convinced Krenek to adapt a dissonant idiom, which caused Krenek's subsequent estrangement from Schreker. Erdmann and Schnabel later influenced Krenek's turn to American jazz idioms which lay at the heart of *Jonny spielt auf*.

Although Krenek probably heard some rudimentary jazz or dance music before he went to Berlin, Schnabel provided him with a regular exposure to American popular music.[1] While on tours of the United States in December of 1921 and during the 1922–23 season, Schnabel acquired sheet music and possibly recordings which furnished both Krenek and Erdmann with examples of the popular new music. Schnabel was fascinated with America, according to Krenek, and enjoyed playing his examples of American popular music for Krenek and his friends. Krenek remembers this music as consisting of popular songs by George Gershwin, Irving Berlin, and other Tin Pan Alley composers.[2]

Erdmann had been in Berlin since 1916 studying composition with Heinz Tiessen, a member of the *Novembergruppe*. Though several of Erdmann's compositions, including the *Symphony I* (1920) and the orchestral *Rondo* (1921), received prestigious premieres and were published during this time, Erdmann was known primarily as a concert pianist, and he would become the leading interpreter of Krenek's piano works. As a pianist, Erdmann served as a juror for several early Donaueschingen Music Festivals, demonstrated mechanical pianos in London for the Aeolian company, and performed at the 1926 opening of the Dessau Bauhaus. From 1925 on, Erdmann taught at the Cologne Hochschule für Musik. He resigned in 1935 in protest over the treatment of his Jewish colleagues, and he would not perform in public again until 1946, when he gave a series of four concerts featuring the works of composers who had been banned under the National Socialists.[3]

In 1922 Krenek composed his first works which show the influence of American jazz dance music: the op. 13 *Toccata und Chaconne* and a single-movement "Tanzstudie" published in the Universal Edition *Grotesken Album* piano anthology.[4] Charles Selig noted that the works contained therein demonstrated how young composers such as Grosz, Alois Hába, Petyrek, Egon Wellesz, and Bartok had turned away from the traditional formal and harmonic principles and had sought inspiration in folk music or popular dance. Krenek's "Tanzstudie," with its pervasive tango rhythms, is the only work in the anthology which relies on popular dance idioms.

The *Toccata und Chaconne,* based on the chorale "Ja, ich glaub an Jesum Christum," was published in 1923 along with an appendix, op. 13a, entitled *Eine kleine Suite von Stücken über denselbigen Choral verschiedenen Charakters.* The "Toccata" and "Chaconne" were serious studies in old contrapuntal forms enlivened with dissonant harmony and perhaps were meant as homage to Busoni, whose *Toccata* with a "Ciacona" movement had appeared two years earlier. The appendix contains movements neo-classical in nature: "Allemande," "Sarabande," "Gavotte," "Walzer," and "Fuge." The concluding movement and longest section of the suite, however, is a "Foxtrott," whose oom-pah oom-pah bass line and dotted, swingable melody shows Krenek's sure understanding of the dance's character, which he combined with his dissonant harmonic idiom (see example 5.1). Erdmann performed the work in Berlin in 1923 as part of the Internationale Gesellschaft für Neue Musik.

Krenek composed the op.13a *Suite* in June of 1922, and the "Tanzstudie" was probably written earlier in the same year. Thus both works postdate Schnabel's first American tour and were probably direct results of Schnabel's musical imports and may, as well, have been modelled on Schnabel's own compositional experiments. Schnabel composed as a leisure activity, and Erdmann performed one of his works, *Eine Tanzsuite* with its first movement "Fox-trott," on a 19 March 1922 concert sponsored by the *Novembergruppe.*[5] Erdmann later responded to Schnabel and Krenek with a *Fox-trot in C-Dur* composed in 1923 and dedicated to Krenek and his wife, Anna Mahler.[6]

Der Sprung über den Schatten

In 1922, Krenek also began work on his first large-scale opera, *Der Sprung über den Schatten,* which received its premiere in Frankfurt on 9 June 1924. Krenek's libretto explores some of the same issues of freedom and individual fulfillment

Example 5.1.   Ernst Krenek, *Suite,* op. 13a, "Foxtrott"

later found in *Jonny spielt auf,* and the musical score incorporates the jazz idioms already present in the op. 13a "Foxtrott" and "Tanzstudie."

The title came from a German saying which means that individuals cannot entirely rid themselves of their inhibitions, just as they cannot jump over their own shadows. The dramatic action revolves around a Doctor Berg who claims that through hypnosis he helps his patients leap over their shadows (see synopsis, appendix C). With its theme of personal fulfillment and loss of inhibitions, the opera also presents a satirical view of modern marriage and sexual mores. The leading characters, a Prince and a Princess, become attracted to other people and eventually are divorced, though as the character Marcus, a detective, points out at the end of the opera, nothing has really changed and the characters' inhibitions remain.

Krenek's theme reflects the larger societal interest in the unconscious mind and inhibited behavior which was a result of Sigmund Freud's research and the later work by his student Carl Jung. Freud's *Three Essays on Sexuality* were published as early as 1905, his *General Introduction to Psychoanalysis* in 1915, and in 1923, the year of the completion of *Der Sprung über den Schatten, Id, Ego and Super-Ego* appeared with its discussion of human personality. Sexual taboos had become topics for public discussion, and Freud's controversial theories and psychoanalysis were especially popular in Berlin.[7] Thus Dr. Berg, the hypnotist, is a topical reference to contemporary mental health practitioners. *Der Sprung über den Schatten* also displays the enlightened contemporary attitude towards marriage and divorce, topics treated later in Hindemith's *Neues vom Tage* and Schoenberg's *Von Heute auf Morgen.*

Krenek had treated this theme of individual freedom in his earlier work, *Zwingburg,* also composed in 1922, and expounded on it again in his third opera, *Orpheus und Eurydike,* completed in 1923.[8] The preoccupation with individual liberation reflects the philosophy of prewar expressionism, which continued to exercise a hold on contemporary art. Krenek may also have been influenced by his teacher Franz Schreker, whose operas, such as *Der ferne Klang,* dealt with issues of personal, even sexual, freedom. However, *Der Sprung über den Schatten* is a comic work and pokes fun at psychoanalysis, modern poets with writing blocks, and unhappily married couples. Although Krenek stated that the action takes place in the present, the reliance on regal characters prevents it from possessing the true *Alltäglichkeit* of *Jonny spielt auf.* The stage settings, designed for the Frankfurt premiere by Ludwig Sievert, underscored the expressionistic qualities of the work, with their abstract designs and antinaturalistic coloring.[9]

Krenek cast *Der Sprung über den Schatten* in the form of a number-opera, showing his early allegiance to a post-Wagnerian ideal inspired by the Handel revival. The orchestration of *Der Sprung über den Schatten* is unusual for the amount and variety of percussion, including xylophone, tambourine, castanets, and tam-tam, as well as the inclusion of banjo.[10] Krenek's score combines his early dissonant, complex style with elements borrowed from American popular music, and he further relies on the sociological symbolism of American dance to underscore his theme of personal freedom.

Krenek designated the overture as a "Tempo di Foxtrot," and the bass line and melody, with its dotted rhythms and two-note slurs, resembles that of his op. 13a. The majority of the first act takes place at a masked ball, and Krenek designates one large ensemble number as a *Foxtrot.* Members of the chorus call to the "Jazzband" to strike up a "hotter" version of the dance. And they proceed to dance and sing about a "Nigger-boy" from the free land of America, who knows all the new dance steps. The music, in cut-time, utilizes the standard accompaniment figure as in the op. 13a coupled with a dotted melodic line. The choral refrain is a hymn to the corporeal, liberating power of dance:

Round in a circle, turn, stamp, dance wildly. O let me sink in you, I stand still in life no more. Frantic swaying tottering. When swaying, you think no more. This is the dance machine of our time. All are ready to trot and step. Twirl in a wild, whirling dance, you will become light and free.[11]

The foxtrot idiom continues through this scene, and Krenek's orchestration, utilizing xylophone, banjo, and castanets, underscores the rhythmic quality of the dance. The inclusion of the banjo results in the identifiable timbre of a dance band.

Towards the end of this same act, which includes more on-stage dancing at the masked ball, Krenek designates another number as *Introduction und Jazz*. This *Jazz* section is in two-four meter with a dotted, syncopated melodic line for solo violin, over a standard foxtrot bass line. Tango rhythms enter later, accented with castanets. During this number, Prince Kuno and Odette, his future lover, meet. The inhibited Kuno expresses his hatred for dance music but Odette responds that jazz is good and powerful.

Foxtrot idioms return in the last two numbers of the opera as part of another dance scene. The penultimate number, a *Tempo di foxtrot,* is in cut-time, and the work ends with an *Introduction and Finale (a la Jazzband)*. During this final number Marcus, the private detective, gives the moral of the story, and the happy couples—the Prince and Princess having obtained a divorce and with new lovers—lead the rest of the chorus in a grand dance in which all try vainly to jump over their shadows. The finale is in two-four meter, and at one point the violin and banjo share the melody. The music becomes increasingly percussive towards the end as Krenek uses dissonant chord clusters, in the tango rhythm, orchestrated for the battery of percussion.

Der Sprung über den Schatten was one of four operas which received premieres in Frankfurt during the summer of 1924 as part of the *Tonkünstlerfest des Allgemeinen deutschen Musikvereins*. Critics generally remarked on the clear number-opera organization of the work and its reliance on jazz dance idioms. *Der Sprung* did not prove to be a critical or popular success, received only a few performances after its premiere, and was not staged again until 21 May 1927 in Leningrad. Perhaps its confusing combination of topical satire and psychological expressionism contributed to its unenthusiastic reception.

Although not a success, *Der Sprung* acted as an important proving ground for *Jonny spielt auf*. Krenek used jazz idioms to accompany topical stage action and symbolically with regard to the theme of personal freedom. His use of banjo and solo violin also show a rudimentary knowledge of instrumentation in popular dance bands. Krenek also met Gustav Brecher and Walther Brügmann, who were then employed in Frankfurt and who contributed much to the later success of *Jonny*.

From 1924 to the Composition of *Jonny spielt auf*

Between 1924 and 1925, Krenek and Erdmann embarked on new projects which brought them closer to the aesthetic expressed in *Jonny spielt auf*. Schnabel explained:

Ernst Krenek and Eduard Erdmann told me one day that they were going to write light opera, to make quicker money than with the heavier type of music they usually composed. . . . They had studied all the most popular and effective work in the field and would simply imitate it—on purpose—and probably do it better.[12]

Krenek completed a piano-vocal score for his attempt, *Bluff,* on a text by Gribble-Levetzov sometime in 1925.[13] Krenek does not mention the work in any of his various autobiographical essays, nor was it published. He apparently abandoned the idea for other projects. However, Schnabel's description of Krenek's interest in a more popular and commercially successful genre suggests Krenek's beginning concern with reaching a larger audience, a concern which would come into sharper focus after his trip to Paris.

Erdmann did not finish his attempt, *Die entsprungene Insel,* on a libretto by his friend Gustav Sprecht. But the few completed numbers were "jazzy" and similar to the kind of pieces Erdmann improvised at the piano for friends.[14] More illuminating, though, is the opera's black American character, Bosco. Hans Holtorf's sketches of the opera's various characters depict a businessman, Moloch; army officer, Knesebeck; circus or possibly nightclub performer, Leontine; and Bosco.[15] Bosco is shown wearing a loud, red-checked suit, white shirt, black tie, and a yellow hat. Erdmann's Bosco may well have been an inspiration for Krenek's Jonny. Letters between Erdmann and Krenek suggest that Erdmann continued to work on the opera at least into 1927.[16]

In December of 1923, Krenek, who was no longer studying with Schreker, accepted the offer of Werner Reinhart, a patron of contemporary music, to spend time as his guest in Switzerland. Krenek welcomed the chance to "take up contact with the 'outside' world, the fabulous free peoples that had defeated the reactionary forces of the Central Powers."[17] Krenek maintained close contacts with his Berlin friends during his stay in Switzerland, and he returned to Germany for the premieres of *Der Sprung* in June of 1924 and *Zwingburg* the following October.

Reinhart shared Krenek's fondness for American popular music as well as for neo-classicism, then popular in Paris and apparent in Krenek's op. 13a with its dance movements characteristic of the Baroque suite. Krenek combined aspects of both in his *Kleine Suite* for clarinet and piano, dedicated to Reinhart, an amateur clarinetist.[18] The movements consist of a "Präludium," "Air," "Bourée," "Adagio," and "'Moderner' Tanz." As in his op. 13a, Krenek reserved the idioms of popular dance for the last movement, combining a syncopated clarinet melody over a piano accompaniment marked "Tempo Guisto."

Krenek went to Paris in late November of 1924, having just separated from his wife of less than two years, sculptor Anna Mahler. In his various autobiographical essays, Krenek has written consistently about the trip's effect on him personally and on the subsequent evolution of his new aesthetic.

> I was fascinated by what appeared to me the happy equilibrium, perfect poise, grace, elegance, and clarity which I thought I perceived in the French music of that period. . . . I decided that the tenets which I had followed so far in writing "modern music" were totally wrong. Music according to my new philosophy had to fit the well-defined demands of the community for which it was written; it had to be useful, entertaining, practical.[19]

Krenek indicated, in one of two letters written from Paris to Paul Bekker, that he originally came to Paris to arrange for a performance of his third opera, *Orpheus und Eurydike,* which would have its premiere in Cassel in 1926.[20] But Krenek was totally unprepared for the Parisian environment. His letters to Bekker, as well as to his parents upon returning to Switzerland, are effusive in their praise for this magical city and the opportunities it offered him. To his parents he wrote that it was "extraordinarily stimulating." In a letter to Bekker, Krenek discussed the philosophical ramifications:

> It all comes together here—even life itself—in a completely altered sense: all the problems of art which we have discussed for so long and so often. I go about in this enchanting city as if in a dream. . . . I've come so far from middle Europe, as if I had journeyed to another planet.[21]

And after he returned to Switzerland, Krenek made some prophetic statements.

> I believe that my stay in Paris will have an entirely decisive meaning for me. . . . The people understand something there which we never got or have forgotten: to live. Thus art occupies a completely different sphere, and daily I experience new surprises, such as those I might find in South America. . . . I doubt that my original plan for which I came to Paris—to find performance possibilities for Orpheus—will come about. . . . To perform Orpheus [in Paris] would be like translating Palestrina into Chinese. No one would understand the piece. Instead, I now have the greatest desire to write something especially *for Paris.*[22]

By the date of this last letter, 14 December 1924, Krenek was back in Switzerland. In June of the following year, he accepted Paul Bekker's offer of employment at the opera house in Cassel. Many of Krenek's duties were mundane, but they provided a direct contact with the opera-going public and the opportunity to test his Parisian ideas about the artist's relationship with his society. Krenek wrote program notes, spoke on the radio, and supplied incidental music for the theatrical productions performed in the opera house. More importantly, he received practical and invaluable experience with theatrical production. The opera house became his "fabulous toy," and his first-hand knowledge of live theater contributed to the success of *Jonny spielt auf.*[23] During his first year with Bekker, Krenek began to work on and completed *Jonny spielt auf,* the work he vowed to write for Paris.

Jonny spielt auf

Krenek finished *Jonny spielt auf* in Cassel on 19 June 1926 and dedicated the work to his second wife, actress Berta Hermann. Hermann had suggested the opera's title, literally "Jonny strikes up [the band]," which provided the energetic vision of the hero setting the mood or giving the beat. Once again, Krenek's idea of freedom is central to the opera, but the work also shows his aesthetic preoccupation with the role of the artist in society and his further immersion in the world of American popular music. Krenek sets up a dichotomy within the opera between two prevailing views of the artist's role in modern society. Jonny, the hero or to many the antihero, represents Krenek's French model where artist and society are in harmony, and the artist's role is to serve the public. Max, Jonny's antithesis, represents the Central European studio composer. Max embodies the elitism and lack of concern for his audience which Krenek decried in his article "Musik in der Gegenwart."

The actual story of *Jonny spielt auf* revolves around the escapades of a black jazz violinist and band leader, Jonny (see synopsis, appendix C). Jonny not only represents Krenek's ideal as a composer, he is the free man, or *Triebmensch.* Having jumped over his shadow, Jonny has no inhibitions, sexual or musical, but rejoices in the vitality of life. Jonny is at the center of things, even though he remains above the action and acts as a catalyst and ultimately as the figure of salvation.

Max, as the product of the Central European studio mentality, wants as little to do with humanity as possible, preferring instead the solitude and isolation of the glaciers. Krenek admitted that Max was autobiographical and that his character development during the opera followed Krenek's own transformation. But Krenek's depiction of the elitist artist as a mountaineer had special contemporary appeal. Siegfried Kracauer, in his study of German post-World War I film, discusses "mountain films," a popular genre akin to American westerns, created by director Arnold Fanck, himself a geologist and mountain climbing enthusiast.[24] While Fanck's early films documented the beauties of the mountains, his *Der Berg des Schicksals* (1924) treated mountain climbing as symbolic of the human struggle against seemingly insurmountable odds. Later films, such as *Der heilige Berg* (1927) and *Die weisse Hölle vom Piz Palü* (1928), which starred Leni Riefenstahl, continued to use this nature symbolism. Kracauer further notes that Fanck's movies reflected the cult of mountain climbing among German intellectuals of the time, for whom the lofty peaks symbolized their high-minded endeavors and superiority over the "valley-pigs."[25] Thus Max was a potent caricature of the German artistic intelligentsia.

Max, this *Gletscher-Mensch,* also caricatured members of Schoenberg's circle, specifically Anton Webern. In their biography, *Anton von Webern,* the Moldenhauers remark on the composer's continual need to seek, as Webern himself said, "this rarified air of the heights."[26] Max's opening hymn to his glaciers not only defines his view of the artist's role, but with the hardly coincidental pun on beautiful mountain, *schöner Berg,* provides evidence of Max's probable identity.

> You beautiful mountain,
> you entice me,
> you propel me away from home,
> away from work.[27]

The word-play continues in scene 4, which Krenek described as "Max in Erwartung," a play on Schoenberg's expressionist work which was first performed in 1924. In this scene Max awaits in great agitation a lover who does not return, similar to the action of Schoenberg's *Erwartung.*

This Schoenberg-Krenek antagonism dates back to Krenek's public condemnation in "Musik in der Gegenwart" of the "head-in-hands." Krenek may have been responding then to the philosophy espoused by Schoenberg in *Die glückliche Hand* which, like *Erwartung,* was first performed in 1924. In *Die glückliche Hand,* Schoenberg preached that artists should renounce earthly happiness and popular success.

Schoenberg retaliated against Krenek's essay with the *Drei Satiren* (1926). In the foreword, Schoenberg describes the objects of his satire as neo-classicists, folklorists, and those who search for a comfortable middleground. In the discussion of neo-classicism, he refers to "the mediocre one" (*der Mediokre neckisch*) creating a pun on Krenek ("—kre neck.") And Schoenberg's comments on the state and future of opera, made in 1927 at the request of the *Neues Wiener Tagblatt,* show how clearly his view contrasted with that expressed by Krenek in *Jonny spielt auf:* "It is self-evident that the highest art can never address itself to the many. . . . So the drama of the future and the opera of the future cannot be art for the masses."[28] Schoenberg knew the piano-vocal score of *Jonny spielt auf* from Stuckenschmidt, who managed to keep on good terms with both Krenek and Schoenberg.[29] Schoenberg responded to *Jonny spielt auf* with his *Von Heute auf Morgen,* discussed in the final chapter, which criticized the *Zeitoper.*

The aesthetic opposition of Max and Jonny is offset by three other characters. Anita is an emotional opera singer who falls in love with Max and tempts him off his glacier. Daniello, a slick, shallow, classical violinist, momentarily lures Anita away from Max and loses his life after pursuing Jonny and his stolen violin. As performers, both Anita and Daniello have a more direct relationship with the public than does Max. A French maid and Jonny's love, Yvonne, is a young coquette who acts entirely from her heart.

Related to the Max-Jonny dichotomy is the nature of their respective musics. Jonny is the true entertainer whose music is appreciated by the general public, whereas Max's music is appreciated by a limited audience and reflects his isolated character. Max, who isolates himself on the glacier, cannot create music which is useful or understandable to a larger community. Krenek emphasizes this musical dichotomy when in scene 7 the hotel guests react harshly to Anita's performance of Max's modern opera aria, but cheer wildly when Jonny starts to play. Ultimately, Max's glaciers refuse to shelter him, and he is forced to return to his society. His change of heart takes place in the penultimate scene when he decides to accompany Anita on her tour of the United States.

> Now, the moment has come!
> I must catch the train
> Which heads for life.[30]

Daniello, the self-declared King of the Violin, parodies sensitive performers. He understands Anita's need for a more sympathetic and worldly lover, but he has no scruples. And though popular within society, his egotism prevents him from serving his populace in the down-to-earth manner of Jonny. When Daniello falls in front of the train, his death is scarcely noticed and never mourned. Jonny is then free to put Daniello's violin to better use in his dance band and is proclaimed by the community as the Jazz Violin King.

Intertwined with Jonny's characterization as a jazz band leader and role model for modern composers are secondary symbols of freedom—dance, Jonny's race, and national heritage. Jonny's depiction as a black American was hardly accidental and proved, at times, to be highly controversial. With the focus on jazz, the choice of a black musician was logical, as Afro-Americans were recognized as responsible for jazz's development. Though Krenek claimed not to have modelled Jonny on any specific black American performer or to have foreseen the possible complications involved, Jonny's race adds to his characterization of the free, uninhibited man.[31] Certainly an aspect of the infatuation with black Americans in general, and jazz in particular, was the often racist perception of its jungle primitivism, of life without societal strictures, of its differentness from the dominant culture. Stuckenschmidt maintains that Krenek's choice of Jonny's race was purposefully radical, given the prejudicial nature of most of German society, and was part of Krenek's avant-garde and provocative nature.[32]

Jonny presents problems today. He is more than a fun-loving entertainer; he is licentious and a thief. In characterizing Jonny as the modern musician who creates out of instinct rather than rational thought, Krenek resorted to obvious racial stereotypes which would probably prohibit the work's performance today in the United States.[33] But it is Jonny whom Krenek favors. Jonny is unrepressed

Figure 5.2.   Gustav Brecher and Max Spilcker as Jonny before the Premiere of *Jonny spielt auf* in 1927
(Reproduced courtesy of Universal Edition, A.G., Wien)

and unbound by legalism. He knows what he wants and takes it. It is no wonder, then, that many critics condemned Krenek—not for his use of racial stereotypes—but for his apparent condoning of such behavior.

Another part of Jonny's characterization as the free man is his nationality as an American. Krenek later described the geographical nature of the Max-Jonny dichotomy: "The main idea of *Jonny spielt auf* is the split between the historically overburdened and brooding European, and especially central European, spirit and the fresh life-asserting mentality of the West symbolized by America."[34] Though the opera is set in Europe—an unidentified Central European city and then Paris—continual references are made to America as a land of freedom and promise. The opera ends with Anita and Max heading to America, Max having left behind his glaciers. America is also credited with creating popular dances. As in *Der Sprung über den Schatten,* these dances represent freedom, and thus America and the American way of life conquer

Europe through jazz and dancing. As Jonny says upon recovering the stolen violin from Anita's apartment:

> And so the new world comes
> Crossing the sea in radiance
> And inherits ancient Europe
> By means of the dance.[35]

And in the finale when Jonny and his jazz triumph, the chorus proclaims:

> The hour strikes for the end of the old era,
> the new age now dawns.
> Don't miss the connecting train.
> The trip begins to the unknown land of freedom.[36]

Thus the freedom advocated by Krenek in *Jonny spielt auf* is more than the loss of personal inhibitions; as in *Der Sprung über den Schatten,* it takes on greater communal ramifications. Having experienced the open society of Paris, and sharing further in the *Amerikanismus* of the time, Krenek presented Jonny as a cultural model for all of postwar Germany, an embodiment of what he called for in his 1925 essay.

Jonny spielt auf rightly deserves its distinction as the first true *Zeitoper*. Its libretto, with its mixture of comedy and social satire, is full of recognizable characters, even caricatures, taken from modern life. The lighthearted spirit is tempered both by an objectivity and a deeper philosophical position regarding the artist in modern culture. Krenek demonstrates his objectivity in Jonny's character, the antihero who exists beyond the rules of society. His theft not only goes unpunished, but helps him triumph. Throughout the work Jonny displays few, if any, emotions; he acts entirely from instinct. And Daniello's death is treated in a matter-of-fact, almost farcical manner. Thus Krenek's libretto shows features of *Neue Sachlichkeit* literature and art in its nonjudgmental approach to its characters and events. But optimism prevails, and the work ends happily.

The libretto depends on settings and stage properties which add to its topical nature. Krenek's choice of locales includes not only Max's alpine glaciers, but Anita's chic apartment, a hotel lobby, a hotel terrace, a police car, and, well serving the image of fast-paced modern life and *Neues Bauen* architecture, a railroad station. The contrast between Max's nature settings and modern industrial ones scenically underscores the dichotomy between Max and Jonny. Krenek brings these two worlds into sharp contrast when the activity on the hotel terrace, Anita's performances of Max's aria, intrudes on Max's glacial refuge and forces him to choose between them.

Modern technology plays an important role. The express train appears on stage and is boarded by the principals while a large station clock ticks away the minutes as Anita waits for Max to arrive. Giant loudspeakers on the terrace of the hotel broadcast Anita's voice over the alps to Max on his glacier, and the radio station XYZ broadcasts Jonny's violin playing within earshot of Daniello. These last two effects rely on everyday objects to solve dramatic or theatrical problems. In earlier operas, chance and coincidence would have brought Anita and Max back together or allowed Daniello to catch up with Jonny. In *Zeitoper,* modern technology steps in and literally plays the role of *deus ex machina.*

Krenek designed the last four scenes of the opera—Jonny's arrival at the railroad station, Max's arrival and subsequent arrest, Anita's arrival with her entourage, Max's ride in the police car and self-realization, and Jonny and Max's rearrival at the station in time to board the train—to occur in quick succession. The innovative and difficult staging requirements, such as the moving police car, the station clock, and the oncoming *D-Zug,* show Krenek's transference of techniques used in modern theater and film into the world of opera. The attention to action and realistic detail gives the final four scenes the quality of a filmed sequence akin to the documentary techniques subscribed to by Piscator.

The staging of Max's scene in the police car is vividly described in the score:

> The auto starts with a snort. At the same moment the iron gate disappears on the right, and lights, illuminated shop windows, electric signs, etc., are visible along the drop curtain closing off the scene, and glide by with increasing rapidity, giving the illusion that the auto is being driven through the brightly-lit streets of the metropolis, to the left.[37]

In the original Leipzig production, the director used a *Trickfilm* [animation] to bring off the scene to Krenek's specifications. The program noted that the *Trickfilm* was realized in the studios of UFA under the direction of architects Haute and K. Tschetverikoff, and that a Leipzig movie theater supplied the necessary projection equipment. Further technical assistance was supplied by Wilhelm Dobra.[38] No doubt fearing that the reliance on innovative staging would impede the production of the work in smaller houses, Universal Edition hastened to note in publicity releases that the work could be staged more simply without losing its effectiveness.[39]

Jonny's apotheosis in the finale (see figure 5.3) necessitated even more special theatrical equipment and expertise. Olin Downes, critic for the *New York Times,* described the finale as performed at the Leipzig premiere:

> This [Jonny and Max's rearrival at the station] is done in time to catch the midnight train which connects with the boat for America. At 11:58, Max and Anita reunited, Jonny skulking about to avoid arrest, the train steams in. In the Leipzig production it sped straight to the rim of the stage and threatened to catapult over the footlights. The guards call out, the hands of the great station clock move by seconds toward the hour. The train starts, but not before Jonny, from a scaffolding overhead, jumps for it. The train disappears. Jonny lands, instead, on the station

clock. The clock becomes the world. Jonny is atop of it, fiddling wildly, scornfully, lackadaisically. The characters of the opera are grouped below him. They are joined by a throng of men and women in every kind of dress and undress, who dance to the Bacchanalian jazz about the base of the whirling globe. At Leipzig the stars in the sky tottered, then whirled, until, at last, the globe had become a record disk, which came gradually to a stop, with the inscription "Jonny spielt auf: Ernst Krenek, Opus 45" upon it.[40]

Krenek's choice of staging, with Jonny atop the world, had special iconographical significance for German audiences.[41] Nineteenth-century newspapers and music journals often depicted violinists Joseph Joachim and Johann Strauss the younger playing astride the world as symbolic of their international popularity. Thus Jonny the jazz violinist, fiddling atop the world, had dethroned nineteenth-century musicians, as witnessed by Daniello's demise. His jazz, and all it stands for, now ruled over the modern age.

The stage directions in the score give some idea of how this final scene was realized. With the aid of an elevated platform, the clock could have been lowered, once it struck twelve, and replaced with the lighted, whirling globe. Krenek also called for colored spotlights and a changing light show [*Lichterspiel*] to add to the spirit of the final scene.

The Musical Score

Krenek's assimilation of jazz idioms in the score shows various levels of understanding. He frequently uses dominant seventh chords and blue notes, the flat third and seventh, both common features of twenties jazz harmony. As was true of most composers of the age, his most skillful use of jazz is his exploitation of popular dance idioms, a maturation of his use of the foxtrot and tango in *Der Sprung über den Schatten.*

The jazz-inspired sections appear as on-stage or behind-the-scenes music which logically proceeds from the dramatic action. But this music does more than characterize a locale; certain sections have further dramaturgical significance. Although he left behind the number-opera format of *Der Sprung,* Krenek clearly marked the jazz dance sections in the score, again showing his intent to set apart these sections within the opera.

Jonny spielt auf requires a standard orchestra, supplemented with *Schlagwerk und Jazzinstrumente.* The large percussion section includes bass, snare, and tenor drums occasionally played with wire brushes [*Jazzbesen*], gong, woodblocks, castanets, tamborine, xylophone, glockenspiel, and high-hat cymbal. Other special effects require a harmonium, glass harmonica, celeste, swanee whistle, electric signal bell, siren, and flexatone. The specific jazz instruments include solo violin, two saxophones, banjo, and piano.

Krenek's use of the solo violin as a jazz instrument was ridiculed by many, especially in the United States. Krenek later admitted that his characterization of

Figure 5.3.   The Final Scene of *Jonny spielt auf* as Staged at the Leipzig Premiere
(Reproduced courtesy of Universal Edition, A.G., Wien)

Jonny as a jazz violinist showed his lack of knowledge, as did the misspelling of
the character's name. But the violin as a legitimate jazz instrument had a basis in
reality, given the presence of violins in a number of jazz and dance ensembles
popular in Germany. Sam Wooding reportedly signed a black British violinist,
Jimmy Boucher, for his band before leaving for Russia in 1926.[42] Jonny carries a
saxophone for his first on-stage appearance, and the cover of the published
piano-vocal score, as well as later publicity photographs, show Jonny with a
saxophone, rather than a violin. In terms of Krenek's aesthetic philosophy,
which theatrically turned on Jonny's theft of a classical instrument which he then
used to entertain his public, a violin was a logical choice. Jonny, as a
saxophonist, would have required casting Daniello as a concert saxophonist,
rarer at the time than a violin-playing band leader.

Krenek sets the tone for the opera with the opening dominant thirteenth
chord (see example 5.2). The melodic movement of the descending fourth
returns in one of the opera's most popular jazz-inspired sections. However,

Example 5.2.   Ernst Krenek, *Jonny spielt auf,* Opening

Example 5.3.   Ernst Krenek, *Jonny spielt auf,* Glacier *Leitmotiv*

Krenek immediately shifts back to a more dissonant idiom for the short overture, which features a *Leitmotiv,* fittingly for Max's glacier, which represents the soon-to-be-vanquished past tradition (see example 5.3).

The first jazz section appears when the action shifts, again fittingly, to Paris and Anita's hotel in scene 3. This instrumental interlude, designated in the score as a "Shimmy," with the added parenthetical remark *schnelles 'Grammophon' tempo,* characterizes the specifically Parisian atmosphere into which Anita has entered. The music, performed on stage, supposedly comes from Jonny's band playing in the hotel lobby and is scored for alto and tenor saxophones, trumpet, trombone, piano, banjo, woodblocks, and drums, an ensemble roughly the dimensions of Sam Wooding's band. Krenek's cut-time shimmy features solos for muted trumpet and saxophone, and a melody line which contains blue notes

Example 5.4.   Ernst Krenek, *Jonny spielt auf,* "Shimmy"

Example 5.5.   Ernst Krenek, *Jonny spielt auf,* "Shimmy," Piano Solo

in the shift between C and C-sharp (see example 5.4). The second half of the shimmy, scored for solo piano and banjo, features a repeated rhythmic pattern which creates the racy, gyrating quality typical of the dance (see example 5.5). The prominent banjo timbre is reminiscent of Wooding's 1925 recordings. This section is the only place in the entire score to which Krenek gives a key signature.

A "Blues" section, so designated in the score, appears in this same scene as Jonny and Yvonne decide to part company. Again, the music is ostensibly supplied by Jonny's band, and Krenek used the same instrumentation as in the

Example 5.6.   Ernst Krenek, *Jonny spielt auf,* "Blues"

previous "Shimmy." The music does not adhere to a traditional 12-bar harmonic scheme; instead, Krenek employs a 16-bar chorus, more common in ragtime. The "Blues" opens with a five-four measure for solo piano, reminiscent of Gershwin's *Rhapsody in Blue,* a work well known in Germany. The melody contains the descending fourth first heard in the opening measures of the opera and moves to the muted trumpet and trombone. A repeated chordal ostinato in the piano and banjo accompanies the second and third repetitions of the chorus. Besides blue notes, both the flat third and seventh, Krenek's "Blues" contains syncopated passages, and the section ends on a dominant seventh chord reminiscent of the opera's opening measures (see example 5.6). An off-stage chorus joins in the third repetition while Jonny and Yvonne pantomime their departure.

This stage action, lovers departing, was a common theme in traditional blues lyrics; thus Krenek's text befitted its casting as a blues:

> Farewell, my love, farewell.
> I'm leaving my home.
> Be happy without me,
> I'll try it without you, and I'll never
> come back here again.[43]

In the ensemble finale which closes part 1 of the opera, strains of the "Blues" return, as Anita, Jonny, and Yvonne all leave the hotel. The melody appears in the vocal lines and in the orchestral coda, as a logical depiction of the departure of all the principals.

This "Leb wohl, mein Schatz' Blues," as it came to be called, was one of the most popular tunes of the opera, and Universal Edition published separate arrangements for voice and piano and jazz band. Stuckenschmidt claimed it was not uncommon to hear the number in nightclubs or as part of revue shows, and several soloists recorded the work for commercial release.[44] Baritone Ludwig Hoffmann recorded a version true to the original with members of the Berlin Städtische Oper. The arrangement released by Gabriel Formiggini and his orchestra contains a prominent trumpet solo, a saxophone line with pitch bends, and a piano accompaniment with tango rhythms. And a third version, by violinist Diez Weismann and pianist Johann de Leur, turned the piece into a virtuoso violin solo worthy of Fritz Kreisler. Weismann's violin playing is highly syncopated, perhaps even containing rudimentary improvisation.

A "Tango" section, marked "lento, molto espressivo," almost immediately follows the "Blues" in scene three. Again, this tango is performed by Jonny's off-stage band and an appropriate French-texted chorus and tango rhythms add further dramatic meaning. This number accompanies Daniello's on-stage seduction of Anita and Krenek elaborates upon the seductive action by relying on the tango's preexisting sexual connotations (see example 5.7). Both rhythms associated with the tango are used throughout, and the chorus adds a special dramaturgical counterpoint to Anita and Daniello's dialogue.

> Oh sweet, infinite memory.
> Seductive melody, mysterious sound,
> fill my heart, fill my heart with rapture's breath,
> with the sadness of eternal love.[45]

The solo violin, supposedly being played by Jonny, appears for the first time here in its context as a jazz instrument, replacing the trumpet and trombone used in the earlier sections. Krenek also adds contrabass and castanets to the rhythm section.

The only part of the score which Krenek designates as "Jazz" appears in part 2, scene 7, where Krenek juxtaposes Max's mountain world with the freer urban world of the hotel. Anita finishes her radio performance of Max's opera aria, which reaches him in the mountains, whereupon Max decides to return to her. To underscore Max's resolve, Jonny comes in over the radio with a syncopated duet for violin and piano that does not imitate any specific twenties dance. Krenek seems to have used the term "Jazz" here to imply generic dance music, as he did in *Der Sprung über den Schatten,* or perhaps the term implied an imitation of the earlier type of ragtime (see example 5.8).

Example 5.7.   Ernst Krenek, *Jonny spielt auf,* "Tango"

Example 5.8.   Ernst Krenek, *Jonny spielt auf,* "Jazz"

Towards the end of the second part another section appears in a style reminiscent of a blues, although Krenek does not so designate it in the score. The melodic line, sung by Anita and then Yvonne as they wait for Max at the train station, contains blue notes and is accompanied by a repeated chordal bass line (see example 5.9). Dramatically, the use of this melancholy musical style fits Anita's emotional state: "Why doesn't he come? I feel it now—perhaps I did not do the right thing by him. Oh come, do come, I'm waiting for you."[46] Yvonne also has an appropriate text. "Ah, where are you now? I feel it now, I alone am to blame for your error."[47]

Krenek also makes musical references to Jonny's race and national heritage apart from the use of dance idioms. After Jonny has stolen the violin and hidden it under Anita's banjo case, he sings a lullaby to the stolen violin, accompanying himself on Anita's banjo. The solo, in an unambiguous E minor, has no dance character; instead, Krenek states that the music should be sung *im Ton eines Niggerliedes.* In light of the banjo accompaniment and simple tune, Krenek probably wanted to imitate the comic vaudeville style of minstrel songs popular since before World War I. This "Niggerlied" returns in Jonny's part during the final chorus scene of part 1, as all the principals leave the Parisian hotel.

A second example of Krenek's racial and musical characterization is the so-called "Triumph-Lied," a title applied later to the number after it became the opera's second most popular tune. This "Triumph-Lied," which appears in scene 6, contains Jonny's primary statement concerning his role as a musician, as he has just regained possession of the stolen violin.

Example 5.9.   Ernst Krenek, *Jonny spielt auf,* Scene 9

> And now the violin is mine, and I shall play on it as David of old did upon the harp. I will praise Jehovah, who created Black people. Everything that is worth having in this world belongs to me. The old world gave birth to good things, but it doesn't know what to do with them. And so the new world comes crossing the sea in radiance and inherits ancient Europe by means of the dance.[48]

This solo is preceded by a lighter cut-time duet between the reconciled Jonny and Yvonne. Krenek sets off Jonny's special solo from this previous music with the designation *Maestoso ma non troppo lento (im Ton eines Neger-Spirituals)* (see example 5.10). The simple melodic line and choral accompaniment, orchestrated for brass choir, demonstrate Krenek's recreation of spirituals which had been sung in Europe by touring black American choirs before World War I and as late as 1927, when a black choir performed as part of the Frankfurt Summer Music Festival. Krenek's opening measure borrows the rhythm from the opening of Stephen Foster's "Swanee River," a song considered to be a true spiritual, having been used in the nineteenth century in dramatizations of *Uncle Tom's Cabin* and appearing in *The Chocolate Kiddies Revue.*[49] Krenek's lyrics show a textual affinity for spirituals with their religious sentiment and references to Jehovah and the harp-playing King David. The melody of the "Triumph-Lied" returns as Jonny's second tune broadcast over the radio (scene 11) which sends Daniello in pursuit.

Example 5.10.   Ernst Krenek, *Jonny spielt auf,* "Triumph-Lied"

The "Triumph-Lied" was also recorded, and Universal Edition published a special piano-vocal arrangement. Ludwig Hofmann recorded the "Hymne des Jonny," as it is called on the label, as side one of his "Leb wohl, mein Schatz" release and violinist Diez Weismann recorded "Jonnys Triumph-Gesang" as the flip side to his "Blues" recording with the pianist Johann de Leur.[50]

Krenek made a third reference to Jonny's heritage and borrowed again from "Swanee River." In scene 8, one of the many short scenes towards the end of part 2, Jonny flees from the police and decides to return to his home in Alabama via the train to Amsterdam. Jonny's melody line borrows the tune of "Swanee River" (see example 5.11). In the score Krenek footnoted this short seven-bar quotation as *Altes amerikanisches Negerlied,* and the quotation is the same part borrowed by Irving Berlin in "Alexander's Ragtime Band," popular in Europe as true ragtime. Krenek no doubt knew that the audience would recognize this extramusical delineation of Jonny's character; thus the need for the explanatory footnote, except to prove his own knowledge, remains a mystery.

The music accompanying the final scene reuses both the melodies of the "Blues" and the "Triumph-Lied," thereby combining pre- and postwar musical

Example 5.11. Ernst Krenek, *Jonny spielt auf,* "Negerlied"

*)Altes amerikanisches Negerlied.

images of America and black Americans. An orchestral version of "Leb wohl, mein Schatz" opens the scene, and the chorus, proclaiming that the dawn of a new age has occurred, picks up the tune. After an orchestral interlude, the chorus returns with music reminiscent of the "Triumph-Lied." Another interlude, spiced with blue notes and harkening back to "Leb wohl, mein Schatz," gives way to an ensemble sung by the principals to the tune of the "Triumph-Lied" combined with the piano ostinato of "Leb wohl, mein Schatz." They provide the moral:

> Thus Jonny struck up the band for us to dance. If you've enjoyed it, thank him. And remember, all of life is nothing but a game. May the sound of his violin accompany you wherever you go. Look, Jonny steps down among us, and Jonny strikes up the band.[51]

The opera ends with Jonny playing "Leb wohl, mein Schatz" on his violin, accompanied by string pizzicato. The full orchestra returns and brings the opera to a close in G major (see example 5.12). This closing gesture, moving from

Example 5.12.   Ernst Krenek, *Jonny spielt auf*, Final Cadence

complex harmony to the unambiguous G, is a paradigm for the entire opera. It provides one final juxtaposition of the difficult world of Max and the intelligible world of the triumphant Jonny.

Other innovative musical sections, unrelated to Jonny's character or the use of jazz idioms, are the glacier music and Max's opera aria. The glaciers respond to Max's plea for aid with a supernatural injunction to return to life orchestrated for off-stage women's chorus, celesta, and glass harmonica and using the *Leitmotiv* which opened the opera. Max's opening aria, which Anita practices in the second scene and then sings over the radio, parodies chromatic, atonal writing (see example 5.13). The text, with its second line, "I looked for my home in the land of dreams,"[52] both characterizes Max's personality as an individual uncomfortable with reality and parodies expressionist texts with their other-worldly sentiments.[53]

Performance History and Critical Reception

Jonny spielt auf was rejected by four opera houses before the Leipzig Neues Theater agreed to stage the work. Instrumental in bringing the work to Leipzig and to its success on the stage were general manager Walther Brügmann and conductor Gustav Brecher (see figures 5.1 and 5.2). The Leipzig opera house possessed little of the Gewandhaus's national reputation for excellence until the arrival of Brügmann and Brecher in 1924. The combination of Brecher's sure musical sense and Brügmann's training in modern theater made Leipzig a center

Example 5.13.   Ernst Krenek, *Jonny spielt auf,* Max's Aria

for operatic innovation in the late twenties and early thirties, on a par with any other house in Germany or Austria.

Walther Brügmann (fl. 1919–46) came to Leipzig after having served for five years as *Oberspielleiter* at the Frankfurt am Main opera house, where he conducted the premiere of *Der Sprung über den Schatten.*[54] The success of *Jonny spielt auf* brought Brügmann much recognition, and reviewers, regardless of their other opinions, consistently praised him for his deft and clever staging. As a result, he staged and directed the evening of chamber operas at the 1928 Baden-Baden Festival, which earned him international recognition within avant-garde circles. Brügmann supported the operatic experiments of the younger generation and had an especially good working relationship with Krenek and Weill, producing Weill's *Aufstieg und Fall der Stadt Mahagonny* in the face of political opposition. Brügmann remained at Leipzig unil he lost his job in 1933 for political and artistic reasons. He lived in Bern until his death early in 1946 before his planned return to his native country.

Gustav Brecher (1879–1940) also came to Leipzig from Frankfurt am Main, and he had trained as a conductor under Gustav Mahler in Vienna. Brecher made a name for himself with his ability and willingness to tackle contemporary scores. Krenek called him "an excellent man, great conductor, [and a] very original person."[55] Reviews of the time praised his conducting in a town known for its conductors. Brecher also lost his job in 1933. He fled to Prague, then to Italy, and finally to Belgium, where he attempted to obtain a visa to emigrate to the United States.[56] He and his family committed suicide in 1940 before Belgium fell to Hitler.

Gustav Brecher appears to have been most responsible for bringing *Jonny spielt auf* to Leipzig and reportedly even helped finance the venture.[57] His artistic gamble paid off more than anyone could have imagined, as the work proved to be the sensation of the year, if not the decade.[58] It received a tremendous amount of press coverage, largely positive. Reviewers remarked on the opera's tumultuous reception, its innovative staging, and the original features of its libretto and score. Because of its up-to-date libretto and use of jazz and dance idioms, critics were reluctant to call it an opera; instead they devised terms to help describe its unusual operatic character: *Opernrevue, Musikkomödie, Buffo-Opera, Jazzoper, Gegenwartsoper* and *Zeitopernrevue,* which eventually gave way to the term *Zeitoper.*

Leipzig critics rejoiced that the work's success finally provided the opera house with national distinction. Adolf Aber, critic for the *Leipziger Neueste Nachrichten,* exulted:

> The Leipzig opera has its sensation. Now, at last a bit of current events recorded to the fullest extent in a musical work. Thrilling and entertaining both, effective as a grotesque and a revue. . . . Musically certain of its revelation, full of wit and appropriate delineation of situations. The success was already assured after the first act. After the second . . . there was a storm of applause for the composer, the conductor Brecher and the director Brügmann, who together had realized something hardly imaginable.[59]

In a second review, Aber analyzed the work and its production in detail. Noting that while other arts had taken new postwar directions, opera, prior to *Jonny spielt auf,* had not taken part in the prevailing *Zeitgeist.*

Alfred Baresel, critic for the *Neue Leipziger Zeitung* and proponent of American jazz, shared Aber's view that *Jonny spielt auf* was important as the first opera to put modern life, with all its attendant trappings, on the stage. Baresel called the triumphant hero *Neue Sachlichkeit in Schwarz* and the work itself, the first *Jazzoper.* He lauded Krenek's synthesis of jazz techniques and preexisting operatic styles, and he especially liked the contrasting musical styles which characterized Max's glacial world and modern life.

The Berlin critics shared this enthusiasm. Oskar Bie claimed that *Jonny spielt auf* was "one of the most fantastic works of all opera history," and incorporated the *Naturromantik* of the glacier world, the *Gefühlsromantik* in

Max and Anita's music, and thirdly, music which was "technical poetry of today
. . . an elementary utterance of the *Menschentempo.*"[60] Walther Schrenk
similarly noted that the work "embodied our technical era of the machine."[61]
Adolf Weissman astutely noted one of the reasons for the spectacular success of
Jonny spielt auf: "From beginning to end the score is fascinating, always ringing.
We're given, undisguised, F Major, C Major, D Major. All modern 'in between'
sounds disappear. This is the music for the general public."[62]

Paul Bekker, then *Intendant* of the Wiesbaden Staatstheater, produced
Jonny spielt auf in Wiesbaden in October of 1927. One enthusiastic patron wrote
to Bekker at length after attending the opera. His letter bears out Weissmann's
judgment of how successful Krenek was in his mission.

> Yesterday evening, I heard Krenek in the theater. It was the strongest stage
> experience—visually and musically—that I've had in many years. . . . It has not been possible
> for me until now to enjoy a modern work spontaneously and from the heart. . . . Now,
> yesterday, I became acquainted with a work embodying a larger, newer, musically vital power.
> . . . Until now, it had not been important for me to be acquainted with anything which comes
> so genuinely and essentially out of our time. These were the tunes of the future! What a relief! I
> conclude from various opinions, that the majority of people understand the decisive thing, the
> "modern" in it, with its connections to the dance, negros, even jazz. And I enjoy these
> elements. They are grand in the style found here.[63]

The Städtische Oper gave the Berlin premiere of *Jonny spielt auf* on 8
October 1927. A distinctive feature of the Berlin production was its program
cover in the style of the photo collages of John Heartfield (see figure 5.4). The
individual images, such as an express train, dancer, and Berenice Abbott's
photograph of drummer Buddy Gilmore, fit the libretto. And the publicity photo
shows that the Städtische Oper tried to live up to the Leipzig premiere—the
chorus is more elaborately costumed but Jonny is not playing atop a spinning
globe (see figure 5.5).[64] The work was well received in Berlin, and the 19
October performance was broadcast over the Berlin radio.[65] Most reviewers
noted that the opera's popular numbers were greeted with great applause; "Jetzt
ist die Geige mein" had to be repeated.

Critical reception was mixed. Oskar Bie faulted the production, directed by
Karlheinz Martin, claiming that the sets designed by Gustav Vargo could not
compare with those used in Leipzig.[66] He also admitted that his initial
excitement about the work had lessened somewhat. Hanns Eisler, critic for the
Communist newspaper *Die rote Fahne,* lamented the extraordinary amount of
time, trouble, and money expended by the house in its production of a work he
found to be dull, trite, and entirely bourgeois. "Despite autos and locomotives,
there is nothing of our time, nothing which interests or captivates us."[67] The
jazz-inspired music was poor; he had heard better in Berlin coffeehouses.

Stuckenschmidt and Max Marschalk, both writing for the Berlin *Vossische Zeitung,* continued to applaud the work. Marschalk's review, though less glowing than his review of the Leipzig premiere, was still positive and voiced none of Bie's criticism for the Berlin production.[68] Alfred Einstein, in the *Berliner Tageblatt,* was even more complimentary both towards the work and the Berlin production.[69]

The Munich premiere of *Jonny spielt auf* on 16 June 1929 was hampered by politically inspired racism resulting from the Rheinland occupation by French troops from 1918–23. President Wilson ordered the black American units home immediately after the Armistice was signed, but the French continued to use its Senegalese soldiers in the Rheinland. Factual and spurious incidents of Senegalese violence towards local inhabitants were constantly reported in the German press.[70]

Reports in the Munich press, prior to the opera's opening night, misrepresented the opera's theme and stated that a black singer would perform the title role. Protesters gathered outside the theater before the start of the sold-out premiere. A full-fledged riot broke out when Alfred Jerger, the Munich Jonny, began "Jetzt ist die Geige mein." Stinkbombs went off, fights broke out, the manager stopped the performance, and the police were required to restore order. Jerger claimed a large crowd then assembled outside his dressing room and threatened to lynch the supposedly black performer.[71] However, they quieted down upon realizing their mistake, and some carried Jerger upon their shoulders back to his hotel.

Newspaper reports blamed the Munich National Socialist Workers Party, under the leadership of businessman Karl Ostberg, for the riot. Later performances were a success, as one critic noted; a good demonstration was powerful advertising.[72] Other critics attempted to counter what the protesters had said concerning the opera's true message. "It is not a question of glorification of the black race. Jonny, the jazz band violinist, steps in as a representative of the uninhibited impulse. . . . Jonny strikes up the band, and Europe dances to his violin. Is that not so?"[73]

As with the discussion of the opera crisis and related topics, the German musical press was deeply divided concerning the opera's merit and influence. Though *Signale für die musikalische Welt* published Adolf Aber's positive review of the Leipzig premiere, they condemned later productions in Berlin and Zurich.[74] The *Rheinische Musik- und Theater-Zeitung, Allgemeine Musikzeitung* and *Zeitschrift für Musik* all questioned the worth of the opera from the start. The *Zeitschrift für Musik* attacked it and rejoiced at the problems it encountered in Munich, Budapest, Paris, and New York City.[75] Hans Mersmann, treating Max's aria as indicative of Krenek's faulty style, misunderstood Krenek's parodistic intentions.[76] Hans F. Schaub lamented what Krenek had done to and

Figure 5.4.   Program Cover from the Berlin Production of *Jonny spielt auf* in 1927

with Busoni's theories, and Georg Gräner contrasted the superficial spirit of *Jonny spielt auf* with the spiritual nature of Bruckner, for whom he longed.[77] "Atonality, quarter-tone music, *Neue Sachlichkeit,* new Hellenism, jazz symphony, jazz opera—what do these more or less interesting events of the day have to do with the creation of inner, metaphysical life, with spiritual and mental rebirth, with the art of genius?"[78]

As was to be expected, both *Anbruch* and *Auftakt* were highly complimentary of the work. Walter Harry, a medical doctor and perhaps a psychologist, wrote an article for *Anbruch* which attempted to prove how *Jonny spielt auf* was more than a jazz opera or a work concerned only with mirroring its time.[79] Applying Jungian psychology, Harry showed how Krenek's characters reflected personality archetypes and depicted the triumph of the Dionysian character, Jonny, over the Apollonian figure of Max.[80]

Figure 5.5. The Final Scene of *Jonny spielt auf* as Staged at the Berlin Städtische Oper in 1927

Jonny spielt auf—Outside Germany

No British house produced *Jonny spielt auf.* As a reviewer after the Viennese production reported in the *London Times,* the libretto by the "ultra-modern" Krenek "would not pass the censor in England in its present form."[81] Paris was the one place where *Jonny spielt auf* failed. Even where productions were hampered by outbreaks of violence, as in Munich and Budapest, or were severely criticized, as in Vienna, the opera still managed to be popular with most audiences. However, in Paris, according to one American critic, a capacity crowd at the Théâtre des Champs-Elysées found the premiere on 21 June 1928 to be boring and disappointing. Since Paris had been the first place where American popular music took hold, the average Parisian may have had a more developed sense of what jazz was or should be. And as Milhaud noted in 1925, the French infatuation with jazz had become a thing of the past. Or, as Krenek himself should have known, performing *Jonny spielt auf* in France was preaching to the converted.

The Metropolitan Opera House produced *Jonny spielt auf* less than two years after its Leipzig premiere, a further testament to its international success. American composer John Alden Carpenter, having been present at the Leipzig premiere, was credited with having brought the work to the attention of the Metropolitan Board of Directors.[82]

The news media generated considerable excitement for the New York premiere. The *New York Times* claimed that the production, which required a record 25 rehearsals, was going to cost as much as $100,000. And a week before the premiere, the *New York Times* music critic, Olin Downes, devoted the entire front page of the Sunday arts section to an article entitled "The Generation of Krenek: What Lies behind This Week's Opera Premiere." Downes summed up his feelings about Krenek, his peers, and the opera: "It [the opera] could not have been written before the war. It could not have appeared even ten years ago. It is of this moment, which in the topical sense, it has hit on the head. And it is amusing on stage."[83]

The management of the Metropolitan Opera felt compelled to make changes in the opera. In Krenek's original libretto, Jonny was black, but out of necessity, white singers played the role in make-up. However, the Metropolitan management cast Jonny as a white jazz band leader in blackface, so as not to raise any objections about his actions with the white female characters. Thereby Jonny becomes a throwback to American minstrelsy rather than being true to New York City or even Parisian nightlife. The Metropolitan also deleted all references in the script to race, black or white. Thus, instead of Jonny declaring "Oh, by Jove, die weisse Frau ist schön," upon first seeing Anita, he says, "Oh, by Jove, die Frau ist schön."[84] And when Jonny finally obtains the violin from Anita's apartment he originally vows to praise Jehovah, "der die Menschen schwarz erschuf" [who created black men]. In New York, Jonny praises Jehovah, "who created violins for jazz violinists."[85]

The premiere in New York was another success. Downes, after noting the work's enthusiastic reception, mentioned how the the issue of race had been "tactfully avoided," and that apparently no one was upset with Jonny, as had been feared by the management.[86] He described Michael Bohnen's characterization of Jonny as inspired by Al Jolson, whose movie *The Jazz Singer* (1927) would have provided a logical model for a musician performing in blackface. The *New York Times* also reported that Al Jolson attended the premiere, having postponed a trip to California just so he could see the production.[87] And after the final curtain, Jolson supposedly made a special trip backstage to congratulate Bohnen and to give him some tips on his make-up. Thus the management clearly attempted to draw connections between blackface comedians, still in vogue, and the possibly controversial Jonny.

Downes criticized the Metropolitan's staging of the climactic final scenes. Set changes were too slow and thereby failed to attain the "kaleidoscopic" effect present in the Leipzig production, although the Metropolitan claimed to have more sophisticated stage equipment. Downes described the apotheosis as "an American music hall extravaganza of the vintage of the '90s."[88] "Krenek did not dream of American flags or the Statues of Liberty, or pickaninny dancers, or any of the effects gratuitously wished upon him in the final scene at the Metropolitan."[89] A photograph of the final scene shows Jonny atop his globe, in the shadow of the Statue of Liberty.[90] The entire male chorus, in blackface, red and white striped pants, blue tail coats, top hats and white gloves, join the women, costumed in short dresses and large bonnets, in the final chorus.

Oscar Thompson, in the *New York Evening Post,* voiced a hostility towards jazz shared by critics writing for the German conservative musical press.

> [The opera] crams into twelve scenes about every objectionable characteristic of the age of jazz. It is vulgar, profane, speed-mad, sexy, soulless, superficial, spoofing, brassy, hard: a blend of the mechanical and animal. And, so, we have at last the equivalent on the operatic stage of much cheap magazine literature and many even cheaper productions of the so-called legitimate stage. Thus opera has caught up with the times.[91]

Similarly, a reviewer for the *Commonweal* misinterpreted the role of Jonny.

> The real meat of Jonny is not that Jonny himself is a Negro, but that the spirit which he typifies has eaten so deeply into the body of the white race that such a work as Krenek's has become possible of general acceptance. . . . What does matter is whether civilization and Christianity are prepared to fight for their very existence, whether they are fully aware of what the triumph of Jonny would mean.[92]

The five remaining performances continued to be well received. The one on 8 February was a benefit for the Babies' Hospital, a part of the New York Medical Center which provided care for infants "regardless of race, nationality or place of residence."[93] In the fifth performance, on 17 February, Lawrence Tibbett replaced Michael Bohnen in the title role and further exaggerated the grotesque blackface minstrel show imagery.

> He [Tibbett] costumed the part in a high water black coat and checker-board trousers of as loud a hue as possible. In coloring Mr. Tibbett was jet black with large white circles around the lips and eyes. He emphasized as much as possible the comic elements of the role, with steps and gestures popular in American cabaret and vaudeville houses.[94]

By the end of the 1927–28 season, the popularity of the opera in the United States had run its course. Downes, in his retrospective article on the Metropolitan's season, discussed *Jonny spielt auf* as a past novelty which suffered from a faulty New York production.[95]

Jonny spielt auf was not ignored by American composers or members of the musical avant-garde. Herbert Peyser, in an article for *Modern Music* which appeared before the New York City premiere, attacked the work. He claimed that the opera should never have been brought to the United States. Having been written by a European ostensibly about American ideas, the work was a musical and philosophical anachronism. Krenek's jazz was a poor imitation at best, and Peyser suggested that

> it would have been doing the young man a greater service if the Metropolitan Board of Directors had chipped in, raised a few thousand dollars to bring him over here for 5 or 6 months and then shipped him back to rewrite his stuff after he had assimilated what the night clubs and "nigger-belts" could teach him.[96]

Henry Cowell wrote a scathing review of the New York premiere.[97] Only George Antheil, in his articles for *Modern Music* and Nancy Cunard's *Negro: An Anthology,* expressed support for the work.[98] Although describing Krenek's jazz imitations as "beery" and teutonic, he still lauded Krenek's attempt to create a new operatic genre. Antheil himself would try to duplicate the style and success of *Jonny spielt auf* with his *Transatlantic*.

After *Jonny spielt auf*

After a highly successful second season, the number of productions of *Jonny spielt auf* decreased as its popularity waned. Writing two years after the premiere, Adolf Weissmann still found Krenek to be the truest representative of the contemporary *Zeitgeist* and claimed that "the sensation [of *Jonny spielt auf*] was so great that it became a rallying point for the younger generation."[99] But by the 1930–31 season, only four performances of the work were given, and by the 1932–33 season, it had disappeared from the scene.[100]

Krenek has maintained that the philosophy espoused in *Jonny spielt auf* was largely misunderstood, and that the opera became a sensation for entirely the wrong reasons: its infusion of popular dance music and its black protagonist. He rejected its designation as a "jazz opera," which ignored its true aesthetic aim. Krenek was accused of betraying his earlier compositional beliefs by pandering to the masses. Paul Bekker took his side, proclaiming in 1932: "Poor Krenek. What did this "Jonny" bring about! Not the royalties, which were smaller than those malevolent, envious people maintained. No, instead, jealousy, hatred, defamation, moral and aesthetic proscription, judgments of inferiority, and other charming musical accompaniments to a world success."[101]

Stuckenschmidt concurred that the success of *Jonny spielt auf* created enormous personal problems for Krenek, if for no other reason than that his new found financial security set him apart from the majority of his peers.[102] The popularity of the opera supposedly caused a rift between Krenek's supporters and followers of Hindemith. Planned productions of Hindemith's *Cardillac* were cancelled in the rush by houses to stage *Jonny spielt auf*.[103] There is no indication, however, that Krenek and Hindemith shared any of this antagonism.

Krenek's next stage works, three one-act operas (1928), retained many of the stylistic and aesthetic features of *Jonny spielt auf* (see appendix C for synopses). *Der Diktator* is a tragic work with none of *Jonny spielt auf*'s comic elements or jazz idioms. The libretto, with its story of a ruthless dictator, was not without some topical relevance. Krenek claimed the central character was loosely based on Mussolini.[104] However, the *Alltäglichkeit* of *Jonny spielt auf* is missing. *Das geheime Königreich,* on a libretto living up to its magical, fairytale title, and set "Im Märchenland," again borrows jazz dance features. A chorus of women dance with the court jester, accompanied by music marked *Tempo Giusto (Tango con moto),* which relies on the tango rhythm.

The third one-act opera, *Schwergewicht, oder die Ehre der Nation,* follows directly in the footsteps of *Jonny spielt auf*. The opera, or "burleske Operette" as Krenek called it, is humorous, lighthearted, and parodistic in its caricatures (see figure 5.6). Here Krenek mocked the infatuation with sports heroes, taking as his starting point a comment made by the German ambassador to the United States that athletic stars had become more important than political leaders.[105] Krenek depicts just such a hero, who, in reality, is duped by both his wife and his manager.

The score of *Schwergewicht* relies heavily on jazz idioms, and the orchestration includes banjo, swanee whistle, and piano. The piano is used very much in the style of jazz practices to lend harmonic support and occasionally to take the melody. As in *Jonny spielt auf,* this music helps characterize the stage action and lend an up-to-date air. One of the characters, Gaston, is a dance instructor, and thus references to dancing and dance music, as well as America, are numerous. Noticeable jazz-inspired sections include a "Tempo di blues" where Evelyn, the boxer's wife, and her dance teacher confess their feelings for one another, and a "Tango Milonga" when Anne-Marie, a medical student, asks the boxer for his autograph. Sections towards the end of the work, as the action becomes increasingly slapstick, are clearly reminiscent of the shimmy music of *Jonny spielt auf.*

The three one-act works received their premiere under Bekker in Wiesbaden on 6 May 1928. Otto Klemperer, following the success of *Jonny spielt auf,* expressed an interest in Krenek and the three works were produced at the Krolloper. Klemperer expressed his dissatisfaction with *Schwergewicht* because it came too close to an operetta for his taste, and he even tried to convince Krenek to substitute another work.[106] The Berlin premiere on 2 December 1928 featured innovative and realistic sets designed and executed by Oskar Strnad.

Reviews of the one-acts were mixed. Critics expected another success on the line of *Jonny spielt auf,* which did not materialize. Many were surprised by the *verismo* of *Der Diktator* and the neo-romanticism of *Das geheime Königreich.* Alfred Einstein remarked on the amount of applause which greeted this second work, thereby proving Krenek's ability to once again satisfy the audience.[107] *Schwergewicht* proved to be the most popular and was produced apart from its other two accompanying works.

Leben des Orest (1930), Krenek's last major stage work before his 12-tone opera *Karl V,* maintains vestiges of the *Zeitoper* while also demonstrating Krenek's departure from the aesthetic of *Jonny spielt auf,* which is reflected in his essays as well. With its basis in Greek mythology, Krenek returned to the Greek revivalism of his *Orpheus und Eurydike.* Krenek called the work a "Grand Opera," further indicating his return to an older tradition predating the *Zeitoper.* In his article "From *Jonny* to *Orest,*" Krenek explained how similar the two operas were in their portrayals of the animal and spiritual sides of human beings.[108] Krenek explained why he also no longer relied on "present-day material" for *Leben des Orest.* "I see more gulfs than bridges in the present period and so to present the bridge I had to go into the past."[109]

True to its grand opera designation, *Leben des Orest* is long and requires a large cast. The work takes place in pre-Christian-era Greece, though Krenek at one time considered setting part of the opera in America of the 1920s. Krenek did borrow some of the philosophy of freedom found in *Jonny spielt auf,* in his contrast of north and south Greece or repressed and free cultures. And, similarly to *Jonny spielt auf,* he used jazz dance idioms to characterize the freer culture of southern Greece. *Leben des Orest* received its premiere on 19 January 1930 in Leipzig, and it was later produced at the Krolloper with set designs by Giorgio de Chirico. A reviewer in Hamburg aptly noted that *Leben des Orest* marked "the

Figure 5.6.   Publicity Photo from the Berlin Städtische Oper's Production of *Schwergewicht* in 1928

death of *neue Sachlichkeit*."[110] And Theodor Wiesengrund-Adorno saw Krenek as a voice for a new romanticism.[111]

By 1933, Krenek had reconciled with Schoenberg, as evident in his adoption of the 12-tone method for *Karl V,* and with it, he turned his back completely on the world of *Jonny spielt auf.* Krenek, who once spoke for a new dramatic age in tune with its time and people, now joined the ranks of the intellectual studio musician, soon to be attacked by the National Socialist government for their degenerate music. If *Jonny spielt auf* did not give rise to a lasting new school of opera, as some predicted, other composers, influenced by the same artistic, literary, and musical ideas which fascinated Krenek, and cheered by the success of *Jonny spielt auf,* produced their own *Zeitopern.* The next original contribution to the genre was Kurt Weill's *Der Zar lässt sich photographieren.*

Figure 6.1.   Kurt Weill in 1928
(Courtesy Lotte Jacobi Archive, Media Services, Dimond Library, The University of New Hampshire; photo by Lotte Jacobi)

6

Kurt Weill:
Der Zar lässt sich photographieren

Berlin Years, 1920–1926

Kurt Weill arrived in Berlin in 1920, having been invited to join Busoni's private composition class offered through the Academy of Arts. A stint as a *Kapellmeister* at the Lüdenscheid theater had already stimulated what would be an abiding interest in musical theater and had further provided Weill with practical experience with live theater. By the time the Leipzig opera house premiered *Der Zar lässt sich photographieren*, Weill, not yet 28, had earned a reputation for musical and theatrical innovation. His one-act opera *Der Protagonist* (composed 1924–25) was the most successful opera by a young composer prior to *Jonny spielt auf*. *Royal Palace*, a second one-act work, received a prestigious Berlin premiere in 1927, coupled with his cantata *Der neue Orpheus*. And the *Mahagonny-Songspiel*, Weill's first collaboration with Bertolt Brecht, was highly acclaimed at its premiere at the 1927 Baden-Baden Festival. The *Mahagonny-Songspiel* demonstrated Weill's new song style, for which *Die Dreigroschenoper*, his best-known work, would become famous. The premiere of *Die Dreigroschenoper* followed that of *Der Zar* by only six months.

After the expressionist tone of *Der Protagonist* Weill changed direction, in keeping with the twenties spirit. Thus *Der Zar lässt sich photographieren* is a work, like *Jonny spielt auf*, which betrays its composer's commitment to a new time and a new audience, a commitment which, for Weill, was indicated by his membership since 1922 in the *Novembergruppe*. It was also during these early Berlin years that Weill came in contact with jazz and American dance music, which he experimented with by 1921 and later wrote about in 1926.[1]

His first use of popular music idioms appears in his cantata, *Der neue Orpheus*, composed in September of 1925 on a text by Ivan Goll (1891–1950). Weill met Goll through their mutual friend, the playwright Georg Kaiser, who supplied the libretto for both *Der Protagonist* and *Der Zar*, and Goll later wrote the libretto for *Royal Palace* (1926). Goll, born in Alsace-Lorraine, wrote poetry in both French and German and amalgamated literary trends associated with both his mother tongues. His early work from 1915 on, with its emphasis on the struggle of the individual within society, reflected prewar expressionism. Goll lived and worked in Paris after 1919, and in 1924 he published a *Manifeste du surréalisme,* which showed his conscious adoption of this French literary movement associated with André Breton.[2]

Goll's text for *Der neue Orpheus* updated the myth of Orpheus in the underworld, which had also been the subject of Krenek's opera *Orpheus und Eurydike* (1923). The hero of *Der neue Orpheus,* in this case a successful violinist, travels around the world only to return home to find that his Euridice has become a prostitute. Goll's hero, in true expressionist fashion, struggles against his society, which is responsible for the ruination of his beloved. Much of the text's poetic images and its free-verse form, however, is more characteristic of the surrealist movement. The text makes many references to modern technology, as Goll was both fascinated with and repelled by contemporary society.[3] Goll enjoyed the fast pace of urban life and adopted a writing style which, through its short, disjunct phrases, attempted to duplicate this new pace. But Goll was equally horrified by the materialism and spiritual emptiness he perceived as another result of modern technology. Thus *Der neue Orpheus* presents his ambivalent views about postwar life.

As Goll's text describes modern life and popular entertainments—the *Kabarett,* surburban movie houses, Yankee girls, the gramophone, and the circus—it was natural for Weill to employ topical musical idioms. Specific jazz dances, so designated in the score, are not present. A set of seven variations, whose corresponding textual images suggest seven skits in a revue, make up the central part of the work. And variation 2, with its oom-pah-pah bass line and dotted melodies, provides an updated waltz suitable for the revue or *Kabarettrevue* (see example 6.1).

Royal Palace

As *Der Sprung über den Schatten* served as a proving ground for *Jonny spielt auf,* so *Royal Palace,* Weill's second opera, fulfilled a similar function for *Der Zar lässt sich photographieren.*[4] Even with its incorporation of jazz idioms, *Royal Palace* remains outside the defined realm of *Zeitoper,* largely as a result of the subject matter and its dramatic treatment, which combines both expressionism and surrealism typical of Goll (see synopsis in appendix C).

Goll described the libretto as "a fairy tale of life first perceived in death."[5] The heroine Dejanira, whose dissatisfaction with her life and rebellion against her society is the central issue, could be the heroine of a number of expressionist plays. Her husband and lovers, part of her detestable life, are referred to simply

Example 6.1.   Kurt Weill, *Der neue Orpheus*

as *Der Ehemann, Der Geliebte von gestern* and *Der Verliebte von morgen,* again in keeping with the convention of nameless characters common to much expressionist drama. Goll's surrealism is evident in Dejanira's past and future lovers, who try to woo her with visions, dreams, and fantasies. Dejanira's final act of suicide is again characteristic of expressionist literature. Goll also liked word-play. At the close of the opera, the chorus, husband, and lovers chant variations of Dejanira's name (De-ja-ni-ra, Ja-ni-ra-de, Ra-ji-di-na) as if they were incantations.

Royal Palace is not without dramatic topicality. The work is set in the present, and the opening scene at the Royal Palace hotel was depicted with great realism on stage. Goll and Weill further depended on up-to-date theatrical techniques carried out by director Ludwig Hörth and set designer Franco

Aravatinos at the Berlin Staatsoper premiere on 2 March 1927. The promises of
the husband and lovers required the use of quick set changes, a revolving stage
[*Drehscheibe*], and a highly touted filmed sequence.[6]

Goll had used film in his plays as early as *Die Unsterblichen* of 1920 and
had even tried to adapt aspects of film technique to his poetry with the use of
sudden verbal "close-ups."[7] The piano-vocal score stated somewhat
ambiguously: "Film: All through the performance actual choice morsels are
depicted. Dejanira in Nice, in a porter car on the way to Constantinople, at a ball
and a Russian ballet, in a plane heading for the North Pole, and so forth."[8] In the
Berlin production, the filmed sequence reportedly showed Dejanira flying to
Berlin, Paris, London, New York City, and Africa.[9] The promise of the lover of
the future was depicted in a ballet and a revue scene celebrating a fantasy world
of technical wonders.[10] Aravatinos's set design featured a mechanistic, abstract
collage of geometric shapes.

As with *Der neue Orpheus,* the topical allusions in Goll's libretto logically
suggested the use of popular idioms in Weill's score. Weill was reported to have
told the Associated Press when asked about his reliance on popular music: "I
didn't sit down to write jazz for its own sake, but rather opera for its own sake. In
so doing, I naturally found myself running into jazz as an expression of our
time."[11] Two main sections in *Royal Palace* display Weill's use of popular music
idioms: the music which accompanies the film and the final "Tanz der
Wasserfrau" preceding Dejanira's suicide. Early on in the work, a chorus of
bellhops, the hotel manager, and a porter execute a ballet as they tempt Dejanira,
at her husband's request, with delectable foods. The accompanying music, while
meant for dancing, does not resemble a particular modern dance despite its
prominent use of an ostinato.

The music accompanying the film is in the style of a foxtrot well suited to
the modern images on screen. The cut-time meter suggests the shimmy, while
the music retains the character of the older foxtrot. Weill's choice of instrumentation clearly imitates dance band ensembles. The piano begins the dance,
with the left hand maintaining the steady quarter note pulse under a typically
dotted melody in the right hand, reminiscent of the solo piano foxtrots of Krenek
and others (see example 6.2). The violin and saxophone have solos before the
piano returns. Perhaps imitating the sound effects used by the Original Dixieland
Jazz Band or Sam Wooding's Band, Weill introduces an auto horn at the close,
before "The Beloved of Yesterday" appears. This lover, as if the next star in a
revue skit, enters and coaxes Dejanira with memories from her past, accompanied by starkly different music.

Weill used the tango rhythm early on in the opera, when Dejanira first
enters, but he did not set off this brief use in the score. The tango rhythm returns
in the final scene of the opera, designated in the score simply as the "Tanz der
Wasserfrauen." A woman's chorus, situated in the orchestra pit, joins the

Example 6.2.   Kurt Weill, *Royal Palace*, Film Music

principals in chanting Dejanira's name. Weill's use of the tango here does not supply the same direct musical topicality as did the foxtrot accompaniment to the film. Weill may have been attempting, however, to draw a musical correlation between this dance of seduction and Dejanira's ultimate temptation by the *Wasserfrauen* which results in her suicide by drowning. The musical effect of the tango is heightened by prominent saxophone solos.

Weill limits his use of jazz dance idioms in *Royal Palace* to the lighthearted foxtrot and the seductive tango. He further shows his knowledge of jazz sonorities through the use of solo piano and saxophone. And as with Krenek, the presence of a violin solo in the foxtrot section shows that Weill, too, recognized it as a legitimate dance band instrument. Notably missing from Weill's score are banjo and muted brass.

Reviewers generally found Weill's score and the Berlin Staatsoper production unable to withstand the bad libretto. Adolf Weissmann described the effect of Goll's *tragische Revue* as "comic melancholy which borders on the ludicrous."[12] Paul Schwers claimed that an artist of taste would have summarily rejected such a text, but that Weill chose it in order to prove himself up-to-date.[13] Some critics, still finding fault with the libretto, applauded Goll's attempts to make a statement on the role of women in modern society. The novel introduction of film led Alfred Baresel to proclaim *Royal Palace* the first *Film-Oper*.[14] And other critics felt that the elaborate stage action, especially during the scenes in which husband and lovers make their promises, overshadowed Weill's score. Weissmann stated: "So much is presented to the eye that the spectator can hardly attend to the music which is almost relegated to the role of accompaniment for a movie."[15]

The close proximity of the dates of their first performances and the shared musical and theatrical topicality led many reviewers to compare *Royal Palace* and *Jonny spielt auf*. Alfred Baresel, Paul Stefan, and Karl Westermeyer discussed *Royal Palace* in light of Weill's self-proclaimed commitment to new operatic genres, a commitment they saw in Krenek's operas as well.[16] Both Krenek and Weill, they noted, sought to bring new theatrical techniques and other features of twenties art and culture—film, revue, and, of course, jazz—into the world of opera. While reviewers judged *Jonny spielt auf* the more successful of the two works, they also recognized that the two works were different and that *Royal Palace* was not intended to be a copy of *Jonny spielt auf*. Adolf Aber later wrote: "[The] two works [*Royal Palace* and *Jonny spielt auf*] fundamentally have nothing to do with one another. *Royal Palace* was entirely a clever attempt to bring into accord the powerful drama of *Der Protagonist* with the entertainment requirement of the time."[17] And Hans Gutman explained the notable differences in their jazz usage:

> In the voices above the water, eclipsed by the high-soaring soprano solo, and in the finale, constructed on the rhythm of a truly fluid tango, lie the highest values of the score. Naturally, Weill does not present the jazz as obviously here as did Krenek. He employs it in a moderate, even stylized way. This discretion is documented by the orchestration where a single saxophone and piano appear alongside various percussion.[18]

Gutman voiced what later writers continued to note as a marked difference between Weill and Krenek.[19] Although Krenek and Weill shared much in the way of artistic philosophy and dramatic content, their reliance on and employment of jazz idioms, again coming out of a similar need to voice the musical language of the day, took individual turns. Weill typically wove jazz idioms into the overall structure of sections within an individual work. Thus the jazz dance and timbres become integral formal and orchestrational constructs, however much they also characterized the setting or added to the dramaturgy. In this way, Weill resembles Schulhoff and others who found in jazz convenient modern absolute forms, twentieth-century versions of the minuet.

Krenek, on the other hand, tended to set up clearer contrasts between his jazz-inspired sections and the rest of his score. In *Jonny spielt auf,* the "Shimmy," "Tango," and "Jazz" numbers are on-stage music, resulting from logical, obvious stage action, though adding much to the impact of the drama. This distinction, often used to argue Weill's superiority, does not always hold. The *Tango-Angèle* of *Der Zar lässt sich photographieren* enters as part of logical on-stage action, while in *Jonny spielt auf,* the blues section of the last scene, sung by Anita and Yvonne, as well as Jonny's solos, are not treated as on-stage numbers and could rightly have been set in a variety of ways.

From 1926 to the Premiere of *Der Zar lässt sich photographieren*

Prior to his composition of *Der Zar lässt sich photographieren*, a work whose comic nature set it apart from both *Der Protagonist* and *Royal Palace*, Weill tries his hand at another comic opera, *Na Und?* Composed during 1926 on a two-act libretto by music critic Felix Joachimson, *Na Und?* remained unpublished and unperformed and has subsequently been lost except for 34 pages of incomplete sketches. The satirical libretto about the American adventures of an Italian emigrant appears not to have suited Weill's publishers. One of three musical excerpts which remains shows Weill's retention of jazz dance idioms to characterize the American milieu; a "Shimmy-Trio" also referred to by Weill as "der Nigger-Song."[20] The use of America as a setting, reference to black Americans, and the shimmy, are tantilizing, and David Drew rightly argues for the importance of this work in charting Weill's operatic development and for the singular tragedy of its loss.

Before *Der Zar* received its premiere, Weill scored a success with the *Mahagonny-Songspiel* at the 1927 Baden-Baden Chamber Music Festival. The festival directors specially commissioned the *Mahagonny-Songspiel* for an evening of short chamber operas, in keeping with their original emphasis on chamber music. Included on the bill with the *Mahagonny-Songspiel* were Hindemith's revue sketch *Hin und zurück*, Ernst Toch's treatment of a Hans Christian Andersen fairy tale, *Die Prinzessin auf der Erbse*, and Darius Milhaud's *L'Enlèvement d'Europe*, a further contribution to his preexisting genre, the *opera minute*.

Composed after *Der Zar lässt sich photographieren*, the *Mahagonny-Songspiel* shows Weill's continued interest in topical subject matter and reliance on popular music idioms while at the same time he was moving towards his simpler *Song* style.[21] With regard to the development of this *Song* style and self-contained musical numbers, often borrowed from popular music, Weill considered the *Mahagonny-Songspiel* to have been a study for his later collaborative work with Bertolt Brecht, *Aufstieg und Fall der Stadt Mahagonny* (1930).

Weill found inspiration for the *Mahagonny-Songspiel* in the five Mahagonny songs published in Brecht's 1927 collection *Die Hauspostille* and succeeded in convincing Brecht that these poems would make an effective libretto. As Brecht wrote the texts of the "Alabama Song" and the "Benares Song" in a kind of broken English, and with the further references to whiskey bars, telephones, and the characters' names—Jimmy, Bobby, Billy, Bessie, Jessie—an American locale suggested itself for the entire *Songspiel*.[22] Brecht may not have subscribed to an *Amerikanismus* which sentimentalized or idealized modern industrial American society, but his Mahagonny texts certainly reflected another kind of fascination with America as the land of decadence and rampant capitalism, which later infected Berlin.[23]

Walther Brügmann, fresh from the success of *Jonny spielt auf*, directed the operas on the program, although Brecht is listed in the original program as the sole director of the *Mahagonny-Songspiel*.[24] The staging was very much in keeping with the style of Piscator productions, with which Brecht was familiar; Brügmann, who knew modern theater, may have had a hand in the final outcome as well. Caspar Neher, a friend of both Brecht and Piscator, designed the sets and the projections, which were shown on a screen behind the center stage platform, designed to look like a boxing ring. Both Piscator and Brecht had used a boxing ring as settings in earlier separate productions. Brecht, in particular, sought to cultivate a sporting atmosphere in his theatrical works and wished to recreate the enthusiasm and sense of fun that was present in audiences at sporting events.[25] The boxing ring set also suggests the fascination with American sports typical of the age and shared by Krenek in *Schwergewicht*.

Of the four works, the *Mahagonny-Songspiel* and Hindemith's *Hin und zurück* received the most attention. With Hindemith's clever adaptation of film techniques and the innovative staging and musical style of the *Mahagonny-Songspiel*, these two works were easily the most unusual and thought-provoking of the four chamber operas. Eberhard Preussner branded Weill an *enfant terrible*, and Otto Klemperer, whose wife Johanna sang in *Hin und zurück*, was quite impressed with him.[26] But not everyone shared Klemperer's newfound respect. Aaron Copland, who reviewed the entire festival for *Modern Music*, agreed that the *Mahagonny-Songspiel* "aroused the most discussion" but found the work strained in its attempt to be revolutionary.[27] Instead, he deemed Milhaud's *opera minute* the best work on the program.

Der Zar lässt sich photographieren

From the outset, Weill conceived of *Der Zar lässt sich photographieren* as a special exercise in comic opera. As *Der Protagonist* had attained a respectable place in the operatic repertory, Weill wished to supply it with a suitable companion to provide a convincing double bill. *Royal Palace* had originally been intended to fulfill this function for *Der Protagonist*, but was judged a failure after its seven performances at the Staatsoper. It is clear from an interview that Weill gave on the eve of the Leipzig premiere of *Der Zar lässt sich photographieren* that he intended the work as more than a mere companion to *Der Protagonist*:

> It was a matter here of creating a complementary work for *Der Protagonist* . . . a contrasting work of another genre yet not inferior in intensity or effectiveness. My ideal subject would lack that private quality of earlier operas and instead turn towards the larger issues of our time which are subjects worthy of theatrical treatment.[28]

As a complementary work, then, *Der Zar* was able to be as comic as *Der Protagonist* was tragic. While both *Der Protagonist* and *Royal Palace*, works expressionist in nature, dwelt upon the intensely personal or private side of their main characters, *Der Zar,* with its social satire, would comment upon the problem of the public role of an individual within modern society.

Weill described the comic nature of *Der Zar* as akin to *Die Fledermaus,* though the work was still to be understood as an opera and not an operetta.[29] And his further identification of *Der Zar lässt sich photographieren* as an *opera buffa* underscored his traditional conception of the work's comic nature. The term *opera buffa* was not commonly used at the time, and many composers no longer even identified their works as either comic or tragic; Ernst Krenek called *Jonny spielt auf* merely "an opera in three parts." Weill's use of this older operatic term suggests his acquaintance with and fondness for such pre-Wagnerian models as Italian *opera buffa,* French *opéra bouffe,* and German *komische Oper.* And in his articles for *Der deutsche Rundfunk* written during this period, Weill specifically discussed the works of Mozart, Rossini, Offenbach, and Lortzing that were typical of the various national traditions of comic opera.[30] And Weill shared Busoni's great love for Mozart, the acknowledged master of the *opera buffa.* As Weill had already voiced the prevailing skepticism for Wagnerian music drama, his labeling of *Der Zar lässt sich photographieren* shows a conscious alignment with older comic genres or even the *commedia dell'arte,* which inspired Busoni's first two operas.[31]

For this new comic opera, Weill returned to his first successful collaborator, playwright Georg Kaiser (see illustration 6.2). As one of the preeminent contributors to expressionist drama, Kaiser was an unlikely candidate for a comic librettist. Although his early play, *Die jüdische Witwe* (1911), was a satirical comedy, Kaiser's later works, such as *Von Morgens bis Mitternachts* (1916) and the *Gas* trilogy (1917–20), were anything but lighthearted. Expressionist dramatic features still appear in *Der Zar lässt sich photographieren,* although they are often couched in parody.

In the same Leipzig interview, Weill credited Kaiser with the idea for the plot concerning the seemingly innocent attempt by a czar visiting Paris to get his photograph taken, and his subsequent involvement in an attempted assassination plot (see synopsis in appendix C). Anti-czarist conspirators have taken over the studio of the famous Angèle, replacing the lovely photographer and her assistants with impostors. A false Angèle plans to shoot the czar with a gun concealed in her camera. Unwittingly, the czar foils the plot by falling in love with his photographer. He attempts to take her picture, thereby stalling for time until the police arrive. The assassin and her fellow conspirators escape over the rooftops of Paris. An assassination as part of a comic work and the matter-of-fact and nonjudgmental treatment of events—the assassins go unpunished—show Kaiser's adoption of the cool, wry detachment of *Neue Sachlichkeit* literature.

As complementary works, *Der Zar* and *Der Protagonist* both have the lead character in the title role, both of whom experience a tension between their

Figure 6.2.   Georg Kaiser, ca. 1924

public roles and their private selves and get caught up in the problem of reality versus illusion. As an actor performing theatrical roles, the hero of *Der Protagonist* confuses his own identity with the stage characters he portrays. The protagonist immerses himself so completely in his role-playing that he is unable to distinguish between the false reality of his dramatic roles and the actual events in his life. This confusion leads him to murder his beloved sister, whom he mistakes for the unfaithful wife of one of his stage personae.

The czar is equally trapped by his limiting public role. Kaiser and Weill's concern for individual freedom echoes Krenek's continuing thematic concern with uninhibited individuals and societies. When the czar is ensnared in the elaborate assassination plot involving impostors, he too becomes unable to distinguish between what is real and what is merely role-playing. When the real Angèle returns after the departure of the conspirators, the czar is surprised by her appearance, but accepts her explanation that his confusion resulted from the darkened studio. Once light is literally shed on the subject, the czar relinquishes his wish for personal satisfaction and once more takes on his social role. The opera ends with the assassination attempt foiled, order restored, and the czar maintaining his public façade in front of the real Angèle's camera. Throughout the work, the czar remains an unwitting victim of his detestable public persona, bewildered by the topsy-turvy reality. In contrast, the protagonist, who has chosen the profession of a public role-player, is responsible for his actions and their tragic personal outcome.

Whereas *Der Protagonist* is set in the Shakespearean past, *Der Zar* captures the vitality of the twenties central to *Zeitoper*. The political references at the heart of the plot—the dictatorial aristocrat and the proletarian assassins—were certainly topical. The assassination of Archduke Franz Ferdinand in 1914, which precipitated World War I, and the murder of Czar Nicholas II and his family in 1918 would have been all too familiar references for the audience. And in the Weimar Republic, political assassinations continued to be a grim reality, although the victims were not always of the aristocracy, as in the murders of Karl Liebknecht and Rosa Luxemburg in 1919.

The opera's setting in a Parisian photographer's studio further underscored the work's modernity. The Parisian geographical location, shared with *Jonny spielt auf,* carried with it similar implications that this city and its attendant culture were special, even if Weill had never been there. As he remarked in his interview: "Almost spontaneously the atmosphere of Paris suggested itself. . . . I have almost no personal sense of the city and don't really know it."[32] The czar, a visitor to the Paris, expresses similar views about the special city when he first arrives at Angèle's studio: "How lovely is this view of Paris . . . Montmartre! Moulin Rouge! Even more interesting at night," and later bemoans upon learning of the plot that "The dream of Paris now dies."[33]

Casting Angèle as a photographer added another topical reference. Photographic portraiture was evolving into a popular new art form in the 1920s, and photographers Lotte Jacobi and Elli Marcus were both known in Berlin at the time for their stunning portraits. Jacobi later photographed both Weill (see figure 6.1) and Lotte Lenya (ca. 1929). And finally, with an attitude also characteristic of the time, the opera does not shy away from sexual candor. Weill describes the czar's antagonist as "a modern woman with political tendencies" and the czar openly attempts to seduce her.

Again as in *Jonny spielt auf* and other *Zeitopern, Der Zar lässt sich photographieren* incorporates stage properties and sound effects common to modern life. Besides the modern portraits which adorn the studio and upon which the czar comments, a telephone call announces the czar's visit and the doorbell rings throughout the work. Two modern mechanical stage properties, Angèle's camera and the gramophone, are central to the action. The camera contains the hidden revolver and becomes the mechanical device over and around which the czar and the false Angèle quarrel. A gramophone takes on special prominence, as a recording is the sole accompaniment for the *Tango-Angèle* at the opera's high point. Kaiser's suggestion of the camera and Weill's dependence on the gramophone both fit the mechanistic spirit of the *Zeitoper*.

Kaiser constructed the libretto largely as an extended duet between the two main characters, the false Angèle and the czar. Both roles are caricatures. Weill claimed that the czar's character as a postwar ruler was modelled on the screen persona of Paramount Pictures' film star Adolphe Menjou.[34] Menjou's roles, such as in the 1926 picture *Ace of Cads,* typified his perennial characterization as the debonair "ladies' man" with his smoothed-back hair and thin triangular moustache. And the anti-czarist assassin, this modern woman, parodied both the liberated New Woman of Weimar who had been given the right to vote in 1919 and aggressive proletarian, even Communist, sympathizers so prevalent in the postwar period. As Krenek set up a dichotomy between Jonny and Max, so, too, did Kaiser with the false Angèle and the czar. Rather than presenting opposing ideas about the artist's role in society, the czar and Angèle characterize opposing social and political views. The czar represents a moribund political system and its society while the false Angèle literally calls for his end and the start of a new political era.

Kaiser's central dialogue for the czar and Angèle turns on dramatic irony, as the audience recognizes that these characters are discussing different subjects. The unknowing czar voices matters of love and photography, while the false Angèle's responses betray her murderous intentions.

Czar: Enough light? It's almost dark. How long must I sit here so stiff and still?
False Angèle: I have a flash in the camera.
Czar: Will it frighten me?

False Angèle: We'll see!
Czar: Do you really believe it will get me right?
False Angèle: Like a sharpshooter, I hit my target.[35]

The action becomes increasingly slapstick, in the nature of a revue skit, as the czar and Angèle each try to force the other in front of the deadly camera.

Kaiser's witty libretto contains social satire in its aristocratic and proletarian caricatures and treatment of the modern problem of the individual in society, and literary satire in its parody of expressionism. The czar struggles against his social role, not unlike Dejanira, in true expressionist fashion. He longs to be a freer man, a man unrestricted by his social position. Other Kaiser plays, such as *Die Koralle* (1917), contained wealthy aristocrats or capitalists uncomfortable with their social position. However, the czar's predicament is treated in such a manner that he becomes a comic rather than tragic figure. The use of impostors, central to the story, was another expressionist dramatic device. Again Kaiser's play *Die Koralle* featured an impostor or *Doppelgänger,* as the wealthy businessman seeks to trade places with a more content underling. In *Der Zar,* the impostors are used for comic effect rather than psychological impact.

Other features of the libretto suggest a further connection with the pre-Wagnerian comic opera repertory already implied by the distinction of the work as an *opera buffa.* The reliance on class distinctions, buffoonish aristocrats, deception, impostors, and unwitting actions on the part of main characters are conventions characteristic of many eighteenth-century *opera buffa*s. The czar, with his roving eye for underlings, updates Mozart's Count Almaviva in *Le Nozze di Figaro.* The false Angèle, like a modern Susanna, is able to get the best of her master. Pretending to succumb to his sexual advances, she manages to extricate herself at the last minute, leaving the embarrassed ruler to face public scrutiny.

The choice of a czar as a central character also suggests, at least superficially, a connection with *Zar und Zimmerman* by Gustav Albert Lortzing (1801–51). This *komische Oper* was regularly performed in the 1920s, and Weill reviewed a Berlin performance in 1925 and wrote another article in 1926 commemorating the one hundred twenty-fifth anniversary of Lortzing's birth.[36] Weill expressed a high regard for Lortzing's work, singling out his sure theatrical sense, masterly treatment of small forms, and his use of truly German national characteristics [*Volkstümlichkeit*]. Displaying once more his anti-Wagnerian sentiment, Weill credited Lortzing with the creation of "a coherent, far-reaching operatic form which is remembered not only as an expression of its time but as a genre worthy in itself."[37] Weill's later coinage of the term *Songspiel* for the *Mahagonny-Songspiel,* in order to stress his adoption of the simpler *Song* style, suggests a backward glance both to the older German *Singspiel* and to Lortzing's *Spielopern.*

Lortzing's *Zar und Zimmermann* had a basis in reality, with its story of Peter the Great's exploits while travelling incognito as a shipbuilder. In both works the czars attempt to shed their public roles and become ordinary citizens and neither is successful. When Peter the Great's identity is revealed, he resumes his royal duties and sails back to Russia, just as Weill's czar finally poses for his offical portrait. Other nineteenth-century comic works, such as Jacques Offenbach's *La Grande Duchesse de Gérolstein,* featured rulers who also tried to escape the public duties of their office.[38]

Critics quickly noted the superior literary quality of Kaiser's libretto, with its combination of social satire and its objective treatment of an assassination in the manner of a farce. Other writers noted the burlesque qualities of the libretto with its parody of musical and dramatic conventions and juxtaposition of serious and comic elements. Some writers judged these juxtapositions as so incongruous as to warrant calling the work a *Groteske.* Though imbued with topicality and possessing a relation to the twenties shared by *Jonny spielt auf,* Kaiser and Weill's conception of *Der Zar* follows, more closely than did Krenek, Busoni's injunction to create an operatic world of pretense, of life reflected and distorted in a comic mirror.

Weill initially referred to the opera in letters to his publisher as *Photographie und Liebe,* and the work was announced in *Die Musik* (July 1927) under that title.[39] On 4 August, Weill wrote to Universal Edition that he now wanted to call the work *Der Zar lässt sich photographieren.* But a mere two days later, Weill wrote Universal Edition with another change. After visiting Kaiser, he changed the title to "Der Zar lässt sich. . . . ." Weill specified that this new title should not end with a mere ellipsis but with nine widely-spaced dots. He and Kaiser felt the new title would suggest more effectively the ambiguity of the work. In German, the many possible implications of the title convey a wide range of activities that the czar might be "having done for himself," from innocently having his palace cleaned to more obscene activities. Many expressionist authors, including Kaiser, favored titles with double entendre or multiple meanings. But before the premiere, Weill wrote once more to ask if there was time to return to *Der Zar lässt sich photographieren.*[40] He explained that he and Kaiser had received comments that the abbreviated title might be a little offensive [*anstössig*].

The Musical Score

Weill's treatment of Kaiser's libretto emphasizes its topical comic spirit. Weill described the opera's formal scheme as consisting of self-contained units—arias, duets, and ensembles—which led into one another or were linked by recitativelike sections.[41] Weill did not provide numbers or titled sections in the score, as Krenek did in *Der Sprung über den Schatten* or as Hindemith would in *Neues vom Tage,* but the individual sections are easily discernable through his use of ostinati and changes of tempo and affect and show his pre-Wagnerian formal approach. Weill's choice of instrumentation also fits the *opera buffa* distinction in its limited size. Notably absent is the saxophone; thus the jazz-related numbers rely solely on brass, woodwind, piano, and special percussion timbres.

Weill's foremost comic and organizational device was a male chorus situated in the orchestra pit, an expansion of the women's chorus in *Royal Palace.* In his Leipzig interview Weill summarized the chorus's function:

> A male chorus, added later by myself, has the primary function . . . of juggling the action and at times even comments in a somewhat unfitting manner on the stage action without influencing this action, and it underscores the *opera buffa* character of the work.[42]

Weill also noted that the chorus provided a useful connection [*Verbindung*] between the dramatic action and the audience.[43] The placement of the chorus in the orchestra pit, situated between the stage and the house floor, heightened its role as an intermediary.

Weill's chorus, standing apart from the stage and commenting upon the action for the benefit of the audience rather than participating in it, functions as a modern Greek chorus and spoofs the Greek revivalism in French and German art of the time. Composers such as Egon Wellesz and Milhaud favored a return to the use of the old-fashioned chorus. Wellesz had also been influenced by the Handel revival, whose productions relied on large, static choruses. Weill himself had a passing flirtation with Greek drama; in a 1927 letter to Universal Edition, in which he first mentioned working on *Der Zar,* Weill also mentioned his intention to compose a *klassische Tragödie* on *Antigone* or a similar subject for the Baden-Baden Festival.[44]

Stravinsky's *Oedipus Rex* may have provided both the model for Weill and a target for his spoof. Stravinsky's opera received a concert performance in Paris on 30 May 1927 during the gestation period of *Der Zar.* In an article published in October 1927, Weill even discussed the new French preference for ancient subject matter and singled out *Oedipus Rex* as an example.[45] One of the notable features of *Oedipus Rex* was its Greek chorus, situated to the side of the stage, which commented on the action throughout the opera. The gala production of *Oedipus Rex* at the Krolloper, which Weill reviewed, calling it a "landmark work in the evolution of the new opera," followed the premiere of *Der Zar.*[46] The Paris premiere was widely reviewed in French- and English-language music journals. It is probable that Weill knew something of the work already in 1927, as he was quite fond of *L'Histoire du soldat,* and would certainly have kept abreast of Stravinsky's latest works. Weill may not have known the musical score of *Oedipus Rex* before the Krolloper production, but he could have read descriptions of the chorus in reviews.

The similarity between *Oedipus Rex* and *Der Zar* did not escape producers or critics of the time.[47] And *Oedipus Rex,* rather than *Der Protagonist,* shared the bill with *Der Zar* on a number of occasions, apparently with Weill's approval.[48] Not only did the two works share the Greek chorus, but *Oedipus Rex* is similar to *Der Protagonist* in its tragic story of an individual forced to take responsibility for his rash actions. Thus a double bill of *Oedipus Rex* and *Der Zar* maintained the tragic-comic dichotomy. Given the comic nature of *Der Zar lässt sich photographieren,* its Greek chorus is a tongue-in-cheek use of Stravinsky's ancient convention. And it further maintains the work's burlesque spirit of incongruous juxtaposition: a Greek chorus in an opera with an up-to-date plot.

The costuming of the chorus added to its comic effectiveness. Although neither the full score nor libretto gives any indication of the chorus's appearance or demeanor, a publicity photograph from the Leipzig premiere (see figure 6.3) shows a group of men, described by one critic as "old geezers" [*Mummel-greise*],[49] sporting exaggerated mustaches, long white beards, and costumed in dark coats and top hats.[50] Which collaborator was responsible for this visual aspect is unclear; it may have been the invention of director Walther Brügmann, who had garnered such praise for his innovative staging in *Jonny spielt auf.* Later houses maintained this costuming, as is evident in the photograph from the Berlin Städtische Oper production (see figure 6.4) with its similarly attired chorus carrying briefcases.[51]

The chorus's distinctive dress also suggests a dramatic convention popular with expressionist playwrights, typification. Through typification, characters were costumed to represent their social function or communal identity, thereby eliminating the need for personal names or individual traits. Many expressionist plays dating from the early 1920s and critical of modern society have characters costumed in dark coats and top hats or other evening dress who represent decadent, capitalist figures such as businessmen, industrialists, or bankers. Kaiser's own early play, *Von Morgens bis Mitternachts* (1916), generally considered to be his first expressionist work, includes several male characters [*Jüdische Herren*] dressed in smoking jackets and silk hats [*Seidenhut*] who act as umpires at a bicycle race. The play's main character, known only as a bank cashier, arrives at the race dressed in evening clothes and top hat, ready to partake in the new delights of capitalism. At the end of the play, the bank cashier is robbed by four men dressed in evening clothes [*Herren im Frack*].[52]

Ernst Toller's *Massemensch* (1920) contains a scene in which the heroine dreams that "the bankers in top hats dance a foxtrot around the stock exchange table."[53] A character in one of Toller's later plays, *Hinkemann* (1922), is a *Budenbesitzer* or showman, and he comes to represent the evils of capitalist society as he forces the hapless Hinkemann to perform in a freak show. Near the end of the play, when the *Budenbesitzer* refuses to release Hinkemann from his contract, this corrupt capitalist is costumed in a dress coat and top hat.[54] The

Figure 6.3.   Publicity Photo from the Leipzig Premiere of *Der Zar lässt sich photographieren* in 1928

Figure 6.4.   The Male Chorus of *Der Zar lässt sich photographieren* in the Berlin
Städtische Oper's Production of 1928

Example 6.3. Kurt Weill, *Der Zar lässt sich photographieren,* Opening

Piscatorbühne's 1924 production, *Revue Roter Rummel,* also costumed its caricatures of the wealthy in top hats and evening dress.[55] And Dr. Caligari, the title character in one of the most famous contributions to expressionist cinema, *Das Kabinett des Dr. Caligari,* sports a top hat. So it may have been Kaiser himself who suggested this recreation of an expressionist dramatic convention. As the chorus's typification is out of place in a comic work, this visual aspect adds another burlesque touch to this *opera buffa,* while further parodying theatrical expressionism.

The chorus sings a total of 10 times. Some entries are brief, consisting of only a measure or two of music, but several passages are lengthy and represent self-contained choral numbers in keeping with Weill's description of the number-opera organization of the work. The chorus performs in unison, in two-, three-, and four-part harmony, both accompanied and a cappella, humming and with the text. As Weill indicated, the chorus does not participate in the stage action. In an often mock-serious manner, coupled with distinctive music, the chorus serves to remind the audience that regardless of what transpires on stage, the opera is a comedy. Although Weill claimed to have added the chorus independently of Kaiser, it is unclear whether Weill supplied the new texts or whether Kaiser wrote them later at Weill's request.[56] Weill cautioned his publisher to use the piano-vocal score to derive the authentic libretto; the typewritten manuscript of the text then in their possession, he warned, had undergone significant revision.[57]

The chorus opens the opera by stating the title of the work in the manner of a *Kabarett conférencier* or variety show emcee announcing the evening's comedy sketch. The attendant music (see example 6.3), with its cymbal downbeat, melodic fifth, and triplet rhythms, is reminiscent of a fanfare suitable for the czar's regal public character. The full orchestra then proceeds with a short overture. The chorus reenters before the curtain rises to state the title, again in three-part harmony and with an orchestral accompaniment which echoes the opening triplet rhythm. Humming in slower four-part harmony as the curtain rises on Angèle's studio, the chorus brings the overture to a close.

The chorus closes the opera as part of a finale in keeping with the tradition of earlier comic operas. As the real Angèle prepares to photograph the czar, a group of his followers march on-stage, giving way to a return of the opening choral and orchestral fanfare. The work closes with the chorus reiterating the title, as in the opening measures, but transposed up a semitone and now followed by a final jazzy cymbal tag. This repetition of the opening choral gesture stresses the opera's paradox of role-playing and reality. For once the assassination plot and the czar's attempted seduction have failed, all that has transpired is that indeed "the czar has had his picture taken." The implicit circularity of the returning chorus shows that the plot has come full circle, and with the true Angèle behind the camera, order has been restored and the status quo maintained.

The chorus enters two other times to clarify the opera's title and central action. When the real Angèle learns of the czar's impending visit, she states the title to the same triplet rhythm as in the opening gesture, but to a different melody. The chorus follows Angèle's restatement of the title with eight measures of hummed four-part harmony. The chorus's slower moving a capella part is in marked contrast to the preceding music, distinguished by rapid sixteenth-note scalar passages, and it musically underscores Angèle's proud announcement. When the false Angèle makes her first attempt to *shoot* the czar, the chorus again declaims the title to the triplet fanfare rhythm and in three-part harmony. This repetition reminds the audience that the czar is only supposed to be photographed.

The remaining choral entrances spoof the stage action and add moments of false tension to the drama. When the political terrorists first enter the studio, the leader reveals the assassination plot; time is expensive and the czar will pay with his blood. And the five other assassins emphatically respond, "With a czar's blood."[58] The chorus repeats this phrase in pianissimo and heightens the dramatic impact. Later the entire group of terrorists swears allegiance to its political mission. This murder, they claim, will be a signal for the oppressed who hunger for liberation; it will open the door to freedom and justice and break the chains of their imprisoned brothers. The male chorus chimes in that the assassination shall, will, and must succeed, after which the terrorists exit with their hostages, leaving the false Angèle to await the czar.

The chorus then reenters with a much longer passage set off from the surrounding music as a separate choral number. The text restates the location of the revolver in the camera and repeats the gist of the assassins' philosophy. The number closes with a final reminder to the audience of the loaded camera, as

Example 6.4.   Kurt Weill, *Der Zar lässt sich photographieren,* Chorus

members of the czar's retinue search the studio. Weill sets this passage in a mock military style in three-part harmony, making prominent use of open fourths and fifths with the accompaniment reduced to a single drum (see example 6.4). The tongue-in-cheek military manner and the mysterioso melodramatic quality created by the rapid crescendi and decrescendi prevent the terrorists' philosophy from receiving the credence it otherwise might have. The number also serves as a suspenseful interlude before the czar's arrival. A shortened version of this choral reminder appears later as the czar first takes a seat in front of the loaded camera.

The chorus also interacts directly with the czar. After the czar receives news that his guards suspect an attempt on his life, a predicament he finds boring, he launches into a soliloquy in which he laments his fate, in true expressionist fashion, and the loss of his personal identity: "A czar can rule everything except his own life. I'm just a concept."[59] Weill's musical treatment effectively reduces any tendency on the part of the audience to sympathize with the czar's situation. Weill sets the czar's solo in the style of recitative, so marked parenthetically in the score, and the chorus, intoning a major second, serves as his accompaniment. After a more lyrical outburst from the czar accompanied by full orchestra, the humming chorus returns as he reflects on his life and compares himself to Napoleon entombed in the nearby Invalides.

Weill's use of recitative for the czar's soliloquy suggests a direct connection with Mozart's *opera buffa*s, except that Weill's recreation burlesques the old-fashioned technique. In resorting to recitative for a comic effect, Weill shows further the probable influence of Lortzing. Like Offenbach, Lortzing abandoned recitative in favor of spoken dialogue, but he occasionally used recitative for comic characterization. Van Bett, the *Bürgermeister* in *Zar und Zimmermann,* is allotted recitative for all of his solo entrances. As a character who takes himself too seriously, the *Bürgermeister*'s pompous nature is revealed

Example 6.5.   Kurt Weill, *Der Zar lässt sich photographieren*, The Czar's Foxtrot

through this outmoded style. Weill repeated this comic device in the recitative of the mounted messenger in the "Third Finale" to *Die Dreigroschenoper*.

Although the chorus played a major role in *Der Zar lässt sich photographieren,* Weill also employed other distinctive musical means which clarified the theme of the private versus public individual. Most notably he borrowed the dance idioms of jazz as well as gestures from the march. Next to the male chorus, Weill's use of jazz, in particular the *Tango-Angèle,* was the feature most often discussed by contemporary critics. Weill claimed he only relied on jazz sounds for special dramatic purposes:

> For me, jazz elements are not illustrative of modern life, but are absolute means of musical expression. Where I employ them I wish to conjure up an effect attainable only through their use. What is astonishing in this opera is that I saved jazz sounds [the *Tango-Angèle*] for the climax.[60]

Weill is not entirely accurate, for before the climactic *Tango-Angèle,* other musical sections appear with overt modern dance characteristics which cannot help but illustrate twenties life. Weill is correct that the *Tango-Angèle* relies on the timbral qualities most associated with jazz and is the most important jazz-inspired section.

The czar makes his first entrance to the strains of a foxtrot (see example 6.5). Solo trumpet and clarinet carry the foxtrot melody and dotted-rhythm countermelody respectively, over the standard accompaniment figure supplied by piano and lower strings.[61] (This foxtrot is strikingly similar to the foxtrot prologue of the *Mahagonny-Songspiel;* see example 6.6.) The accompaniment and dotted rhythm melody appear before the czar's first entrance when Angèle's assistant pretends to be the czar as they make preparations for his arrival. Thus

Example 6.6.   Kurt Weill, *Mahagonny-Songspiel,* Foxtrot Prologue

this earlier appearance presages the association of the foxtrot with the czar's sojourn in Paris. The dancelike character remains through this first encounter between the czar, whose opening line takes up the foxtrot melody, and the false Angèle. The melody returns after the czar states his wish to be photographed not as a ruler but as "a man who walks the street with other men who are all equals."[62] A shorter version of the foxtrot recurs as the czar poses for Angèle after he has been assured that he will be repaid for his royal favor.

Weill's use of this modern dance characterizes the czar caught up in the Paris of the 1920s and heightens the public versus private issue at the heart of the opera. The foxtrot clarifies the personality of the czar, an individual who longs to be an ordinary man and to appreciate this common, popular music and the more common pleasures of a relationship with his photographer. The dancey music contrasts markedly with the dramatic, deadly serious music of the assassins which precedes it, thereby adding a burlesque touch and bringing the worlds of the czar and assassins into conflict.

The *Tango-Angèle,* so designated in the score and announced by the false Angèle, appears at the climax of the opera and received the most comment from critics because a gramophone recording provided the sole accompaniment (see example 6.7). Again Weill described the dramatic reasons for creating this special section based on a modern dance:

> I proposed achieving the [climactic] effect through a completely new sound form, and for me this was the gramophone, which enters for the first time as a soloist while the orchestra is silent, and whose melody is countered by the singers. . . . The opposition of an action rising to its greatest tension [the arrival of the police] and a simple dance-like recording seemed to be precisely the way to achieve the climactic effect.[63]

Example 6.7.   Kurt Weill, *Der Zar lässt sich photographieren,* Two Excerpts
from *Tango -Angèle*

Although Weill suggests that he alone conceived of the dramatic and musical role of the gramophone, he may have been influenced by his earlier collaborator Goll. With his love of modern technology, Goll experimented with the gramophone in his dramatic works dating from 1927.[64]

Weill's music captures the languorous quality of the tango through the use of the common tango rhythm. Missing from this tango is the habanera rhythm relied upon by Krenek and associated with the dance in its earlier adaptations to art music. The full score of the opera does not list the instrumentation for the tango, the original recording of which was made in Berlin on 11 January 1928 by the Dobbri Saxophone Orchestra in Weill's presence and perhaps under his direction.[65] The recording, which was leased with the orchestra parts to opera houses, is still available for rental from Universal Edition, but the score and parts have been lost.

Based on the recording, the big band orchestration of the *Tango-Angèle* consisted of two or three saxophones, one or two violins, trumpet, trombone, piano, accordion, banjo, tuba, and percussion, including a highly audible woodblock.[66] The piano fulfills both harmonic and melodic functions, trumpet, saxophone, and violin provide other solo breaks, and the banjo and accordion fill out the rhythm section.[67] The *Tango-Angèle* proved to be one of Weill's first popular tunes and was commercially released. An advertisement in the Leipzig opera house program, appearing less than two months after the opera's premiere, boasted that the *Tango-Angèle* was released only on the Parlophon-Beka label and was currently available at a local Leipzig music store.[68]

Weill's choice of a tango as Angèle pretends to submit to the czar's advances is dramatically appropriate and echoes Krenek's use of the tango for a scene of seduction in *Jonny spielt auf.* The entrance of the tango, immediately following the czar's recitative soliloquy, creates another comic juxtaposition: the unlikely contrast of an eighteenth-century operatic convention and a twentieth-century popular one. The strains of the tango continue as the false Angèle and her co-conspirators make their escape over the rooftops of Paris. Their frenzied departure, accompanied by the tango rhythm, which creeps into their vocal lines, maintains the burlesque incongruity as the comedy reaches its climax. After so many false highpoints, which Weill treats in a standard way through the use of increased rhythmic activity and building crescendi, the actual climax arrives in the guise of a tango. This popular dance diffuses dramatic tension which would detract from the comedy.

Although Weill claimed he did not resort to jazz idioms solely to make *Der Zar lässt sich photographieren* topical, they do add to the opera's up-to-date spirit as well as to the dramatic construction of the entire work. As in *Royal Palace,* Weill used foxtrot and tango gestures; blues are conspicuously absent, although he used them in the "Alabama-Song" from the *Mahagonny-Songspiel.* Weill was correct in claiming that he reserved the most obvious jazz timbres for the *Tango-Angèle,* with its big band ensemble and special solos and transmission via recording.

As Krenek relied on other American musical sources to delineate Jonny's character further, so Weill relied on additional musical gestures to depict the regal side of the czar's character. A *Gemessener Marsch,* scored for brass and piano, appears after the second, shorter use of the foxtrot as the czar first sits for his photograph. The czar has just stated his wish to leave his public duties behind, and he complains to Angèle that the formal pose is uncomfortable. The false Angèle, at last behind the deadly camera, sees the czar only as a political symbol, not as a human being trapped in a role. The *Gemessener Marsch* identifies the czar's political and public nature as understood by the false Angèle.

A second martial section, marked *Alla marcia,* features another prominent trumpet solo and forms part of the finale discussed earlier. At this point, the plot has been uncovered and the true Angèle reappears to take the czar's picture. The czar is so confused by this turn of events that he wonders if he is still czar. A group of his followers march on stage with sabers swinging and sing of their loyalty to him. This march answers the czar's question; after all that has transpired he is indeed still czar. As the male chorus closes the work, the czar is photographed, not as the ordinary man of the foxtrot or tango, but as the political figure of the military march.

Weill's use of the march to characterize the old-fashioned regal nature of the czar may reflect the rediscovery of march music as a genre of chamber music for the 1926 Donaueschingen Festival. And Krenek's *Drei lustige Märsche* appeared on the program. In light of the postwar era, critics viewed the Donaueschingen march music as humorous and irreverent attacks on the Austro-Germanic musical heritage. So, too, for Weill, the march represents the czar, who like Napoleon, is of a past age.

Performance History and Critical Reception

Throughout his correspondence with his publisher, Weill stressed the importance of having *Der Zar* and *Der Protagonist* performed together as companion pieces. He spent considerable time and energy trying to convince opera houses to mount the works as a double bill, and he persistently urged his publisher, when acting as his agent, to present the works as two halves of a whole. Initially Weill hoped for a premiere at the Krolloper. Hans Heinsheimer of Universal Edition offered Klemperer the premiere of *Der Zar lässt sich photographieren* instead of Krenek's projected three one-act operas which Klemperer had specifically requested.[69] Klemperer persisted in his original request, although he subsequently showed interest in producing *Der Zar* after the success of the *Mahagonny-Songspiel*.

Weill abandoned his hopes for a Berlin premiere and entered into negotiations with the Leipzig opera house. He had become acquainted with Walther Brügmann through the *Mahagonny-Songspiel* performance at the Baden-Baden Festival. And Brügmann and Brecher, no doubt, hoped to repeat their success of the previous season by giving the premiere of a second topical comic work conposed by another up-and-coming young composer. Weill also hoped that the work might be more favorably received in Leipzig, which was now more predisposed to modern works than was Berlin.[70]

The Leipzig premiere was hampered by various problems. Gustav Brecher claimed that his schedule at the Gewandhaus prevented sufficient rehearsal time to premiere *Der Zar* on the same bill with *Der Protagonist*, but he promised performances of *Der Protagonist* for the following fall.[71] In place of *Der Protagonist*, Brügmann coupled *Der Zar* with Nicola Spinelli's *A basso porto*. Weill then complained that Brecher was "pedantic," that he overexaggerated the difficulties of the score, had an outmoded musical sense, and that he forced an inappropriate style of declamation on the opera.[72] Given the high regard both critics and Krenek had for Brecher's musicianship, as well as Weill's later dedication of *Der Jasager* to him, such complaints seem to indicate Weill's state of mind prior to the premiere. In any case, Weill subsequently claimed it was necessary to make changes in the score to allay Brecher's fears, changes which did not appear in the full score.[73] The date of the premiere, 18 February 1928, conflicted with the opening in Berlin of a Gluck revival; thus many Berlin critics were not in attendance.

The Leipzig premiere was well received and considered to be another success for Brecher and Brügmann. Adolf Aber, perhaps aware of the problems, claimed that the work could not have received a better first production.[74] Most critics praised Kaiser's superior libretto for its antisentimentality and social satire and credited Brügmann with having brought Kaiser's story to life. Critics, too, found Weill's music for the most part well suited to the witty libretto and entirely in keeping with its *opera buffa* distinction. Critics most often singled out for special mention Weill's use of the chorus, reliance on jazz rhythms, use of distinct formal units, and the score's overall aggressive, rhythmic quality.

Alfred Baresel, in his enthusiastic review for the *Neue Musik-Zeitung,* vividly described the function of the chorus and the nature of Weill's jazz usage:

A Greek chorus in the orchestra pit comments upon the mysteries of the pernicious camera and wrinkles the just freshly pressed tension: A triumph of the grotesque! Jazz rhythms are captured as absolutes in themselves, and break out at the end in a gramophone tango like a hit tune.[75]

He further praised Weill's popularizing of the modern musical idiom through the use of clearly audible triads at cadences and half-cadences which provided "anchors for the inexperienced listener" [*Rettungsanker für die Ungeübten*].

Adolf Aber, who shared Baresel's enthusiasm, described Weill's chorus as providing a witty way to prevent the possibly serious action from clouding the *opera buffa* character of the work. Aber described Weill's use of jazz and the *Tango-Angèle* as part of Weill's search for economy of musical means: "It [the score] becomes even more economical as things come to a point of crisis on stage. Ultimately the gramophone must replace the entire orchestra in the studio of the beautiful Parisian photographer, and, to be sure, with a masterly conceived tango."[76] Heinrich Strobel further remarked that Weill's use of jazz, so symptomatic of the time, helped him create a comic language [*Buffosprache*] which proved to be highly versatile.[77]

Der Zar lässt sich photographieren did not receive universal acclamation. The notable Berlin critics Adolf Weissmann and Alfred Einstein expressed reservations. Einstein, though complimentary of Kaiser's libretto and acknowledging Weill's witty score, still found the score "a bit too slight . . . a sketch of what really might have been written."[78] He later implied that the sparse score showed Weill's belief "that the absence of music is a way towards a new operatic form."[79] Weissmann was more critical and did not even share Einstein's appreciation for Kaiser's libretto.[80] He judged the plot so full of action that Weill's score could scarcely keep pace. Weissmann seconded Weill's criticism of Brecher, finding him not up to the intricacies of the modern score.

More detailed discussions of the work appeared in several larger music journals. Paul Stefan, editor of *Anbruch,* in "Antimonie der neuen Oper," discussed *Der Zar* and *Oedipus Rex* as representative of the current operatic spectrum with regard to both subject matter and musical treatment.[81] Stefan stressed that both works were likewise related to each other in their new understanding of the theater. He went on to describe Weill as a true man of the theater through his collaborations with Brecht and Kaiser and claimed that Weill's music subtly adapted itself to every nuance of the stage. Stefan also praised Brügmann as a man trained first in live theater production and whose gift for staging helped make *Der Zar* a success. Stefan rightly concluded that if Weill continued in his present innovative manner, he would earn a place for himself in musical history.

Heinz Jolles, in "Paraphrase über Kurt Weill," stated that the Leipzig premiere of *Der Zar* confirmed his belief, shared by others as well, that Weill was one of the truly gifted young composers.[82] In particular, Jolles found Weill's score, which "resisted the enticements of the highly-imaginative buffa libretto while meeting it half-way on his own terms," entirely equal to the satirical qualities of Kaiser's text.[83] He further claimed that Weill might prove to be the one composer of the day to bring a new essence to modern opera.

The Piscatorbühne expressed an interest in staging the Berlin premiere of *Der Zar*. Weill felt such a possibility had distinct advantages—both monetary and artistic—even in the face of considerable musical obstacles.[84] Preferring to have the work produced by one of the three opera houses in Berlin, Universal Edition showed little enthusiasm for the idea. Bruno Walter then expressed interest, and Hans Curjel at the Krolloper indicated that if Klemperer would not conduct it, he might pass it on to his assistant Alexander Zemlinsky.[85] Ultimately the work received its Berlin premiere on 14 October 1928 at the Städtische Oper under Robert Denzler in tandem with *Der Protagonist*. Gustav Vargo designed new sets, and Brügmann served as guest director.

Most critics expressed views similar to those given after the Leipzig premiere. The Berlin production was judged successful, and most reviewers enjoyed the combination of *Der Protagonist* and *Der Zar*, although few seemed to appreciate the relationship between the companion works which so obsessed Weill in his negotiations with opera houses. Fritz Ohrmann, in the conservative journal *Signale für die musikalische welt,* gave the most radical opinion of the work, characterizing Weill as a new exponent of extreme modernity and describing the libretto as nothing but a "humorless concoction" [*humorloser Schmarren*].[86] He found the chorus to be an offensive parody of the German tradition of male choruses.

Der Zar lässt sich photographieren was successful within German-speaking countries. Nine other houses presented a total of 39 performances of the work in its first season (see statistics in appendix D). However, performed more in its first season than *Jonny spielt auf* was in its, *Der Zar* was not performed in Paris or in the United States during the 1920s.[87] Weill expressed further intentions to his publisher of arranging a chamber orchestra version of *Der Zar* for American productions, as Kaiser had some notoriety in the United States.[88] He also hoped to arrange performances in Russia, although he conceded that a Russian production would necessitate making the czar an even more ridiculous character.[89] Neither adaptation nor performance seems to have materialized.

After *Der Zar lässt sich photographieren*

In its own time *Der Zar* was quickly overshadowed by *Die Dreigroschenoper,* which proved to be the unexpected success of 1928. Although this work also possessed topicality and used popular music idioms, *Die Dreigroschenoper,* as well as its failed successor *Happy End,* cannot be considered *Zeitopern.* Both works were conceived outside the realm of traditional comic opera, as compositions to be performed in more modest theatrical surroundings.

With *Aufstieg und Fall der Stadt Mahagonny,* Weill and Brecht returned to a traditional conception of opera. Although it would be incorrect to call the work a *Zeitoper, Aufstieg und Fall der Stadt Mahagonny* carried some features of the genre within its embodiment of a new epic opera. Likewise, nascent features of epic opera are discernable within *Der Zar.*[90] *Aufstieg und Fall der Stadt Mahagonny,* though satiric and containing didactic comments on modern life and society, lacks the bald comedy of either *Jonny spielt auf* or *Der Zar.* But the musical score resounds with jazz idioms, and the innovative staging harkens back to the experiments of earlier *Zeitopern.* And, for all its seeming reflection of the Weimar age, *Aufstieg und Fall der Stadt Mahagonny* possesses a surreal quality with its make-believe city of Mahagonny.

Aufstieg und Fall der Stadt Mahagonny was not Weill's last opera written during his time in Germany. Two works followed which show his departure from the satiric and comic just as *Leben des Orest* and *Karl V* demonstrated Krenek's similar change of heart. *Die Bürgschaft,* on a text by Caspar Neher, who designed the projections for the *Mahagonny-Songspiel,* was composed in 1931 and premiered in Berlin in March of 1932. Based on a story by Johann Herder, the opera's tone is serious as it explores the destruction of friendship through greed. Weill collaborated once more with Kaiser on *Der Silbersee* (1933). This work reflects Weill's continued interest in addressing social or public issues and the responsibility humans must take for one another. In both of these last two works, Weill did not draw upon elements of popular music or infuse the operas with overt topicality. Weill had changed, and these later works show a new, personalized language, as well as reflecting the different political and cultural climate of the early 1930s. With the forced departure of both Krenek and Weill from Germany in 1933, only Paul Hindemith was left to speak for the postwar generation of German composers.

Figure 7.1.   Paul Hindemith in the mid-1920s
(Courtesy of the Paul-Hindemith-Institut, Frankfurt a.M.)

7

Paul Hindemith: *Neues vom Tage*

1917–1927

Paul Hindemith was one of the first non-French composers to experiment with jazz idioms in his compositions, but he came after Krenek and Weill to the composition of *Zeitoper*. His one-act opera *Hin und zurück*, which shared the 1927 Baden-Baden Festival program with the *Mahagonny-Songspiel*, marked his first foray into the genre. By that time he was recognized as the leading postwar composer and had accepted a prestigious appointment to the Berlin Hochschule. His full-fledged *Zeitoper*, *Neues vom Tage*, did not appear until 1929, by which time Eugen d'Albert's *Die schwarze Orchidee* and Max Brand's *Maschinist Hopkins* had already been produced.

 Hindemith shared Krenek and Weill's early interest in opera. In January of 1924, with the critical successes of his three one-acts behind him, Hindemith wrote Willy Strecker, his editor at the Schott Brothers, to ask for Strecker's help in finding suitable libretti.[1] He boasted that if a good text were to be found, he could produce a new and original work in a minimum of time. Less than a month later, Hindemith wrote Strecker and explained the differences of opinion he had been having with one possible collaborator about the importance of opera.[2] Unlike his potential librettist, Hindemith felt that opera should be to modern music what beef steak was to a meal. Strecker complied with Hindemith's initial request, and among many ideas he suggested were collaborations with Bertolt Brecht and a new setting of Gay's *Beggar's Opera*.[3]

 By the summer of 1925, Hindemith was at work on *Cardillac*, which he finished in 1926. In *Cardillac*, Hindemith turned to a number-opera scheme to which he adapted absolute instrumental forms such as the passacaglia and fugue. The work was successful after its Dresden premiere on 9 November 1926 (see appendix D), and it might well have become a significant success of the 1920s if it had not had to compete with the phenomenon of *Jonny spielt auf*.

 The libretto, by Ferdinand Lion after E. T. A. Hoffmann, treats the theme of the artist's role in society, as in *Jonny spielt auf*. But *Cardillac* retained expressionist overtones from his one-act works *Sancta Susanna* and *Mörder, Hoffnung der Frauen* which are alien to *Jonny spielt auf* and suggest, instead, an

Example 7.1.   Paul Hindemith, *In einer Nacht,* Opening Rhythm

affinity with Schoenberg's *Die glückliche Hand.* Cardillac the jeweler is unable to part with his creations, as is the main character of *Die glückliche Hand,* and becomes so obsessed by them that he murders his customers so as to keep his works for himself. Hindemith would return to the theme of the artist in society with *Mathis der Maler,* a work which both marked his departure from the aesthetic of *Zeitoper* and brought about his exile from Germany.

Hindemith's early use of jazz musical resources may have resulted from his lifelong activity as a professional performer. Hindemith described the eclectic nature of his performing experience in a 1922 autobiographical statement published in the *Neue Musik-Zeitung:* "As a violinist, violist, pianist, or percussionist, I have 'cultivated' extensively the following musical genres: chamber music of all kinds, cinema, coffee house, dance music, operetta, jazz bands, military music."[4] It is difficult to know what he meant, in 1922, by jazz band and dance music; however, one of Hindemith's early performing experiences can be documented. Before his induction into the military in 1917, he played in a Frankfurt ensemble, the Kurkapelle, which performed various kinds of light entertainment music [*Unterhaltungsmusik*]. The ensemble consisted of three violins, viola, cello, bass, two clarinets, flute, trumpet, trombone, and possibly a drummer or pianist.[5] This combination of strings, woodwinds, and brass suggests that the group most likely performed light classics or waltzes, although it is possible that they may have performed some rudimentary ragtime and social dance music.

Hindemith continued to perform during the war, having been able to escape front line military duty on the grounds that he was more valuable as a musician. And it may have been during this time that he became exposed to the new popular music then drifting into and out of France. After the war, he performed with the Amar Quartet, a group which championed French and German contemporary music and toured all over Europe. These tours afforded direct contact with both popular music and French composers similarly interested in the fusion of popular and concert musics.

American popular dance idioms appear in Hindemith's music as early as the unpublished piano work, *In einer Nacht, Träume und Erlebnisse,* op. 15, composed between 1917 and 1919. The work, a series of 14 short character pieces, has as its penultimate section a "Foxtrott" which is then followed by the "Finale: Doppelfuge." The foxtrot movement is in two-four meter with the marking "Sehr rhythmisch" and with its distinctive rhythms it resembles the "Golliwog's Cake Walk" from Debussy's *Children's Corner* (1908) (see example 7.1).[6] After the opening measures, Hindemith's foxtrot takes on the

Example 7.2.   Paul Hindemith, *Tuttifäntchen,* "Foxtrott"

standard features already noted in other art music foxtrots: a faster, dotted melody over a regular bass line. As with Krenek, Erdmann, Schnabel, and Weill a piano foxtrot marked Hindemith's first synthesis of popular culture and the cultivated tradition.

From this time on, Hindemith continued his experiments with the new resource, so that in 1920 he could write to his publisher and ask, "Could you also use foxtrots, bostons, rags and other *Kitsch?* When respectable music no longer comes to me, I always write such things."[7] Such *Kitsch,* which Schott Brothers apparently would not or could not use and thus remained unpublished, included the *Lyonel-Foxtrott, Young Lorch Fellow-Rag,* both from 1920, the *Ragtime (wohltemperiert)* (1921), *Bobby's Wahn-Step,* and *2 Shimmies* (1924).[8]

Three published works from 1922—*Tuttifäntchen,* the *Kammermusik No. 1,* op. 24, and the *Suite 1922,* op. 25—show Hindemith's further cultivation of dance idioms, in particular, the foxtrot. *Tuttifäntchen,* a choreographed Christmas fairy tale, contains a "Tanz der Holzpuppen" which was designated as a "Foxtrot" when published apart from the full score.[9] This foxtrot, with its two-four meter, unison opening and pervasive use of dotted rhythms, is reminiscent of the earlier "Foxtrott" from the op. 15 unpublished piano pieces (see example 7.2).

Hindemith had already achieved recognition at the Donaueschingen Festival with his *String Quartet No. II,* which was performed on the 1921 program. The *Kammermusik No. 1* dramatically signaled Hindemith's embrace of popular American music at its premiere on the 1922 Donaueschingen Chamber Music Festival. And everything about the *Kammermusik No. 1* was deemed radical and out of accordance with a traditional understanding of chamber music, making it perfect for the avant-garde forum of Donaueschingen. The instrumentation of flute, clarinet, bassoon, trumpet, two violins, viola, cello, bass, and piano is not out of the ordinary, but the inclusion of accordion and percussion is, especially with the siren and sand-filled tin can [*mit Sand gefüllte Blechbüchse*]. A second unusual feature was Hindemith's recommendation "that the performers be situated out of sight of the audience," and most important for his development was its "Finale: 1921," which incorporated a quotation of a supposedly well-known foxtrot by Wilm Wilm.[10]

The entire four-movement work is characterized by its rhythmic drive and vitality, with tempo and affect markings such as "Sehr schnell und wild," "Sehr streng im Rhythmus," and "Furioso." Only the third movement, "Quartett," for the unlikely combination of flute, clarinet, bassoon, and the F-sharp note of a glockenspiel, provides a respite from the rhythmic activity.

The "Finale: 1921" opens in a twelve-eight meter with a piano solo in the bass against an aggressive eighth-note pattern in the strings. This string pattern continues relentlessly throughout the rest of the movement, changing timbral color only through the addition of other instruments. The quotation from Wilm Wilm's *Fuchstanz* enters halfway through the movement in the trumpet and stands out from the rest of the ensemble (see example 7.3). In the cut-time coda, a dotted-rhythm melody, derived from both the foxtrot and Hindemith's own opening theme, dominates, only to be silenced by the siren. The dotted melody makes one last appearance before the final cadence.

Hindemith's *Kammermusik No. 1* shows a sophisticated understanding and appreciation of jazz on a par with that demonstrated by Milhaud a year later in *La Création du monde*. Hindemith left behind the solo piano, for which so many composers wrote their jazz-inspired music, and used the resources of a soloistic ensemble. The instrumentation may have been a recreation of Hindemith's own Kurkapelle ensemble or a similar dance band. Hindemith stressed the soloistic nature of the ensemble, both in the title, *Kammermusik mit Finale 1921 für zwölf Solo-Instrumente,* and in the score where the instrumentation is given as *"Besetzung/(solistisch)."* Hindemith obviously understood and appreciated that jazz was a soloist's art. The rhythmic vitality and stratified counterpoint in the "Finale: 1921" further suggest the collective improvisational techniques of early jazz bands, such as the Original Dixieland Jazz Band and others, which Hindemith could have heard in France or elsewhere.

The recommended placement of the group out of sight of the audience may have been an attempt to create the dance salon ambiance in stark opposition to traditional concert performance practices. The band does not take center stage; its music functions as a backdrop to other social activities. The invisibility of the group may have also been Hindemith's way of celebrating contemporary technological phenomena, the gramophone and radio, two media which he would continue to explore, with their invisible musicians on record.

The *Kammermusik No. 1* proved successful at its premiere, and the foxtrot finale no doubt served as further inspiration for Krenek and others who were attracted to American popular music. Naturally, not everyone approved of Hindemith's new direction. Alfred Heuss, critic for the *Zeitschrift für Musik,* was shocked when Wilhelm Furtwängler programmed the *Kammermusik No. 1* on a Gewandhaus concert in 1923. Heuss decried the work's French influences. "It is the most corrupt, frivolous, and, at the same time, the most topical music one can think of."[11]

The success of the *Kammermusik No. 1* was such that Hindemith's publishers could hardly ignore his jazz-influenced musical style any longer. In 1923 Strecker wrote to Hindemith with an idea for a puppet play based on the Faust legend.[12] The legend could be updated with Faust representing modern man. Faust's descent into hell could be musically set as an "infernal foxtrot," Strecker suggested, or a modern bacchanal, similar to what Hindemith had already produced in his *Kammermusik No. 1*. Hindemith appears not to have acted upon Strecker's well-meant idea.

Following the success of the *Kammermusik No. 1,* Hindemith composed the *Suite 1922*. In the tradition of the baroque solo keyboard suite, he brought together movements in contrasting styles and emotional character. The suite opens with a "Marsch," and a number of Hindemith's early unpublished works were marches, such as the "Gouda-Emmental Marsch." Although not a modern dance, Hindemith regarded the march as another genre or style suitable for musical parody, as did Weill with the czar's regal music in *Der Zar*.[13]

A faster, cut-time "Shimmy" follows the opening march. The third movement, "Nachtstück," functions similarly to the "Quartett" movement in the *Kammermusik No. 1,* serving as a respite from the frenetic activity of the surrounding movements. The fourth movement, a "Boston," captures the then old-fashioned character of the three-four meter dance. The *Suite 1922* ends with a "Ragtime," a tour-de-force of syncopated, virtuosic solo piano writing. It is in this final movement that Hindemith again betrays his preoccupation with the rhythmic quality of jazz and his understanding of the objective machinelike quality which brought jazz into line with *Neue Sachlichkeit:* "Play this piece wildly, but with strict rhythm, like a machine. Think here of the piano as an interesting kind of percussion instrument and treat it accordingly."[14] Hindemith's interest in jazz rhythms and percussion would be repeated once more in the *Kammermusik No. 4* (1925), in which he described the intended sound of its four drums. They should sound like "small rings covered on one side—similar to tambourines without jingles—such as have only been used in jazz bands."[15]

The *Suite 1922* had as great a success as the *Kammermusik No. 1*. Franz Willms, who later wrote on *Neues vom Tage* and also produced its piano-vocal arrangement, described the *Suite 1922* as a set of powerful caricatures or

Example 7.3.   Paul Hindemith, *Kammermusik No. 1*, "Finale: 1921"

*)„Fuchstanz" von Wilm Wilm mit Genehmigung des Verlegers Fritz Schubert jun.,Leipzig

grotesques, not unlike those published by Universal Edition in the *Groteskes Album,* to which Krenek had contributed.[16] Hindemith and other young composers, he pointed out, now used these weapons of ridicule [*Spott*] and irony against their musical elders.

Hindemith, an artist of considerable talent, designed the cover for the *Suite 1922.* Adolf Weissmann saw the character of the entire work reflected in Hindemith's depiction of modern metropolitan life. "The cover design, drawn by the composer himself, is already a mirror of the chaos and folly of the cabaret man, which is further reflected in the score: the pell-mell activity of the people, of the vehicles, and of the arched street lamps, the offspring of electricity."[17]

Between the composition of these works and *Hin und zurück* five years later, Hindemith became increasingly involved with organizing the Donaueschingen/Baden-Baden Festivals, which became forums for his interest in mechanical instruments, music for film, and *Sing- und Spielmusik.* As discussed in chapter 2, these *Gebrauchsmusik* activities were part of a larger interest in forging new music in keeping with the republican age. Although Hindemith wrote little on his aesthetic philosophy, the *Novembergruppe* performed his works on their concerts, suggesting his approval of their radical commitment to the mass audience. And from his early days with the Amar Quartet, Hindemith had direct contacts with French artists, especially Milhaud; thus he may have perceived and wished to emulate as well the special quality of French art which inspired Krenek.

Hin und zurück

Hindemith's position at the Berlin Hochschule provided him with another institutional basis for his musical experimentation. And that same year his *Hin und zurück* appeared on the program of chamber operas at the Baden-Baden Music Festival. With this *Sketch mit Musik,* on a libretto by Marcellus Schiffer based on Schiffer's own revue *Hetärengespräche,* Hindemith adopted the comical and topical features of the *Zeitoper.*[18] The work, which lasts some ten minutes, parodies old-fashioned operatic conventions, modern domestic life, and the film industry.

Unlike Krenek or Weill, Hindemith focused his attention on the intimate, domestic arena (see synopsis in appendix C). A jealous husband shoots his unfaithful wife and then commits suicide. In its use of a domestic scene set in the 1920s, Hindemith followed the lead of Richard Strauss, whose opera *Intermezzo* (1924) also dealt with private family matters, in Strauss's conscious effort to leave behind the "love and death affairs" [*Liebes- und Mordaffären*] of earlier operas.[19] Hindemith retained this focus of modern marital strife in *Neues vom Tage,* which Schoenberg would also use in *Von Heute auf Morgen.*

The unusual aspect of *Hin und zurück*'s well-worn plot is its sudden reversal, as suggested in the title "There and Back." A *deus ex machina,* in the guise of a bearded sage, appears via a trap door and explains that "Looking down from above, it makes no difference whether man goes forward with life from the cradle until he dies, or whether he dies first and is born afterwards."[20] Thus the sage orders the action reversed, and the plot proceeds backwards in imitation of the common, even hackneyed, film technique. Neither Hindemith nor Schiffer strove for a complete reversal of the action in the manner of a palindrome; instead, entire sections of the libretto and attendant music return in preceding order. However, the sneeze of the deaf, unobservant aunt, which opens the work, returns backwards as "Ptsch-haa."

The imitation of a filmed sequence thrown into reverse hardly indicates a sophisticated understanding of the modern cinema, but Hindemith had a serious interest in film music. As a young man he supplied, under a pseudonym, a score entitled "In Schnee und Eis" for Arnold Franck's early mountain film *Im Kampf mit den Bergen* (1921).[21] And he contributed film scores to the Festival programs of 1927 and 1928, and later wrote music for advertising and feature films. Along with his establishment of a radio department at the Berlin Hochschule, he taught a special course on film music techniques.[22]

Although the score for *Hin und zurück* makes no direct use of modern dances, the music shows a marked resemblance to both the *Kammermusik No. 1* and the *Suite 1922*. As *Hin und zurück* was a chamber opera, Hindemith orchestrated the work for an ensemble of nine instruments with ten performers: flute, clarinet, alto-saxophone, bassoon, trumpet, trombone, piano two-hands, and a second piano four-hands, and a harmonium used solely behind the scenes to accompany the sage's monologue. Notably absent from the ensemble are strings and percussion. As the work is based on a revue sketch, Hindemith may have been attempting to imitate the small ensembles typically found in revue theaters.

As in the *Kammermusik No. 1* and *Suite 1922,* an aggressive rhythmic vitality pervades the entire work, and syncopation rules. The small ensemble allows for a soloistic treatment of the instruments, and Hindemith singles out the saxophone, flute, trumpet, and trombone in particular. The pianos, likewise, receive special handling, and they function almost entirely in a role of harmonic and rhythmic support, as was common in jazz or dance bands. Only rarely does one pianist double a melody in the woodwinds or brass. In the absence of percussion, the pianos become the lone members of the rhythm section, thus once again becoming a "new kind of percussion instrument" as in the *Suite 1922*.

Hindemith retained the number-opera format in *Hin und zurück*. An instrumental prelude is followed by Helene's ariette, Helene and Robert's duet, and a trio for the doctor, his attendant, and the remorseful husband. The central solo for the sage is unnumbered, and then the trio, duet, and ariette return. The

Example 7.4.   Paul Hindemith, *Hin und zurück*, "Ariette"

opening ariette pokes fun at traditional opera arias. The text consists of four words—"Froh und früh erwacht" [I awoke cheerful and early]—which are repeated for maximum comic effect. The final line (see example 7.4) is a mocking imitation of an operatic cadenza complete with cadential trill. The trio parodies operatic ensemble numbers, in which individual characters vent their personal feelings, unaware of what is being said around them. In this case, the doctor and attendant go about examining the murdered Helene. The doctor states and restates that nothing can be done while his attendant recites a list of possible medications to apply. Both of them are oblivious to Robert's overblown declaration of remorse, "Now the tooth of repentance gnaws at me."[23] And the sage's monologue, with its repeated pitches and free rhythm, is obviously a recreation of the old-fashioned recitative, as Weill would use it in *Der Zar.*

Hin und zurück was well received at its premiere, and reviewers commented upon its wit and clever staging, again executed by the talented Walther Brügmann. A picture of the Baden-Baden premiere shows Brügmann's use of an obviously unrealistic two-dimensional set and properties: a flat breakfast table with dishes, flowers in a vase, and even a cardboard dog.[24] Brügmann's purposefully unrealistic stage set underscored the two-dimensional aspect of Schiffer's sketch and its cinematic cliché, maintained in Hindemith's parodistic score.

Unlike the *Mahagonny-Songspiel, Hin und zurück* received many performances after its premiere, including an April 1928 production in Philadelphia under the aegis of the Society for Contemporary Music (see appendix D). Marc Blitzstein, writing after this Philadelphia performance, described the music as "serious, purposeful, and so cunningly adapted to the dimensions of the comic ideas involved."[25]

Hin und zurück was often combined with Ernst Toch's *Die Prinzessin auf der Erbse,* another of the original Baden-Baden chamber operas, but it also appeared alongside Stravinsky's *Mavra* and Krenek's *Schwergewicht. Hin und zurück* received its Berlin premiere on 7 January 1931 at the Krolloper with Klemperer conducting, Hans Curjel directing, and sets designed by Bauhaus artist Laszlo Moholy-Nagy. The production was arranged by the Berlin tennis club Rot-Weiss and included performances of Ravel's *L'Heure espagnole,* Debussy's *Jeux,* and Weill's *Kleine Dreigroschenmusik.*[26]

Neues vom Tage

With the success of *Hin und zurück* behind him, Hindemith began work on a second large opera. Willy Strecker, on the lookout for suitable libretti, suggested that Hindemith work with expressionist playwright Ernst Toller.[27] But on 10 February 1928, Hindemith wrote Strecker of his plans for a second collaboration with Schiffer. A mere two months later Hindemith announced that the new work was almost completed.[28] The choice of Schiffer shows Hindemith's desire to continue in the direction of the one-act *Zeitoper* sketch.

Many features of *Hin und zurück* appear in *Neues vom Tage. Neues vom Tage* maintains the domestic arena of *Hin und zurück* with its central focus of a husband and wife, Eduard and Laura, and their marital problems (see synopsis in appendix C). Here, however, the domestic drama is both extended and modernized. Instead of marital squabbles leading to the cliché murder-suicide of *Hin und zurück,* Laura and Eduard decide to get divorced. Although divorce had become a more acceptable practice since World War I, grounds still had to be proven in court. Schiffer and Hindemith thus explored the modern problem of obtaining such grounds, in this case, staging a false incident of marital infidelity with a rented lover, the handsome Herr Hermann. Hindemith indicated that Schiffer consulted with a lawyer for accuracy.[29] Hindemith, however, chose not to stretch the limits of the work's modernity; he did not include the character of a whore, as Strecker had suggested.

Schiffer and Hindemith also maintained the circular nature of *Hin und zurück.* When all is said and done, Eduard and Laura decide they might as well stay together. And in their revue skit at the end of the opera, they reenact the scenes of their married life with which the opera opened. A second couple, Frau and Herr M, having successfully obtained a divorce through the services of the "handsome Herr Hermann," remarry at the end, thus ending up as they started. Along with this return of dramatic elements from the beginning, Hindemith reused corresponding musical sections as well. Thus Hindemith and Schiffer's work suggests some of the philosophy already put forth in *Hin und zurück* and by Weill in *Der Zar lässt sich photographieren;* with all the convoluted, frenetic stage activity, life comes full circle and the status quo is maintained.

Neues vom Tage also shares with *Der Zar lässt sich photographieren* its social satire. Schiffer and Hindemith good-naturedly mock aspects of modern life, not just twenties sexual mores, but the legal system and modern bureaucracies. And most importantly, they lampoon the commercialization of life, resulting from the increased power of the news media. As the title suggests, Schiffer shows how the contemporary interest in reportage has turned private life into subject matter for public newspaper stories.

Schiffer suggested two possible titles for the work: *Das kann Jedem passieren* [It could happen to anyone] and *Neues vom Tage.*[30] Strecker preferred the first, though came to understand the choice for the latter upon receiving the last act. In order to earn money for their debts, Laura and Eduard, having had their stories told in the press and thereby creating a public scandal, can now reenact their marital plight as part of a revue or *Kabarettrevue* show which plays to packed houses. They are media stars; their actions have made them the "news of the day." And at the end of the opera, Laura and Eduard are trapped in these public roles. The commercial success prevents a return to the anonymity of their former lives. Thus Schiffer and Hindemith also explored the public versus private theme found in *Der Zar lässt sich photographieren.*

Neues vom Tage shares with both *Jonny spielt auf* and *Der Zar lässt sich photographieren* a Parisian locale, again suggesting that Paris was the magical place where such modern events took place. References are also made to America, the land of opportunity. Eduard, like Anita in *Jonny spielt auf,* is promised an American contract. Individual scene locations, as in *Jonny spielt auf,* stress the *Alltäglichkeit* of the work. The opera opens in the couple's living room and moves to modern offices, a hotel room, a jail cell, a theater foyer, and to the interior of the Alkazar revue theater.

Schiffer's use of a revue theater for a stage setting was a direct reference to modern life, and director Ernst Legal was careful to make the representation as true to life as possible. A photograph of this scene shows Eduard and Laura in evening clothes suitable for an entertaining revue.[31] The couple are surrounded by a number of women dressed similarly to Laura, thereby recreating the popular feature of a chorus line common to many revue and *Kabarettrevue* shows.

The work also incorporates some modern staging requirements. The simultaneous sets of Piscator's theater are required for scene 6, with Laura's hotel room and Eduard's jail cell. Other modern mechanisms include typewriters in the offices, a bathroom with running water, and signal bells indicating the start of the revue numbers. Chorus members also call out newspaper headlines in the manner of street corner paper carriers and add another documentary touch. Some of the topical headlines include "Tomorrow evening Furtwängler conducts a special Beethoven concert" and "In Rome, Mussolini opens a house for poor coin collectors."[32]

The Musical Score

As was true of *Hin und zurück,* Hindemith formulated *Neues vom Tage* in the manner of an eighteenth-century number opera. The work is in three acts and eleven scenes, and each scene is subdivided into two to five separate numbers. The individual numbers, clearly marked in the score, include solo arias, choruses, duets, trios, quartets, and a special finale. The score of *Neues vom Tage* also has much in common with that of *Hin und zurück.* Hindemith's orchestration favors brass and woodwinds, calling for two flutes, oboe, English horn, clarinets in B-flat and E-flat, bass clarinet, alto saxophone, two bassoons, contrabassoon, horn, two trumpets, two trombones, and tuba, offset by six violins, four violas, four celli, and four basses. Percussion includes xylophone and glockenspiel, and harp, mandolin, and banjo are required for certain sections. Most telling is the presence of a piano two-hands and a second piano four-hands. The pianos have an important function, acting once again as harmonic and rhythmic support for the melodic colors of the woodwinds and brass.

The score also shares the rhythmic energy and vitality of *Hin und zurück.* The overture, marked "very fresh and tight," is lively with its syncopated off-beat rhythms and occasional cymbal outburst. Three sections show Hindemith's continued reliance on jazz idioms, although none of the titles of the separate numbers indicate the presence of dance jazz idioms as was done in the *Kammermusik No. 1* and *Suite 1922.* The opening duet between Laura and

Example 7.5.   Paul Hindemith, *Neues vom Tage,* Scene 1

Eduard, in which they express their disgust for one another, moves into an identifiable foxtrot with its four-beat bass line against a dotted melody for solo trumpet (see example 7.5). Further on in the same scene, Herr and Frau M enter, having just returned from their honeymoon, and join Eduard and Laura. This quartet is cast as a triple-time Boston section, not unlike the "Boston" movement of the *Suite 1922.* The ostinato bass line and woodwind melody contain blue notes as well (see example 7.6). The argumentative foxtrot returns as Herr and Frau M begin to take sides in the other couple's marital dispute and decide to dissolve their own marriage as well.

Both of these dance sections return towards the end. Laura and Eduard's revue number recreates their argumentative foxtrot with the addition of a chorus. Frau and Herr M's entrance into the Alkazar theater, having just returned from their second honeymoon, reuses the bluesy Boston. In both these cases, Hindemith's use of jazz and dance idioms is organic; the dances are not handled

Example 7.6.   Paul Hindemith, *Neues vom Tage,* Quartet

as on-stage music, but rather are integrated into the drama, in the manner of Weill's foxtrot for the czar. Thus, the popular music stresses the overriding *Alltäglichkeit* of the opera; commonplace domestic scenes are set to everyday music.

Naturally the final revue scene uses identifiable materials from popular music. The saxophone figures prominently here, as well as the banjo and mandolin, which add their peculiar jazz timbre to the rhythm section. Laura and Eduard's strophic revue song is straightforward, and not unlike a foxtrot, with its steady bass line and mildly syncopated melody (see example 7.7). In this scene, the jazzy number grows directly out of logical stage action as in *Jonny spielt auf* and the *Tango-Angèle* of *Der Zar lässt sich photographieren.*

It is not surprising, with Hindemith's interest in technology and machines, that he would bring machines into the musical score. Scene 3, in the Office of Family Affairs, opens with a chorus of typists who type while singing about handsome Herr Hermann. Hindemith depicts this mechanical action with

Example 7.7.   Paul Hindemith, *Neues vom Tage,* Scene 11

repeated sixteenth-note passages in the pianos and xylophone, and oboe, B-flat clarinet, bass clarinet and bassoon entering with scalar passages as the typists throw the carriages of their machines (see example 7.8). The mood changes upon the regal entrance of the pompous Herr Hermann, but the chorus of typists returns at the end of the scene with staccatissimo strings adding to the mechanical nature of the music.

Within his number-opera format, Hindemith carries over the spirit of musical parody from *Hin und zurück* and other earlier works. He burlesques a number of operatic conventions by combining musical ideas which were serious in their origin with texts which are everyday to the point of being mundane or are otherwise antithetical to the musical nature. Such a burlesque, Laura and Eduard's duet, opens the work. Instead of declaring their love, as would be expected, they voice their mutual hatred. After separate outbursts of name-calling, the two join together for a long, unison, melismatic phrase on the text "Wir lassen uns scheiden," [we want a divorce] which is repeated for effect

Example 7.8.   Paul Hindemith, *Neues vom Tage,* Scene 3

(see example 7.9). Later, in scene 2, Frau and Herr M have a similar divorce duet as they extol their happiness in having obtained a divorce. And throughout the opera, Hindemith sets the noun and verb form of divorce in an overblown, melismatic manner, thereby giving this modern word a special comic treatment.

A love duet appears in scene 4, but again the effect is burlesque. This "Duett-Kitsch" involves false declarations of love between Laura and Herr Hermann, her rented lover. The text is overly sentimental, and Hindemith's music, with its diminished chords, chromaticism, and harp arpeggios, parodies nineteenth-century operatic literature (see example 7.10). Adding to the humor of the situation are Herr Hermann's continual interruptions as he gives Laura pointers in the staging of this marital infidelity.

One of the burlesques most commented upon at the time was Laura's "Arioso" in scene 5. This aria, sung while Laura bathes in a hotel bathroom, praises the plentitude of the electrically heated hot water. The melody line contains dramatic skips, long sustained notes, and virtuosic passages at odds with her text (see example 7.11). "Hot water, daily, nightly, a bath ready in three minutes. No gas smell, no explosion, no danger to life. Out, out with the old gas water heaters."[33] This scene ends with an ensemble, Herr Hermann having come in on Laura, and then his presence with her having been discovered by others. All the characters—Laura, Herr Hermann, Frau M, and hotel employees—express their horror over the situation. Hindemith sets the soloist's lines off from the homophonic chorus, and the repetition of "wie peinlich" [how embarrassing] is particularly comical. In an overdone example of how opera suspends naturalistic action, no one makes any move to rectify the situation, only to voice repeatedly their horror.

Hindemith knew that a woman in a bathtub might be considered risqué, and

Example 7.9.   Paul Hindemith, *Neues vom Tage,* Scene 1

this scene did have later political repercussions. When he first mentioned the scene to Strecker, Hindemith hastened to add that it would be executed so tastefully that even Dr. Heuss, the critic who so despised the *Kammermusik No. 1,* would have no objections.[34] *Neues vom Tage,* after all, was to be a family opera. All descriptions of the scene from the time indicate that only Laura's head and shoulders, or just her head, were visible to the audience.

Hindemith also used recitative; small sections occasionally appear for passages of dialogue within longer numbers. In two instances the recitatives are extended and serve similar comic functions as in *Der Zar* or *Hin und zurück.* The fourth scene, set in the Louvre museum with the *Venus di Milo,* opens on a tour group being led through the room. To a sparse string pizzicato accompaniment, the guide drones on about the *Venus di Milo* to the distinctly uninterested group (see example 7.12). "Notice the missing arms. Genuinely classical. Three stars in Baedecker."[35] The guide returns at the end of the scene with the same speech, and he and his unobservant group are oblivious to the fact that the three-star statue has been destroyed during Eduard's jealous rampage.

Example 7.10.   Paul Hindemith, *Neues vom Tage,* "Duett-Kitsch"

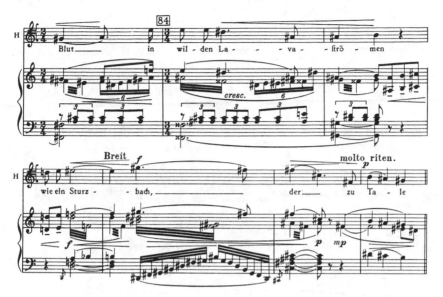

Performance History and Critical Reception

Neues vom Tage received its premiere in June of 1929 as part of the annual Berlin Festspiele. That summer the festival boasted not only the premiere of *Neues vom Tage,* but numerous other opera productions. Arturo Toscanini conducted the cast of La Scala in six different works, and Richard Strauss conducted six of his own operas. Though not part of the Krolloper's regular season, the Festspiele performance of *Neues vom Tage,* with Ernst Legal as director and sets designed by Piscator's collaborator Traugott Müller, was conducted by Otto Klemperer. *Neues vom Tage* was the only work Klemperer's Krolloper premiered in its entire history. Klemperer also conducted performances of *Don Giovanni, Der fliegende Holländer,* and Krenek's three one-acts, as well as an all-Stravinsky orchestral concert.[36] Thus *Neues vom Tage* had formidable competition.

Klemperer expressed early enthusiasm for the work, writing to his wife that "everything fits together charmingly . . . the orchestration is a marvel."[37] But he demanded such thorough rehearsing that orchestra members openly complained.[38] Hans Curjel, who probably had some hand in the staging of the work, concurred with Klemperer's opinion of the score. In a letter to Kurt Weill before the premiere Curjel stated, "The orchestra sounds fascinating, a lot goes on on stage, [Klemperer's] *élan* compensates for much."[39]

Example 7.11.   Paul Hindemith, *Neues vom Tage,* "Arioso"

Even with all the competition during the Festspiele, *Neues vom Tage* was well received by the capacity crowd. In an interesting case of life imitating art, the *Berliner Börsen-Courier* ran a story entitled "The Picture as Divorce Grounds" the day before the premiere.[40] The reception, though, could hardly compare with that received by *Jonny spielt auf, Der Zar,* or Hindemith's own *Hin und zurück.* There was, however, universal praise for Klemperer's conducting; his numerous rehearsals had paid off.

Most critics, including Heinrich Strobel of *Melos,* who supported Hindemith, and H. H. Stuckenschmidt, found the work flawed. In particular,

Example 7.12. Paul Hindemith, *Neues vom Tage,* Recitative

they thought it did not succeed in its attempt to combine Schiffer's revue sketch libretto and Hindemith's rigorous formal models. Critics acknowledged that Schiffer was a masterful writer for the *Kabarett* and revue stage, and, likewise, that Hindemith was a master of opera and wrote much witty, energetic, and parodistic music. But somehow the collaboration between the two talents had failed to jell. Alfred Einstein noted the "incongruity between the *light-weight* demands of this text, this cabaret-like dramatic string of scenes, and the *less light-weight* demand of the music."[41] Other critics, such as Hans Gutman, felt that Schiffer was truly at fault.[42] Schiffer's conception of the story was better than his execution; therefore Hindemith's music was largely wasted on the libretto. Paul Bekker expressed this same concern about the combination of Schiffer's text and Hindemith's music as late as 1932.[43]

H. H. Stuckenschmidt, who liked the work in general and applauded Hindemith's retention of Schiffer as a librettist, found the opera to suffer from another dramatic flaw.

> My strongest dramaturgical objection to the work is the conclusion. The final chorus scene, with Laura and Eduard's duet, is weak, theatrically bankrupt, and destroys much of the distinguished impression already made throughout the evening. They will have to revise it fundamentally in order to make the work viable.[44]

Arno Huth agreed that after a strong first act, the work went downhill.[45] Hindemith himself expressed dissatisfaction with the Krolloper production, in particular with Legal's staging, about which he complained to Strecker, "to put it very crudely, but accurately, [it] was a load of crap."[46]

It was for the *Neues vom Tage* edition of *Die Blätter der Staatsoper* that Hans Curjel wrote his "Triumph der *Alltäglichkeit,*"[47] in which he described the current interest in the everyday. Although such an aesthetic stance had existed well before *Neues vom Tage,* of all the *Zeitopern* discussed, it was by far the most down-to-earth: no czars, no political sentiments, no apotheosis of the new artist, no temperamental opera singers, just an unhappily married couple caught up in modern commercial society.

It is not surprising then that critics responded in particular to this aspect of the opera. Both Gutman and Heinrich Strobel saw the work as clearly indicative of an artistic support for *Alltäglichkeit.* Gutman maintained that *Neues vom Tage*

> is of considerable importance because it not only is characteristic of the author's present status but also throws light on the general condition of opera in Germany today. . . . [T]hat a serious composer like Hindemith should decide to compose to a farce created by a cabaret mentality, is symptomatic.[48]

Gutman also noted that this introduction of everyday life, though by no means a novelty in 1928, represented an anti-nineteenth-century stance, as romantic opera had largely excluded reality. Strobel, writing before the premiere, described the work as significant in its combination of art and entertainment: "The play, drawn from the everyday, replaces the stirring private drama of the suffering of the soul. What could happen to anyone, any day, is shown on the stage."[49] But Max Marschalk questioned whether the work did incorporate *Alltäglichkeit* or just mocked the current fascination with it, along with everything else it parodied.[50]

The nature of Hindemith's musical parody was frequently discussed, and any number of composers and operas were suggested as the source for Hindemith's persiflage. Erich Steinhard, in a review for *Auftakt,* not only raved about the work and its *Bauhausstil* production, but claimed that each number in the entire opera parodied some earlier operatic style.[51] Other writers commented upon the falsely sentimental "Duett-Kitsch," described as in the style of Puccini, Richard Strauss, or Wagner. Others likened the chorus of typists in scene 3 to the opening of *Salome.* Oskar Bie and occasionally other writers misunderstood the burlesques. Bie criticized Hindemith's closing "wie peinlich" ensemble in scene 5, noting that the music was serious enough to be included in a mass and was out of place for the dramatic action.[52]

Neues vom Tage received a respectable number of performances, especially in its second season (see appendix D). And the overture was successful apart from the opera. A production planned for Munich was called off within two months of the premiere, as the opera house management expressed misgivings about the text.[53] The topic of divorce may have been considered too controversial by the standards of the conservative Munich audience, not to mention the objectionable nature of Laura's bathtub aria.

Karl Holl noted that the work's reception in Darmstadt had not been as successful as in Berlin, although he blamed it on the Darmstadt public's notorious hatred for new works and not on the production itself.[54] Publicity photographs from this 1929 production show that this smaller stage used sophisticated and modern theatrical staging techniques.[55] Scene 7 (see figure 7.2), where the various agents try to persuade Eduard to sign a contract, was staged with the agents off to the side on various levels of scaffolding, while their suggestions for how Eduard could capitalize on his notoriety—*Laura und Eduard im Kino, Laura und Eduard im Kabarett*—are shown on the curtain backdrop, perhaps in imitation of Piscator and his projection of scene captions. The Darmstadt company later gave two performances of the work in Frankfurt to a better reception. Strecker noted in 1930 that smaller houses were more interested in producing the work, while larger houses, such as Munich and Frankfurt, held back.[56] Hindemith had already found the October 1929 Magdeburg production very successful and more to his taste, whereas Strecker deemed the May 1931 production in Mannheim as perhaps the best.[57] Klemperer and the Krolloper also produced a revival of *Neues vom Tage* in June of 1930.

Hindemith revised *Neues vom Tage* considerably in 1954, following the establishment of his new compositional principles. He restructured the work into two acts, changed the makeup of individual scenes, deleted Frau and Herr M, and added new characters. The work had its first performance in the United States in 1961 at the Santa Fe Opera. Most recently, it was performed by the Manhattan School of Music in 1979.

After *Neues vom Tage*

Following the composition of *Neues vom Tage*, Hindemith worked on two other related projects. His *Lehrstück, Der Lindberghflug* was written in collaboration with Bertolt Brecht and Kurt Weill for the 1929 Baden-Baden Festival. Its continued success, however, was sabotaged by Brecht.[58] Also in keeping with his concurrent interest in the *Jugendmusikbewegung*, Hindemith's children's opera, *Wir bauen eine Stadt*, received a radio performance and then a staged production in Wiesbaden in 1931.

After *Wir bauen eine Stadt*, Hindemith left behind the aesthetic of *Alltäglichkeit*. He wrote Strecker in March of 1931 and aptly noted that "a new wave of serious and great music is on the way."[59] Indeed, Krenek and Weill had both already begun writing new serious operas. And in Hindemith's cantata *Das*

Figure 7.2. *Neues vom Tage* as Staged at the Darmstadt Hessisches Landestheater in 1929

Unaufhörliche and the opera *Mathis der Maler,* he demonstrated his change of musical direction. Otto Klemperer conducted the first performance of *Das Unaufhörliche,* on a text by Gottfried Benn, on 21 November 1931. Hindemith later pointed to this work, with its renunciation of the lighthearted, energetic music he had produced in the 1920s, as marking the start of his mature style.

Hindemith's change is even more apparent in *Mathis der Maler,* which he began in 1933 and finished in 1935. *Mathis der Maler* is thoroughly grounded in older German operatic tradition, even more so than Krenek's *Leben des Orest* or *Karl V.* It is thus especially perplexing that this opera would have elicited such harsh criticism from the National Socialists.[60] In *Mathis der Maler,* Hindemith sounded the death knell for the *Zeitoper* by again taking up the theme of the artist in society and repudiating once and for all Krenek's model in *Jonny spielt auf.* In *Mathis der Maler,* the artist has no preoccupation with his culture or politics but learns through trial and tribulation to remain true to his private art alone. The era of envying the oneness of French culture, of the *Novembergruppe,* and of *Gebrauchsmusik* was over.

By 1934, Krenek and Weill had left Germany, and Hindemith was falling out of favor with the National Socialist party. He was branded an "international" composer and attacked for his associations with Jewish colleagues. Wilhelm Furtwängler's open letter of support for Hindemith and his subsequent resignation as conductor of the Berlin Philharmonic and State Opera and from his post as deputy president of the Reichsmusikkammer did not help Hindemith's situation.[61] Propaganda Minister Joseph Goebbels responded to Furtwängler's letter of support with his own open letter.[62] He cited Laura's bathtub arioso, which he described as both obscene and sensational, as evidence of Hindemith's musical decadence. He further claimed that the score of *Neues vom Tage* was dissonant and atonal. It is unlikely, however, that Goebbels ever saw the work performed, or knew of it in any way, except perhaps from secondhand reports or the reviews of such conservative critics as Alfred Heuss.

Willy Strecker tried to come to Hindemith's aid. He informed Hindemith that he would write a letter in which he would address all the charges made against him.[63] Strecker planned to counteract the contention that *Neues vom Tage* had a "dirty" libretto by suggesting that the ending could be read tragically and as a condemnation of the time. Hindemith was nonetheless branded a cultural Bolshevik.[64] Thus, with few other options remaining, he left Germany in 1938, thereby joining the other foremost representatives of his generation in America, or to quote from *Jonny spielt auf,* in "the unknown land of dreams."

8

Conclusion: Works by Schreker, d'Albert, Toch, Brand, Rathaus, Grosz, Antheil, and Schoenberg

Krenek, Weill, and Hindemith, as the dominant members of the postwar generation of German composers, produced the most celebrated *Zeitopern*. Other composers who shared their concerns for new opera produced works much like those already discussed. As early as 1924, Franz Schreker (1878–1934), Krenek's teacher at the Berlin Hochschule, was at work on his opera *Christophorus* which contains features of the *Zeitoper*. Schreker earned a reputation for opera as early as 1912 with *Der ferne Klang,* and he was one of several prewar composers who embraced, at least partially, the postwar *Zeitoper*. Schreker finished *Christophorus* in 1928, and a piano-vocal score was published in 1931.[1] The National Socialists, objecting to Schreker's Jewish heritage, stymied plans for a premiere in that same year, and the work remained unperformed in Schreker's lifetime.[2]

Dedicated to Arnold Schoenberg, *Christophorus,* subtitled "The Vision of an Opera," relates the story of a young composition student, Anselm, who must chose between human love and a dedication to his music. The libretto, by Schreker himself, is actually an opera within an opera. Anselm envisions himself caught in a love triangle with his colleague Christoph and Lisa, the daughter of his composition teacher Meister Johann. This jealousy leads Christoph to murder Lisa, and other scenes show Anselm and Christoph in an opium den and nightclub before Anselm returns to reality. Schreker initially referred to the work as "eine moderne Legende," and the story of St. Christopher figures first as the suggested theme for a student composition and then becomes part of Anselm's operatic vision.[3]

Christophorus lacks the comic spirit of true *Zeitopern,* although Schreker uses parody in his depiction of composition students. The work deals with the role of the contemporary artist in modern society, as does *Jonny spielt auf,* and it incorporates concrete images of modern life. The first scene of act 2 takes place

Example 8.1.   Franz Schreker, *Christophorous*, Act 2

in the Hotel Montmartre, a typical nightclub complete with a *conférencier* who announces the musical numbers. The score requires an on-stage jazz band, which supplies the music for the entire scene and consists of tenor saxophone, piano, and percussion, to be played by black musicians. This music (see example 8.1), with its eighth-note bass line, cut-time meter, and distinctive rhythm, suggests an earlier kind of popular music reminiscent of Hindemith's unpublished piano work *In einer Nacht.*

Another composer whose operatic reputation was made prior to World War I and who turned to *Zeitoper* in the 1920s was Eugen d'Albert (1864–1932). *Die schwarze Orchidee,* his *opera grottesca,* received a premiere in Leipzig on 1 December 1928 and a Berlin production in June of 1929 (see appendix D for more performance statistics). Set in New York City, the libretto by Karl Levetzow deals with a well-to-do cat burglar, Percy, whose trademark is a black

Example 8.2.   Eugen d'Albert, *Die schwarze Orchidee,* "Eros-Foxtrot"

orchid, left at the scene of each of his robberies. This "Break-in King" falls in love with the aristocratic Grace and she with him while both are at the Mt. Everest Bar, situated atop a skyscraper. They are reunited after he breaks into her house, and the kindhearted chief of the secret police, Pinkleton, allows Percy to escape, taking Grace with him.

Besides Pinkleton, whose character parodies law enforcement officers, the cast of *Die schwarze Orchidee* includes Jimmy, Percy's black servant. Jimmy is an ancillary character undoubtedly included for the sake of fashion, and he is subjected to outbursts of racist name-calling by the other characters and chorus. When he is abandoned at the end by Percy, Jimmy breaks into the spiritual "Deep River," accompanied by a saxophone quartet, and then concludes that the white world is certainly a merry [*lustig*] one. A third comic character true to modern life is the snoopy investigative reporter Schmuckele, who hopes to unmask the "Break-in King." D'Albert claimed to have had no prior knowledge of *Jonny spielt auf* and to have finished *Die schwarze Orchidee* before the premiere of Krenek's work.[4] It seems highly unlikely, however, that the composer of *Tiefland* and *Die toten Augen,* works very much of the nineteenth-century tradition, would have created *Die schwarze Orchidee* without the influence of *Jonny spielt auf.*

The scene in the Mt. Everest Bar, described as "a jazz paradise," contains a revue number starring Bessie, who is both Percy's erstwhile girlfriend and Grace's maid. Bessie, accompanied by her Glacier-Girls, invites the guests into her ice palace to dance the "Eros-Foxtrot." This foxtrot (see example 8.2) was orchestrated for saxophone, banjo, percussion, and strings, and it was later published in a separate piano reduction as one of the opera's popular songs.[5]

A third, older composer who was drawn to *Zeitoper* was Ernst Toch (1887–1964) whose *Prinzessin auf der Erbse,* based on the Hans Christian Andersen fairy tale of the princess and the pea, shared the Baden-Baden stage with the *Mahagonny-Songspiel* and *Hin und zurück. Der Fächer* [The Fan], an *Opern-Capriccio,* received a 1930 premiere in Königsberg as part of the *Deutsches Tonkünstlerfest.* The libretto by Ferdinand Lion, who supplied *Cardillac* for Hindemith, is a modern version of a Chinese legend in which a widow vows to remain chaste as long as the dirt covering her husband's grave retains moisture. She then obtains a magic fan which accelerates the crucial evaporation process.

The opera is set in Shanghai, and though no specific time is given, the work makes reference to the modern film industry, the widow having become infatuated with a film director. Besides the references to film the opera utilizes on-stage loudspeakers and radio broadcasts. The second scene of act 2 takes place in the club "Berlin." The accompanying music, designated as a *Tempo di tango,* uses tango rhythms and is performed by an on-stage ensemble consisting of two violins, alto saxophone, trumpet, cello, banjo, piano, and percussion [*Jazzbatterie*].

Maschinist Hopkins, by Max Brand (b. 1896) lacks the comic nature of *Zeitopern* but celebrates the machine and factory worker as symbolic of contemporary life. Brand's depiction of proletarian life and the worker's milieu suggests an affinity with Serge Prokofiev and Alexander Mosolov, whose ballets *Pas d'acier* and *The Foundry,* respectively, were both premiered in 1927. Sets in New York City, *Maschinist Hopkins,* on Brand's own libretto, revolves entirely around the factory where a foreman is murdered by his unfaithful wife and her lover, a fellow worker. This pair proceed to attain success as an actress and business magnate, but the machines, which witnessed the murder, finally get their revenge on the two with the help of an omniscient head machinist known only as Hopkins.

Scenes take place in the factory proper, a factory office, the workers' neighborhood [*Proletariergasse*], a theater dressing room and the backstage, and a bar. The critics lauded the premiere in Duisburg on 13 April 1929, as part of a special citywide festival, for its sets and staging, particularly the large factory scenes where the workers, dressed in identical uniforms, operate the pistons, levers, and cogs of the giant machines. The production also used cinematographic projections which showed the machines coming to life in the darkened factory, and an off-stage speaking chorus provided the machines with a voice.[6] The foreword to the piano-vocal score describes how the speaking parts are to be performed and refers the reader to Schoenberg's preface to *Die glückliche Hand,* which also contained a speaking chorus. Other critics singled out for special comment Brand's accompanying machine music, which required a siren, thunder

Example 8.3.   Max Brand, *Maschinist Hopkins,* "Black-Bottom-Jazzband"

and wind machines, as well as a large percussion section and the chorus. The
work was popular, with 120 performances given in its second season, including a
Berlin production in March of 1930 (see appendix D for more performance
statistics).[7]

Brand used jazz idioms in 2 of the 12 scenes. Scene 4 takes place in an
outdoor nightclub where Nell, the wife of the murdered foreman, works. Brand
entitled the syncopated cut-time interlude which precedes the scene
"Black-Bottom-Jazzband" and orchestrated it for banjo, piano, saxophones, including a soprano saxophone line marked *ad lib.*, clarinet, trombone, and tuba (see
example 8.3). Scene 4 proper opens with a chorus line dancing to the
English-texted "Ma-Bram-Hob-Han" song, performed by six black musicians.
Three of these musicians play banjo, and the other three play saxophone. George
Antheil supplied the text for this song about the Sultan of Turkestan who, while
in drag, attempts to infiltrate the modern harem of a beauty contest. The
accompanying music contains features of the foxtrot combined with the
Charleston rhythm, and is scored with prominent banjo, saxophone, piano, and
violin solos (see example 8.4). This "Ma-Bram-Hob-Han" song was published in
a separate piano-vocal arrangement as a foxtrot.[8] Later on in the same scene, a
couple dance a tango as part of the stage show. This tango music, with its
opening triplet rhythms, is more characteristic of a bolero, but Brand also
incorporates the standard tango rhythms (see example 8.5).

Scene 10 takes place in Bondy's Bar, an establishment frequented by the
factory workers. In the production in Duisburg, the bar was decorated with red
and white stripes in imitation of an American flag.[9] The orchestral interlude

Example 8.4. Max Brand, *Maschinist Hopkins*, "Ma-Bram-Hob-Han" Foxtrot

Example 8.5. Max Brand, *Maschinist Hopkins*, Tango

Example 8.6.   Max Brand, *Maschinist Hopkins,* Bondy's Bar

preceding the scene is in two-four meter and carries the further distinction *Schnelles (Shimmy) Tempo.* In the scene proper, an on-stage electric piano provides music to accompany several couples dancing a foxtrot (see example 8.6).

Fremde Erde, by Karol Rathaus, contains features of the *Zeitoper* combined with a strong political commentary. The story chronicles a group of Russian emigrants who come to America, although the description of their new land appears to be a cross between Mexico and South America. The emigrants are deceived by wealthy mine owners, one emigrant dies, and at the end of the opera, against the backdrop of the New York City harbor, the remaining emigrants long for their homeland.

Rathaus's use of jazz appears in the first act and characterizes the rich ship passengers—who dance to jazz on their voyage to America—in contrast to the lowly emigrants in steerage who cannot partake in the entertainment. Rathaus calls for a dance band, situated on the ship's deck, consisting of solo violin, trumpet, trombone, alto saxophone, banjo, piano, and percussion. Selections of the dance music are designated as in *Shimmy-Tempo* and *Im Zeitmass eines bewegten Tango.* The work concludes with a quotation of "Yankee Doodle." After its December 1930 premiere the work was little performed.

The year 1930 saw premieres in Frankfurt of two *Zeitopern*—Wilhelm Grosz's *Achtung! Aufnahme!* and George Antheil's *Transatlantic*—and Arnold Schoenberg's *Von Heute auf Morgen,* a critical commentary on the genre and a final attack on Krenek. *Achtung! Aufnahme!* was a one-act *Tragikomödie* on a libretto by Béla Balázs, who supplied the scenario for Grosz's ballet *Baby in der*

Bar. The entire opera takes place in a movie studio, reflecting Balázs's own work in the cinema, having supplied the story for the film "The Adventures of a Ten-Mark Bill" (1926), one of the first German "street films." In *Achtung! Aufnahme!,* a young student threatens the life of the leading actress and his "acting" is so convincing that he is signed to a lucrative contract by the director. The score includes lively sections marked *Shimmy-Zeitmass,* a *Slow-Fox-Zeitmass,* with a dotted melody over the standard four quarter-note bass line, and a *Tango-Zeitmass* section which uses both tango rhythms. The orchestration calls for two alto saxophones, *Jazztrompet* and *Jazzposaune. Achtung! Aufnahme!* was not successful at its premiere in Frankfurt on 23 March 1930 on a double bill with Stravinsky's *Petrushka,* and it appears to have been little performed after the premiere.

Transatlantic shared the fate of *Achtung! Aufnahme!* Its mammoth staging demands precluded its performance by all but the largest opera houses, and it remained unperformed, although critically acclaimed, after its 25 May 1930 premiere in Frankfurt. Antheil first called the work *Glare,* and then *Transatlantic,* subtitled "The People's Choice." The story, devised by Antheil perhaps at the suggestion of Stuckenschmidt with encouragement by Krenek, centers on an American presidential election marred by political corruption. Ajax, an unscrupulous political boss, with the help of his mistress Helena attempts to control Hector, the favored presidential candidate. Good eventually triumphs, although Hector loses the election, shoots one of Ajax's henchmen, and tries to strangle Helena. Ajax is arrested, and Hector and Helena, having fallen in love, are reunited on the Brooklyn Bridge as the sun rises over New York City and the chorus praises that American institution, hard work. Theodor Wiesengrund-Adorno, who praised the work, described the libretto as a synthesis of love and *Sachlichkeit.*[10]

Antheil clearly tried to make his *Zeitoper* as theatrically up-to-date as possible and appears to have borrowed many of Piscator's innovations. The work opens on a ship approaching the New York City harbor, and the following scenes of the first two acts include the interior of Helena's Fifth Avenue apartment, a New York City cabaret, a restaurant, an ascending elevator, and Ajax's office. The last act contains 27 scenes played on 4 simultaneous sets—a bathroom, Helena's apartment, Ajax's office, and a hotel room—connected by stairways so the principals can move from one set to another. A "Review [*sic*] Dancer" provides a commentary on the action, and captions for each scene are projected onto a central screen. The final scene consists of a movie, again projected on the center screen, which depicts Hector's dream of meeting Helena five years hence; he is a tourist in Paris; she has become a prostitute. This cinematic reverie causes Hector to look for Helena and reconcile. Other modern staging effects include projected headlines from a New York City newspaper, typewriters and tele-

Example 8.7. George Antheil, *Transatlantic*, "Tango"

graphic equipment in Hector's campaign office, people acting like robots, and an imitation of a filmed sequence run in slow motion.

The score of *Transatlantic* abounds with jazz idioms and other identifiably American music. Sections are designated as *Tempo di tango* with corresponding rhythms. The cabaret scene includes dance music for chorus girls and a black bottom dancer, as well as a blues. A choral number is described as a *Jazz-Chorus*, and the music which accompanies the "Review Dancer" is a cut-time shimmy. Other American musical references include a quotation of "The Erie Canal" and a representation of Salvation Army Band music. The piano-vocal score provides only clues to instrumentation—two saxophones and banjo added to a standard orchestra—and no full score was published.[11] Universal Edition did publish a solo piano "Tango" derived from the *Tempo di tango* sections in scene 2.[12] The music (see example 8.7) shows Antheil's combination of both tango rhythms.

Antheil wished to attain a major commercial success with *Transatlantic*. In letters to his patron Mary Curtis Bok, founder of the Curtis Institute of Philadelphia, Antheil refers to the success of Krenek and others and suggests he can achieve the same.[13] (By 1929 Antheil knew both Krenek and Weill, whose libretto for *Der Lindberghflug* he translated into English for the 1930 publication.) And he had hopes that his "American Grand Opera" would be performed at the New York Metropolitan, thereby earning him the respect in the United States he felt he was due.[14] The work, though clever in many respects, did not find the hoped-for success, though it received favorable coverage in

Germany and in the United States.[15] It was simply too difficult for most houses to produce. The Frankfurt production was well done and well received, and in the opening night audience were many of Antheil's Parisian friends, including Ezra Pound, Sylvia Beach, and Nancy Cunard.

As early as November of 1928, Schoenberg wrote to Universal Edition of his interest in writing a new one-act comic work.[16] Early in 1929 he was eliciting comments from his students Alban Berg, Anton Webern, Josef Rufer, and Erwin Stein about the libretto for *Von Heute auf Morgen*.[17] The libretto, by Max Blonda, a pseudonym for Gertrud Schoenberg, is a modern domestic drama not unlike *Neues vom Tage*. The couple, known only in expressionist terms as *Frau* and *Mann*, experience marital problems as the husband becomes infatuated with the wife's more modern, and therefore more desirable, girlfriend. In retaliation, the wife pretends to be in love with a singer. The husband realizes his foolishness, and the work ends with a general condemnation of modern ideas which change overnight, or "von Heute auf Morgen," an expression Schoenberg had previously used in the foreword to the *Drei Satiren* in which he condemned the faddish nature of neo-classicism and other postwar trends.

Though a domestic drama like *Neues vom Tage*, *Von Heute auf Morgen* was no doubt Schoenberg's final response to Krenek and to *Zeitoper*. Other allusions to Krenek in particular may be the use of "Max" for Gertrud Schoenberg's pseudonym, as a way of reaffirming the philosophy first espoused by Max in *Jonny spielt auf*, and the opening line "Schön war es dort" [it was beautiful there], which repeats the opening word of *Jonny spielt auf*. In *Von Heute auf Morgen*, the first line is uttered by the foolish, gushing husband, whose foolish, even immature infatuation is repudiated at the end of the opera, thus paralleling Max's opening line in *Jonny spielt auf* which was likewise repudiated at the end of Krenek's opera. Schoenberg may have also been suggesting that, like the foolish husband, many composers and critics thought the *Zeitoper* more modern and desirable, while Schoenberg knew differently.

Schoenberg claimed that the score for *Von Heute auf Morgen* was light, cheerful, and even comic, and his orchestration included saxophones, piano, mandolin, and guitar.[18] Although he included instruments popular with composers of *Zeitopern* for their recognizable jazz timbres, Schoenberg did not adapt popular idioms for his score. At one point the wife does hum nine measures of a modern dance, so called in the score, as she attempts to dance with her husband, and the alto saxophone doubles her melody line.[19] For the most part, Schoenberg chooses to use the instruments identified with jazz in a straightforward, absolute manner. He demonstrates that saxophones are still saxophones and do not necessarily carry with them preexisting social and aesthetic connotations.

Von Heute auf Morgen received its premiere in Frankfurt on 1 February 1930. Although Schoenberg expressed dissatisfaction with the production, the work was popular with the opening night audience.[20] It received three other

Frankfurt performances and a later performance over the Berlin radio which featured soprano Margot Hinnenberg-LeFevre, wife of H. H. Stuckenschmidt. The work ultimately fell from the repertory.

In 1943 Ernst Krenek published his first article on opera since his departure from Germany and Austria. By this time he had settled in the U. S. and had made his peace with the American avant-garde. In "Opera between the Wars," which appeared in the American avant-garde journal *Modern Music,* Krenek assessed the contributions to modern opera he and other young composers had made and concluded that the last 20 years had produced nothing of permanent value.[21] *Jonny spielt auf* was remembered only for its "mechanical contrivances enlivening the plot." At best these operas represented the first steps in a post-Wagnerian evolution, but as of yet, no one composer had displayed the single-minded dedication to opera that characterized Wagner and his achievements.

As Krenek tacitly acknowledged, the *Zeitoper* did not or could not live up to its expectations. And perhaps in this respect it must be considered a failure even as the Weimar Republic itself was. The *Zeitoper* was a short-lived trend, one of many in a decade of rapidly changing and quixotic artistic experiments. By our standards and theirs, as the Republic declined, *Zeitopern* had at times become overly optimistic and faddish, and they soon became dated. In their aim to forge new roles and be of their time, these composers did choose, as their critics decried, the topical at the expense of the eternal. And thus they ultimately found themselves caught in a trap of their own conscious making, having created works on purpose which would not necessarily wear well through the century.

The *Zeitoper,* however, was important even without having had a lasting influence. Fundamentally the composers of the *Zeitoper* affirmed a commitment to opera as a genre which needed to evolve in the twentieth century. These experiments enlarged the definition of modern opera and musical theater and acted as a proving ground for their own more mature works. Secondly, these same composers reflected on the problem of the role of the artist in society. Although their commitments to new roles were temporary—only Kurt Weill with his later career in American musical theater could be said to have continued with his twenties perspective—they sought to provide an alternative view to the musical isolationism which marked, and to an extent still marks, the music of this century. The *Zeitoper* provides food for thought for those of us concerned about the future of contemporary music. Are the topical and eternal mutually exclusive? How do composers make peace with the popular music of their own age? Why are popular successes so suspect? How do composers and audiences reconcile their often different artistic needs?

The *Zeitoper* was profoundly an artistic consequence of the Weimar Republic. It was self-consciously republican opera for what many hoped would be a new social and political age. Composers turned their backs on what they thought had been an age marked by elitism and separation and sought to create a postwar art which was democratic and communal. Walter Jacob, writing in *Die Musik* after the premiere of *Jonny spielt auf,* tried to reconcile these conflicting issues of currency and historical value. His assessment of *Jonny spielt auf* can stand for the genre as a whole:

> It may be that this work which speaks so strongly to us today may appear to a later time as unfit, an individual experiment only of historical value. Possibly, but this *Jonny* is also worthwhile as one of the strongest and most characteristic operatic works of our time.[22]

The *Zeitoper* supplies a missing piece in our perception and understanding of Weimar cultural life. Its significance rests in how it speaks for that fragile time, what people wanted to write, and what others wanted to hear.

Appendix A

Jazz-Influenced Works

The following lists were compiled from a variety of sources including biographies of composers, catalogues of works, reviews, advertisements in journals, and various articles from the time. The year given for a work is the date of publication when known or the year of a first recorded performance. Although the actual year of composition would better chronicle the spread of this compositional trend, it was impossible to find such dates for the majority of works. Wherever possible, the score was obtained so as to document more precisely the jazz idioms present. In particular, I looked for references to jazz dances or the use of instruments which indicated an interest in jazz timbres. When the scores were unobtainable, I had to rely solely on references, often made in passing and without adequate documentation, or titles which suggested the influence of jazz.

European, 1917 to 1933

1917

Francis Poulenc. *Rhapsodie nègre* (rev. 1933). Represents an infatuation with black Americans rather than the use of jazz idioms.
Erik Satie. *Parade*. Ballet. "Petite fille americaine," use of syncopated ragtime idiom.

1918

Igor Stravinsky. *Rag-Time for 11 Instruments*.
———— . *L'Histoire du soldat*. "Three Dances: Tango, Waltz, Ragtime."

1919

Paul Hindemith. *In einer Nacht*. Piano. Penultimate section "Foxtrott." Unpublished; composed between 1917 and 1919.
Darius Milhaud. *Le Boeuf sur le toit*. Ballet. Use of tango rhythms, although in a South American context.
Erwin Schulhoff. *Fünf Pittoresken*. Piano. "Zeitmass-Foxtrott," "Ragtime," "In Futurum," "Onestep," "Maxixe" (dedicated to George Grosz).
Igor Stravinsky. *Piano-Rag-Music*.

1920

Georges Auric. *Adieu, New York!* Solo piano and chamber ensemble versions. Subtitled "Fox-Trot."
Paul Hindemith. *Lyonel-Foxtrot* and *Young Lorch Fellow-Rag*.
Darius Milhaud. *Caramel mou (Shimmy)*. Voice and small jazz band. Text by Jean Cocteau; first performed in 1921.
Erwin Schulhoff. *Ironies*. Piano. Last movement "Tempo di fox."

1921

Paul Hindemith. *Ragtime (wohltemperiert)*. Orchestra.
———— . *Das atonale Kabarett*.

1922

Eduard Erdmann. *Foxtrot*. Piano.
Paul Hindemith. *Kammermusik No. 1*. "Finale: 1921."
———— . *Suite 1922*. Piano. "Shimmy," "Boston," and "Ragtime" movements.
———— . *Tuttifäntchen*. "Christmas Fairytale for Voices with Choreography." Number 4: "Tanz der Holzpuppen," called a foxtrot.
Ernst Krenek. *Tanzstudie*. Piano. Pervasive syncopated rhythms.
Artur Schnabel. *Eine Tanzsuite*. Piano. First movement "Foxtrott"; unpublished; performed by Eduard Erdmann on 19 March 1922 *Abend der Novembergruppe*.
Erwin Schulhoff. *Ragmusic*. Piano. "Tempo di Foxtrott," "Jazz-like," "Tango-Rag," "Tempo di Foxtrott" movements.

1923

Artur Bliss. *Bliss, a One-Step*. Piano or chamber ensemble.
Ernst Krenek. *Toccata und Chaconne über den Choral "Ja, ich glaub an Jesum Christum."* Anhang: *Eine kleine Suite von Stücken über denselbigen Choral verschiedenen Charakters*. Piano. "Allemande," "Sarabande," "Gavotte," "Walzer," "Fuge," "Foxtrott" movements, composed in 1922.
Darius Milhaud. *La Création du monde*. Ballet.
———— . *Trois rag-caprices*. Piano or small orchestra. Dedicated to Jean Wiéner; first performed on a Concert-Wiéner.
Jean Wiéner. *Sonatine syncopée*. Dedication thanks the black American jazz bands for their influence; second movement "Blues."

1924

Eduard Erdmann. *Fox-trot in C-Dur*. Piano. Composed in 1923; dedicated to Ernst Krenek and Anna Mahler.
Wilhelm Grosz. *Jazzband*. Violin and piano. Performed at the 1925 Venice I. S. C. M. festival.
Paul Hindemith. *Two Shimmies*. Piano.
Ernst Krenek. *Kleine Suite*. Clarinet and piano. Last movement "Moderner Tanz" (finished in 1924 though not published until 1969); dedicated to Werner Reinhart.
———— . *Der Sprung über den Schatten*. Opera. Different sections in popular dance tempi.
Francis Poulenc. *Les Biches*. Ballet. "Rag-Mazurka."
Jean Wiéner. *Trois blues chantes*. Voice and piano. Textless vocal part written in imitation of a "Saxophoniste nègre."
———— . *Sept petites histoires*. Voice and piano. Movement 3: "Rag-Time."

1925

Arthur Honegger. *Prélude et blues*. Harp quartet.
Marcel Poot. *Paris in Verlegenheid*. Ballet.
Maurice Ravel. *L'Enfant et les sortilèges*. Opera. Ragtime duet between the black Wedgwood teapot and the chinoiserie cup.
Erwin Schulhoff. *Partita*. Piano. "Rag-Music," "Boston," "Tempo di Rag," "Tango," "Jimmy-Jazz" movements; first performed in 1922.
————. *Fünf Stücke*. String quartet. Movement 4: "Alla Tango milonga"; dedicated to Milhaud.

1926

Gerald Berners. *Triumph of Neptune*. Ballet.
Emil Burian. *Koktarly*. Voice and jazz band.
————. *American Suite*. Two pianos.
O. A. Evans. *Jazz-Etude*. Piano. Part of a series of piano studies.
Walter Gieseking. *Drei Tanz-Improvisationen*. Piano. "Tempo di Charleston" movement.
Walter Goehr. *Amerikanisches Liederbuch*. Performed at 1926 Baden-Baden Festival.
Wilhelm Grosz. *II. Tanzsuite*. Piano. "Foxtrot," "Boston," "Tango," "Shimmy," "Quasi-Fivestep" movements.
Arthur Honegger. *Concertino*. Piano and orchestra.
Ernst Krenek. *3 Military Marches*. March idioms combined with syncopated ragtime character; performed at the 1926 Donaueschingen Festival.
William Walton. *Façade*. Suite. On a text by Edith Sitwell.
Kurt Weill. *Der neue Orpheus*. Cantata for soprano, violin and orchestra. Text by Ivan Goll; brief use of dance music idioms to characterize modern life.

1927

Arthur Bliss. *The Rout Trot*. Piano. Composed ca. 1920.
Emil Burian. *Jazz-Requiem*. Soloists, chorus, and jazz band. Premiere given in a Prague church.
Wilhelm Grosz. *Baby in der Bar*. Ballet. Entire work written around various dances.
Alois Hába. *Vier Tänze*. Piano. "Shimmy," "Blues," "Boston," "Tango" movements.
Ernst Krenek. *Jonny spielt auf*. Opera.
————. *Mammon*. Ballet. Use of Charleston rhythm.
Constant Lambert. *Elegiac Blues*. Piano and orchestral arrangements.
Bohuslav Martinů. *Black Bottom*. Piano.
————. *La Revue de cuisine*. Ballet. Sections marked "Charleston," "Tango," "Fox-Trot."
————. *Der Soldat und die Tänzerin*. Opera. Jazz music to accompany barroom scenes.
————. *3 Skizzy moderné tancŭ*. Piano. "Blues," "Tango," "Charleston" movements.
Maurice Ravel. *Sonata*. Violin and piano. Second movement: "Blues."
Erwin Schulhoff. *5 Etudes de Jazz*. Piano. "Charleston," "Blues," "Chanson," "Tango," "Toccata sur le Shimmy 'Kitten on the Keys'" movements.
————. *Bürger als Edelmann*. Incidental music for Molière's play *Le Bourgeois Gentilhomme;* contains a "Foxtrottfuge."
Kurt Weill. *Mahagonny-Songspiel*. Unpublished in Weill's lifetime; first performed at the 1927 Baden-Baden Festival; foxtrot and blues idioms.
————. *Royal Palace*. Opera. Sections in popular dance tempi and use of tango and other dance rhythms.

1928

Emil Burian. *Bubu vom Montparnasse*. Opera.
Eugen d'Albert. *Die schwarze Orchidee*. Opera. Scene in Mt. Everest Bar with appropriate nightclub music.
Ernst Krenek. *Kleine Symphonie*. Much syncopation; habanera rhythms in the third movement; use of banjos, guitar, and mandolin.
———— . *Das geheime Königreich*. One-act opera. Sections in dance tempi and rhythms.
———— . *Schwergewicht, oder die Ehre der Nation*. One-act opera. On-stage dancing; use of modern dance rhythms.
———— . *Potpourri*. For orchestra. Drum with *Jazzbesen;* written in 1927.
Bohuslav Martinů. *Le Jazz*. Orchestra.
———— . *Jazz Suite*. Small orchestra. "Prelude," "Blues," "Boston," "Finale" movements.
———— . *Les Larmes du Couteau*. One-act opera. Orchestra includes saxophone and banjo.
Erwin Schulhoff. *6 Esquises de jazz*. Piano. "Rag," "Boston," "Tango," "Blues," "Charleston," "Black Bottom" movements.
Kurt Weill. *Der Zar lässt sich photographieren*. One-act opera. "Tango-Angèle" and foxtrot sections.

1929

Alban Berg. *Der Wein*. Voice and orchestra. "Tempo di Tango" sections.
Boris Blacker. *Jazz-Koloraturen*. Voice (textless soprano part), alto saxophone, bassoon. "Slow fox" and "Allegro molto (Charlestontempo)" sections.
Max Brand. *Maschinist Hopkins*. Opera. Scenes in a nightclub and bar with appropriate dance music.
Paul Hindemith. *Neues vom Tage*. Opera. Cabaret scene and use of foxtrot, Boston and blues idioms.
Constant Lambert. *Rio Grande*. Chorus, orchestra and solo piano. Use of tango rhythms though more to suggest Latin America, first performed in February of 1928.
Bohuslav Martinů. *Les trois souhaits*. Film-opera. Orchestra includes two saxophones, banjo, harmonica, accordion.
———— . *8 Preludes*. Piano. Movement 1: "In the Form of a Blues" and movement 8: "In the Form of a Foxtrot."
———— . *Sextet*. Piano and winds. Movement 4: "Blues."
Serge Prokofiev. *L'Enfant prodigue*. Ballet. Written for Diaghilev; first performance 1929.
Erwin Schulhoff. *Hot Music, zehn synkopierte Etüden*. Piano.
———— . *II. String Quartet*. Movement 2: "Tempo di Fox."
Mátyás Seiber. *2 Jazzolettes*. Scored for two saxophones, trumpet, trombone, piano, and percussion.
Kurt Weill. *Die Dreigroschenoper*. Opera. Various numbers borrowing foxtrot, blues, and tango idioms as well as using jazz band instrumentation.
Jean Wiéner and Clement Doucet. *Album Wiéner-Doucet*. Contents: "Blues," "A Six Cylinder Rag-Time," "Haarlem (Tempo di Blues)," "Chicken Pie-Novelty Foxtrot."

1930

Ralph Benatzky. *Im weissen Rössl*. Operetta. Includes various foxtrot and tango numbers.
Wilhelm Grosz. *Afrika-Songs*. Voice and orchestra. Scored for *Jazztrumpet* and *Jazzposaune;* movement 8: "Blues-Zeitmass."
Ernst Krenek. *Leben des Orest*. Opera. Sections with dance rhythms.
Karol Rathaus. *Fremde Erde*. Opera. On-stage dance band.
Erwin Schulhoff. *H. M. S. Royal Oak*. Jazz concerto, for *Jazzsänger*, chorus, and symphonic jazz orchestra.

_____ . *Hot Sonate*. Saxophone and piano. Subtitled "Jazz-Sonate."
Ernst Toch. *Der Fächer*. Opera. Cabaret scene.
Kurt Weill. *Aufstieg und Fall der Stadt Mahagonny*. Epic opera. Various numbers borrowing from popular dances.
Jean Wiéner. *Cadences pour deux pianos*. Movement 1: "Jazz"; dedicated to Paul Whiteman.

1931

Paul Abraham. *Die Blume von Hawaii*. Operetta. Character Jim-boy is a jazz singer; work premiered in Leipzig.
Eugen d'Albert. *Blues*. Piano.
Edmund Nick. *Leben in dieser Zeit*. Chorus and orchestra. On texts by Erich Kästner; various dance tempi and rhythms.
Maurice Ravel. *Concerto pour la main gauche*. Piano and orchestra. Blue notes and syncopation present.
Franz Schreker. *Christophorus*. Opera. Contains nightclub scene with black performers playing ragtime, composed between 1924 and 1928.
Erwin Schulhoff. *Suite dansante en jazz*. Piano. "Stomp," "Strait," "Waltz," "Tango," "Slow," "Fox-Trot" movements.
Alexandre Tansmann. *Sonatine transatlantique*. Piano. "Fox-Trot," "Spiritual et Blues," "Charleston" movements

1932

Mario Castelnuovo-Tedesco. *Piano Sonata*. Composed in 1928; contains "Blues I" and "Blues II" sections in the second movement, as well as melodies marked "quasi saxofoni" and "quasi clarinetti."
Rio Gebhardt. *Dreisätzige Jazz-Suite*. Piano.
Wilhelm Grosz. *Zwölf kleine Negerlein*. Voice and piano. "Tango" and "Valse-Boston" tempi.
Gustav Holst. *Jazz-band Piece*.
Walther Neimann. *Tango nobile*. Piano.
Gabriel Pierné. *Divertissement sur un thème pastoral*. Orchestra. "Cortège-Blues" movement.
Maurice Ravel. *Concerto*. Piano and orchestra. Blue notes and syncopation present.
Erwin Schulhoff. *Flammen*. Opera. Uses orchestra and separate jazz band.
Kurt Wolf. *Jazz-Etude*. Piano.

1933

Marcel Poot. *Jazz Music*.

Additional Works
Publication Date or Premiere Date Unknown

Conrad Beck. *Tanzstücke*. Piano. "Boston," "Foxtrot" movements; ca. early 1920s.
Emil Burian. *Synkopische Etüden*. Piano.
Henri Cliquet-Pleyel. *Deux blues*. Piano. "Come Along" and "Far Away"; ca. 1920.
_____ . *Cinq tangos*. Piano. Ca. 1920.
Rio Gebhardt. *Concerto*. Piano and jazz orchestra.
Hanns Jelinek. *Musik in Jazz*, op. 6. For large orchestra. Ca. 1931.
_____ . *Rondo in Jazz*, op. 7. For large orchestra. Ca. 1931.

Kurt Kern. *Jazz Symphonie*.
Edmund Nick. *Boston-Intermezzo*. String orchestra. Ca. 1931.
Walther Niemann. *Der gelbe Tango*. Piano.
Jean Wiéner. *Franco-American Concerto*. Piano and strings. Ca. 1930.
S. A. Polovinkin. *Foxtrot*. Piano. Ca. 1928.
P. Wladigeroff. *Foxtrot*. Piano. Ca. 1928

American, 1915 to 1933

1915

John Alden Carpenter. *Piano Concertino*. Use of ragtime.
Henry F. Gilbert. *Dances in Ragtime Rhythm*.

1920

John Alden Carpenter. *Tango americaine*. Piano.

1921

John Alden Carpenter. *Krazy Kat*. Jazz pantomime. Includes a "Katnip Blues."
Aaron Copland. *Trois esquisses*. Juvenelia. Movement 3: "Jazzy."

1922

George Antheil. *Symphony 1*. Movements described in a letter to Mary Curtis Bok as "II. Vivo: alla
    Zingaresco, poi Ragtime," "IV. Ragtime: Faces: Ada (Spiritual)."
Henry F. Gilbert. *The Dance in Place Congo*.
George Gershwin. *Blue Monday Blues*. One-act jazz opera.

1923

George Antheil. *Jazz Sonata*. Piano.
Aaron Copland. *Two Pieces*. String quartet. Movement 2: "Rondino"; first performed in 1928.
Virgil Thomson. "Two Sentimental Tangos."

1924

Henry F. Gilbert. *Dance for Jazzband*.
Louis Gruenberg. *Daniel Jazz*. Voice and orchestra. Performed at 1925 I. S. C. M. in Venice.
John Alden Carpenter. *Skyscrapers*. Ballet.
George Gershwin. *Rhapsody in Blue*.
Edward Burlingame Hill. *Jazz Studies*. 2 pianos.

1925

George Antheil. *A Jazz Symphony*. Carnegie Hall performance with W. C. Handy and his band.
Aaron Copland. *Two Choruses*. Second chorus, "An Immorality," on a text by Ezra Pound.
————— . *Music for the Theater*.
Louis Gruenberg. *Jazz Masks*. Piano. Reworkings of melodies by Mendelssohn, Chopin, Rubinstein,
    Offenbach.

_____ . *Jazzberries*. Piano. "Fox-Trot," "Blues," "Waltz," "Syncopep" movements.
George Gershwin. *Concerto in F*. Piano and orchestra.
Leo Sowerby. *Monotony* and *Syncopation*. Written for Paul Whiteman's orchestra.

1926

John Alden Carpenter. *Jazz Orchestra Pieces*. Movement "A Little Bit of Jazz"; dedicated to Paul Whiteman.
Aaron Copland. *Two Pieces for Violin and Piano*. "Nocturne" and "Ukelele Serenade."
Louis Gruenberg. *Jazzettes*. Violin and piano.
_____ . *The Creation*. Chorus and orchestra.

1927

John Alden Carpenter. *4 Negro Songs*. Texts by Langston Hughes; includes the song "Jazz-Boys."

1928

Randall Thompson. *Jazz Poem*. Piano and orchestra.

1930

George Antheil. *Transatlantic*. Opera. Use of dance rhythms to characterize sections.
Hamilton Forrest. *Camille*. Opera. Updating of *La Traviata* with foxtrots and Charlestons.
William Grant Still. *Afro-American Symphony*. Second movement uses blue notes.

1932

Jerome Moross. *Those Everlasting Blues*. Cantata for voice and small orchestra. Text by A. Kreymborg; first performed in 1933.

1933

George Gershwin. *Second Rhapsody*. Piano and orchestra.
Louis Gruenberg. *Three Jazz Dances*.
_____ . *Emperor Jones*. Opera.

Additional Work
Publication Date or Premiere Date Unknown

Louis Gruenberg. *Jazz Suite*. Orchestra. "Foxtrot," "Boston," "Blues," "One-Step" movements; ca. 1925–26.

Appendix B

"Music of Today"

Address by Ernst Krenek, presented on 19 October 1925 to the Congress of Music Aesthetics in Karlsruhe. Reprinted in *25 Jahre neue Musik,* ed. Paul Stefan and Hans Heinsheimer (Vienna: Universal Edition, 1925): 43–59.*

One day in Switzerland, I went into a confectioners shop to get a few things. Since I needed matches and saw some lying out for sale on the counter, I asked the clerk to throw in a box along with everything else. I was convinced that I was bringing matches home with me. When I got home, I tried to use my newly acquired kindling devices. The first match didn't work, but that didn't shake my conviction that I had real matches. The second one broke off during striking. Such a thing often happens with matches, so I didn't give it another thought but went right on attempting to light a third, a fourth and even a fifth one. By that time, the uselessness of the matches appeared to exceed what one would normally expect, and I realized I would have to correct my belief that I was dealing with real matches. Through trial and error and reflection on my part, it became evident to me that these items were really candy in the shape of matches.

Why am I telling this anecdote? Just to point out to you how permanent our convictions really are. Based on my observations alone, I had this theory that there were matches in that box. Had I never opened the package, my theory would still be standing unassailed. However, one of life's necessities caused me to put my theory to the test in such a way that revealed the true nature of my would-be matches beyond any mere outward appearance. My theory was useless because my observations didn't agree with it. I had to come up with a new theory.

From these personal experiences, I would like to suggest two applications. The first one concerns my own theory, or—let me be more modest—my own tentative ideas that I will develop here. I myself am well aware of the relativity of these so-called insights and the theories derived from them. No theory has any

---

*This reprint translated with the help of Conrad Henderson.

value or meaning apart from a subjective one. Every assertion about the nature of things, no matter how objective it appears to be, is a production of the basic nature of the observer. Moreover, such assertions do not get their appearance of objectivity from any abstractly existing agreement with the so-called "facts." Rather they appear objective because the observer in question, as a representative of a general attitude of his time, finds himself in a special state of consensus with his contemporaries, whose similar attitude toward things he is able to articulate.

The second application of my experience with matches leads me into the realm of my rather sketchy views on music, which I will attempt to develop here. These views are concerned with the peculiar paralysis of academic music theory, which has shown itself in recent years to be more and more of an absurdity. Music theory, as a science, that is the study of harmony and counterpoint, can only be as descriptive as in the natural sciences. Whenever it begins to set up axioms about how things must be, it becomes grotesque, as botany would be if it tried to stipulate that blossoms with more than ten stamens should be outlawed and their existence denied, even if such a flower through some creative malice of God were suddenly to turn up. Music theory can only gather its information from the observation and analysis of existing works and then put them in order. However, its practitioners should never draw the conclusion that this system is incapable of expansion.

How then does music theory arrive at the pretension of being an obligatory rule book for yet-to-be-created works of art rather than a systematic description of existing music? It results from the double role of music theorists—that of being both scientific cataloguers and introductory teachers. Teaching, by its very nature, must set limits and requirements for students. This in no way implies, however, that the other side of music theory, the research end, should get bogged down in the same place. Academic music theory is derived from an aesthetic ideal which corresponds roughly to the developmental state of music at the time of Beethoven. Even then, however, elements of Schubert's music could no longer be easily classified. And the closer we come to the present the more comical become the stilted attempts at derivation perpetrated by harmonic theory. Indeed, they remind us of the epicycle theory that Ptolemy used to explain the orbits of the planets. In harmonic theory, we also have derivations of derivations, which lack any connecting elements or constructs, and whose formation no longer shows any trace of a natural process. Here and there, with considerable strain, some parts still fit. However, I believe that the retrograde planet which throws the whole system into total absurdity has already been knocking about for some time in the musical cosmos. Periodically, attempts are made to put music theory on a new footing. Still, I don't believe such attempts, though they may contain much that is new and correct, can lead to a satisfactory general concept as long as they continue to be derived from traditional ideas and precepts. A revolution that is continually out to prove its legitimacy is a contradiction in terms.

The necessities of an educational method alone will not suffice to explain such a striking phenomenon as music theory's bondage to a long-vanished stage of musical development. There must be a deeper reason. I will attempt to find an explanation for this in a parallel situation in which a large part of our public finds itself. If one considers the concert public of Central Europe, one finds the so-called regular concert subscriber, who wants to hear over and over classical music up to Brahms, but who is quite adverse to anything beyond that, in the vast majority. Can't one see in this a parallel phenomenon to the above-mentioned condition of music theory? I believe this parallel has already been noticed and a partial attempt has been made to establish a causal connection between the two. That semi-musical education produced by popular introductions, music guides and the like—all based on academic foundations, of course—was given as the reason for the paralysis of public taste. Although I can't come out strongly enough against this type of dilettantish education, which leads to the complete corruption of the public's aesthetic instincts and culture, it would be ascribing demonic powers to the writers of these well-meaning instructional guides if one were to hold them completely responsible for the public's bad taste. It is probably more of a case of these authors' writing in a tone that the public wants to hear rather than the other way around.

There must be some basic psychological fact at the root of all these phenomena. The phenomena themselves are only superficial forms that, while they do have some conditioning influence on each other, are actually subordinate to the following basic phenomenon: music in the nineteenth century is subject to an ever-intensifying movement towards isolation [*Individualisierung*].* It is clear that the music of old always and without much pressure turned to a natural community of listeners. In the oldest period—the Middle Ages—it was church music and thus had the community of believers as its natural public. This community later underwent all sorts of changes which are of no importance for our subject here, but even Bach's music still had its basically cohesive public within the protestant church.

In the second half of the eighteenth century, the community to which the music of the time was addressed clearly shifted out of the church and into secular society. Now the highly cultured and finely educated nobility became the societal group to which the music of the time was speaking. Shortly after that, there occurred another sharply dramatic shift in the relationship of music to the public. Beethoven became the first composer to address himself to an unlimited community of listeners. Viewed ideally, this music was intended for all mankind who live under democratic rule. However, with this step, Beethoven reached a

---

*Though "individualization" would seem to be a closer English translation of *Individualisierung*, what Krenek appears to be stressing here is not a move to a personal or individual art, but rather that art was becoming progressively isolated from its community, thereby possessing greater cultural autonomy.

stage of development that could neither be surmounted nor maintained. Beginning with Beethoven, music started to withdraw to an even narrower circle of listeners. Firstly during the romantic period, this trend manifested itself in a common bond of basic human feelings which both stimulated the creation of music in the composer and caused smaller or larger groups of similarly spirited listeners, who never existed before as a group, to form. Wagner made a conscious effort to enlarge his circle of listeners to the whole of the German nation. And it is actually this attempt to expand his influence that linked him inwardly to Beethoven and not so much the aesthetics of expression that he constructed and more or less artificially tried to project into Beethoven's music. Wagner's attempt had to fail because he set out from the premise of creating through art a nation that did not yet exist, whereas art must be created by a nation if it is to address itself to that nation.

Recent developments teach us that the inner line of evolution in music is leading to an even more narrowly limited circle of appreciators. Two kinds of attempts to keep the circle of appreciation large should not deceive us. The first attempt is that of stylistic imitation, as found in Brahms, and the other is the retention of the monumental apparatus, as in Bruckner and Mahler. The absolute music of the present, in contrast to the music of the romantic period, no longer addresses itself to those who share certain emotions, but rather to those who have reached the same stage of musical sophistication. It has become a game that is only interesting to those who know the rules. It has neither the capacity nor the inclination to address itself to the uninitiated community. It can even exist without participating players; that is, without providing the rules of performance or inviting similarly oriented persons to a performance. Taken to its conclusion, it becomes the self-gratification of an individual who sits in his studio and invents rules according to which he then writes down his notes. In transforming these notes by means of musical instruments into audible substance, none of this adherence to his rules will be passed on to the listeners unless they are prepared for it in the most exacting way. In fact, then, the very act of listening itself has become totally superfluous, since the artistic nature of these works will most likely only have an effect on those who read through them carefully after first having become knowledgeable about their rules of composition. Whoever does this can take delight in that state of perfection found in the masterful realization of an artistic form—a feeling not to be underestimated—something that I can best refer to as intellectual intoxication.

One proof that music has actually taken this route into the esoteric and solipsistic is the peculiar split between so-called "light" and "serious" music that has been developing since the second half of the nineteenth century. One can describe these two steadily diverging branches—leaving aside their content for the time being, but taking into account the psychological effect they produce—as either desirable or undesirable music, whereby it is naturally understood that the so-called light music is the desirable one. At first—I'm thinking here of Offenbach's time and the decades that immediately followed, say, up to about Johann Strauss—there existed, at least in substance, no fundamental difference between the two categories. From a purely musical standpoint, we can well imagine "Tristan chords" occurring as an expressive device in an operetta. Indeed, it occasionally happened that the techniques of serious music were enriched by some advancement in light music—the *sixte ajoutée* of the Viennese waltz comes to mind. Today, however, things are quite different. An operetta that uses the expressive devices of serious music would be a total absurdity. We must look for the cause of this development by considering the psychological effects of this music. At an earlier time, one and the same public attended on one day a serious opera, a symphony concert, or an evening of chamber music, and on the next day an operetta or some similar musical event. Today there are circles of the public, and they represent the overwhelming majority of concertgoers, who only attend operettas. The results of this can be seen in the striking change that the operetta has undergone since the time of its inception. Beginning as a purely lighthearted though sometimes satirical or parodistic art form, today it is pervaded with sentimentalism and false tragedy. The people who enjoy operettas today use this one genre to meet both their need for spiritual uplift on the lighter side and their need for an emotional catharsis on the serious side, whereas before, there existed a homogeneous public that allowed itself to be moved one evening by a serious piece and then, as a counterbalance, entertained the next night by the lighter touch of an operetta.

With that we come to an important difference that I would like to discuss. The art of the past was always a functional art. Church music was never considered an end in itself, but was composed with an eye toward its usefulness in fulfilling its religious function. The primary matter was not the will or the urge of the composer to create artistic entities, but rather the public's need for such works.

Church music arose out of the compelling demands of the community of believers. To what overwhelming greatness this music developed, if we consider it from a purely artistic point of view separated from its purpose, need not be delineated further. But it is clear that at the time, the aesthetic element of music did not play the role it does today. I believe that from our vantage point we cannot even call the thinking of that time "aesthetics." We have instead technical discussion by people for whom the justification, scope, contents, and form of their activity did not present the slightest problem, who had their secure place in the world, and who at most were able to reach a consensus about how best to achieve the goals of their craft, and are therefore merely discussing their trade.

Also during the later era, which I designated earlier as that of the educated nobility, music was also a functional art. The function of music at that time was the diversion of a genteel society—a much more pedestrian function than earlier to be sure—but nonetheless, a function. Already the individual creative will of the composer had begun to play a greater role, since the circle of interested persons was smaller and their needs were not so demanding. In spite of that, however, we see the composer bowing willingly to the wishes of his public; he had become a court employee of a music-loving prince.

But even this period came to an end, superseded by that of the bourgeoisie during the French Revolution. This new period basically no longer needed art. People who are oppressed or have only recently been freed from oppression no longer have any use for entertainment in the form of refined "divertissement." And for the community of the liberated, a need for expression analogous to that of the community of believers existed only in a fictive sense, as we can see from the history of the nineteenth century. Nevertheless, the ideology of the democratic revolution, which certainly hung in the air at the time, brought forth a Beethoven. And he became the standard-bearer for an imaginary multitude, in contrast to the artists of previous times who were exponents of an actual community. Beethoven was addressing a public that did not yet exist and wouldn't come into existence until the turn of the century. Nonetheless, this fiction carried him forward and helped his music achieve that strong rallying power that continues to be effective even to this day, though the public submits to it now only out of force of habit.

But what does the public, that is, the most recent faction to make fictive demands on music, want now? The answer will perhaps be somewhat frightening: none other than dance music. The bourgeoisie, long secure in its democratic achievements, demands from art only entertainment in the form of dance music. However, any sort of guiding principle that would guarantee the expression of music in a way demanded by, and thus capable of being understood by, society as a whole is completely lacking. The artists produced by this latest faction are only treating individual specialized problems that are uninteresting because they merely interest but do not move us. They are psychologically isolated cases. Let us consider the situation from a completely objective standpoint by posing the question: which type of music would people demand first if all composers were to go on strike? One would have to admit that a strike, say, of chamber music composers would only provide material for the joke page of a popular dance music journal. A strike of the producers of popular dance music is not just something I thought up—it actually happened in America, and if I am informed correctly, it resulted in the complete success of the striking composers because the general public was unwilling to go without dance music for a longer period of time.*

This brings me to a remarkable, though purely superficial, parallel between modern dance music and old church music. The products of both are intended to

---

*There appears to be no factual basis for Krenek's American anecdote.

be purely ephemeral items of the day. The composers of older church music were contractually obligated to turn out a new cantata every Sunday, whose further destiny was of little concern to either subscriber or composer. If it was particularly well liked, that is, if it fulfilled its purpose in an extraordinary way, it might be repeated a time or two. However, the desire to create in every musical piece something of lasting value, which today can be observed in even the lowliest scribbler, was completely absent in those healthier times. This is because the composers then knew they could draw upon an inexhaustible source of creative power and didn't feel the urgent need, as we do now, to preserve philologically even the most insignificant scrap of cultural material. I don't need to carry the parallel any further. Modern dances are created at a particular time for that time, and their immortality doesn't bother the consumers at all, and the composers are only concerned with this aspect from a pecuniary standpoint at best. The lifespan of the product is in direct proportion to its usefulness. We can object that dance music of today is a *genre honteux,* a sad and shameful phenomenon, which unfortunately exists but which has nothing to do with music and *true* art. It doesn't do us any good, however, to close our eyes to a phenomenon of the times. Though the enormous and incomparable success of this music may appear to us to be a symptom of decline and decay, we still can't blame the composers as if they were Beelzebub's emissaries sent to poison the world with their filth. No one can get around the fact that the existence or nonexistence of symphonies is of absolutely no consequence to the members of today's bourgeoisie. On the other hand, if the output of dance music were to cease for some reason, they would demand, through their newspapers or in some other way, the immediate resumption of its production.

The next obvious step is to consider the potentialities of the proletariat, a class that finds itself in approximately the same place the bourgeoisie did 130 years ago. Without becoming overly speculative, we can see from the facts that this class has yet to produce an artist who can give it the kind of art it wants. Furthermore, it isn't difficult to extrapolate from this that the proletariat has yet to demand any new kind of art at all. All the needs of any social group are capable of being met within the group itself, if such needs really exist. The proletariat has not advanced enough yet to desire its own art, only to understand it. This situation will last as long as the proletariat is not class-conscious in the most fundamental and purest sense, that is, as long as it strives to assimilate the accomplishments of the bourgeoisie rather than produce its own culture. Until that happens, the worker will be happy to listen to Beethoven's works, as long as his organization provides the opportunity and foots the bill. Indeed to a certain extent, he will even let himself be caught up in the previously mentioned suggestive power of this art, which was actually written for the benefit of another social group. Left to his own devices, the worker would take his hard-earned money to the operetta theater in order to experience the fulfillment of his fantasies, namely, to see finely dressed ladies and gentlemen, counts and countesses, parading on stage, and to hear them expressing themselves in a musical language that is unfortunately all too understandable to him. From that day on, when the accomplishments or achievements of the bourgeoisie no longer seem worth striving for and have become uninteresting and irrelevant to the worker, we can begin to hope for a new art that the proletariat will create simply because it wants such an art. Perhaps someone will come along then and give a new sense and shape to the ancient order of things—that the trees are green and the eternal mountains white. Such possibilities have been lost to us; we must be clear about this or we will end up living in a fantasy realm.

Perhaps all this sounds very bleak. I find today, however, that we shouldn't spend our time looking for consolation and trying to preserve by hook or crook a situation based on completely false premises. The only thing one can say as a consolation is that this condition exists in such a radical state only in Central Europe. In France, there is still a certain kind of rapport between the music maker and his public. There are fairly large circles in Paris who still have a real need to hear contemporary music now and then, chiefly in the theater to be sure. The reason for this state of affairs lies in the fact that France still retains the last vestige of a homogeneous public, which I characterized earlier when differentiating light and serious music. This means that the receptive capability of this relatively large audience is on a higher level than that found in the Central European public of the same size. On the other hand, the production of the French artist is instinctively geared to this same level, which by our standards seems superficial and shallow. Whatever you may think of this, I am only interested in demonstrating that a relationship exists between the production of this music and the needs of the audience. No matter what objections one may raise against it, it has certain vital charm that is generally lacking in the products of Central European studio intellectuality.

As I conclude my thoughts here, one question seems to arise; *should* we continue to create art, and if so, what kind of art *should* it be? When it comes right down to it, art doesn't *have* to exist at all; at any rate, it doesn't *have* to exist in any certain way. It either exists or it doesn't. The question about "what should be" in regard to art is, in my view, the very core of aesthetics. However, at the very moment this question arises, a dangerous lesion simultaneously appears on the living organism of art. It represents a weakening, perhaps even to the incipient decay of art itself. In spite of all this, the artist has no choice in the matter, even if he is clearly aware of living in a time of decadence. Knowledge about what is going on in no way obligates one to act in any certain way. The only thing that is compelling is feeling and belief. Nonetheless, we can discuss what possibilities still exist for at least a limited expansion of music. I am of the opinion that the strongest possibilities in this direction lie in the realm of the theater. The theater is still up to a certain point a vital necessity for a large number of the public. When the curtain goes up in the theater, we still see the formation of that communal body which is an essential part of any community, i.e., a functional work of art. I would like to take the opportunity here to elaborate on several ideas that I touched on in a small article entitled "On the Problem of Opera," which appeared in the 1925 yearbook *Von neuer Musik,* published by the Verlag Marcan in Cologne.* There I attempted to delineate my views on what I considered to be the proper subject matter for an opera, and in so doing, I put the main emphasis on the inner adherence to musical rules [*Gesetzmässigkeit*] and the musically correct completion of the score in an aesthetic sense. Seen from the perspective of my present discussion, I was still approaching this subject from the point of view of a Central European.

The result was that the subject matter of the opera as such became largely insignificant. As a result of my present investigation, however, I must modify my findings to the extent that I have posited the necessity for a musical work to have a psychological impact as well as inner musical correctness. It is clear too that isolated psychological events cannot be effective in forming a cohesive social body. Drama is not an art form that has to be automatically interesting because of milieu, costuming, a special method of exposition, or some unusual turn of the plot. Consider, for example, the ancient Greek tragedies where it was assumed that the basic story line was already well known to the great mass of the audience. Or take Shakespeare, who sometimes dramatized well-known material or sought to remove any tension or curiosity on the part of the spectator by using prologues or sometimes even crude means to let the audience know what was coming. To a far higher degree, the same requirements also applied to the opera, where for purely practical reasons every complication of the story must be avoided because even the slightest deviation from a simple linear plot will render the opera unintelligible when sung. In drama in general, and particularly opera, *how* something is portrayed is more important than *what* is portrayed. And therein lies the problem of opera today: the need to locate the basic premises [*Selbstverständlichkeiten*] of our time. As far as the material itself is concerned, it is a matter of finding that all-encompassing circle of character types, facts, situations, and data that we can sagely assume will be well known and interesting to the greatest number of our contemporaries. The musical expression of this kind of material must be kept as simple as possible if it is to be effective. Characteristically, the above-mentioned move towards isolation experienced by music in the nineteenth century made an ever-increasing use of chromaticism in the musical material. It is quite fitting that this process of isolation manifested itself in a search or a new means of expression. Since these composers wanted to create extraordinary works in the first place, it is easy to see how their instincts

---

*Ernst Krenek, "Zum Problem der Oper," in *Von neuer Musik,* eds. H. Grues, E. Kruttge, and E. Thalheimer (Cologne: F. J. Marcan, 1925): 39–42.

drove them to extraordinary means to do it. Thus we see a continuing individualization of the chromatic scale in a way that runs parallel to the dismembering of the old community-oriented creative process for the sake of a society that is itself disintegrating more and more. Whoever doesn't find this situation extraordinary enough will split up these scales even further in order to give adequate expression to his own special psychology by means of fractions of half-steps. And whereas I indicated before that the artist who wants to create for a new society will have to perceive and reformulate anew the old eternal verities and the obvious truths, I would like to add that I believe the artist will also have to rediscover perceptually and reshape the universal means of musical expression to one which all are capable of understanding. The style of this music will be determined by the way in which this new perception and reshaping of the musical material takes place. Essentially it will be a matter of reexperiencing the relationship between the tonic and the dominant within the diatonic scale. That this relationship still represents a viable aspect of music can be seen now and then in individual cases that are the exceptions in the field of contemporary music. I am thinking here, for example, of the Czech Janeček who, without actually using the typical devices of "modern" music, still manages to seem absolutely new and original. He is only one example of a whole series of composers whose work is rooted in the national folksong. They have it easier than we Central Europeans, who, in this respect, are left hanging in the air. The folksong is an inexhaustible source of power for those who are able to find roots in it thanks to favorable circumstances within their various countries. We lack this source, however, and we must attempt to arrive at a new perception of the old truths on our own through our own experience.

Perhaps we will find a cue for this in the inclination of nationally rooted composers toward the folksong, for it is no accident that these artists in particular have developed out of the rediscovered simplicity of the folksong. The human voice, which is the basis of this art form, as well as the creator and prime mover of everything that happens musically, should occupy our attention in a much more intense and profound way. The voice unites within itself two things: first, the constancy and immutability of the musical elements, and secondly, the inexhaustible potential for individual expression as the purest and most personal organ of the perceiving human being. This also brings us back to the theater, that multiplicity, organized and bound into a single dramatic unit encompassing the profusion of human voices which represents the whole gamut of individual expression. And to the extent that the age-old inner laws of this material seem to require it, the simplicity in expression and composition that I referred to earlier will come naturally in an organic and unartificial way, without looking backward, but occurring spontaneously. In this regard, I would especially like to call to mind the relativity of our ideas that I mentioned at the outset. A creative artist's views about musical style can only be a product of his state of development at the present, but this is an underground stream, and he himself is the least clear about which direction it will take.

I would like to formulate one last thought at the end of these musings, and that is that art is not as important as we would all like to believe. Whoever places art at the beginning of his credo will, in my modest opinion, get nowhere. *Vivere necesse est, artem facere non,* is what I say. We want to live, look life in the face and say yes to it with a passionate heart. Then we will suddenly have art and not know how it happened. It should never serve to express our lack of this thing or that, but should always flow out of the abundance of life; then it will be right and above all our muddlings.

Appendix C

Synopses of Opera Plots

Ernst Krenek: *Der Sprung über den Schatten*

Libretto by Ernst Krenek, synopsis adapted from Wolfgang Rogge, *Ernst Kreneks Opern* (Wolfenbüttel: Möseler Verlag, 1970), 16–17.

Act I

The private detective Marcus, a specialist in uncovering cases of adultery, receives an assignment over the telephone from Prince Kuno to track Kuno's wife, Princess Leonore. The prince suspects Dr. Berg, at whose séances the princess has been a frequent participant, of being his wife's lover. Dr. Berg, Marcus's friend, who has eavesdropped on the conversation, offers to play the role of detective so as to be nearer Princess Leonore. However, Laurenz Goldhaar, a "blocked," inhibited poet, is also attracted to Princess Leonore, and she returns his feelings.

A séance takes place at Dr. Berg's. The princess cannot decide whether she should attend a masked ball that evening, where she expects to find the poet Goldhaar. Hypnotically, Dr. Berg encourages her to leap over her shadow and to attend the party.

The party begins with an agitated chorus number. They sing of a Negro boy "in the free land of America." Leonore discovers Goldhaar in disguise, but avoids giving away her own disguise. The unsuspecting Goldhaar searches further for his lover. Prince Kuno, likewise deceived, dances with Odette, who urges him on as he resists the enchanting rhythms of the jazz dance music. The maid, Blandine, attempts to rendezvous with Dr. Berg, whom she has mistaken for the poet Goldhaar. Leonore prevents the disclosure of Goldhaar's true identity. Blandine arranges a meeting at midnight at the back door of the palace with Goldhaar, the presumed Dr. Berg. The signal: a small rose.

Act II

Prince Kuno comes home from the dance exhausted. Secretly informed by his supposed detective, Dr. Berg, that his wife was also at the party, he regrets not having looked for the suspicious Dr. Berg. Blandine then confides to the supposed detective her love for the unknown Dr. Berg. Dr. Berg continues to play his dual role. Blandine asks Berg to get the hypnotist and arrange for a palace séance. Prince Kuno, who has overheard the conversation, orders the detective to catch the hypnotist in the act. As Goldhaar appears at the back door, already regretting his "shadow-leap," he is persuaded to come inside the castle. The darkness of the hypnotic séance results in a further mix-up; Goldhaar is arrested by the palace guards as the suspected hypnotist.

Act III

In prison, Goldhaar laments his fate, but Leonore comes to comfort him. In a scene of courtroom parody, the disguised Dr. Berg now takes on the role of the lawyer. As the trial concludes, Dr. Berg summons the true private detective as the last witness and asks for his advice. Marcus suggests that the royal couple get a divorce. Only this solution can prevent both scandal and the impending revolution of their subjects. But such is not the case. The people still revolt.

The divorce proceedings take place. In the meantime, the prince and Odette meet, and Leonore goes to her poet Goldhaar, who is still in jail. To give himself one last chance of winning Leonore's affection, Dr. Berg proclaims the kingdom a republic. But he soon finds out that Leonore has already run off with the poet Goldhaar.

As *deus ex machina,* Marcus, the real detective, comes to the rescue. The dual role of Dr. Berg is revealed, and he is proclaimed president by the people. Marcus then gives the moral of the story: "You see, they no sooner think they have carried out the leap, than the old shadow reappears." All the parties bring the opera to a close with a big dance in which they try in vain to leap over their shadows.

Ernst Krenek: *Jonny spielt auf*

Libretto by Ernst Krenek, synopsis translated from that printed in the original Leipzig program found in the collection of the Museum für Geschichte der Stadt Leipzig.

Scene 1

While up in the mountains on a narrow rock plateau above a glacier, the composer Max and the singer Anita meet. He is a completely internalized, unworldly man, full of love for nature and its wonders. Max has come this way so as to be alone with the mountains and his splendid glacier. She has not come looking for such sights; rather she has lost her way and is overcome with a tormenting fear of isolation in this mountainous world. She is looking for someone to take her back to humanity, to the scene of her artistic triumph. She is doubly happy, therefore, to meet the composer, whom she has not met but in whose opera she has already sung the title role. He attempts to make the mountains and glaciers appealing to her, but she wants to leave, begging him to come with her.

Scene 2

Max and Anita, after their meeting in the mountains, have fallen in love and are living together in Anita's artistic abode. She is now getting ready to leave for Paris to sing the lead role in one of his operas. This separation pains him. He is, as he exclaims, "jealous of my own child," for which she must leave him. During the emotional departure, he gives her the manuscript of another opera, and she runs through the important second act aria with him. Her manager then appears to take her to the train station. Max then implores her to renounce all fame and to live alone with him, existing only on their love, but she presses forth. Anita takes her banjo, which she needs for her role, off the piano and hastens away.

Scene 3: In Paris

Anita is staying in a modern hotel. The stage shows a part of the corridor with the entrance to Anita's room. Nearby is the room of the famous violinist Daniello, who is to give a concert that evening. The sound of a jazz band, whose leader is the famous Negro Jonny, drifts up from the hotel lounge. The maid Yvonne is busy straightening up Daniello's room. During an intermission, Jonny rushes up to see her, and they exchange caresses. He changes his lovers as often as he changes the hotel in which he plays. Daniello comes back from the concert, surrounded by a troop of admirers who seek his autograph. He carries his violin into the room and disappears into the restaurant with his adoring fans. Anita also returns to the hotel following the end of the opera. She has scored another success, but she wants nothing to do with her enthusiastic public. She longs for her home and her beloved. A hastily prepared telegram will notify him of her early arrival. A hotel bellhop takes over relaying the message, while Anita goes to the restaurant to have a meal before her departure.

On the way she runs into Jonny. He has been observing her admiringly during the last scene and suggests—in a blunt and obvious manner—that he should be her companion for the rest of the evening. The violinist Daniello, returning from the restaurant, finds Anita in this difficult situation. He chases the Negro away, but gives him a thousand franc bill as a "consolation," and then accompanies Anita into the restaurant. Yvonne reproaches Jonny for his infidelity, and they separate expressing their disgust for one another. Daniello returns from the restaurant with Anita. His fulsome speech has flustered the hot-blooded artist. She's forgotten her beloved waiting at home and puts up no resistance as Daniello leads her into her room. Jonny comes sneaking up the stairs. He listens at Anita's door and makes sure that both of them are in the room. Quickly his decision is made; Daniello took the woman from him, so he will take the costly violin from Daniello. He enters the violinist's room, takes the instrument out of its case and hides it in the banjo case which hangs on the door of Anita's room. He plans to follow Anita home and steal the violin out of her house.

Scene 4

The hotel is in an uproar! The maid Yvonne is upset over her break-up with Jonny and argues with the hotel manager, who is in turn upset that Anita's room is not yet vacated. Anita gets ready to leave and bids farewell to Daniello. She tells him of her beloved at home, thereby depriving him of any hope for a repetition of the previous night. The violinist thinks he can stop her if he plays something for her on his costly violin. Thus he discovers the robbery. He accuses the entire hotel. Yvonne is fired by the hotel manager, but is then engaged by Anita to accompany her on the trip. Daniello, who with one stroke has lost both his beloved from the previous night and his violin, plots revenge. He gives the ring which Anita gave him as a remembrance to Yvonne with the instructions to give it to Anita's beloved with his greetings. During all this Jonny appears, informs the distraught hotel manager of his resignation as jazz band leader and leaves the hotel. Anita and her manager, who has arranged an especially good tour of America for her, follow suit.

Part 2. Scene 5: Max in Anticipation [in Erwartung]
of the Homecoming of His Beloved

A telegram has announced her impending arrival. He arranges flowers in the room and impatiently counts the minutes until her return. The arrival time of the train from Paris passes. Anita has not returned.

Scene 6: The Next Morning

Max wakes up, having dozed overnight in the armchair. Anita returns to this somewhat tense, strained atmosphere. She answers all his questions absent-mindedly and finally withdraws to her room. Yvonne comes in with her new mistress's luggage. She waits until she and Max are alone, then she gives him Daniello's ring. Max realizes what has taken place and storms out. "Away from her. Back to you, my glacier." Through the window comes Jonny, who has followed Anita home. He spots the violin lying on the piano in the banjo case and takes it. He puts Yvonne off and then leaves the same way he came. Anita comes in and learns that Max has run off after Yvonne gave him Daniello's ring. Anita recognizes the ring as the present she gave earlier to Daniello. She knows now that tragedy has struck.

Scene 7

Max, deeply injured, has withdrawn to the mountains, to the isolation of the glacial world. The glacier itself begins to speak and sends him back to the land of the living. Suddenly Anita's voice rings out from a loudspeaker situated on the terrace of a nearby mountain hotel. She is singing the aria that she practiced with Max just before her trip to Paris. Overcome by this experience, Max rushes away—back to the land of the living, back to find his beloved. After Anita's performance, a jazz band comes on the radio: Jonny strikes up the band! All the hotel guests are inspired by his playing. Out of the hotel comes Daniello. He recognizes the sound of his violin and now knows who stole the instrument from him. He sets off in pursuit of the thief.

Scene 8

Jonny has the violin, and, hounded by his pursuer, is on the way to the train station. Three policemen are right behind him. They almost think they've lost his trail. Then one of them finds a ticket to Amsterdam. Thus the chase is on, to the railroad station!

Scene 9: On the Platform

Max appears for his rendezvous with Anita, who will take him with her on her American tour. Jonny arrives. Still pursued by the police, he decides to abandon the violin and puts it on top of Max's luggage. The police discover it there and arrest Max. When Anita appears in search of Max, he has already been taken into custody at the railroad station. Daniello tries to make Anita believe that Max, out of jealousy, stole the violin and has now been arrested. Anita begs Yvonne to go to the police and testify to Max's innocence. Daniello tries to stop her. The two struggle. Yvonne pushes Daniello off the platform, onto the tracks, and in front of the oncoming train.

Scene 10

At the outside entrance of the train station, a police car waits for the arrested man. Yvonne spots Jonny, who is making his last attempt to get the violin. She tells him quickly what has transpired, that Max is her new mistress's beloved, and she implores Jonny to save him. Jonny knocks out the driver and puts on his police uniform. The police appear with Max to take him to jail. Jonny, in the driver's seat, takes off. Max, in his despair, cries out "to the train station." To the amazement of the accompanying guards, the driver turns back. Jonny silences the two policemen.

Scene 11

Max arrives just in time for the train to Amsterdam and jumps for the departing train where Anita, Yvonne, and the manager wait. Jonny appears larger than life on the railroad clock. The new world has conquered the old, and the whole world pays homage to Jonny, the black jazz band king!

Ernst Krenek: Three One-Act Operas

Libretti by Ernst Krenek, synopses adapted from Ernst Krenek, "Meine Drei Einakter," *Anbruch* 10 (May 1928): 158–61.

Der Diktator

The hero, the dictator of a country at war, is recuperating at a sanitarium along with his wife. He has become infatuated with the lovely wife of one of his officers. This officer, staying at the same sanitarium, was blinded in the war. The officer's wife decides to kill the dictator to avenge her husband's accident. The dictator's wife, overcome with a sense of foreboding, hides in his office, where he has an audience with the assassin. His wife is at first appalled, and then becomes the indignant witness of a scene in which the dictator, through his simple, suggestive power, forces the desired wife of another to lay down her revolver and give it to him. He then utters scornful words about his own wife, causing her, out of jealousy, to threaten him with another revolver. The now converted former assassin throws herself in front of the dictator and takes the bullet meant for him. The dictator gives an official account of this "suicide" of an unknown woman. The motive: unhappy love. The blind officer, having heard the shot and believing that the act of revenge has taken place, gropes about in the room. Still unsuspecting, he steps in front of the corpse of his wife and screams "Maria, where are you. I am afraid."

Das geheime Königreich

Das geheime Königreich takes place in a fairy-tale land and concerns the story of a good, but weak, king, who doesn't know how to wield the inherent power of his crown over his rebellious subjects. The covetous and ambitious queen, on the contrary, has only two desires: the crown and a handsome, strong man. The latter she has found in the captured rebel leader. The crown she hopes to take from the jester, to whom the despairing king has given it for safekeeping during the last attack on the castle by the rebels. She conspires, through seduction, wine, and card tricks to obtain possession of the crown and to free her beloved rebel from the royal dungeon. However, the rebel doesn't use his freedom to be with her, but rather to storm the palace with his comrades and to lead a siege against the poor king. The queen flees with the crown. Her ladies-in-waiting disguise the king in the jester's clothes. The rebel pursues the queen to get the crown. In a nearby wood, he finds her and threatens her with death. In desperation, she tries to confuse him by undressing. Dazzled by her beauty, he rushes at her—but a mighty power transforms her into a tree to punish her for her sins. The rebel is horrified. The pursued king enters in the jester's costume. Two drunk revolutionaries ask the alleged fool where the king is, and whether they would earn a reward for his death. The real jester arrives, without his usual dress, and observes the action. The king, his noble feelings taking effect, identifies himself to the rebels and asks to die as a sacrifice for his people. The two drunks take this for great wit and leave in laughter to search for the "real" king, teased and pushed on by the real fool. The king, in desperation, decides to hang himself from the tree into which the queen was transformed. She begins to talk to him, and, as if in a dream, he understands what the tree says. He begins to understand that the outward symbols of power do not give life; rather, resignation and inner superiority do. Here, in the beautiful, quiet wood, he will stay and live with the stars, trees, and animals. He will contemplate the wonder of God, which he never found in the confusing activity of his rule, in the microcosm of a flower. A longed-for peace envelopes him, and he lies down at the foot of the magic tree to sleep. The fool enters, puts his old clothes on the sleeping figure who has now found his true kingdom, and hangs the crown on a branch of the tree. The wood sings a lullabye.

Schwergewicht, oder die Ehre der Nation

The master boxer, Adam Ochsenschwanz [oxtail] is deceived, through time-honored means, by his wife and her shrewd dance instructor. A number of drastic events, in imitation of well-worn operatic disguise manouvers, take place. In order to more fully contrast the outward regard for the he-man and his true inner worth, an ambassador, acting on behalf of the country hosting the next olympiad, appears to negotiate the hero's contract. In vain the ambassador asks Ochsenschwanz to put down his training equipment so they can have a private consultation. Ochsenschwanz can't spare a minute of his precious training—he must become "the pride of the nation."

Kurt Weill: *Royal Palace*

Libretto by Ivan Goll, synopsis adapted from Karl Westermeyer, "Berlin. Kurt Weill: *Royal Palace,*" *Rheinische Musik- und Theater-Zeitung* 28 (1927): 108–10.

The action takes place in the present and is set on the terrace of the luxury hotel Royal Palace, on the shore of an Italian mountain lake. Dejanira, the heroine, is sick and tired of the grandeur of her life supplied by her rich "Husband." He promises her even more (depicted in a film sequence: The Rich Continent). The "Beloved of Yesterday" makes an appeal to her memories and paints her a picture of the auspicious "Heavens of our Nights" (ballet: Dance of Passion). The "Beloved of Tomorrow" lastly offers Dejanira "The World of Fantasy" (ballet and revue scene). Ultimately, they only want to possess her. She heeds the enticing call of the water women to pass into the unknown land of death.

Kurt Weill: *Der Zar lässt sich photographieren*

Libretto by Georg Kaiser, synopsis based on the one which Weill sent Universal Edition on 4 April 1927.*

Setting: The Angèle Studio of Photography in Paris

The telephone rings. The boy answers it, becomes alarmed and calls the assistant. He comes, talks into the phone, is alarmed and calls out agitatedly. Angèle enters, listens in on the call, and learns that a czar from XXX, on a short stay in Paris, will come to her, the beautiful Madame Angèle, to be photographed. A major flurry of activity ensues; the studio is straightened up, the equipment readied, Angèle pretties herself. The doorbell rings. The boy opens it ceremoniously. A group of men push their way in, led by a commander. The beautiful Frau Angèle, the assistant, and the boy are captured. A woman takes

---

*Though this copy of the synopsis is in Weill's hand, the style, with its clipped sentences and occasional obscure telling of events, suggests Kaiser's manner. It may well have been one synopsis that Kaiser supplied to Weill for his use or even the first version of the plot the two concocted. I have tried to maintain the flavor of the original.

Angèle's scarf, a man takes the assistant's jacket, and a young man the boy's smock. Angèle learns of the assassination plot: a pistol will be hidden in the camera which can be activated by the shutter's rubber ball. Angèle, despairing, is hidden in the next room. The woman [false Angèle] remains behind with the false assistant and false boy. The doorbell rings. The czar, elegant, distinguished, and bold, enters and dismisses his attendants in order to be alone with the beautiful woman. He perceives only himself and the pictures standing guard. She thinks fanatically only of her task. Finally he sits in the chair. She aims the camera directly at his heart, takes the rubber ball in her hand and counts: 1 . . . 2 . . . The czar jumps up—it will be nice to be photographed, but first she should come over there as he wants to take her picture. She resists, he forces her into the chair, takes the rubber ball. At the last second, the false assistant comes to her rescue. The czar throws him out and tries again to take the snapshot. The false boy disrupts him and runs off. [In actuality, the false Angèle extricates herself from the hazardous situation with no help from her fellow conspirators.] He has fallen in love with her, but she must continue with the assassination plot. Then an announcement from outside: the Paris police have learned that an assassination of the czar has been planned, and soon they will arrive to protect him. The czar is upset that someone wants to disrupt his little affair of the heart. She must shoot him now at any cost. He sits in the chair, she grabs the rubber ball, he jumps up, tries to kiss her, and forces her into the chair. She pretends to submit to his desire, they become passionate. Suddenly the doorbell rings, and knocking comes from all sides—the police have arrived. Flight alone remains for her now. The czar lies buried beneath cushions on the couch. She tells him he should wait a bit while she undresses. He waits under the cushions. The knocking gets louder. The assassins flee from the next room over the rooftop. The real Angèle is upset—if the police find the pistol, she will be ruined. She depresses the rubber ball, and the shot goes off. The assistant puts the camera away and brings out a new one. The boy opens the door to the police, and the czar comes out from under the cushions. He is bewildered and cannot figure anything out. "A Shot?" "No!" "It smells of gunpowder?" "No, only magnesium." The camera is set, the czar sits in the chair, the policemen salute, Angèle is in place—the czar has his picture taken. The End.

Paul Hindemith: *Hin und zurück*

Libretto by Marcellus Schiffer after his own revue, *Hetärengespräche*. Synopsis taken from Marc Blitzstein, *"Hin und Zurück* in Philadelphia, " *Modern Music* 5 (May–June 1928): 34–36.

The play opens with a sneeze from an old deaf aunt who sits knitting. In the incredibly short time of four minutes the entire first section has taken place: Hélène has her morning coffee, greets Robert, her husband, who presents her with a birthday gift; a letter is brought in which is discovered to be from her lover; Robert draws a cap-pistol, shoots her on the spot; a doctor and attendant enter—too late—carry her off; Robert in despair throws himself out the window. The lights go out; a wise man appears who pedantically explains the silliness of the situation and announces a reversal of the plot as proof that it makes as much sense backwards as forwards. The lights go on, Robert jumps back through the window, Hélène is carried on the stage, and the play unravels itself back to the starting point. The curtain lowers itself upon a final sneeze from the old aunt.

Paul Hindemith: *Neues vom Tage*

Libretto by Marcellus Schiffer, synopsis translated from Franz Willms, *"Neues vom Tage:* Zu Hindemiths lustiger Oper," *Blätter der Staatsoper* 9 (June 1929): 5–9.

After a short introductory orchestral overture, the opera begins in the midst of a quarrel between the married couple Laura and Eduard. Cups and plates are being smashed. Divorce becomes the saving word. A newly married couple, Herr and Frau M, make their entrance. They also want to get divorced; a quartet in a foxtrot style concludes the first scene. At the register's office, scene 2, the two couples meet again. Herr and Frau M are recently divorced. Laura and Eduard must still attend to the necessary papers. After much to and fro the business ends unsuccessfully with a dispute between the bureaucrat and Eduard. To help with dispatching the necessary formalities, Herr and Frau M recommend the Office of Family Affairs G.m.b.H., which, with its head, the handsome Herr Hermann, is shown in scene 3. A chorus of typists frames Herr Hermann's aria. His heart regularly goes out to the lovely clients he serves. Near the famous statue of *Venus di Milo* at the museum, scene 4, Laura waits at the agreed upon time for the man who will provide her with the necessary grounds for her divorce. The handsome Herr Hermann undertakes this business himself and arranges a love scene with Laura. Eduard comes in, but he takes the scene to be in earnest, flies into a rage, and finally throws the priceless statue of *Venus* at the fleeing pair. With that, the first act ends.

While Laura, in an aria, praises the advantages of the warm water supply in the bathroom of the Hotel Savoy, scene 5, Herr Hermann enters. Laura shows him the door, but he will not leave and explains to her that he—against his better business sense—has truly fallen in love with her. Frau M, who after her divorce has become Herr Hermann's lover, comes in. She first preaches to her unfaithful lover, whose explanation she sees right through. With a vengeance coming from her rage towards her rival, she calls together all the hotel personnel: the scandal is made known. A large chorus ensemble, on the text "how awful, how awful," closes the scene. The following scene, 6, shows, simultaneously, Laura in a hotel room and Eduard in a jail cell. Each one finds out from a newspaper what the other has been up to. Indignation and anger dissipate into calm confidence that now nothing more stands in the way of their divorce. Eduard, discharged from the jail, scene 7, enumerates in a legalistic "catalog aria" the fines which he must pay. His situation is in doubt. Then the handsome Herr Hermann appears like a tempter and offers Eduard the necessary money for the divorce. For a while Eduard suppresses his growing anger towards this rival, who now has his eye on his wife, but when the rejected helper presents him with the bill, Eduard throws him out. The rescue comes from elsewhere: six managers rush in excitedly and try to engage Eduard. His divorce process is the sensation of the day—and is worth exploiting. Gigantic sums are promised; Eduard shakes on it. A triumphal march crowns this seven-person finale.

The beginning of the third act starts back at the Office for Family Affairs, scene 8. The typists are again at their machines, but their boss, the handsome Herr Hermann, has changed as a result of what has occurred. He vows to live from now on only for his business and to keep his heart out of it. In the meantime, Herr and Frau M have found one another again. Returning from their second honeymoon, they meet Eduard and Laura in the foyer of the Alkazar variety theater, scene 9, where Eduard and Laura have been engaged. Frau and Herr M will watch the not-yet-divorced couple. The dividing curtain is raised and allows a view of the sold-out house and open stage, scene 10. After one cabaret number, which is enthusiastically commented upon by the audience, Laura and Eduard come on-stage and display, for the delight of the public, their household squabbles and the destruction of Venus.

The last scene is an epilogue played behind the curtain. Laura and Eduard have earned enough money and can now pay all of their debts. They are reconciled and want to remain together as peaceful private citizens. But the chorus—voices of a higher power—won't allow it: Laura and Eduard belong to the public; they can no longer do what they want but must live by the law to which they agreed. That means they must always argue and always be awaiting their divorce. Thus everyone can read about it in the paper, for what is recorded as *Neues vom Tage* must exist in reality, even if it makes for a colorful mess, as is served up in the quodlibet chorus finale.

Appendix D

Statistics on Opera Performances

The following table provides an idea of the relative popularity of the operas by Krenek, Weill, Hindemith, and others discussed in this work. The statistics given (number of performances/number of houses producing) were largely taken from Wilhelm Altmann's series of yearly "Opernstatistik" articles (see bibliography) published in the *Allgemeine Musikzeitung, Anbruch,* and elsewhere. Altmann's source for such production information was the *Deutsche Bühnenspielplan,* a monthly publication begun in 1899, which listed all German-language theatrical and operatic works performed on European stages.

1926–1927

Cardillac. 68/16. Most performed new work of the season.
Jonny spielt auf. 26/3. Staged in Leipzig, Hamburg, and Prague in its first season.
Royal Palace. 7/1. Premiered at the Berlin Staatsoper.

1927–1928

Jonny spielt auf. 421/45. Most performed opera of all for this year with twenty-five performances at the Berlin Städtische Oper alone.
Der Zar lässt sich photographieren. 39/10. Represents seven more houses and thirteen more performances than *Jonny spielt auf* had in its first season.
Hin und züruck. 38/10. Premiered as part of the 1927 Baden-Baden Music Festival.
Der Protagonist. 11/3.
Der Diktator, Das geheime Königreich, Schwergewicht. 7/1. Premiered in Wiesbaden.
Cardillac. Performed three times by Klemperer at the Krolloper; other performances unknown.

1928–1929

Schwergewicht. 81/21. Includes eight performances of all three one-acts at the Krolloper.
Der Zar lässt sich photographieren. 75/26. Includes three performances with *Der Protagonist* at the Berlin Städtische Oper.
Das geheime Königreich. 67/9.
Der Diktator. 58/14.
Hin und züruck. 43/17.
Cardillac. 43/ . Number of houses not available.

Jonny spielt auf. 24/8. Includes five performances at the Berlin Städtische Oper, the second season they produced the work.

Die schwarze Orchidee. 17/2. Premiered in Leipzig and later produced at the Berlin Städtische Oper with five performances.

Der Protagonist. 16/5.

Maschinist Hopkins. 14/2. Premiered in Duisburg and later produced in Bochum.

Neues vom Tage. 8/1. Premiered at the Krolloper as part of the Berlin Music Festival.

Royal Palace. 2/1. Only its second production after the premiere, staged in Essen.

1929–1930

Maschinist Hopkins. 120/20. Includes productions at the Berlin Städtische Oper and Frankfurt.

Neues vom Tage. 57/12. Includes two performances at the Krolloper.

Leben des Orest. 42/7. Includes nine performances at the Krolloper.

Schwergewicht. 29/7.

Jonny spielt auf. 18/4. Still produced in Leipzig.

Cardillac. 17/ . Staged by at least two houses, including two performances at the Krolloper.

Aufstieg und Fall der Stadt Mahagonny. 16/4. Premiered in Leipzig. Further productions in Cassel, Braunschweig, and Prague.

Die schwarze Orchidee. 13/3.

Das geheime Königreich. 12/3.

Der Diktator. 12/3

Transatlantic. 6/1. Premiered in Frankfurt.

Von Heute auf Morgen. 4/1. Premiered in Frankfurt.

Der Zar lässt sich photographieren. 3/1.

Achtung! Aufnahme! 3/1. Premiered in Frankfurt with Stravinsky's *Petruschka.*

Der Fächer. 3/1.

Der Protagonist. 2/1.

1930–1931

Neues vom Tage. 29/4. Includes six performances at the Krolloper.

Hin und zürück. 16/4. Includes three performances at the Krolloper.

Aufstieg und Fall der Stadt Mahagonny. 12/2.

Der Zar lässt sich photographieren. 11/4.

Cardillac. 4/1.

Schwergewicht. 5/2.

Jonny spielt auf. 4/2. Produced in Leipzig and Vienna.

Leben des Orest. Only one recorded performance at the Krolloper.

(No performances recorded of either *Maschinist Hopkins* or *Die schwarze Orchidee.*)

1931–1932

(Altmann changed his format with this season and only provided the total number of performances for each work.)

Aufstieg und Fall der Stadt Mahagonny. 52.

Schwergewicht. 11.

Leben des Orest. 6.

Cardillac. 6.

Maschinist Hopkins. 5.

Neues vom Tage. 4.

1932–1933

Hin und zurück. 8.
Mahagonny-Songspiel. 3.
Schwergewicht. 1.
(Altmann remarked on the 1932–33 season that *Leben des Orest, Cardillac, Neues vom Tage, Maschinist Hopkins, Aufstieg und Fall der Stadt Mahagonny,* and *Der Protagonist* had been relegated to the archives of operatic history, with little chance of revival.)

The other unexpected success of the 1920s was Jaromir Weinberger's *Schwanda, der Dudelsackpfeifer.* Its record of performances, for comparison with *Jonny spielt auf,* was: 1928–29, 110; 1929–30, 490 (topping *Carmen* as the most performed work of the season); 1930–31, 125; 1931–32, 54; for 1932–33 Altmann lists no performances.

Notes

Chapter 1

1. Peter Heyworth, *Otto Klemperer: His Life and Times,* Vol. 1: 1885–1933 (Cambridge: Cambridge University Press, 1983), 375.

2. Paul Zschorlich, "Fidelio auf Eis," *Deutsche Zeitung,* 21 November 1927. Reprinted in Hans Curjel, *Experiment Krolloper, 1927–31* (Munich: Prestel, 1975), 221–23.

3. Hans Heinsheimer, "German Music on the Breadline," *Modern Music* 9 (March–April 1932): 116.

4. Alfred Einstein, "German Opera, Past and Present," *Modern Music* 11 (January-February 1934): 66.

5. Hans Heinsheimer, "The Plight of German Opera Houses," *Musical Courier,* 27 February 1932.

6. Hans Heinsheimer, "A New Patron for Music," *Modern Music* 8 (January–February 1931): 14.

7. Neither Prof. Krenek nor H. H. Stuckenschmidt could remember, when I interviewed them, when or how the term was first used.

8. Kurt Weill, "Zeitoper," *Melos* 7 (March 1928): 106–8. Translated in Kim Kowalke, *Kurt Weill in Europe* (Ann Arbor: UMI Research Press, 1979), 482.

9. For example, the term *Zeitoper* appears in the essay on twentieth-century opera and in the Hindemith article in the *New Grove,* although it is not defined elsewhere as a separate term. *The New Grove Dictionary of Music and Musicians,* s.v. "Opera: 20th century" and "Hindemith, Paul."

10. Kim Kowalke, ed., *A New Orpheus* (New Haven, Conn.: Yale University Press, 1986) and David Drew, *Kurt Weill: A Handbook* (Berkeley: University of California, 1987).

Chapter 2

1. Berlin critic Adolf Weissmann, in *Die Musik der Weltkrise* (1922), translated by M. M. Bozman as *The Problems of Modern Music* (London: J. M. Dent, 1925), was one of the first writers to describe the postwar "age of anarchy" and its effect on opera, which he viewed as a particularly endangered genre. Articles discussing the opera crisis are given in the bibliography.

2. See Scott Messing, *Neoclassicism in Music: From the Genesis of the Concept through the Schoenberg/Stravinsky Polemic* (Ann Arbor: UMI Research Press, 1988) for an excellent discussion of prewar reactions to Wagner in France and Germany.

3. Alfredo Casella, "Reflections on the European Scene," *Modern Music* 5 (May–June 1928): 16–17.

4. Egon Wellesz, "Die Oper und diese Zeit," in *25 Jahre neue Musik*, eds. Hans Heinsheimer and Paul Stefan (Vienna: Universal Edition, 1925), 112.

5. Ferruccio Busoni, "Entwurf einer neuen Ästhetik der Tonkunst," in Rosamund Ley, trans., *The Essence of Music and Other Papers* (London: Rockcliff Publishing Corp., 1957). See also Scott Messing, *Neoclassicism in Music*.

6. *Anbruch* 3 (January 1921). *Melos*, the journal published by Schott Brothers in Mainz, covered Busoni's theories several months earlier. See Hermann Scherchen, "Neue Klassizität?" *Melos* 1 (16 July 1920): 242–43.

7. Busoni, *The Essence of Music and Other Papers*, 5.

8. Lazare Saminsky, "More about Faustus," *Modern Music* 5 (November–December 1927): 39.

9. Busoni, *The Essence of Music and Other Papers*, 40.

10. Alfred Einstein, "Gay German Opera," *The New York Times*, 22 April 1928,

11. See Ferruccio Busoni, "'Neue Klassizität'?" *Frankfurter Zeitung* [first morning edition], 9 February 1920, and Paul Bekker, "Impotenz oder Potenz," *Frankfurter Zeitung*, 15 January 1920.

12. See Giselher Schubert, "Aspekte der Bekkerschen Musiksoziologie," *The International Review of Music Aesthetics and Sociology* 1, no. 2 (1970): 179–85.

13. Paul Bekker, "Die Kunst geht nach Brot," in *Kritische Zeitbilder* (Berlin: Schuster and Loeffler, 1921), 217: "der eigentlich produktiven, wesensunmittelbaren Inkarnation des neuen Staatsgedankens überhaupt. Das kulturelle Gemeinschaftsleben ist die Rechtfertigung und Krönung des wirtschaftlichen, beide bedürfen, stützen und ergänzen einander: der 'Staat des sozialen Rechts' bedingt den Staat der sozialen Kunst."

14. Paul Bekker, *Richard Wagner: His Life in His Work*, trans. M. M. Bozman (Freeport, N.Y.: Books for Libraries, 1931).

15. Paul Bekker, *The Changing Opera*, trans. Arthur Mendel (London: J. M. Dent, 1936), 275.

16. Paul Bekker, "The Opera Walks New Paths," *Musical Quarterly* 21 (July 1935): 268.

17. Claudia Maurer Zenck provides an extensive bibliography of Krenek's writings in *Ernst Krenek: Ein Komponist im Exil* (Vienna: Lafite, 1980), and Kim Kowalke does likewise for Kurt Weill in *Kurt Weill in Europe* (Ann Arbor: UMI Research Press, 1979). See also Kurt Weill, *Ausgewählte Schriften*, ed. David Drew (Frankfurt: Suhrkamp, 1975) which contains a number of Weill's essays, 27 of which Kowalke translates in *Kurt Weill in Europe*.

18. Paul Bekker's correspondence, including some 12 letters from Ernst Krenek, is located in the Music Division of The Library of Congress. The letters from Krenek span the years 1922–29, and quotations from them are published with the permission of Mr. Krenek.

19. Ernst Krenek, "Zum Problem der Oper," in *Von neuer Musik*, eds. H. Grues, E. Kruttge, E. Thalheimer (Cologne: F. J. Marcan, 1925) 39–43. The article was reprinted in *Österreichische Musikzeitschrift* 5 (September 1950), 178–81.

20. Ernst Krenek, "Musik in der Gegenwart," in *25 Jahre neue Musik*, 43–59.

21. Krenek, "Musik in der Gegenwart," 54–55: "In Frankreich besteht heute noch eine gewisse Art von Rapport zwischen dem Musiker und seinem Publikum. Es gibt bedeutend grössere Kreise in Paris, die ein wirkliches Bedürfnis haben, ab und zu zeitgenössische Musik, vorwiegend freilich im Theater zu hören. Der Grund für diese Erscheinung liegt darin, dass Frankreich noch einen Rest von jenem homogenen Publikum besitzt. . . . Das bedeutet, dass das Niveau der Aufnahmefähigkeit eines relativ grossen Publikums höher ist als die eines gleich grossen mitteleuropäischen Kreises. Andererseits ist die Produktion der französischen Künstler instinktmässig auf gerade diese Niveau eingestellt, ist also, von unserem üblichen Masstab aus gesehen, oberflächlich und seicht. . . . Sie hat auf diese Weise bei allem, was man gegen sie einwenden mag, einen lebendigen Charme, der den Produkten mitteleuropäischer Ateliergelehrsamkeit durchschnittlich fehlt."

22. Letter of Krenek to Bekker, 9 December 1924. Krenek's trip to France and its influence on the creation of *Jonny spielt auf* is discussed further in chapter 5.

23. H. H. Stuckenschmidt, "Die neue Musik Frankreichs," *Kunstblatt* 6 (1922): 84–85. Virgil Thomson expressed similar feelings in his autobiography when he described his reasons for going to Paris to study. German music had "failed to keep contact with our century." Virgil Thomson, *Virgil Thomson* (New York: E. P. Dutton, 1985), 117.

24. Kurt Tucholsky, "Ein Pyrenäenbuch" in *Gesammelte Werke II* (Reinbeck: Rowohlt, 1960), 703–5. "Dank, dass ich in dir leben darf, Frankreich . . . da stehe ich auf der Brücke und bin wieder mitten in Paris, in unser aller Heimat."

25. See "Französisches und deutsches Musikempfinden," *Anbruch* 11 (February 1929): 53–57, and "Darius Milhaud," *Anbruch* 12 (April–May 1930): 135–40.

26. Krenek, "Musik in der Gegenwart," 56. "Typen, Tatsachen, Zuständen und Gegebenheiten aller Art zu finden."

27. Krenek, "Musik in der Gegenwart," 59. "Wir wollen leben und dem Leben in die Augen sehen und mit heissem Herzen 'ja' dazu sagen, und dann werden wir sie plötzlich haben und nicht wissen wie. Nie darf sie die Gestaltung unserer Mängel an dem und jenem sein, immer soll sie aus dem Überfluss des Lebens strömen, dann wird sie richtig und jenseits aller Überlegungen sein."

28. Ernst Krenek, "'Materialbestimmtheit' der Oper," *Anbruch* 9 (January–February 1927): 48–50. *Materialbestimmtheit* is a compound noun of Krenek's own devising and implies the directed or particular applications of operatic materials.

29. Paul Stefan, "Einleitung: Die Oper nach Wagner," and Paul Pisk, "Das neue Publikum," *Anbruch* 9 (January–February 1927): 3–10, 95–96. Pisk voiced similar concerns for the proletariat in an earlier essay, "Musikalische Volksbildung," in *25 Jahre neue Musik*, 155–68.

30. Krenek, "'Materialbestimmtheit' der Oper," 50. "Es ist ganz klar, dass diese Betonung der Tanzhaftigkeit den Komponisten, wenn er die gegebenen Möglichkeiten der Szene mit dem Konventionsleben der Gegenwart erfüllen will, zu den zeitgenössischen Tanzformen führen wird. Ihre gesellschaftsbildende Macht, die wir Tag für Tag erleben, wird niemand in Abrede stellen."

31. Ernst Krenek, "Über Sinn und Zweck des Theaters," *Anbruch* 9 (August-September 1927): 281–82.

32. Krenek, "Über Sinn und Zweck des Theaters," 282. "Ist nicht Freude ein Lebenselement und eine Lebensnotwendigkeit wie das Mittagessen für den der sie braucht?"

33. Ernst Krenek, "Opernerfahrung," *Anbruch* 11 (June 1929): 235–37.

34. Ernst Krenek, "Zur Situation der Oper," *Auftakt* 12 (1932): 131–37. His article "Forderung auch an diese Zeit: Freiheit des menschlichen Geistes!" *Anbruch* 14 (January 1932): 1–4, from a 1931 lecture, makes a similar call to create art which speaks to the beauty of the human heart.

35. "Richtlinien der 'Novembergruppe'," in *Zehn Jahre Novembergruppe,* ed. Will Grohmann, *Sonderheft: Kunst der Zeit* 3 (1928): 11. See also Helga Kliemann, *Die Novembergruppe* (Berlin: Gebr. Mann, 1969).

36. H. H. Stuckenschmidt, "Musik und Musiker in der Novembergruppe," in *Zehn Jahre Novembergruppe,* 94–107. Reprinted in *Anbruch* 10 (October 1928): 293–95.

37. Kurt Weill, "Bekenntnis zur Oper," in *25 Jahre neue Musik:* 226–28. Translated in Kowalke, *Kurt Weill in Europe,* 458–60.

38. Kurt Weill, "Die neue Oper," *Der neue Weg* 55 (16 January 1926): 24–25. Translated in Kowalke, *Kurt Weill in Europe,* 464–67.

39. Ibid., 466.

40. See Kurt Weill, "Busoni und die neue Musik," *Der neue Weg* 54 (16 October 1925): 282–83; "Busonis *Faust* und die Erneuerung der Opernform," *Anbruch* 9 (January-February 1927): 53–56; "Ferruccio Busoni: Zu seinem 60. Geburtstag," *Der deutsche Rundfunk* 4 (28 March 1926): 972. All three essays are translated in Kowalke, *Kurt Weill in Europe.*

41. Kurt Weill, "Verschiebungen in der musikalischen Produktion," *Berliner Tageblatt,* 1 October 1927. Translated in Kowalke, *Kurt Weill in Europe,* 478–81.

42. Ibid., 478.

43. Kurt Weill, "Zeitoper," *Melos* 7 (March 1928): 106–8. Translated in Kowalke, *Kurt Weill in Europe,* 482–84.

44. See Kurt Weill, "Tanzmusik," *Der deutsche Rundfunk* 4 (14 March 1926): 732–33; and "Notiz zum Jazz," *Anbruch* 11 (March 1929): 138. Both translated in Kowalke, *Kurt Weill in Europe,* 473–75 and 497–98, respectively.

45. Adolf Weissmann, "Das Donaueschinger Kammermusikfest 1925," *Die Musik* 17 (September 1925): 910.

46. For a detailed discussion of the origin of the term, see Stephen W. Hinton, "The Idea of Gebrauchsmusik: A Study of Musical Aesthetics in the Weimar Republic (1919–1933) with Particular Reference to the Works of Paul Hindemith" (Ph.D. dissertation, University of Birmingham, 1984).

47. The March 1929 issue of *Die Musik* was devoted to the topic of *Gebrauchsmusik* with articles by Licco Amar, Hans Möser, H. H. Stuckenschmidt, Eberhard Preussner, and Georg Schünemann.

48. Kurt Weill, "Die Oper—Wohin," *Berliner Tageblatt,* 31 October 1929. Ernst Krenek, "Neue Humanität und alte Sachlichkeit," *Neue Schweizer Rundschau* 24 (1931), reprinted and translated in Krenek, *Exploring Music* (New York: October House, 1966), 43–60. Paul Hindemith, *A Composer's World* (Cambridge, Mass.: Harvard University, 1952), viii.

49. Such views of Hindemith are expressed in the following: Arthur G. Browne, "Paul Hindemith and the Neo-Classic Music," *Music and Letters* 13 (1932): 42–58; Andrew A. Fraser, "Paul Hindemith," *Music and Letters* 10 (1929): 167–76; and Willi Reich, "Paul Hindemith," *Musical Quarterly* 17 (1931): 486–96.

50. Paul Hindemith, "Über Musikkritik," *Melos* 8 (1929): 106. "Was uns Alle angeht ist dies: das alte Publikum stirbt aus; wie und was müssen wir schreiben, um ein grösseres, anderes, neues Publikum zu bekommen; wo ist dieses Publikum?"

51. Adolf Weissmann, "Germany's Latest Music Dramas," *Modern Music* 4 (May–June 1927): 20–26.

52. Hans Mersmann, "Probleme der gegenwärtigen Operndichtung," *Anbruch* 9 (January–February 1927): 15–19.

53. Ibid., 17. ". . . ein Drama, durchpulst von dem Tempo unserer Zeit mit allen ihren Ausdrucksmitteln arbeitend."

54. Adolf Aber, "Zeitgenössische Oper in ihren Hauptströmungen," *Auftakt* 7 (1927): 151.

55. In 1930 Hanns Eisler published a cantata for alto and bass soloists, mixed choir, and small orchestra entitled *Tempo der Zeit*. The work makes references, not always complementary, to modern culture. Edmund Nick and poet Erich Kästner collaborated on a similar work, *Leben in der Zeit*, a *lyrische Suite* in three movements published in 1931. One number, "Hymnus auf die Zeitgenossen," makes use of a telephone bell and railroad signal. Other numbers used jazz dance rhythms in the style of foxtrots and tangos.

56. Kurt Westphal, "Die moderne Oper," *Blätter der Staatsoper* 9 (October 1928): 5–7.

57. Siegfried Günther, "Gegenwartsoper," *Die Musik* 20 (July 1928): 718–26.

58. Hans Curjel, "Triumph der Alltäglichkeit, Parodie, und tiefere Bedeutung," *Blätter der Staatsoper* 9 (June 1929): 1–4.

59. Ibid., 3. "Das Werk soll beim Zuhörer oder Zuschauer einen bestimmten Zweck erfüllen, es ist in einem neuen Sinn für den Abnehmer geschaffen.

60. Ibid., 4. "Nüchternheit ist Prinzip, *Alltäglichkeit* ist Stoff der gestaltenden Darstellung—das Ergebnis ist ein höchst kompliziert funktionierendes, geschliffenes Kunstwerk, das bei allem heiteren und lockeren Schein die Tiefen und Untiefen eben der reinen Kunst besitzt."

61. Hermann W. von Walterhausen, "Die Krise der zeitgenössischen deutschen Oper," *Schweizerische Musikzeitung und Sängerblatt* 68 (1928): 41–42; (1928): 56–57.

62. Julius Kapp, "Gibt es eine Krise der Oper," *Blätter der Staatsoper* 9 (April 1929): 10–12.

63. Fritz Ohrmann, "Trimuph [*sic*] der Alltäglichkeit," *Signale für die musikalische Welt* 87 (1929): 815–19.

64. Hans Tessmer, "Zeitfragen des Operntheaters: Die Oper am Scheidewege," *Zeitschrift für Musik* 97 (1930): 172–76.

65. Karl Lüthge, "Musik in der Gegenwart," *Signale für die musikalische Welt* 88 (1930): 442–47.

66. See the following two articles for examples of pessimism voiced by formerly optimistic critics: H. H. Stuckenschmidt, "Ist die Oper überlebt?" *Das Kunstblatt* 14 (1930): 225–33; Alfred Baresel, "Pessimismus der Oper," *Rheinische Musik- und Theater-Zeitung* 32 (1931): 4–5.

67. Hans Tessmer, "Hat die deutsche Oper eine Zukunft?" *Zeitschrift für Musik* 100 (1933): 1000–1002. For a further discussion of the political and anti-Semitic tone of other German journals at this time, see Joel Sachs, "Some Aspects of Musical Politics in Pre-Nazi Germany," *Perspectives of New Music* 9 (Fall–Winter 1970): 74–95.

68. For examples of such protests see: Hans Heinsheimer, "Neues vom Tage," *Anbruch* 13 (January 1931): 1–4; Karl Wörner, "Was ist Kulturbolschewismus," *Melos* 11 (1932): 397–99; X. T., "Kultur Terror," *Modern Music* 10 (May–June 1933): 209–13; H. H. Stuckenschmidt, "Nightmare in Germany," *Modern Music* 10 (January–February 1933): 115–17; and "Under the Swastika," *Modern Music* 11 (November–December 1933): 49–52; Alfred Einstein, "German Opera, Past and Present," *Modern Music* 11 (January–February 1934): 65–72; and "National and Universal Music," *Modern Music* 14 (November–December 1936): 3–11; Fugitivus, "Inside Germany," *Modern Music* 16 (May–June 1939): 203–13.

69. Kurt Weill, "Busoni und die neue Musik," translated in Kowalke, *Kurt Weill in Europe,* 464.

Chapter 3

1. H. H. Stuckenschmidt, "Musik und Musiker in der Novembergruppe," *Anbruch* 10 (October 1928): 293–95.

2. John Willett in *Art and Politics in the Weimar Period* (New York: Pantheon, 1978) was the first author in English to apply the concept of *Neue Sachlichkeit,* which he translates as "new sobriety," to Weimar culture in general. His discussion of musical life at the time is both limited and flawed. See also Thomas Koebner, "Die *Zeitoper* in den zwanziger Jahren," in *Erprobungen und Erfahrungen zu Paul Hindemiths Schaffen,* ed. Dieter Rexroth (Mainz: Schott, 1978), 60–115, and Stephen Hinton, "Weill: *Neue Sachlichkeit,* Surrealism and *Gebrauchsmusik,*" in *A New Orpheus,* ed. Kim H. Kowalke (New Haven, Conn.: Yale University Press, 1986), 61–82.

3. Jost Hermand, "Unity within Diversity? The History of the Concept 'Neue Sachlichkeit'," trans. Peter and Margaret Lincoln, in Keith Bullivant, ed., *Culture and Society in the Weimar Republic* (Manchester: Manchester University Press, 1977), 166.

4. Wieland Schmied, "Neue Sachlichkeit and German Realism in the Twenties," in Louise Lincoln, ed., *German Realism of the Twenties* (Exhibition Catalogue) (Minneapolis: Institute of Art, 1980), 41.

5. Peter Salz, "The Artist as Social Critic," in Lincoln, ed., *German Realism of the Twenties,* 29, 32.

6. Schmied, "Neue Sachlichkeit," 43.

7. H. Wieynck, "Die künstlerische Bildgestaltung in der Photographie," *Photographische Rundschau* (1926): 277, quoted in Ute Eskilden, "Exhibits," trans. J. C. Horak in *Avant-Garde Photography in Germany 1919–1939* (Exhibition Catalogue) (San Francisco: Museum of Art, 1980), 43.

8. Bernd Ohse, "Cameras," in *Avant-Garde Photography in Germany 1919–1939,* 47.

9. Van Deren Coke, "Introduction," in *Avant-Garde Photography in Germany 1919–1939,* 18.

10. Ruth J. Hofrichter, "Erich Kästner as a Representative of 'Neue Sachlichkeit'," *German Quarterly* 5 (1932): 176.

11. Ibid., 175.

12. Quoted in Lisa Appignanesi, *The Cabaret* (New York: Macmillan, 1975), 105.

13. H. H. Stuckenschmidt, "Ausblick in die Musik," *Das Kunstblatt* 7 (1923): 221–22.

14. Siegfried Kallenberg, "Zur modernen Musik," *Zeitschrift für Musik* 91 (1924): 562–64.

15. Heinrich Strobel, "'Neue Sachlichkeit' in der Musik," *Anbruch* 8 (June 1926): 254–56.

16. H. Strobel, "'Neue Sachlichkeit' in der Musik," 256. "Dieser neue Stil ist Konsolidierung nach revolutionärem Aufbrausen, Beginn einer Periode ruhigen Reifens."

17. H. H. Stuckenschmidt, "Neue Sachlichkeit in der Musik," *Vossische Zeitung*, 19 February 1927. Later reprinted in *Auftakt* 8 (1928): 3–6 and in *Die Musik eines halben Jahrhunderts: 1925–1975 Essays und Kritik* (Munich: R. Piper, 1976), 36–41.

18. Ibid., 41. "Dass wir am Anfang einer neuen musikalischen Kultur stehen, die sich aus soziologischen Umschichtungen ergab, dass die überlieferte künstlerische Ideologie im Sterben liegt, wird das Publikum mit Schrecken erst dann wahrnehmen, wenn es zu spät ist."

19. Ernst Krenek, "*Neue Sachlichkeit* in der Musik," *i 10* 1 (June 1927): 216–18.

20. Ernst Krenek, "Mechanisierung der Künste," *i 10* 1 (October 1927): 376–80.

21. See in particular Walter Berten, "Mensch und Maschine Sachlichkeit," *Rheinische Musik- und Theater-Zeitung* 28 (4 June 1927): 219.

22. Ernst Krenek, "Neue Humanität und alte Sachlichkeit," *Neue Schweizer Rundschau* 24 (April 1931), reprinted in Krenek, *Exploring Music* (New York: October House, 1966), 43–60.

23. Ludwig Misch, "*Neue Sachlichkeit*," *Allgemeine Musikzeitung* 54 (1927): 613–15. Ernst Schliepe, "Musik und Neue Sachlichkeit," *Signale für die musikalische Welt* 87 (1929): 1206–10.

24. Schliepe, "Musik und Neue Sachlichkeit," 1210. "Die angeblich 'sachlichen' Komponisten der Gegenwart, die Genie haben, können zum Glück auch nicht gegen ihre Natur, und es ist erfreulich und trostreich zu sehen wie sie in ihren besten Momenten höchst unsachlich werden. Womit sie selbst den Beweis liefern, dass es auf die Dauer nichts ist mit der Sachlichkeit in der Musik."

25. See Fritz Neumeyer, "Nexus of the Modern: The New Architecture in Berlin," in Tilman Buddensieg, ed., *Berlin 1900–1933: Architecture and Design* (New York: Cooper-Hewitt Museum of Decorative Arts and Design, 1987), 34–83.

26. Franz-Peter Kothes, *Die theatralische Revue in Berlin und Wien 1900–1938: Typen, Inhalte, Funktionen* (Wilhelmshaven: Heinrichshoffen, 1977), 14, 98.

27. Rudolf Hösch, *Kabarett von Gestern nach zeitgenössischen Berichten, Kritiken und Erinnerungen*, 2 vols. (Berlin: Henschelverlag, 1969), I:140.

28. Ibid., I:215, 218.

29. Ibid., I:224.

30. Ibid., between I:224–25, illustrations numbered 261, 268.

31. Alfred Rosenzweig, "Die Revuetechnik in Operette und Oper," *Melos* 6 (December 1927): 525.

32. Maria Ley-Piscator, *The Piscator Experiment: The Political Theatre* (New York: James H. Heinemen, 1967), 13.

33. C. D. Innes, *Erwin Piscator's Political Theatre: The Development of Modern German Drama* (London: Cambridge University Press, 1972), 5.

34. Leo Lania, *Today We Are Brothers: The Biography of a Generation*, trans. Ralph Marlowe (Boston: Riverside, 1942), 273.

35. Innes, *Erwin Piscator's Political Theatre*, 72,81.

36. This song has been recorded by Teresa Stratas on *The Unknown Kurt Weill*, Nonesuch D-79019, 1981.

Chapter 4

1. I am indebted to Prof. James Dapogny of The University of Michigan for the formulation of this definition. I have tried to use the term "jazz" with as much specificity as possible.

2. Edmund Wilson, Jr., "The Aesthetic Upheaval in France: The Influence of Jazz in Paris and Americanization of French Literature and Art," *Vanity Fair* (February 1922): 49.

3. H. H. Stuckenschmidt, interview with author, Berlin, West Germany, 8 December 1981.

4. Jean-Francis Laglenne, "Boxeurs," *L'Esprit nouveau* 14 (1923): 1673–74.

5. For example, in 1929 Bertolt Brecht, Paul Hindemith, and Kurt Weill collaborated on *Der Lindberghflug*, which was subsequently premiered at the Baden-Baden Festival. Weill later set Brecht's entire text himself.

6. Erich Mendelsohn, *Amerika: Bilderbuch eines Architekten* (Berlin: Rudolf Mosse, 1926).

7. Ibid., foreword. "Seine Bevölkerung, eine aus allen Erdteilen zusammengewirbelte Masse, bildet den Unterwind dieses Babylonischen Kessels. . . . Dass dieses Land alle Möglichkeiten in sich trägt, ist ohne Frage."

8. There were also black American performers who toured Germany prior to World War I and popularized earlier dances such as the cakewalk. Ranier Lotz is currently documenting this prehistory of jazz, as he calls it. See his "The 'Louisiana Troupes' in Europe," *The Black Perspective in Music* 11 (Fall 1983): 133–42, and "Black Diamonds Are Forever: A Glimpse of the Prehistory of Jazz in Europe," *The Black Perspective in Music* 12 (Fall 1984): 216–34.

9. Irene F. Castle, *Castles in the Air* (New York: Doubleday, 1958), 54.

10. Louis Erenberg in *Steppin' Out: New York Nightlife and the Transformation of American Culture* (Chicago: University of Chicago Press, 1981) chronicles the changing nature of American nightlife as part of changing social behavior between men and women. His fifth chapter deals specifically with the Castles, public dancing, and Irene Castle as a symbol of the modern American woman.

11. Castle, *Castles in the Air*, 88.

12. Ibid., 86.

13. Mr. and Mrs. Vernon Castle, *Modern Dancing* (New York: Harper and Row, 1914).

14. Castle, *Castles in the Air*, 92.

15. Ibid., 133–34; Southern, *The Music of Black Americans*, 350; and W. C. Handy, *Father of the Blues* (New York: Macmillan, 1944), 226.

16. Several of these early recordings have been reissued on *A History of Jazz: The New York Scene*, RBF RF3 and *Steppin' on the Gas: Rags to Jazz, 1913–1927*, New World NW 269.

17. Arthur W. Little, *From Harlem to the Rhine: The Story of New York's Colored Volunteers* (New York: Covici-Fried, 1936), 133.

18. Ibid.

19. Emmett J. Scott, *Scott's Official History of the American Negro in the World War* (Washington, D. C., 1919), 307–8.

20. "Memphis Blues" has been rereleased as part of *Steppin' on the Gas,* NW 269.

21. "A Negro Explains Jazz."

22. Scott, *Official History,* 300.

23. Southern, *The Music of Black Americans,* 361.

24. Scott, *Official History,* 310–11, and Southern, *The Music of Black Americans,* 361.

25. Ernst Ansermet, "Sur un orchestre nègre," *La Revue romande* (15 October 1919): 10–13. Reprinted in *Ecrits sur la musique,* ed. J-Claude Piquet (Neuchâtel: Baconnière, [1983]), 177–78. "Il y a au *Southern Syncopated Orchestra* un extraordinaire virtuose clarinettiste qui est, parait-il, le premier de sa race à avoir composé sur la clarinette des blues d'une forme achevée. . . . Je veux dire le nom de cet artiste de génie, car pour ma part je ne l'oublierai pas: c'est Sydney Bechet."

26. Victor Silvester and Philip J. S. Richardson, *The Art of the Ballroom* (London: Herbert Jenkins Ltd., 1936), 24.

27. Armand Lanoux, *Paris in the 20s,* trans. E. S. Seldon (New York: Golden Griffen, 1960), 47.

28. Prof. James Dapogny notes the presence of the habanera rhythm in the accompaniment of "The Memphis Blues" (1912) and "St. Louis Blues" (1914), two popular works associated with W. C. Handy, and in Jelly Roll Morton's "Jelly Roll Blues" (1914), the work generally considered to be the first jazz publication.

29. Mae West, *Goodness Had Nothing to Do with It* (Englewood Cliffs, N.J.: Prentice-Hall, 1959), 65.

30. Marshall Stearns and Jean Stearns, *Jazz Dance* (New York: Macmillan, 1968).

31. Lanoux, *Paris in the 20s,* 49.

32. Francis Steegmuller, *Cocteau: A Biography* (Boston: Little, Brown, 1970), 17.

33. Born Frederic Sauser, Cendrars chose his new name with the play on words—*braise* [embers] *cendres* [ashes]—to signify the burning passion for writing which consumed his life. See Blaise Cendrars, *Complete Postcards from the Americas,* trans. and intro. by Monique Chefdor (Berkeley: University of California Press, 1976), 7.

34. John Dos Passos, "Homer of the Trans-Siberian," in *Orient Express* (New York: Jonathan Cape and Harrison South, 1930), 118–204.

35. Blaise Cendrars, *L'Anthologie nègre* (Paris: Editions de la Sirène, 1921). Translated by Margery Bianco as *The African Saga* (1927; reprint Negro University Press, 1969).

36. Lynn Haney, *Naked at the Feast* (New York: Dodd, Mead, 1981), 59.

37. Janet Flanner, *Paris Was Yesterday* (New York: The Viking Press, 1972), xx–xxi.

38. Quoted in Hösch, *Kabarett von Gestern nach zeitgenössischen Berichten, Kritiken und Erinnerungen,* I: 217. "Langbeinig und paradiesisch. . . . Das straffgekämmte blauschwarze Haar, die wippende Hüfte und das blitzend weisse Gebisse aus dem das helle, lustig-gutturale Französisch purzelte, sprach den ganzen Inhalt der neuen Vokabel aus, die damals aus Amerika über den Ozean nach Berlin herübergeschwebt war: Sex-Appeal."

39. Hans Heinsheimer, *Best Regards to Aida* (New York: Alfred A. Knopf, 1968), 23.

40. Haney, *Naked at the Feast*, 88–89.

41. Ibid., 67–68, 104.

42. A number of Whiteman's recordings have been rereleased on *An Experiment in Modern Music: Paul Whiteman at Aeolian Hall*, The Smithsonian Collection, RO28 DNN2–0518.

43. Whitney Balliett, "Jazz," *The New Yorker*, 16 April 1984.

44. Darius Milhaud, *Notes without Music* (1953; reprint New York: Da Capo Press, 1970), 136.

45. H. H. Stuckenschmidt, "Jean Cocteau," *Blätter der Staatsoper* 8 (February 1928): 18.

46. Milhaud, *Notes without Music*, 238–39.

47. Steegmuller, *Cocteau*, 201.

48. Even Ansermet referred to Berlin as the "most celebrated composer of ragtime" in his review of the Southern Syncopated Orchestra, "Sur un orchestre nègre," 174.

49. Jean Cocteau, "Le Coq et l'harlequin," in *A Call to Order*, trans. Rollo H. Myers (London: Faber and Gwyer, 1926).

50. Ibid., 27.

51. Steegmuller, *Cocteau*, 243.

52. Cocteau, "Order Considered," in *A Call to Order*, 192–93.

53. For more information on Wiéner's reputation as a pianist, see H. H. Stuckenschmidt, "Der neue Klaviervirtuose," *Auftakt* 6 (1926): 79–82.

54. Jean Wiéner, *Allegro Appassionato* (Paris: Pierre Belford, 1978), 88, 213–18.

55. Count Harry Kessler, *In the Twenties* (New York: Holt, Rinehart, and Winston, 1971), 209, and H. H. Stuckenschmidt, interview with the author, Berlin, West Germany, 16 November 1981.

56. Darius Milhaud, "Les Resources nouvelles de la musique," *L'Esprit nouveau* 25 (n.d.): no page numbers printed.

57. Brian Rust, comp., *Jazz Records 1879–1942*, 2 vols. (London: Storyville, 1969), I:71. I have been unable to locate the released recording.

58. Milhaud, "Les Resources nouvelles."

59. Albert Jeanneret, "Les Concerts Wiéner," *L'Esprit nouveau* 14 (1923): 1664.

60. Milhaud, *Notes without Music*, 128.

61. Jeanneret, "Les Concerts Wiéner," 1664. "La batterie: bruiteuse ou sourde avec la cymbale ou la grosse caisse, mate avec la caisse de bois, une mativité aux rapports troublants. Cette batterie, tout un arsenal à déclanchement de rythme. Cénesthesie. Les entrailles s'émeuvent."

62. André Coeuroy and André Schaeffner, *Le Jazz* (Paris: Claude Aveline, 1926).

63. Ibid., 33–34. "Même sécheresse brisante du coup directement porté sur la caisse de bois; même alternance entre cette sécheresse ligneuse et la matité moindre de la peau frappée; même moyen de répartir sur deux timbres distincts les périodicités différentes de la mesure et du rythme."

64. Ibid., 145. "En vain fermera-t-on l'oreille au jazz. Il est vie, il est art. Il est ivresse des sons et des bruits. Il est joie animale des mouvements souples. Il est mélancholie des passions. Il est nous d'aujourd'hui."

65. Appendix A contains a list of such European jazz-influenced works.

66. Steegmuller, *Cocteau*, 242, 260.

67. Milhaud, *Notes without Music*, 120.

68. Ibid., 136–37.

69. Ibid., 135–36.

70. Ibid., 148–49.

71. Ibid., 135–36.

72. Darius Milhaud, "Les Resources nouvelles"; "The Jazz Band and Negro Music," *Littel's Living Age* (18 October 1924): 169–73; "The Day after Tomorrow," *Modern Music* 3 (November-December 1925): 22–24; "Die Entwicklung der Jazz-Band und die Nordamerikanische Negermusik," *Anbruch* 7 (April 1925): 200–205.

73. Wiéner, *Allegro Appassionato*, 106.

74. Jean Wiéner, *Sonatine syncopée* (Paris: Max Eschig, 1923). "Merci, chers orchestres nègres d'Amerique, merci magnifiques jazz-bands, de la bienfaisante influence que vous avez eue sur la vraie musique de mon temps."

75. Jean Wiéner, *Trois blues chantes* (Paris: Max Eschig, 1924). "La voix est traitée ici comme un instrument, et comme un instrument de cuivre—l'auteur avait pensée d'abord à composer ces mélodies pour un Saxophoniste nègre—on devra donc chanter 'souple' en usant beaucoup, des soufflets < > sur une même note, et chanter 'tendre.' On devra aussi respecter les valeurs, et aller tout à fait en mesure, tout en s'efforçant de rendre expressif chaque son, même le plus court."

76. Maurice Ravel, *L'Enfant et les sortilèges*, piano-vocal score (Paris: Durand, 1925), 18–20.

77. Virgil Thomson, "Paris, April 1940," *Modern Music* 17 (May-June 1940): 204, although in his article "Tanzmusik," *Der deutsche Rundfunk* 4 (14 March 1926): 732–33, Kurt Weill called for more radio coverage of jazz.

78. *Funkstunde*, 22 March 1925; 14 October 1927.

79. Rudolf Lothar, "Die Musik," in *Fünf Jahre Berliner Rundfunk: Ein Rückblick 1923–28* (Berlin: Funk-Stunde, 1928), 90.

80. *Funkstunde*, 20 October 1927.

81. Horst H. Lange, *Die Geschichte des Jazz in Deutschland* (Lübeck: Uhle and Kleimann, 1960), 7. Lange provides a discography of these early Germany recording artists. Rainer Lotz has also published a number of short studies through "Der Jazzfreund" documenting early jazz in Germany.

82. Lange, *Die Geschichte des Jazz in Deutschland*, 8.

83. Björn Englund, "Chocolate Kiddies," *Storyville* 62 (December 1975–January 1976): 45.

84. The Schomburg Center for Research in Black Culture has six photographs of Wooding and his group from various times in his career.

85. Björn Englund, "Redan för Ar Sedan," *Orkester Journalen* (December 1964): 16.

86. These recordings have been reissued on *Sam Wooding and His Chocolate Dandies*, Biograph BLP-12015.

87. According to Garvin Bushell, whose memoirs are being edited by Mark Tucker for The University of Michigan Press.

88. Eric Borchard recorded an "O Katherina" in 1924 and the two tunes may be related.

89. Art Napoleon, "A Pioneer Looks Back," *Storyville* 9 (February–March, April–May 1967): 37.

90. *Funkstunde,* 13 July 1928, 927.

91. Brian Rust, comp., *Jazz Records,* 2:1862–63.

92. These recordings are also found on the Biograph reissue of *Sam Wooding and His Chocolate Dandies.*

93. Heinz Greul, *Bretter, die die Zeit bedeuten* (Cologne: Kiepenheuer and Witsch, 1967), 250.

94. E. Mauck, "Die Musik im Kabarett," *Berliner Tageblatt,* 22 February 1925.

95. Hösch, *Kabarett von Gestern,* between pages 224–25, photograph no. 269.

96. Ibid., 225.

97. H. H. Stuckenschmidt, *Musik am Bauhaus* (Berlin: Bauhaus-Archiv, 1976), 9–13. Two photographs of the band from around 1928 and possibly by Lux Feininger are reproduced in Harvey Mendelsohn, ed., *Bauhaus Photography* (Cambridge, Mass: MIT Press, 1985), 105, 303. However, composer Paul Arne, who worked at the Bauhaus from 1928 on, remembers no jazz ensemble (letter from Paul Arne to the author, 4 July 1987).

98. Mendelsohn, *Bauhaus Photography,* 104, 107.

99. H. H. Stuckenschmidt, "Die heutige Musik," *Kunstblatt* 8 (1924): 189. "Dieses Land Amerika hat der Welt die neuen Tanzrhythmen gegeben. Es wird ihr die Erlösung aus dem künstlerischen Krampf geben, in dem Europa sich windet."

100. Erwin Schulhoff, "Der mondäne Tanz," *Auftakt* 4 (1924): 73–77.

101. Anbruch 7 (April 1925). Contents: Paul Stefan, "Jazz"; Alexander Jemnitz, "Der Jazz als Form und Inhalt"; Louis Gruenberg, "Der Jazz als Ausgangspunkt"; Darius Milhaud, "Die Entwicklung der Jazz-Band"; Cesar Saechinger, "Jazz"; Percy Grainger, "Jazz."

102. Louis Gruenberg, "Vom Jazz und anderen Dingen," in *25 Jahre neue Musik,* eds. Stefan and Heinsheimer, 229–36. Gruenberg, along with a number of other Americans, composed jazz-inspired works. See appendix A.

103. Louis Gruenberg, "Der Jazz als Ausgangspunkt," 199: "einer, der dem Blute, der Erziehung und dem Herzen nach Amerikaner ist."

104. Erwin Schulhoff, "Eine Jazz-Affaire," *Auftakt* 5 (1925): 220–22.

105. Auftakt 6, no. 10 (1926). Contents: A. Simon, "Jazz"; Alfred Baresel, "Jazz als Rettung"; E. J. Mueller, "Jazz als Karikatur"; André Schaeffner and André Coeuroy, "Die Romantik der Jazz"; Erich Steinhard, "Whiteman's Jazzorchestra in Paris"; Artur Iger, "Jazz-Industrie"; "Jazz-Mosaik."

106. Alfred Baresel, *Das neue Jazzbuch,* rev. ed. (Leipzig: Wilhelm Zimmermann, 1929).

107. Ibid., 5. I have not located this article, but it may well make Baresel the earliest German writer on jazz.

108. Baresel and N. Fedorow, *Schule für Saxophon* (Leipzig: Zimmermann, 1926); Baresel, *Instruktive Jazz-Etüden für Klavier* (Leipzig: Zimmermann, 1929); Baresel and Rio Gebhardt,

Jazz-Klavier Schule (Leipzig: Zimmermann, 1932); Baresel, "Formeln des Jazz," *Die Musik* 22 (February 1930): 354.

109. Hermann Schildberger-Gleiwitz, "Jazz-Musik," *Die Musik* 17 (September 1925): 914–23.

110. Alois Melichar, "Walzer und Jazz," *Die Musik* 20 (February 1928): 345–49.

111. Rudolf Sonner, "Caféhausmusik," *Die Musik* 21 (March 1929): 440–43.

112. Paul Bernhard, *Jazz: Eine musikalische Zeitfrage* (Munich: Delphin, 1927).

113. Adolf Weissmann, *Die Entgötterung der Musik* (Berlin: Max Hesse, 1926). Translated by Eric Blom as *Music Come to Earth* (London: J. M. Dent, 1930).

114. For examples of such reactions see Neil Leonard, "The Reactions to Ragtime," in *Ragtime,* ed. John Hasse (New York: Schirmer, 1985), 102–13, and Mary Herron DuPree, "'Jazz,' the Critics, and American Art Music in the 1920s," *American Music* 4 (Fall 1986): 287–301.

115. J. A. Rodgers, "Jazz at Home," in *The New Negro,* ed. Alain Locke (New York: Arno Press, 1968), 216–24.

116. Sam Wooding, "8 Years Abroad with a Jazz Band," *Etude* 57 (April 1938): 233–34, 282.

117. Karl Holl, "Jazz im Konservatorium," *Frankfurter Zeitung,* 25 November 1927.

118. Pages from the conservatory's catalog appear in Peter Cahn, *Das Hoch'sche Konservatorium 1878–1978* (Frankfurt: Kramer, 1979), 292–93. Other teachers listed are: saxophone, Eduard Liebhold; trumpet, Friedrich Herold; trombone, Heinrich Böhm; percussion, Arthur Sitz; and banjo, Josef Grosch. Only Grosch was a new member; the other four also taught in the orchestra division.

119. Cahn, *Das Hoch'sche Konservatorium,* 378.

120. Mátyás Seiber, "Jazz als Erziehungsmittel," *Melos* 7 (1928): 281–86; "Jazz-Instrumente, Jazz-Klang und neue Musik," *Melos* 9 (1930): 122–26; "Jazz und die musikstudierende Jugend," *Artist* (Düsseldorf, 21 February 1930); and "Welche Rolle spielt die Synkope in der moderne Jazzwerke?" *Musik-Echo* (1931).

121. It has been suggested to me that Seiber, as a student of Kodály, may well have come to an appreciation of jazz through improvisation, as the Kodály education method places great emphasis on improvisation.

122. Mátyás Seiber, *Schule für Schlagzeug* (Mainz: Schott, 1929).

123. Mátyás Seiber, "Rhythmic Flexibility in Jazz?" *Music Review* 6 (1945): 30–41, 89–94, 160–171.

124. "Jazz-Klasse an Dr. Hochs Konservatorium," *Zeitschrift für Musik* 94 (1927): 706.

125. Max Chop, "Jazz als Lehrfach," *Signale für die musikalische Welt* 86 (1928): 43–44.

126. Alfred Pelegrini, "Jazz-Unfug," *Rheinische Musik- und Theater-Zeitung* 29 (1928): 317–18.

127. Paul Schwers, "Die Frankfurter Jazz-Akademie im Spiegel der Kritik," *Allgemeine Musikzeitung* 54 (1927): 1246–48.

128. Heinrich Strobel, "Unzeitgemässe Proteste," *Anbruch* 10 (January 1928): 25.

129. Erich Steinhard, "Modemusiker Erwin Schulhoff," *Auftakt* 9, no. 3 (1929): 80. See also *Bibliographisches Verzeichnis der Kompositionen von Erwin Schulhoff* (Berlin: Tschechoslowakischen Akademie der Wissenschaften, 1967).

130. Erich Steinhard, "Flammen," *Auftakt* 12 (1932): 78–80.

131. J. Jezek, "E. F. Burian," *Auftakt* 8 (1928): 197–98.

132. Lothar, "Die Musik," 52.

133. For more information on this cycle see Malcolm S. Cole, "Afrika Singt: Austro-German Echoes of the Harlem Renaissance," *Journal of the American Musicological Society* 30 (Spring 1977): 72–87.

134. Joseph Wulf, *Musik im Dritten Reich: Eine Dokumentation* (Gütersloh: Sigbert Mohn, 1963), 348.

135. Wulf, *Musik im Dritten Reich;* between 224–25, 423.

136. The cover is reproduced in Minna Lederman, *The Life and Death of a Small Magazine,* ISAM Monographs, no. 18, 1983, after page 142.

137. Mike Zwerin, in his anecdotal study *La Tristesse de Saint-Louis* (New York: Morrow, 1987), claims that jazz merely went underground during the Nazi years, surfacing in private record parties and even in prison camp performances.

Chapter 5

1. Ernst Krenek, telephone interview with the author, 21 April 1982.

2. Ibid.

3. Christof Bitter and Manfred Schlösser, eds. *Begegnungen mit Eduard Erdmann* (Darmstadt: Eratro, 1968), 364–65. There is no article on Erdmann in *The New Grove.*

4. Charles Selig, ed. *Grotesken Album* (Vienna: Universal Edition, 1922).

5. The program for this *Abend der Novembergruppe* is reproduced in Helga Kliemann, *Die Novembergruppe* (Berlin: Gebr. Mann, 1969), 36.

6. Eduard Erdmann, *Fox-trot in C-dur* (Stockholm: Nordiska Musikforlaget, 1924). I have been unable to obtain a copy of this work.

7. Walter Laqueur, *Weimar: A Cultural History, 1918–1933* (New York: G.P. Putnam's Sons, 1974), 213.

8. Krenek, *Horizons Circled,* 37. For a discussion of Krenek's philosophy of freedom from the time, see Hans F. Redlich, "Heimat und Freiheit: Zur Ideologie der jüngsten Werke Ernst Kreneks," *Anbruch* 12 (February 1930): 54–58.

9. Photographs of Sievert's designs are reproduced in Albert Mohr, *Das Frankfurter Opernhaus, 1880–1980* (Frankfurt: Waldemar Kramer, 1980), 209.

10. Only the piano-vocal score of *Der Sprung über den Schatten* was published. An autograph manuscript of the full score is in the Universal Edition archive.

11. Ernst Krenek, *Der Sprung über den Schatten* (Vienna: Universal Edition, 1924), 49–51. "Rund im Kreise drehen, stampfen, wilder Tanz! O lass mich in dir untergehn, ich bleibe nie mehr im Leben stehn. Tolles Schwanken, Wanken! Schranken kennen nicht mehr Gedanken. Das ist die Tanzmaschine dieser uns'rer Zeit, zu Trot und Step sind alle allbereit. Drehet euch im wilden Wirbeltanz, ihr werdet leicht und frei sein."

12. Artur Schnabel, *My Life and Music* (New York: St. Martin's, 1963), 79.

13. Ernst Hilmar, ed. *Ernst Krenek: Katalog zur Ausstellung* (Vienna: Universal Edition, 1982), 62.

14. Krenek, telephone interview with the author, 21 April 1982.

15. Bitter and Schlösser, *Begegnungen mit Eduard Erdmann,* 277.

16. Letters between Erdmann and Krenek, published in Bitter and Schlösser, *Begegnungen mit Eduard Erdmann,* 274–78.

17. Krenek, "Self-Analysis," *New Mexico Quarterly* 23, no. 1 (1953): 14.

18. Ernst Krenek, *Kleine Suite für Klarinette und Klavier* (Cassel: Bärenreiter, 1969).

19. Krenek, "Self-Analysis," 14.

20. Ernst Krenek to Paul Bekker, letter of 14 December 1924. All Krenek-Bekker correspondence is from the Bekker papers at the Music Division of The Library of Congress and is quoted with the permission of Prof. Krenek.

21. Krenek to Bekker, letter of 9 December 1924.

22. Krenek to Bekker, letter of 14 December 1924.

23. Krenek, telephone interview with the author, 21 April 1982.

24. Siegfried Kracauer, *From Caligari to Hitler: A Psychological History of the German Film* (Princeton N.J.: Princeton University Press, 1947), 110.

25. Kracauer, *From Caligari to Hitler,* 111.

26. Hans and Rosaleen Moldenhauer, *Anton von Webern* (New York: Alfred A. Knopf, 1979), 158.

27. Ernst Krenek, *Jonny spielt auf,* piano-vocal score (Vienna: Universal Edition, 1926), 4–5. "Du schöner Berg! der mich anzieht, der mich antreibt, zu gehn fort von der Heimat, fort von der Arbeit."

28. Arnold Schoenberg, "The Future of Opera," *Neues Wiener Tagblatt,* 1927. Translated in *Style and Idea,* ed. Leonard Stein (New York: St. Martin's Press, 1975), 336–37.

29. H. H. Stuckenschmidt, interview with the author, West Berlin, 16 November 1981.

30. Krenek, *Jonny spielt auf,* piano-vocal score, 195. "Jetzt ist der Moment gekommen! Ich muss den Zug erreichen, der ins Leben führt."

31. Krenek, telephone interview with the author, 21 April 1982.

32. H. H. Stuckenschmidt, interview with the author, West Berlin, 16 November 1981.

33. *Jonny spielt auf* has been performed in the last two decades in Florence (1963, 1965), Regensburg (1968), Vienna (1980), Leeds (1984), and most recently, Palermo (1987) without any apparent problems and using black singers in the title role.

34. Ernst Krenek, in a letter to Nicholas Slonimsky, reprinted in *Music since 1900,* 4th ed (New York: Charles Scribners's Sons, 1971), 447.

35. Krenek, *Jonny spielt auf,* piano-vocal score, 129–30. "Da kommt die neue Welt übers Meer gefahren mit Glanz und erbt das alte Europa durch den Tanz."

36. Krenek, *Jonny spielt auf,* piano-vocal score, 201–3. "Die Stunde schlägt der alten Zeit, die neue Zeit bricht jetzt an. Versäumt den Anschluss nicht. Die Überfahrt beginnt ins unbekannte Land der Freiheit."

37. Krenek, *Jonny spielt auf,* piano-vocal score, 191. "Das Automobil setzt sich mit einem Hupenton in Bewegung. Im gleichen Augenblick verschwindet das Gittertor nach rechts und man sieht, den die Szene abschliessenden Vorhang entlang, Lichter, beleuchtete Fenster, Lichtreklamen u. dgl. mit wachsender Geschwindigkeit nach rechts gleiten, so dass die Illusion angedeutet wird, dass das Auto durch beleuchtete Grosstadtstrassen nach links fährt."

38. *Jonny spielt auf:* Programmhefte (Leipzig: Neuestheater, 3 April 1928), from the archive of the Leipzig Museum für Stadtgeschichte.

39. *Ernst Krenek:* Jonny spielt auf. *Der Sensation-Erfolg am Leipziger Stadttheater* (Vienna: Universal Edition, [1927]), 3. Universal Edition also offered to provide houses with further technical advice and suggestions for set designs.

40. Olin Downes, "The Generation of Krenek," *The New York Times,* 13 January 1929.

41. Heinrich W. Schwab, "The Violinist on the Globe," *RIdIM/RCMI Newsletter* 7, no. 2 (1983): 10.

42. Horst J. P. Bergmeier, "Sam Wooding Recapitulated," *Storyville* 74 (December 1977–January 1978): 46.

43. Krenek, *Jonny spielt auf,* piano-vocal score, 45–46. "Leb wohl, mein Schatz, leb wohl, ich geh' hinweg aus meiner Heimat. Sei glücklich ohne mich, ich will es probieren ohne dich und nie komm' ich zurück."

44. H. H. Stuckenschmidt, interview with the author, West Berlin, 16 November 1981. Ludwig Hoffmann, *'Leb wohl, mein Schatz' Blues und Song,* Odeon O-6565; Gabriel Formiggini and his Orchestra, *Blues aus der Oper* Jonny spielt auf, Electro-Vox 08610; and Diez Weismann and Joh. de Leur, *Leb wohl, mein Schatz Blues aus der* Oper Johnny [*sic*] spielt auf, Elektrola E. G. 690. All three recordings are in the collection of the Music Division of the Deutsche Staatsbibliothek, East Berlin.

45. Krenek, *Jonny spielt auf,* piano-vocal score, 54–55. "O rêverie, doucement infinie, mélodie séduisante, son mysterieux, remplis mon coeur, remplis mon coeur de l'ivresse de la tristesse de l'éternel amour."

46. Ibid., 173–74. "Warum kommt er nicht? Ich fühl' es jetzt, ich hab vielleicht recht nicht an ihm getan."

47. Ibid., 175–76. "Ach, wo bist du nur? Ich fühl' es jetzt, ich bin allein nur schuld an deiner Schuld."

48. Ibid., 129–30. "Jetzt ist die Geige mein, und ich will drauf spielen, wie old David einst die Harfe schlug, und preisen Jehova, der die Menschen schwarz erschuf. Mir gehört alles, was gut ist in der Welt. Die alte Welt hat es erzeugt, sie weiss damit nichts mehr zu tun. Da kommt die neue Welt übers Meer gefahren mit Glanz und erbt das alte Europa durch den Tanz."

49. William Austin, *"Susanna," "Jeanie," and "The Old Folks at Home"* (New York: Macmillan, 1975), 226.

50. Ludwig Hofmann, *Hymne des Jonny,* Odeon O-6565; Diez Weismann and Joh. de Leur, *Jonnys-Triumph-Gesang,* Elektrola E. G. 690.

51. Krenek, *Jonny spielt auf,* piano-vocal score, 208–12. "So hat uns Jonny aufgespielt zum Tanz. Hat euch dies Spiel gefallen, dankt es ihm! Und denkt daran, das ganze Leben ist ein Spiel. Begleit euch seiner Geige Ton, wohin ihr auch geht! Denn seht, er tritt unter euch, und Jonny spielt auf."

52. Ibid., *Jonny spielt auf,* piano-vocal score, 20. "Ich suchte mein Heim in der Träume Land."

53. As another stab at Schoenberg, the text may have been meant as a spoof on the text of the last movement of Schoenberg's *String Quartet II* which opens "I feel an air from other planets streaming through darkness."

54. Brügmann's forced departure from Germany and death before he could return has resulted in his virtual absence from all major biographical sources. Only now are his contributions to opera direction being assessed. See Jürgen Schebera, "Herr Brecht, machen Sie doch weiter: Die Ära Brecher/Brügmann," *Theater der Zeit* 1 (1986): 49–52.

55. Ernst Krenek, telephone interview with the author, 21 April 1982.

56. Stefan Stompor, foreword to "Opern-Übersetzung," by Gustav Brecher in *Jahrbuch der Komischen Oper* 2 (Berlin: Henschel, 1962): 49.

57. Paul Schwers, *"Jonny spielt auf," Allgemeine Musikzeitung* 54 (1927): 151–52.

58. See statistics in appendix D. Hans Heinsheimer, in *Menagerie in F Sharp* (1947; reprint, Westport, Conn.: Greenwood Press, 1979), 142–44, discusses the unprecedented popularity of *Jonny spielt auf* which resulted in a brand of Jonny cigarettes and a request from Warner Brothers for the movie rights. Two other houses produced the work in its first season, and in the 1927–28 season, the work swept across Europe with performances on 45 different stages as far apart as Zagreb, Ljubljana, Antwerp, and Paris. The libretto was eventually translated into 14 languages.

59. Adolf Aber, "Ernst Krenek: *Jonny spielt auf,*" *Leipziger Neuste Nachrichten,* 11 February 1927. "Die Leipziger Oper hat ihre Sensation. Endlich einmal ein Stück des Zeitgeschehens mit höchster Plastik in einem musikalischen Bühnenwerk erfasst! Spannend und unterhaltend zugleich, wirkungsvoll als Groteske und Revue. . . . Musikalisch gewiss seine Offenbarung aber voll Witz und treffendster Situations-Schilderung. Der Erfolg war schon noch dem ersten Akt entschieden. Nach dem zweiten . . . gab es Rundgebungen stürmischer Art für den Komponisten, den Dirignten [*sic*] Gustav Brecher und den Regisseur des Werkes Walther Brügmann, der hier das kaum Denkbare möglich gemacht hat.

60. Oskar Bie, *"Jonny spielt auf," Berliner Börsen-Courier,* 12 February 1927. Reprinted in *Ernst Krenek:* Jonny spielt auf, 5. "Eins der phantastischen Werke der gesamten Operngeschichte. . . . die technische Poesie der Gegenwert . . . eine elementare Äusserung des Menschentempos."

61. Walther Schrenk, "Ernst Krenek: *Jonny spielt auf,*" *Deutsche allgemeine Zeitung,* reprinted in *Ernst Krenek:* Jonny spielt auf, 5.

62. Adolf Weissmann, "Ernst Krenek: *Jonny spielt auf,*" *B. Z. am Mittag,* reprinted in *Ernst Krenek:* Jonny spielt auf, 5. "Eine von Anfang bis zum Ende fesselnde, immer klingende Partitur. Da gibt es ja, unverhülltes, F Dur, C Dur, D Dur, die alles Zwischentönige, Neuzeitliche hinwegschwemmen. Dies ist Musik fürs grosse Publikum."

63. Hermann Kesser to Paul Bekker, letter of 28 October 1927, from the Paul Bekker correspondence at the Music Division of The Library of Congress. "Gestern Abend hoerte ich im Theater Krenek. Es war einer meiner staerksten Bühneneindrücke—durch Szene u. Musik—seit manchem Jahr. . . . es war mir auch bisher noch nicht moeglich gewesen, zu einer Leistung der juengsten Musikliteratur—die wirklich groesstenteils nur 'Literatur' zu sein scheint—aus spontanem Herzensurteil bedingungslos ja zu sagen. . . . Nun, gestern ist mir jedenfalls zum ersten Male ein Werk von ganz grosser, neuer musikalischer Lebensschwungkraft begegnet. . . . Mir ist bis jetzt nicht beschieden gewesen, Musik kennen zu lernen, die

so echt und wesentlich aus unserer Zeit kommt! Das sind kuenftige Melodien! Das ist Erholung! Die Mehrzahl sieht wohl—ich schliesse das aus Meinungen, die fragmentarisch zu mir gekommen sind—das Entscheidende, das "moderne" darin in den Zusammenhaengen mit Tanz, Neger, ja Jazz. Auch ich freue mich an diesen Elementen. Sie sind grossartig in den Stil hereingenommen."

64. The photograph from the Berlin production (illustration 5.4) was reproduced in *Funkstunde,* 14 October 1925.

65. *Funkstunde,* 14 October 1925, 1340.

66. Oskar Bie, "Ernst Krenek: *Jonny spielt auf,*" *Berliner Börsen-Courier,* 9 October 1928.

67. Hanns Eisler, "Ernst Krenek: *Jonny spielt auf,*" *Die rote Fahne,* 19 October 1927, reprinted in Eisler, *Musik und Politik* (Munich: Rogner and Bernhard, 1973), 34–36.

68. Max Marschalk, "Jazz-Oper und Mysterium," *Vossische Zeitung,* 11 October 1927.

69. Alfred Einstein, "Ernst Krenek: *Jonny spielt auf,*" *Berliner Tageblatt,* 10 October 1927.

70. Royal J. Schmidt, *Versailles and the Ruhr* (The Hague: Nijhoff, 1968), 38.

71. Alfred Jerger, in the liner notes to Ernst Krenek, *Jonny spielt auf* [excerpts], Amadeo AVRS 5038.

72. "*Jonny spielt auf,*" *A. Z. am Abend,* 18 June 1928.

73. Ibid. "Es handelt sich dabei durchaus nicht um eine 'Glorifizierung' der schwarzen Rasse. Jonny, der Jazzbandgeiger, tritt auf als Repräsentant hemmungsloser Triebhaftigkeit. . . . Jonny spielt auf—und Europa tanzt nach seiner Geige. Ist's etwa nicht so?"

74. Max Chop, "Ernst Krenek: *Jonny spielt auf,*" *Signale für die musikalische Welt* 85 (1927): 1477–80, and A. Laszlo, "Zürcher Stadttheater: *Jonny spielt auf* von Ernst Krenek," *Signale für die musikalische Welt* 86 (1928): 932–34; "Wie es Jonny in München, Budapest und Paris erging," *Zeitschrift für Musik* 95 (1928): 440.

75. "Deutschland nun auch in Amerika durch *Jonny spielt auf* blossgestellt," *Zeitschrift für Musik* 96 (1929): 160–62.

76. Hans Mersmann, "Ernst Krenek *Jonny spielt auf,*" *Melos* 7 (January 1928): 24. Alois Munk made a similar mistake criticizing Krenek as a librettist based on the text of Max's aria. Alois Munk, "*Jonny spielt auf,*" *Berliner Lokalanzeiger,* 9 October 1928.

77. Hans F. Schaub, "Kreneks 'Jonny' im Hamburger Stadttheater," *Allgemeine Musikzeitung* 54 (1927): 731–32; Georg Gräner, "Bruckner und der Geist des 'Jonny'," *Allgemeine Musikzeitung* 54 (1927): 1215–17.

78. Gräner, "Bruckner und der Geist des 'Jonny'," 1217. "Atonalität, Vierteltonmusik, Neue Sachlichkeit, neuer Hellenismus, Jazzsinfonie, Jazzoper—was haben diese mehr oder minder interessanten Tagesereignisse mit dem inneren, metaphysichen Leben, mit geistig-seelischer Neugeburt, mit der Kunst des Genies zu schaffen?"

79. Walter Harry, "Zeitliches und Überzeitliches in *Jonny spielt auf,*" *Anbruch* 10 (January 1928): 14–17.

80. A similarly psycho-literary treatment of the work by Rudolf Majut appeared in the *Germanisch-Romanische Monatschrift* 16 and discussed *Jonny spielt auf* in light of Rousseau's primitivism and Hermann Hesse's *Weltschmerz.* This article was abstracted in *Die Musik* 21 (March 1929): 457.

81. "'Jazz' Opera in Vienna," *The London Times*, 4 January 1928.

82. *"Jonny spielt auf* Excites Interest," *The New York Times*, 11 January 1929.

83. Olin Downes, "The Generation of Krenek," *The New York Times*, 13 January 1929.

84. Ernst Krenek, *Jonny spielt auf: Libretto*, trans. Frederick H. Martens (New York: Fred. Rallman, 1928): 14.

85. Ibid., 41.

86. Olin Downes, *Jonny spielt auf* Opera of this Age," *The New York Times*, 20 January 1929.

87. "Al Jolson greets 'Jonny,'" *The New York Times*, 20 January 1929.

88. Downes, *"Jonny spielt auf* Opera of This Age."

89. Olin Downes, *"Jonny spielt auf* Again," *The New York Times*, 29 January 1929.

90. Alfred Frankenstein, "Jazz Arrives at the Opera," *Review of Reviews* 79 (1929): 138.

91. "Jonny Strikes Up the Band," *Literary Digest* 100 (1929): 20.

92. Grenville Vernon, *"Jonny spielt auf,"* *Commonweal* 9 (1929): 450.

93. "In Aid of Babies' Hospital," *The New York Times*, 8 February 1929.

94. Olin Downes, "Tibbett as Jazz Leader," *The New York Times*, 28 February 1929.

95. Olin Downes, "Metropolitan Repertory," *The New York Times*, 31 March 1929.

96. Herbert Peyser, "Jonny over There," *Modern Music* 6 (January–February 1929): 34.

97. Henry Cowell, "Why the Ultra-Modernists Frown on Krenek's Opera," *Singing and Playing* 4 (February 1929): 15, 39. The citation and a brief annotation are given in Bruce Saylor, *The Writings of Henry Cowell: A Descriptive Bibliography* (New York: ISAM, 1977). Charles Ives, in a letter to Cowell ca. 1930, mentions the opera in the context of his rejection by members of the International Society for Contemporary Music: "Johnny Spiel auf [*sic*] will put it to American Music." Quoted in Frank Rossiter, *Charles Ives and His America* (New York: Liveright, 1975), 225.

98. George Antheil, "The Negro on the Spiral," in *Negro: An Anthology*, ed. Nancy Cunard, ed. and abridg. Hugh Ford (New York: Frederick Ungar, 1970), 218; "Wanted: Opera by and for Americans," *Modern Music* (June–July 1930): 11–16.

99. Adolf Weissmann, "Ernst Krenek," *Auftakt* 9 (1929): 271. "Das Aufsehen war so gross, dass es zum Sammelpunkt für die jüngere Generation wurde."

100. Wilhelm Altmann, "Opernstatistik," *Allgemeine Musikzeitung* 60 (1933): 41–15.

101. Paul Bekker, "An Ernst Krenek," in *Briefe an zeitgenössische Musiker* (Berlin: Max Hesses Verlag, 1932), 93. "Armer Krenek. Was hat dieser "Jonny" Ihnen eingetragen! Nicht an Honorar, denn das war weniger, als böswillige Neider behaupteten. Wohl aber an Missgunst, Hass, Verunglimpfung, moralischer und ästhetischer Ächtung, Minderwertigkeitsfeststellung und anderen lieblichen Begleitmusiken eines Welterfolges."

102. H. H. Stuckenschmidt, interview with the author, West Berlin, 16 November 1981.

103. Adolf Weissmann, "Ernst Krenek," *Auftakt* 9 (1929): 272.

104. Krenek, "Self-Analysis," 18.

105. Krenek, *Horizons Circled*, 49. The publicity photograph was reproduced in *Funkstunde*, 14 December 1928: 1678.

106. Peter Heyworth, *Otto Klemperer: His Life and Times*, vol. 1, 1885–1933 (Cambridge: Cambridge University Press, 1982), 277.

107. Alfred Einstein, "D'Alberts *Schwarze Orchidee* und das 'Triptychon' von Krenek," *Berliner Tageblatt*, 3 December 1928.

108. Ernst Krenek, "From *Jonny* to *Orest*," *Leipziger Neuste Nachrichten*, January 1930. Trans. by Margaret Shenfield and Geoffrey Skelton in *Exploring Music* (New York: October House, 1966), 23–25.

109. Ibid., 25.

110. "Das *Leben des Orest* und der Tod der 'Neuen Sachlichkeit'," *Hamburg Mittagsblatt*, 17 April 1930.

111. Theodor Wiesengrund-Adorno, "Zur Deutung Kreneks," *Anbruch* 14 (February 1932): 42.

Chapter 6

1. David Drew in *Kurt Weill: A Handbook* (Berkeley: University of California, 1987), 129, discusses a foxtrot cabaret number, one of Weill's few surviving early works.

2. Ivan Goll, "Manifeste du surréalisme," in *Oeuvres*, 2 vols. eds. Claire Goll and François Xavier (Paris: Emile and Paul, 1968–70), I:87–89.

3. Margaret A. Parmée, *Ivan Goll: The Development of His Poetic Themes and Their Images* (Bonn: Bouvier, 1981), 164.

4. See Kowalke, *Kurt Weill in Europe*, 47–48 for a more in-depth discussion of *Royal Palace* as a turning point in Weill's compositional development.

5. Ivan Goll, "Flucht in die Oper," *Blätter der Staatsoper* 7 (February 1927): 10–11: "das Märchen vom Leben, das erst im Tode sich erkennt."

6. Undoubtedly the most famous opera requiring a filmed sequence, which also depicted events in the life of the heroine, was Alban Berg's *Lulu*. Berg did not begin work on *Lulu* until some two years after the premiere of *Royal Palace*. The use of the filmed sequence was announced in pre-premiere publicity and all reviews mentioned it, thus Berg must have known of Weill's earlier use.

7. Parmée, *Ivan Goll*, 165.

8. Kurt Weill, *Royal Palace*, piano-vocal score (Vienna: Unversal Edition, 1926), 41. "Alle zur Zeit der Aufführung aktuellen Leckerbissen werden gezeigt. Dejanira in Nizza, im Schlafwagen nach Konstantinopel, ein Ball, russisches Ballett, Flug zum Nordpol u.s.w."

9. Walther Schrenk, "Operndämmerung: *Royal Palace* in der Staatsoper," *Deutsche Allgemeine Zeitung*, 4 March 1927.

10. A photograph of Aravatinos's set appears in Elisabeth Reissig, "Die moderne Idee in der Opern Regie: Franz Ludwig Hörth, *Erlebte Opernkunst* (Berlin: Österheld, 1928): 42.

11. "Berlin Opera Mingles Auto Horn, Films, Jazz," *The New York Times*, 3 March 1927.

12. Adolf Weissmann, "Germany's Latest Music Dramas," *Modern Music* 4 (May–June 1927): 24.

13. Paul Schwers, "Kurt Weill in der Berliner Staatsoper," *Allgemeine Musikzeitung* 54 (1927): 241.

14. Alfred Baresel, *"Royal Palace:* Berliner Uraufführung der Jazzoper von Kurt Weill," *Neue Musik-Zeitung* 48 (1927): 316–17.

15. Weissmann, "Germany's Latest Music Dramas," 25.

16. Alfred Baresel, *"Royal Palace"*; Paul Stefan, "Berlin: Weill *Royal Palace,"* *Anbruch* 9 (March 1927): 133–34; Karl Westermeyer, "Berlin: Kurt Weill: *Royal Palace,"* *Rheinische Musik- und Theater-Zeitung,* 28 (1927): 108–10; and Westermeyer, *"Royal Palace,"* *Signale für die musikalische Welt* 85 (1927): 330–32.

17. Adolf Aber, "Kurt Weill und sein Schaffen," *Leipziger Bühnenblätter* 14 (1928–29): 117: "dass beide Werke im Grunde gar nichts miteinander zu tun haben. *Royal Palace* war ein im ganzen gescheiterter Versuch, die starke und echte Dramatik des 'Protagonist' mit dem Unterhaltungsbedürfnis der Zeit irgendwie in Einklang zu bringen."

18. Hans Gutman, "Kurt Weill: *Royal Palace,"* *Auftakt* 7 (1927): 74–76. "In den Stimmen über dem Wasser, vom hochschwebenden Sopransolo überstrahlt, im Finale, das in den Rhythmus eines schön fliessenden Tangos eingebaut ist, liegen die höchsten Werte dieser Partitur. Natürlich gibt sich Weill dem Jazz nicht so unbedingt hin wie Krenek; er verwendet ihn in gemässigter, ja stilisierter Form, schon im Orchester dokumentiert sich diese Zurückhaltung, wo neben verschiedenartigem Schlagzeug nur ein einzelnes Saxophon und Klavier erscheinen."

19. See Kowalke, *Kurt Weill in Europe,* 46, 283–86; Douglas Jarman, *Kurt Weill: An Illustrated Biography* (Bloomington: Indiana University Press, 1982), 106–7; and Elaine Padmore, "Kurt Weill," *Music and Musicians* 21 (October 1972): 34–40.

20. David Drew, *Kurt Weill: A Handbook* (Berkeley: University of California Press, 1987), 164–70.

21. For more information on Weill's development of his *Song* style, see Kowalke, *Kurt Weill in Europe,* 132–37.

22. See David Drew, *Kurt Weill,* 173, for a discussion of problems with the published editions.

23. Leo Lania, who knew Brecht through their mutual friend Erwin Piscator, talks at some length in his memoir, *Today We Are Brothers* (Boston: Houghton Mifflin, 1942), about how postwar Berlin aped much of decadent American culture.

24. Brecht and Weill, *Mahagonny-Songspel,* piano-vocal score.

25. See Bertolt Brecht, "Mehr guten Sport," *Berliner Börsen-Courier,* 6 February 1926. Translated as "Emphasis on Sport" in John Willett, ed., *Brecht on Theatre* (New York: Hill and Wang, 1964), 6–9.

26. Eberhard Preussner, Deutsche Kammermusik Baden-Baden 1927," *Die Musik* 19 (September 1927): 887.

27. Aaron Copland, "Baden-Baden 1927," *Modern Music* 5 (November-December 1927): 31–34.

28. E. Th. Krojanker, "Kurt Weill über seine Oper," *Leipzig Neuste Nachrichten,* 18 February 1928. "Denn es handelt sich für mich darum, eine abendfüllende Ergänzung zum "Protagonist" zu schaffen. Ein gegensätzliches Werk anderen Genres, doch an Spannung und Wirksamkeit diesem nicht nachstehend. Ein Stoff war mein Ideal, der jenen privaten Charakter früherer Opernstoffe Gedankengängen unserer Zeit zuwendet, die ja reich genug ist an darstellungswerten Typen."

29. Ibid.

30. Kowalke, In *Kurt Weill in Europe*, 545–49, lists the topics of Weill's signed articles in *Der deutsche Rundfunk*. His reviews of various works by Mozart, Lortzing, and Offenbach are reprinted in *Ausgewählte Schriften*, David Drew, ed. (Frankfurt, Suhrkamp, 1975), 141–57.

31. Kurt Weill, "Die neue Oper," *Der neue Weg* 55 (16 January 1926): 24–25. Translated in Kowalke, *Kurt Weill in Europe*, 464–67.

32. Krojanker, "Kurt Weill über seine Oper." "Fast von selbst ergab sich daraus die Atmosphäre Paris . . . ich mit Paris gar keine innere Fühlungnahme habe und es nicht einmal kenne."

33. Weill, *Der Zar lässt sich photographieren*, piano-vocal score, 44, 101. "Wie schön ist diese Aussicht auf Paris . . . Montmartre! Moulin Rouge! Bei Nacht noch interessanter. . . . Nun stirbt der Traum Paris."

34. Krojanker, "Kurt Weill über seine Oper."

35. Kurt Weill, *Der Zar lässt sich photographieren*, piano-vocal score, 61–62. "Zar: Genügt das Licht? Es ist ja Dämmerung. Wie lang muss ich sitzen stocksteifstill? Falsche Angèle: Ich habe Blitzlicht in der Kamera. Zar: Werd' ich erschrecken? F. Angèle: Das wird sich finden! Zar: Sie glauben fest, ich werde gut getroffen? F. Angèle: Ich treffe wie der Schütze seine Scheibe."

36. Kurt Weill, "Albert Lortzing: *Zar und Zimmermann*," *Der deutsche Rundfunk* 3 (26 April 1925): 1069; and "Albert Lortzing: Zu seinem 125. Geburtstag," *Der deutsche Rundfunk* 4 (17 October 1926): 2953. Both reviews are reprinted in *Ausgewählte Schriften*, 146–47 and 122–23, respectively.

37. Weill, "Albert Lortzing.": "eine einheitliche, umfassende Opernform . . . die nicht nur als Ausdruck ihrer Zeit, sondern auch als Gattung an sich immer Geltung behalten wird."

38. This work was also reviewed by Weill in *Der deutsche Rundfunk* 4 (21 November 1926): 3329–32.

39. Letter from Kurt Weill to Universal Edition, 14 May 1927. Copies of the complete Weill-Universal Edition correspondence are available at The Weill-Lenya Research Center at Yale University. All of Weill's correspondence is cited with the permission of The Kurt Weill Foundation for Music.

40. Postcard from Weill to Universal Edition, 2 December 1927.

41. Krojanker, "Kurt Weill über seine Oper."

42. Ibid. "Durch einen später von mir selbständig hinzugefügten Männerchor, der hauptsächlich mit dem Satz: [several words obscured in the original] jongliert um sich manchmal sogar in etwas unpassender Weise zu den Vorgängen gewinnen zu können, ist der Opera-buffa-Charakter des Werkes unterstrichen."

43. Adolf Aber, "Kurt Weill und sein Schaffen," *Leipziger Bühnenblätter*, no. 14 (1927–28): 118.

44. Letter from Weill to Universal Edition, 23 March 1927.

45. Kurt Weill, "Verschiebungen in der musikalischen Produktion," *Berliner Tageblatt*, 1 October 1927. Translated in Kowalke, *Kurt Weill in Europe*, 478–79.

46. Kurt Weill, "Igor Stravinsky: *Oedipus Rex*," *Der deutsche Rundfunk* 6 (16 November 1928): 3180. Reprinted in *Ausgewählte Schriften*, 161.

47. See Paul Stefan, "Antinomie der neuen Oper: Kurt Weill and Stravinsky," *Anbruch* 10 (March-April 1928): 119–122, and T. W. Adorno in *Die Musik* 20 (September 1928): 923–24.

48. Weill to Universal Edition, 18 November 1927.

49. Karl Holl, *"Der Protagonist, Royal Palace,"* *Frankfurter Zeitung*, 21 June 1928.

50. This publicity photograph, the original now in the Leipzig Museum für Stadtgeschichte, was published in *Anbruch* 10 (April–May 1928): 121.

51. Reviews from the Frankfurt, Düsseldorf, and Prague productions also mention the chorus's distinctive dress.

52. Georg Kaiser, *Werke*, ed. Walther Huder (Frankfurt: Propyläen, 1972), I:490, 492, 505.

53. Ernst Toller, *Prosa, Briefe, Dramen, Gedichte* (Reinbek bei Hamburg: Rowohlt, 1961), 303.

54. Ibid., 421.

55. J. L. Styan, *Expressionism and Epic Theatre*, Modern Drama in Theory and Practise 3 (Cambridge: Cambridge University Press, 1981), 129.

56. No mention of the chorus appears in the first scenario Weill sent his publisher (4 April 1927). Weill does not refer to the chorus until a letter of 6 August 1927, by which time the music was largely composed.

57. Letter from Weill to Universal Edition, 4 January 1928.

58. Weill, *Der Zar lässt sich photographieren*, piano-vocal score, 20–21.

59. Ibid., 100.

60. Krojanker, "Kurt Weill über seine Oper." "Jazz-elemente sind mir nicht Illustration des mondänen Lebens, sondern absolutes musikalisches Ausdrucksmittel. Wo Ich sie verwende, wünsche ich eine wirklich nur durch diese erreichbare Wirkung zu erziehlen, was in dieser Oper um so verblüssender ist, als ich mir den Jazz-Klang bis zum Höhepunkt aufgespart habe."

61. A manuscript copy of the full score is available at The Kurt Weill Foundation for Music, New York City.

62. Weill, *Der Zar lässt sich photographieren*, piano-vocal score, 43. "Als Mensch, der auf den Strassen geht mit andern Menschen, die alle seines gleichen sind."

63. Krojanker, "Kurt Weill über seine Oper." "Ich beabsichtige die Wirkung nur durch eine völlig neue Klangform, und das war für mich von vorneherein—das Gramophon. Ich instrumentierte einen Tango eigens für das Gramophon, dass—während das Orchester schweigt—zum ersten Male als Soloist auftritt, und dessen Melodie die Sänger eigene Kantilenen gegenüberstellen. Gerade durch die Gegensätzlichkeit einer bis zur höchsten Spannung gesteigerten Handlung und einer rein tänzerischen Schallplatte schien mir die Wirkung des Höhepunktes erreicht."

64. C. D. Innes, *Erwin Piscator's Political Theatre* (London: Cambridge University Press, 1972), 18.

65. David Drew, *Kurt Weill: A Handbook* (Berkeley: University of California Press, 1987), 169–70.

66. A concert performance of *Der Zar lässt sich photographieren* was performed in Cologne on 3 November 1984 under the auspices of the West German Radio. Members of the Cologne Radio Orchestra and Chorus were conducted by Jan Latham-Köneg. A copy of this performance is in the collection of The Kurt Weill Foundation for Music.

67. The presence of the accordion gives the *Tango-Angèle* a sound quality very similar to that found later in *Die Dreigroschenoper*. Though the circumstances surrounding the recording of the *Tango-Angèle* are unclear, it may have given Weill his first opportunity to work with jazz instrumental sonorities used later with such success in *Die Dreigroschenoper*.

68. Programmhefte: Jonny spielt auf, Leipzig Neues Theater, 3 April 1928, in the collection of the Leipzig Museum für Stadtgeschichte.

69. Peter Heyworth, *Otto Klemperer: His Life and Times*, 2 vols. (Cambridge: Cambridge University Press, 1983), 246.

70. Letter from Weill to Universal Edition, 20 September 1927.

71. Letter from Weill to Universal Edition, 23 October 1927.

72. Letters from Weill to Universal Edition, 23 October, 2 November, and 10 November 1927.

73. Letter from Weill to Universal Edition, 12 February 1928.

74. Adolf Aber, "Oper: Leipzig," *Die Musik* 20 (April 1928): 542.

75. Alfred Baresel, "Der neue Kurt Weill: *Der Zar lässt sich photographieren*," *Neue Musik-Zeitung* 49 (1928): 384. "Ein griechischer Chor im Orchesterraum erläutert die Geheimnisse der verderblichen Kamera und zerknittert die mehrmals frischgebügelte Spannung: Triumph der Groteske! Jazzrhythmen sind als Absolutum eingefangen; und brechen am Schluss als Grammophon-Tango doch zum Schlager."

76. Adolf Aber, "Weill und Spinelli: Uraufführung von *Der Zar* und Neuinszenierung von *A Basso Porto*," *Leipzig neuste Nachrichten*, 20 February 1928. "Sie wird um so sparsamer, je mehr sich auf der Bühne die Dinge zuspitzen. Schliesslich muss ein Grammophon im Atelier der schönen Pariser Photographin das ganze Orchester ersetzen, und zwar mit einem meisterlich gearbeiteten Tango."

77. Heinrich Strobel, "Kurt Weill *Der Zar lässt sich photographieren*," *Melos* 7 (March 1928): 137–38.

78. Alfred Einstein, "Gay German Opera: Reich Provinces Hear Lighter Novelties by Dressel, Weill and Wellesz," *The New York Times*, 22 April 1928.

79. Alfred Einstein, "Unproblematische und problematische Oper," *Berliner Tageblatt*, 15 October 1928: "dass der Mangel an Musik ein Weg zu einer neuen Opernform ist."

80. Adolf Weissmann, "Kurt Weill's New Opera," *Christian Science Monitor*, 24 March 1928.

81. Paul Stefan, "Antinomie der neuen Oper: Kurt Weill und Stravinsky," *Anbruch* 10 (March–April 1928): 119–22.

82. Heinz Jolles, "Paraphrase über Kurt Weill," *Neue Musik- Zeitung* 49 (1928): 541–44.

83. Jolles, "Paraphrase über Kurt Weill." "Wie er den Lockungen eines geistreichen Buffo-Libretto so wohl widersteht, ihnen anderseits auf seine Weise entgegenkommt."

84. Letter from Weill to Universal Edition, 8 March 1928.

85. Letters from Weill to Universal Edition, 16 March 1928, and Universal Edition to Weill, 3 April 1928.

86. Fritz Ohrmann, "Kurt Weill in der Berliner Städtischen Oper," *Signale für die musikalische Welt* 86 (1928): 1279–82.

87. The American premiere took place on 27 October 1949 at the Juilliard School, New York, as *The Shah Has His Photograph Taken,* under the direction of Dino Yannopoulos. Most recently the Camden Festival produced *Der Zar lässt sich photographieren* on a double bill with *Der Protagonist* in 1986 under the direction of John Eaton.

88. Letter from Weill to Universal Edition, 23 February 1928.

89. Ibid.

90. Weill's description of the chorus's function suggests the alienating or distancing effect [*Verfremdungseffekt*] as later articulated by Brecht. Typification, also present in the chorus, was one of the techniques ascribed by Brecht to epic opera as well.

Chapter 7

1. Letter of Hindemith to Strecker, 13 February 1924. Copies of the entire Hindemith-Strecker correspondence are available at the Paul-Hindemith-Institut in Frankfurt am Main.

2. Ibid.

3. Letters of Strecker to Hindemith, 1 October 1923 and 28 January 1925.

4. Quoted in Andres Briner, *Paul Hindemith* (Mainz: Schott, 1971), 17. "Habe als Geiger, Bratscher, Klavierspieler, oder Schlagzeuger folgende musikalische Gebiete ausgiebig 'Beackert': Kammermusik aller Art, Kino, Kaffeehaus, Tanzmusik, Operette, Jazz-Band, Militärmusik."

5. Giselher Schubert, *Paul Hindemith: in Selbstzeugnissen und Bilddokumenten* (Hamburg: Rowohlt, 1981), 20. A picture of the Kurkapelle appears on page 18.

6. A page of the original manuscript is published in Paul Hindemith, *Briefe,* ed. Dieter Rexroth (Frankfurt: Fischer, 1982), 71.

7. Quoted in Schubert, *Paul Hindemith,* 30. "Können Sie auch Foxtrotts, Bostons, Rags und anderen Kitsch gebrauchen? Wenn mir keine anständige Musik mehr einfällt, schreibe ich immer solche Sachen."

8. Schubert, *Paul Hindemith,* 32, 144. Luther Noss, curator of the Hindemith Collection at Yale, in his list of Hindemith's works included in David Neumeyer's recent analytical treatment (*The Music of Paul Hindemith,* New Haven: Yale University Press, 1986) notes that missing from the list are a number of piano entertainment pieces from the 1920s: foxtrots, marches, rags, shimmies, etc.

9. Paul Hindemith, "Tanz der Holzpuppen: Foxtrot aus der Musik zu *Tuttifäntchen*" (Mainz: Schott, 1922).

10. Paul Hindemith, *Kammermusik No. 1* (Mainz: Schott, 1922), 4. Hindemith footnotes the quotation as having been borrowed with permission of the publisher, but I have not been able to discover anything further about Wilm Wilm or the original foxtrot. It is possible, knowing Hindemith's love of jokes, that the quotation is spurious: "Es empfiehlt sich, die Vortragenden dem Publikum unsichtbar zu plazieren."

11. Alfred Heuss, "Der Foxtrot im Konzertsaal," *Zeitschrift für Musik* 90 (1923): 54. "Es ist die lasterhafteste, frivolste und dabei gegenständlichste Musik, die man sich denken kann."

12. Letter of Strecker to Hindemith, 18 September 1923.

13. Hindemith's jesting use of regal and militaristic march music appeared again in 1923 with his *Minimax* for string quartet which contains inside jokes for the Fürstenberg family, the patrons of the Donaueschingen/Baden-Baden Festivals, and parodies several well-known marches.

14. Paul Hindemith, *Suite 1922* (Mainz: Schott, 1922), 19. "Spiele diese Stück sehr wild, aber stets sehr stramm in Rhythmus, wie eine Maschine. Betrachte hier das Klavier als eine intressante [*sic*] Art Schlagzeug u. handle dementsprechend."

15. Quoted in Briner, *Paul Hindemith*, 38: "kleine, einseitig bespannte Ringe—Tambourins ohne Schellen ähnlich—wie sie bis jetzt nur in Jazzbands gebräuchlich sind."

16. Franz Willms, "Paul Hindemith. Ein Versuch," in *Von neuer Musik* (Cologne: F. J. Marcan, 1925), 78–123.

17. Adolphe Weissmann, "La Jeune Musique allemande et Paul Hindemith," *L'Esprit nouveau*, nos. 20, 22 (1925): no page numbers given. "Le dessin de couverture déjà, ce pêle-mêle de gens, de véhicules, de lampes à arc, de fils électriques, crayonnés par l'auteur lui-même, est déjà le miroir du chaos, et la folie de l'homme de cabaret qui s'y reflète."

18. Greul, *Bretter die die Zeit bedeuten* (Cologne: Kiepenheuer and Witsch, 1967), 262.

19. Richard Strauss, *Intermezzo* (London: Boosey and Hawkes, 1952), foreword.

20. Hindemith, *Hin und zurück,* piano-vocal score (Mainz: Schott, [1927]), 14–15. "Von ganz droben gesehn ist es ohne Belang ob des Menschen Lebensgang von der Wiege vorwärts irrt, bis er verdirbt, oder ob er erst stirbt und nachher geboren wird."

21. Helga de la Motte-Haber and Hans Emons, *Filmmusik: Eine systematische Beschreibung* (Munich: Carl Hanser, 1980), 91–93.

22. Particulars on Hindemith's course were reported in "In Studio bei Hindemith," *Filmkurier* 10 (20 March 1930).

23. Hindemith, *Hin und zurück,* piano-vocal score, 16. "Schon nagt an mir der Reue Zahn."

24. *Das Illustrierte Blatt* [Frankfurt], 30 July 1927: 801.

25. Marc Blitzstein, "*Hin und zurück* in Philadelphia," *Modern Music* 5 (May–June 1928): 34–36.

26. Alfred Einstein, "Festvorstellung für den Tennis-Club Rot-Weiss," *Berliner Tageblatt,* 1 December 1930. Reprinted in Hans Curjel, *Experiment Krolloper* (Munich: Prestel, 1975), 302–3.

27. Letter of Strecker to Hindemith, 18 May 1927.

28. Letter of Hindemith to Strecker, 12 April 1928.

29. Letter of Hindemith to Strecker, 16 June 1928.

30. Gertrude Hindemith to Strecker, writing on behalf of her husband, 29 November 1928.

31. *Das Illustrierte Blatt* [Frankfurt], 29 June 1929: 788.

32. Hindemith, *Neues vom Tage,* piano-vocal score, 245–46.

33. Ibid., 97–98. "Heisses Wasser, tags, nachts, ein Bad bereit in drei Minuten. Kein Gasgeruch, keine Explosion, keine Lebensgefahr. Fort, fort mit den alten Gasbadeöfen."

34. Letter of Hindemith to Strecker, 16 June 1928.

35. Hindemith, *Neues vom Tage*, piano-vocal score, 66. "Beachten Sie die fehlenden Arme. Echt klassisch, drei Sterne im Baedecker."

36. Peter Heyworth, *Otto Klemperer* (Cambridge: Cambridge University Press, 1983), 293.

37. Letter of 30 May 1929, quoted in Heyworth, *Otto Klemperer*, 292.

38. Ibid., 293.

39. Letter of 2 June 1929, quoted in Heyworth, *Otto Klemperer*, 292–93.

40. "Das Bild als Scheidungsgrund," *Berliner Börsen-Courier*, 7 June 1929.

41. Alfred Einstein, *Neues vom Tage*, *Berliner Tageblatt*, 10 June 1929. Reprinted in Hans Curjel, *Experiment Krolloper*, 267–69: "ein Missverhältnis zwischen dem (leichten) Anspruch dieses Textes, dieser kabarettistischen dramatischen Bilderfolge, und dem (weniger leichten) Anspruch der Musik."

42. Hans Gutman, "Tabloid Hindemith," *Modern Music* 7 (December-January 1929): 34–37.

43. Paul Bekker, "An Paul Hindemith," in *Briefe an zeitgenössische Musiker* (Berlin: Max Hesse, 1932), 31–43.

44. H. H. Stuckenschmidt, "Bühne und Kunst: Hindemiths *Neues vom Tage*," *Bohemia* (Prague), 9 June 1929. "Dieser Schluss ist der stärkste dramatische Einwand gegen das Stück. Die abschliessende Chorszene mit dem Duett Laura-Eduard ist schwach, theatralisch vergriffen und zerstört vieles von den ausgezeichneten Eindrücken des Abends. Man wird sie gründlich umarbeiten müssen, um die Oper lebensfähig zu machen."

45. Arno Huth, *"Neues vom Tage,"* *Frankfurter Nachrichten*, 11 June 1929.

46. Letter of 25 February 1930, quoted in Geoffrey Skelton, *Paul Hindemith: The Man behind the Music* (London: Victor Gollancz, 1976), 94.

47. Hans Curjel, "Triumph der Alltäglichkeit," *Blätter der Staatsoper*, 9 (June 1929): 1–4.

48. Gutman, "Tabloid Hindemith," 34.

49. Heinrich Strobel, "Hindemiths *Neues vom Tage*," *Melos* 8 (May 1929): 257–59. "Das aus dem Alltag entnommene Spiel löst die aufgepeitschte Dramatik der privaten Seelenschmerzen ab. Was jeden Tag und jedem passieren kann, wird auf der Bühne gezeigt."

50. Max Marschalk, "Hindemiths lustige Oper," *Vossische Zeitung*, 10 June 1929. Reprinted in Curjel, *Experiment Krolloper*, 271–72.

51. Erich Steinhard, "Paul Hindemith: *Neues vom Tage*," *Auftakt* 9 (1929): 181–84.

52. Oskar Bie, *"Neues vom Tage,"* *München-Augsburger Zeitung*, 13 June 1929. Reprinted in Curjel, *Experiment Krolloper*, 272–73.

53. Letter of Willy Strecker to Paul Hindemith, 21 August 1929.

54. Karl Holl, *"Neues vom Tage* in Darmstadt," *Melos* 8 (November 1929): 502.

55. Pictures from the Darmstadt production are reproduced in Walter Panofsky, *Protest in der Oper* (Munich: Laokoon, 1966), 14, 114.

56. Letter of Strecker to Hindemith, 2 January 1930.

57. Letter of Hindemith to Strecker, 29 October, and letter of Strecker to Hindemith, 18 May 1931.

58. Letters between Strecker and Hindemith, as well as additional letters from Brecht, all in the Schott correspondence, give a very good idea of the situation. Hindemith and his publisher had both good intentions towards and considerable patience with Brecht, who wanted to exercise complete authority over all performances of the work and any revision. See also David Drew, *Kurt Weill*, 223–26, for background on Weill's contribution to feelings about this collaboration.

59. Letter of 2 March 1931, quoted in Heyworth, *Otto Klemperer*, 383.

60. Hindemith's struggle with the National Socialists over *Mathis der Maler* and the performance by Furtwängler of the symphonic movements has been well documented. For recent discussions see: James F. Paulding, "*Mathis der Maler*—The Politics of Music," *Hindemith-Jahrbuch* 5 (1976): 102–22; and Claudia Maurer Zenck, "Zwischen Boycott und Anpassung an den Charakter den Zeit. Über die Schwierigkeiten einese deutschen Komponisten mit dem Dritten Reich," *Hindemith-Jahrbuch* 9 (1980): 65–129.

61. Paulding gives the complete text of the letter in "*Mathis der Maler*—The Politics of Music," 104–8.

62. *Berliner Lokal-Anzeiger*, 12 December 1934.

63. Letter of Strecker to Hindemith, 9 March 1935.

64. Hindemith's music, along with Krenek's and Weill's, was later displayed in the 1938 Düsseldorf *Entartete Musik* exhibit. Joseph Wulf, *Musik im Dritten Reich* (Gütersloh: Sigbert Mohn, 1963), 423.

Chapter 8

1. Franz Schreker, *Christophorus, oder Die Vision einer Oper* (Berlin: Adler, 1931).

2. *Christophorus* was not performed until 1978 in Freiburg, as part of the centenary celebration of Schreker's birth.

3. Christoper Hailey, "Zur Entstehungsgeschichte der Oper *Christophorus*," in *Franz-Schreker-Symposium* (Berlin: Schriftenreihe der Hochschule der Künste Berlin, 1980), 116.

4. L. K. M. "Anmerkungen zum Werk [*Die schwarze Orchidee*]," *Blätter der Staatsoper* 9 (June 1929): 105. Another work which contained a black character probably based on Krenek's Jonny was Walter Gronostay's chamber opera *In Zehn Minuten* in which the black character triumphs over the other two white characters, all in ten minutes. It was premiered on the 1928 Baden-Baden Festival program.

5. Eugen d'Albert, *Foxtrot der Bessie* (Vienna: Universal Edition, 1929). Other numbers published separately from the opera include the *Walzer der Grace* for voice and piano and a *Phantasie* for solo piano.

6. Paul Bechert, "59th German Tonkünstlerfest a Tryout for New Operas," *Musical Courier* 99 (3 August 1929): 6–7.

7. The work was most recently revived in 1983 in Bielefeld, West Germany.

8. Max Brand, *Ma-Bram-Hob-Han Foxtrot aus der Oper Maschinist Hopkins* (Vienna: Universal Edition, 1929).

9. Oscar Thompson, "Fly-wheel Opera," *Modern Music* 7 (December-January 1929–30): 39.

10. Theodor Wiesengrund-Adorno, "George Antheil: *Transatlantic*," *Die Musik* 22 (July 1930): 754.

11.   I have been unable to consult copies of the manuscript full score, owned by Universal Edition and in the collection of the Vienna Stadt- und Landesbibliothek and in the Antheil Archive, overseen by Charles Amirkhanian.

12.   George Antheil, *Tango aus der Oper* Transatlantic (Vienna: Universal Edition, 1930).

13.   See letter of Antheil to M. C. Bok, 28 June 1928. The Antheil-Bok correspondence is found in the Music Division of The Library of Congress. For more information on the extent and content of this correspondence, see Wayne D. Shirley, "Another American in Paris: George Antheil's Correspondence with Mary Curtis Bok," *The Quarterly Journal of the Library of Congress* (January 1977): 2–22.

14.   Letter of Antheil to Bok, 22 February 1928.

15.   See Randall Thompson, "Contemporary American Composers V: George Antheil," *Modern Music* 8 (May-June 1931): 17–27; and Theodor Wiesengrund-Adorno, *"Transatlantic,"* *Modern Music* 7 (June-July 1930): 38–41. It has recently been produced (1987) in Bielefeld and Ulm.

16.   See letter of Schoenberg to Universal Edition, 15 November 1928. The Schoenberg correspondence is available in the Music Division of The Library of Congress.

17.   See letters of Berg to Schoenberg, 4 April 1929; Webern to Schoenberg, 19 February 1929; Rufer to Schoenberg, 25 January 1929; and Stein to Schoenberg, 15 April 1929, also contained in the Schoenberg correspondence.

18.   See letter of Schoenberg to Paul Bekker, 22 April 1929. Schoenberg was trying to interest Bekker in staging the premiere in Wiesbaden.

19.   Arnold Schoenberg, *Von Heute auf Morgen,* Sämtliche Werke, Abteilung III, vol. 7 (Mainz: B. Schott's Söhne, 1970), 128–31.

20.   Hans Keller, "Schoenberg's Comic Opera," *The Score,* no. 23 (July 1958): 27.

21.   Ernst Krenek, "Opera between the Wars," *Modern Music* 20 (January–February 1943): 111.

22.   Walter Jacob, "Über den Realismus in Kreneks *Jonny spielt auf,"* *Die Musik* 20 (December 1927): 185. "Mag sein, dass dieses zu uns heute stark sprechende Werk einer späteren Zeit als untauglicher, einmaliger Versuch von nur historischem Wert erscheint; möglich aber auch, dass dieser 'Jonny' einst als stärkstes und charakteristischstes Opernwerk unserer Zeit gilt."

Bibliography

Historical and Cultural Context

Bollert, Werner. *50 Jahre Deutsche Oper Berlin*. Berlin: Bruno Hessling, 1962.

Buddensieg, Tilman, ed. *Berlin 1900–1933: Architecture and Design*. New York: Cooper-Hewitt Museum of Decorative Arts and Design, 1987.

Bullivant, Keith, ed. *Culture and Society in the Weimar Republic*. Manchester: Manchester University Press, 1977.

Cahn, Peter. *Das Hoch'sche Konservatorium, 1878–1978*. Frankfurt: Kramer, 1979.

Curjel, Hans. *Experiment Krolloper, 1927–31*. Munich: Prestel, 1975.

————. *Synthesen*. Hamburg: Claassen, 1966.

Drew, David. "Musical Theatre in the Weimar Republic." *Proceedings of the Royal Music Association* 88 (1961–62): 89–108.

Einstein, Alfred. "National and Universal Music." *Modern Music* 14 (November–December 1936): 3–11.

Eisler, Hanns. *Musik und Politik: Schriften, 1924–48*. Edited by Günter Mayer. Munich: Rogner and Bernhard, 1973.

Fetting, Hugo. *Die Geschichte der deutschen Staatsoper*. Berlin: Henschel, 1955.

Friedrich, Otto. *Before the Deluge: A Portrait of Berlin in the 1920s*. New York: Harper and Row, 1972.

Gay, Peter. *Weimar Culture: The Outsider as Insider*. New York: Harper and Row, 1968.

Georges, Horst. *Deutsche Oper Berlin*. Berlin: Stapp, 1964.

Gutman, Hans. "Berlin and Modern Works." *Modern Music* 5 (November–December 1928): 40–42.

Heinsheimer, Hans. *Best Regards to Aida*. New York: Alfred A. Knopf, 1968.

————. "German Music on the Breadline." *Modern Music* 9 (March–April 1932): 115–20.

————. *Menagerie in F Sharp*. Garden City, N.J.: Doubleday, 1947.

————. "A New Patron for Music." *Modern Music* 8 (January–February 1931): 14–19.

————. "The Plight of German Opera Houses." *Musical Courier*, 27 February 1932.

Henning, Roslyn Brogue. "Expressionist Opera." *American-German Revue* 52 (August–September 1966): 19–22.

Heyer, Hermann. "Spaziergang durch die Geschichte der Leipziger Oper." In *Leipziger Bühnen*. Berlin: Henschel, 1956.

Heyworth, Peter. *Otto Klemperer, His Life and Times*. Vol. 1: 1885–1933. Cambridge: Cambridge University Press, 1983.

Holde, Artur. "Frankfurt." *Anbruch* 9 (May–June 1927): 228–30.

Kapp, Julius, ed. *185 Jahre Staatsoper*. Berlin: Atlantic, 1928.

————. *Das Opernbuch: Eine Geschichte der Oper und ein musikalisch-dramatischer Führer durch die Repertorieopern*. Leipzig: Hesse and Becker, 1929.

———— . *Geschichte der Staatsoper Berlin*. Berlin: Max Hess, 1942.

Kessler, Harry. *In the Twenties: The Diaries of Harry Kessler*. Trans. by Charles Kessler. New York: Holt, Rinehart, and Winston, 1971.

Koebner, Thomas. "Die Zeitoper in den zwanziger Jahren. Gedanken zu ihrer Geschichte und Theorie." In *Erprobungen und Erfahrungen zu Paul Hindemiths Schaffen in den zwanziger Jahren*. Mainz: B. Schott, 1978.

Kracauer, Siegfried. *From Caligari to Hitler: A Psychological History of the German Film*. Princeton: Princeton University Press, 1947.

LaQueur, Walter. *Weimar: A Cultural History, 1918–1933*. New York: G.P. Putnam's Sons, 1974.

Lederman, Minna. *The Life and Death of a Small Magazine*. ISAM Monographs, no. 18, 1983.

Mohr, Albert Richard. *Das Frankfurter Opernhaus, 1880–1980*. Frankfurt: Kramer, 1980.

———— . *Musikleben in Frankfurt am Main*. Frankfurt: Kramer, 1976.

Moldenhauer, Hans, and Rosaleen Moldenhauer. *Anton von Webern*. New York: Alfred A. Knopf, 1979.

"Die Musikpflege in der Weimarer Republik." In *Das Musikleben Leipzig*. Leipzig: 1977.

Nelson, Keith L. *Victors Divided*. Berkeley: University of California, 1975.

Otto, Werner. *Die Lindenoper*. Berlin: Henschel, 1977.

Padmore, Elaine. "German Expressionist Opera, 1910–1935." *Proceedings of the Royal Musical Association* 95 (1969): 41–53.

Panofsky, Walter. *Protest in der Oper: Das Provokative Musiktheater der zwanziger Jahre*. Munich: Laokoon, 1966.

Paris-Berlin, 1900–1933: Rapports et contrastes. Exhibition catalogue. Paris: Centre Nationale d'Art et de Culture G. Pompidou, 1978.

Petzoldt, Richard. "Traditionen fortschrittlicher Opernpflege in Leipzig." In *Festschrift zu Eröffnung des neuen Leipziger Opernhauses*. Leipzig: Seeman, 1960.

Prieberg, Fred K. *Musik im NS-Staat*. Frankfurt: Fischer, 1982.

Reber, Horst, and Heinrich Heym. *Das Frankfurter Opernhaus 1880 bis 1944*. Frankfurt: Kettenhof, 1969.

Sachs, Joel. "Some Aspects of Musical Politics in Pre-Nazi Germany." *Perspectives of New Music* 9 (Fall-Winter 1970): 74–95.

Schmidt, Royal J. *Versailles and the Ruhr*. The Hague: Nijhoff, 1968.

Schrenk, Oswald. *Berlinische Oper*. Berlin: Scherl, 1943.

———— . *Berlin und die Musik: Zweihundert Jahre Musikleben einer Stadt, 1740–1940*. Berlin: Bote and Bock, 1940.

Slonimsky, Nicholas. *Music since 1900*. 4th ed. New York: Charles Scribner's Sons, 1971.

Stein, Erwin. "Schoenberg and the Germanic Line." *Modern Music* 3 (May-June 1926): 22–27.

Stengel, Theo, and Herbert Gerigk, eds. *Lexicon der Juden in der Musik*. Berlin: Bernhard Hahnefeld, 1940.

Stompor, Stephan. "800 Jahre Musikstadt Leipzig." *Musik und Gesellschaft* 15 (1965): 615–23.

———— . "Die Idee kann man nicht töten: Otto Klemperer und die Berliner Kroll-Oper, 1927–1931." *Jahrbuch der Komischen Oper Berlin* 3 (1962–63): 145–72.

Stuckenschmidt, H. H. *Die Musik eines halben Jahrhunderts, 1925–75*. Munich: Piper, 1976.

———— . *Neue Musik*. Berlin: Suhrkamp, 1981.

———— . "Nightmare in Germany." *Modern Music* 10 (January-February 1933): 115–17.

———— . *Oper in dieser Zeit*. Hannover: Friedrich, 1964.

———— . "Oper in dieser Zeit: Versuch einer Orientierung." In *Oper im XX. Jahrhundert: Musik der Zeit* 6. Bonn: Boosey and Hawkes, 1954.

———— . *Twentieth-Century Composers*. Vol. 2. New York: Holt, Rinehart, and Winston, 1970.

———— . *Twentieth-Century Music*. Trans. by Richard Deveson. New York: McGraw-Hill, 1969.

———— . *Zum Hören Geboren: Ein Leben mit der Musik unserer Zeit*. Munich: Piper, 1979.

Thomson, Virgil. *Virgil Thomson.* New York: E. P. Dutton, 1985.

Tucholsky, Kurt. "Ein Pyrenäenbuch." In *Gesammelte Werke II.* Reinbeck: Rowohlt, 1960.

"Warum die jetzige Leipziger Oper keine Uraufführungen bringt!" *Zeitschrift für Musik* 93 (1926): 295.

Willett, John. *Art and Politics in the Weimar Period: The New Sobriety, 1917–1933.* New York: Pantheon, 1978.

Worbs, Hans Christoph. *Welterfolge der Modernen Oper.* Berlin: Rembrandt, 1967.

Wulf, Joseph. *Musik im Dritten Reich: Eine Dokumentation.* Gütersloh: Sigbert Mohn, 1963.

The *Novembergruppe, Gebrauchsmusik,* and Festivals

Burkard, Heinrich. "Die Musikfeststädte Donaueschingen-Baden-Baden." *Anbruch* 9 (May–June 1927): 221–24.

Clossen, Hermann. "The Case against *Gebrauchsmusik.*" *Modern Music* 7 (February–March 1930): 15–19.

Copland, Aaron. "Baden-Baden 1927." *Modern Music* 5 (November–December 1927): 31–34.

Doflein, Erich. "Gegenwart, Gebrauch, Kitsch und Stil." *Melos* 8 (1929): 294–300.

Felber, Erwin. "Step-Children of Music." *Modern Music* 4 (November–December 1926): 31–33.

"Gebrauchsmusik: Sonderheft." *Die Musik* (March 1929).

Grohmann, Will, ed. "Zehn Jahre Novembergruppe." Sonderheft *Kunst der Zeit* 3 (1928).

Gutman, Hans. "The Festivals as Music Barometers." *Modern Music* 8 (November–December 1930): 27–32.

———. "Umschau: Gebrauchsmusik." *Melos* 8 (1929): 74–78.

Hinton, Stephen W. "The Idea of Gebrauchsmusik: A Study of Musical Aesthetics in the Weimar Republic (1919 to 1933) with Particular Reference to the Works of Paul Hindemith." Ph.D. Dissertation. University of Birmingham, 1984.

Holde, Artur. "Das Donaueschingen Musikfest." *Allgemeine Musikzeitung* 53 (1926): 627–28.

Kliemann, Helga. *Die Novembergruppe.* Berlin: Gebr. Mann, 1969.

Kroll, Erwin. "Musik und Tanz in Donaueschingen." *Zeitschrift für Musikwissenschaft* (September 1924): 666–68.

Lucchesi, Joachim. "Einsatz für die 'junge Kunst': Musik und Musiker in der Berliner Novembergruppe." *Musik und Gesellschaft* 1 (1987): 18–22.

"Novembergruppe E.V. Berlin." *Anbruch* 8 (January 1926): 46–47.

Preussner, Eberhard. "Deutsche Kammermusik 1928 in Baden-Baden." *Die Musik* 20 (September 1928): 872–78.

———. "Deutsche Kammermusik: Baden-Baden 1927." *Die Musik* 19 (September 1927): 884–92.

———. "Gemeinschaftsmusik 1929 in Baden-Baden." *Die Musik* 21 (September 1929): 895–903.

———. "Das sechste Donaueschinger Kammermusikfest." *Die Musik* 18 (September 1926): 899–903.

Pringsheim, Heinz. "Aus der Berliner Konzertsaalen." *Allgemeine Musikzeitung* 51 (1924): 53.

Richard, August. "II. Donaueschingen Kammermusikfest zur Förderung zeitgenössischer Tonkunst." *Allgemeine Musikzeitung* 49 (1922): 620–21.

Stefan, Paul. "Ein Sommer der Musik." *Anbruch* 9 (August-September 1927): 269–72.

Stuckenschmidt, H. H. "Musik und Musiker in der Novembergruppe." *Anbruch* 10 (October 1928): 293–95.

Unger, Max. "Deutsche Kammermusik in Baden-Baden." *Allgemeine Musikzeitung* 54 (1927): 877–79.

Weissmann, Adolf. "Das Donaueschinger Kammermusikfest 1925." *Die Musik* 17 (September 1925): 910–14.

The State of Music and Opera in the 1920s

Aber, Adolf. "Zeitgenössische Oper in ihren Hauptströmungen." *Auftakt* 7 (1927): 147–52.

Adorno, Theodor W. "Opernprobleme." *Anbruch* 8 (May 1926): 205–08.

Altmann, Wilhelm. "Die Berliner Opern in der verflossenen Spielzeit 1926/27." *Allgemeine Musikzeitung* 54 (1927): 917–18, 937–38.

————. "Die Berliner Opern in der verflossenen Spielzeit 1927/28." *Allgemeine Musikzeitung* 55 (1928): 935–36, 958–59.

————. "Die Berliner Opern in der verflossenen Spielzeit 1928/29." *Allgemeine Musikzeitung* 56 (1929): 862–64.

————. "Die Berliner Opern in der verflossenen Spielzeit 1929/30. *Allgemeine Musikzeitung* 57 (1930): 822–25.

————. "Die Berliner Opern in der verflossenen Spielzeit 1930/31." *Allgemeine Musikzeitung* 58 (1931): 626–27, 642–44.

————. "Eine gute Aussicht für Opernkomponisten?" *Allgemeine Musikzeitung* 55 (1928): 190–91.

————. "Opernstatistik 1926/27." *Anbruch* 9 (December 1927): 424–31.

————. "Opernstatistik 1927/28." *Anbruch* 10 (November–December 1928): 429–34.

————. "Opernstatistik 1928/29." *Anbruch* 11 (September–October, November–December 1929): 309–15, 352–55.

————. "Opernstatistik 1929/30." *Anbruch* 12 (November–December 1930): 292–98.

————. "Opernstatistik 1929/30." *Anbruch* 14 (January 1932): 24–25.

————. "Opernstatistik von August 1930 bis Juli 1931." *Zeitschrift für Musik* 98 (1931): 948–68.

————. "Opernstatistik von August 1931 bis Juli 1932." *Allgemeine Musikzeitung* 59 (1932): 609–10, 625–26, 637–38, 652–53.

————. "Opernstatistik von August 1932 bis Juli 1933." *Allgemeine Musikzeitung* 60 (1933): 491–95.

————. "Zur Opernstatistik der deutschen Bühnen 1929/30." *Allgemeine Musikzeitung* 59 (1930): 1041–43.

————. "Zur Opernstatistik der Spielzeit 1928/29." *Allgemeine Musikzeitung* 56 (1929): 1129–30.

Anschütz, George. "Stilistische Elemente im Opernschaffen der Gegenwart." *Neue Musik-Zeitung* 49 (1928): 700–04.

Antheil, George. "Opernregie von Morgen." *Kunstblatt* 14 (1930): 234–35.

Aron, Willi. "Opernkrise, Opernreform, Opernregie." *Die Musik* 20 (May 1928): 571–74

Axelrod, Jakow. "Nochmals, 'Das Prinzip des Absoluten'." *Allgemeine Musikzeitung* 55 (1928): 139–41.

Baresel, Alfred. "Ich wittere eine neue 'Richtung' der Musik." *Neue Musikzeitung* 49 (1928): 189–91.

————. "Pessimismus der Oper." *Rheinische Musik- und Theater-Zeitung* 32 (1931): 4–5.

Bennett, Howard G. "Opera in Modern Germany." *Proceedings of the Music Teachers National Association* 29 (1934): 65–73.

Bie, Oskar. "Die Anarchie der Oper." In *Die Oper*. Berlin: S. Fischer, 1920.

————. "Stand der Oper." *Der neue Rundschau* 43 (1932): 124–31.

Blitzstein, Marc. "Coming—The Mass Audience!" *Modern Music* 13 (May-June 1936): 23–29.

————. "Music and Theatre—1932." *Modern Music* 9 (May-June 1932): 164–68.

Brand, Max. "Die bewegte Opernbühne." *Anbruch* 9 (January–February 1927): 62–66.

————. "'Mechanische' Musik und das Problem der Oper." *Anbruch* 8 (October–November 1926): 356–59.

————. "Die Situation der Oper." *Blätter der Staatsoper* 10 (March 1930): 7–9.

Casella, Alfredo. "Reflections on the European Scene." *Modern Music* 5 (May-June 1928): 16–18.

Curjel, Hans. "Neben der Oper." *Blätter der Staatsoper* 8 (October 1928): 1–4.

————. "Triumph der Alltäglichkeit, Parodie, und tiefere Bedeutung." *Blätter der Staatsoper* 9 (June 1929): 1–4.

Einstein, Alfred. "German Opera, Past and Present." *Modern Music* 11 (January–February 1934): 65–72.

————. "Die Wiederentdeckung des Menschen in der Musik." *Die neue Rundschau* 41 (1930): 519–26.

Erhardt, Otto. "Oper in Deutschland." *Neue Musik-Zeitung* 49 (February 1928): 273–80.

Flechtner, Hans Joachim. "Das Problem des Operntextes." *Rheinische Musik- und Theater-Zeitung* 29 (1928): 233.

Fugitivus. "Inside Germany." *Modern Music* 16 (May–June 1939): 203–13.

Grues, H., E. Kruttge, and E. Thalheimer, eds. *Von neuer Musik: Beiträge zur Erkenntnis der neuzeitlichen Tonkunst.* Cologne: F. J. Marcan, 1925.

Günther, Siegfried. "Gegenwartsoper." *Die Musik* 20 (July 1928): 718–26.

Gutman, Hans. "Berlin and Modern Works." *Modern Music* 6 (November–December 1928): 40–42.

————. "Oper in unserer Zeit: Repertoire oder Stagione." *Auftakt* 13 (1933): 166–68.

————. "Young Germany 1930." *Modern Music* 7 (February–March 1930): 3–10.

Guttmann, Oskar. "Opernkrise ist Geldkrise." *Rheinische Musik- und Theater-Zeitung* 29 (1928): 234–35.

Heinsheimer, Hans. "German Music on the Breadline." *Modern Music* 9 (1932): 115–20.

————. "Neues vom Tage." *Anbruch* 13 (January 1931): 1–4.

————. "A New Patron for Music." *Modern Music* 8 (January–February 1931): 14–19.

————. "Nightmare in Germany." *Modern Music* 10 (January-February 1933): 115–17.

————. "The Plight of the German Opera Houses." *Musical Courier,* 27 February 1932.

————. "Youth Leaves the Vanguard." *Modern Music* 9 (November–December 1931): 3–5.

————, and Paul Stephan, eds. *25 Jahre neue Musik.* Vienna: Universal Edition, 1925.

Herzfeld, Friedrich. "Die Möglichkeiten der neuen Oper." *Signale für die musikalische Welt* 89 (1931): 25–27.

Huth, Arno Franz. "Mechanische Musik." *Allgemeine Musikzeitung* 53 (1926): 48.

Kallenberg, Siegfried. "Zur modernen Musik." *Zeitschrift für Musik* 91 (1924): 562–64.

Kapp, Julius. "Gibt es eine Krise der Oper?" *Blätter der Staatsoper* 9 (April 1929): 10–12.

Kobelt, Johannes. "Händel-Opern—Festspiele Göttingen (July 1922)." *Allgemeine Musikzeitung* 49 (1922): 619–20.

Lüthge, Kurt. "Musik in der Gegenwart." *Signale für die musikalische Welt* 88 (1930): 442–47.

"Maschinen." *Auftakt* 6, no. 6 (1926).

Mersmann, Hans. "Probleme der gegenwärtigen Operndichtung." *Anbruch* 9 (January–February 1927): 15–19.

————. "Unser Verhältnis zur neuen Oper." *Melos* 8 (1929): 418–23.

Meyer, Ludwig K. "Rundfrage: Wie denken Sie über zeitgemässe Weiterentwicklung der Oper." *Blätter der Staatsoper* 8 (October 1927): 12–19.

————. "Vom Geist der neuen Musik." *Blätter der Staatsoper* 8 (October 1927): 8–11.

Milhaud, Darius. "The Evolution of Modern Music in Paris and in Vienna." *North American Review* 217 (April 1923): 544–54.

"Musik und Maschine." *Anbruch* 8 (October-November 1926).

Ohrmann, Fritz. "Trimuph [*sic*] der Alltäglichkeit." *Signale für die musikalische Welt* 87 (1929): 815–19.

"Oper Jahrbuch." *Anbruch* 9 (January–February 1927).

"Opernkrise im Ausland." *Melos* 11 (1932): 366–67.

Oppenheim, Hans. "Die Oper und das Operntheater von Morgen." *Melos* 7 (1928): 588–94.

Perl, Carl Johann. "In einer Zeit wie dieser . . ." *Blätter der Staatsoper* 10 (March 1930): 1–3.

Pisk, Paul. "Das neue Publikum." *Anbruch* 9 (January–February 1927): 94–96.

Preussner, Eberhard. "Germany's New Music Literature." *Modern Music* 7 (February–March 1930): 38–41.

Prunières, Henry. "The Departure from Opera." *Modern Music* 3 (January–February 1926): 3–9.

Raskin, Adolf. "Das musikalische Theater der Gegenwart." *Blätter der Staatsoper* 10 (March 1930): 10–13.

––––––. "Symptomatische Musikpolitik." *Melos* 9 (1930): 299–302.

––––––. "Symptomatische Musikpolitik: Querschnitt—West Deutschen 1930/31." *Melos* 10 (1931): 379–82.

Redlich, Hans. "Die kompositorische Situation von 1930." *Anbruch* 12 (June 1930): 187–90.

Reger, Erik. "Die Krise des Opern-Repertoire." *Die Musik* 22 (October 1929): 22–26.

––––––. "Die musikalische Welt im Maschinenzeitalter." *Die Musik* 20 (February 1928): 338–45.

Riesenfeld, Paul. "Der Kampf um die Oper." *Signale für die musikalische Welt* 88 (1930): 357–60.

Scherchen, Hermann. "Die gegenwärtige Situation der Musik." *Das neue Frankfurt* 6 (1926–27): 137–39.

Schiedermair, Ludwig. *Die deutsche Oper*. Bonn: Dümmler, 1940.

Schlee, Alfred. "German Opera in Transition." *Modern Music* 11 (March–April 1934): 147–49.

Schliepe, Ernst. "Händels Opern und die Gegenwart." *Die Musik* 20 (June 1928): 640–43.

––––––. "Krisis der Oper." *Signale für die musikalische Welt* 89 (1931): 1238–41.

Schloezer, Boris de. "The Operatic Paradox." *Modern Music* 4 (November–December 1926): 3–8.

Schoen, Ernst. "Zur Soziologie der Oper." *Blätter der Staatsoper* 9 (October 1928): 13–16.

Schönewolf, Karl. "Operndämmerung." *Die Musik* 20 (May 1928): 561–64.

Schreker, Franz. "Die Zukunft der Oper." In *Deutsche Musikpflege*. Frankfurt: Bühnenvolksbund, 1925.

Schwers, Paul. "Ruhe bewahren!" *Allgemeine Musikzeitung* 60 (1933): 151.

––––––. "Umwälzungen im Opernleben." *Allgemeine Musikzeitung* 60 (1933): 141–42.

"Sonderheft: Wagner." *Melos* 12 (October 1933).

Stefan, Paul. "Bekenntnis zur Oper." *Anbruch* 8 (May 1926): 203–4.

––––––. "Einleitung: Die Oper nach Wagner." *Anbruch* 9 (January–February 1927): 3–10.

Steglich, Rudolf. "Händel und die Gegenwart." *Zeitschrift für Musik* 92 (1925): 333–38.

Stieber, Hans. "Die Krise im deutschen Opernschaffen." *Rheinische Musik- und Theater-Zeitung* 27 (1926): 8–9.

Strobel, Heinrich. "Krise der Oper—Krise der Kritik." *Melos* 9 (1930): 191–93.

––––––. "Neues Operntheater." *Die Scene* 20 (1930): 73–75.

––––––. "Opernpublikum." *Melos* 7 (1928): 111–13.

Stuckenschmidt, H. H. "Ausblick in die Musik." *Kunstblatt* 7 (1923): 221–22.

––––––. "Einbruch des Kabaretts in die Oper." *Blätter der Staatsoper* 9 (June 1929): 13–14.

––––––. "German Season under the Crisis." *Modern Music* 10 (March–April 1933): 163–67.

––––––. "Die heutige Musik." *Kunstblatt* 8 (1924): 189.

––––––. "Ist die Oper Überlebt?" *Kunstblatt* 14 (1930): 225–33.

––––––. "Machines—A Vision of the Future." *Modern Music* 4 (March–April 1926): 8–14.

––––––. "Maschinenmusik." *Auftakt* 7 (1927): 152–57.

––––––. "Mechanisierung." *Anbruch* 8 (October–November 1926): 345–46.

––––––. "Die Mechanisierung der Musik." *Kunstblatt* 9 (1925): 275.

––––––. "Die Musik zum Film." *Die Musik* 18 (August 1926): 807–17.

––––––. "Die neue Musik Frankreichs." *Kunstblatt* 6 (1922): 84–85.

––––––. "Opera in Germany Today." *Modern Music* 13 (1935): 32–37.

––––––. "Short Operas." *Anbruch* 10 (June–July 1928): 204–7.

––––––. "Under the Swastika." *Modern Music* 11 (November–December 1933): 49–52.

Tessmer, Hans. "Hat die deutsche Oper eine Zukunft?" *Zeitschrift für Musik* 100 (1933): 1000–1002.

––––––. "Zeitfragen des Operntheaters: Die Oper am Scheidewege." *Zeitschrift für Musik* 97 (1930): 172–76.

Tiessen, Heinz. *Zur Geschichte der Jüngsten Musik (1913–1928)*. Mainz: Melos, 1928.
Tischer, Gerhard. "Vom Wandel der Zeit." *Rheinische Musik- und Theater-Zeitung* 26 (1925): 547–48.
Waltershausen, Hermann W. "Die Krise der zeitgenössischen deutschen Oper." *Schweizerische Musikzeitung und Sängerblatt* 68 (1928): 41–42, 56–57.
Weissmann, Adolf. "Die deutsche Musik." *Die neue Rundschau* 34 (May 1923): 428–38.
———. "Germany's Latest Music Dramas." *Modern Music* (May–June 1927): 20–26.
———. *The Problems of Modern Music*. Trans. by M. M. Bozman. London: J. M. Dent, 1925. Reprint. Westport, Conn.: Hyperion Press, 1979.
———. "Zwischenzustand der Musik." *Die neue Rundschau* 40 (1929): 551–62.
Wellesz, Egon. *Essays on Opera*. Trans. by Patricia Kean. New York: Roy, 1950.
———. "The Return to the Stage." *Modern Music* 5 (November–December 1926): 19–24.
Westphal, Kurt. *Die Moderne Musik*. Leipzig: Teubner, 1928.
———. "Die moderne Oper." *Blätter der Staatsoper* 9 (October 1928): 5–7.
Wörner, Karl. "Was ist Kulturboschewismus?" *Melos* 11 (1932): 397–99.
———. "Wort und Ton in der neueren Oper." *Signale für die musikalische Welt* 90 (1932): 133–36.
X. T. "Kultur Terror." *Modern Music* 10 (1933): 209–13.
Zimmerseimer, Karl. "Stoff- und Textfragen der neuen Oper." *Melos* 12 (1933): 182–89.
"Zur Opernfrage." *Rheinische Musik- und Theater-Zeitung* 29 (1928): 232.

Neue Sachlichkeit in Art, Literature, and Music

Avant-Garde Photography in Germany, 1919–1939. Exhibition Catalogue. San Francisco Museum of Modern Art, 1980.
Berten, Walter. "Mensch und Maschine Sachlichkeit." *Rheinische Musik- und Theater-Zeitung* 28 (1927): 219.
Curjel, Hans. "Espressivo und objektivierter Ausdruck." *Blätter der Staatsoper* 8 (June 1928): 3.
Finke, Fidelio F. "Neue Sachlichkeit: Eine Temperamentsangelegenheit." *Auftakt* 8 (1928): 145–46.
Fladt, Hermann. "Eisler und die Neue Sachlichkeit." In *Hanns Eisler Argument Sonderband* 5. West Berlin, 1975.
Gutman, Hans. "Grenzen der Simplizität." *Melos* 8 (1929): 304–7.
Hermand, Jost. "Unity within Diversity? The History of the Concept 'Neue Sachlichkeit'." Trans. by Peter and Margaret Lincoln. In *Culture and Society in the Weimar Republic*. Manchester: Manchester University Press, 1977.
Heuss, Alfred. "Was unter 'Sachlichkeit' in der Tonkunst zu verstehen wäre!" *Zeitschrift für Musik* 99 (1932): 495–99.
Hofrichter, Ruth J. "Erich Kästner as a Representative of 'Neue Sachlichkeit'." *German Quarterly* 5 (1932): 173–77.
Last, R. W. *Erich Kästner*. Modern German Authors 3. London: Oswald Wolff, 1974.
Lincoln, Louise, ed. *German Realism of the Twenties: The Artist as Social Critic*. Exhibition Catalogue. Minneapolis: The Institute of Art, 1980.
Mehring, Walter. *The Lost Library: The Autobiography of a Culture*. Trans. by Richard Winston and Clara Winston. New York: Bobbs-Merrill, 1951.
Mendelsohn, Harvey L. *Bauhaus Photography*. Cambridge, Mass.: The MIT Press, 1985.
Misch, Ludwig. "Neue Sachlichkeit." *Allgemeine Musikzeitung* 54 (1927): 613–15.
Riesenfeld, Paul. "Die Romantik der neuen Sachlichkeit." *Signale für die Musikalische Welt* 87 (1929): 1075–78.
Schibli, Sigfried. "Zum Begriff der Neuen Sachlichkeit in der Musik." *Hindemith-Jahrbuch* 9 (1980): 157–78.

Schiedermair, Ludwig. "'Expressionismus' und 'Sachlichkeit'." In *Die deutsche Oper*. Leipzig: Quelle and Meyer, 1930.

Schliepe, Ernst. "Musik und Neue Sachlichkeit." *Signale für die musikalische Welt* 87 (1929): 1206–10.

Schubert, Gisheler. "Aus der musikalischen Vorgeschichte der Neuen Sachlichkeit." *Die Musikforschung* 29 (1976): 137–54.

Strobel, Heinrich. "'Neue Sachlichkeit' in der Musik." *Anbruch* 8 (June 1926): 254–56.

Stuckenschmidt, H. H. "Neue Sachlichkeit in der Musik." *Auftakt* 8 (1928): 3–6.

Winkelmann, John. *The Poetic Style of Erich Kästner*. University of Nebraska Studies: new series 17. The University of Nebraska Press, 1957.

German Theater in the 1920s

Davies, Cecil W. "Working Class Theater in the Weimar Republic, 1919–1933." *Theatre Quarterly* 10 (Summer 1980): 68–96.

Innes, C. D. *Erwin Piscator's Political Theatre: The Development of Modern German Drama*. London: Cambridge University Press, 1972.

Jhering, Herbert. "Zeittheater." *Melos* 7 (1928): 522–24.

Lania, Leo [Lazar Hermann]. *Today We Are Brothers: The Biography of a Generation*. Trans. by Ralph Marlowe. Boston: Riverside Press, 1942.

Piscator, Erwin. *The Political Theatre*. Trans. by Hugh Rorrison. London: Eyre Methuen, 1980.

Piscator, Maria-Ley. *The Piscator Experiment: The Political Theatre*. New York: James H. Heinemen, 1967.

Styan, J. L. *Expressionism and Epic Theater*. Modern Drama in Theory and Practice 3. Cambridge: Cambridge University Press, 1981.

———. *Max Reinhardt*. London: Cambridge University Press, 1982.

Willett, John. *The Theatre of Erwin Piscator: Half a Century of Politics in the Theatre*. London: Eyre Methuen, 1978.

Popular Entertainment in the 1920s

Appignanesi, Lisa. *The Cabaret*. New York: Macmillan, 1975.

Charles, Jacques. *Cent ans de music-hall*. Paris: Jeheber, 1956.

Fesquotte, Jacques. *"Que sais-je?" Histoire du music-hall*. Paris: Presses Universitaires de France, 1965.

Greul, Heinz. *Bretter, die Zeit bedeuten: Die Kulturgeschichte des Kabaretts*. Cologne: Kiepenheuer and Witsch, 1967.

Hollaender, Friedrich. *Von Kopf bis Fuss: Mein Leben mit Text und Musik*. Munich: Kindler, 1965.

Hösch, Rudolf. *Kabarett von Gestern nach zeitgenössischen Berichten, Kritiken und Erinnerungen, Band I 1900–1933*. Berlin: Henschel, 1969.

Klein, Jean-Claude. "Borrowing, Syncretism, Hybridisation: The Parisian Revue of the 1920s." *Popular Music* 5 (1985): 175–87.

Kothes, Franz-Peter. *Die theatralische Revue in Berlin und Wien, 1900–1938*. Wilhelmshaven: Heinrichshoffen, 1977.

"Revue." *Auftakt* 8, no. 8 (1928).

Rosenzweig, Alfred. "Die Revuetechnik in Operette und Oper." *Melos* 6 (1927): 525–59.

Zivier, Georg, Hellmut Kothschenreuther, and Volker Ludwig. *Kabarett mit K*. Berlin: Berlin Verlag, 1974.

Jazz, Social Dance, and Their Cultural Contexts

Baker, Josephine, and Jo Bouillon. *Josephine*. Trans. by Marianna Fitzpatrick. New York: Harper and Row, 1977.

Balliett, Whitney. "Jazz." *The New Yorker*, 16 April 1984.

Baskerville, David Ross. "Jazz Influence on Art Music to Mid-Century." Ph.D. Dissertation. U.C.L.A., 1965.

Bechet, Sidney. *Treat It Gentle*. London: Cassell, 1960. Reprint, New York: Da Capo Press, 1975.

Berlin, Edward A. *Ragtime: A Musical and Cultural History*. Berkeley: University of California Press, 1980.

Bishop, John Peale. "The Formal Translations of Jazz." *Vanity Fair* 23 (October 1924): 57, 90, 100.

Blitzstein, Marc. "Popular Music—An Invasion: 1923–33." *Modern Music* 10 (January–February 1933): 96–102.

Bochner, Jay. *Blaise Cendrars: Discovery and Recreation*. Toronto: Toronto University Press, 1978.

Bricktop and James Haskins. *Bricktop*. New York: Atheneum, 1983.

Castle, Irene Foote. *Castles in the Air*. New York: Doubleday, 1958.

Castle, Vernon, and Irene Foote Castle. *Modern Dancing*. New York: Harper and Row, 1914.

Cendrars, Blaise. *The African Saga*. Trans. by Margery Bianco. New York: Payson and Clarke, 1927. Reprint. Negro University Press, 1969.

———. *Complete Postcards from the Americas*. Trans. by Monique Chefdor. Berkeley: University of California Press, 1976.

———. *Petits contes nègres pour les enfants des blancs*. Paris: Jean Vigneau, 1946.

Charters, Samuel, and Leonard Kunstadt. *Jazz: A History of the New York Scene*. Garden City, N.Y.: Doubleday, 1962.

Chisolm, Anne. *Nancy Cunard*. London: Sigwick and Jackson, 1979.

Cocteau, Jean. *A Call to Order*. Trans. by Rollo H. Myers. London: Faber and Gwyer, 1926.

Cole, Malcolm S. "Afrika singt: Austro-Germanic Echoes of the Harlem Renaissance." *Journal of the Americam Musicological Society* 30 (Spring 1977): 72–87.

Collins, Joseph. "The Dance 'Mania': Some Explanation of America's Present Popular and Persistent Diversion." *Vanity Fair* 25 (February 1926): 68, 84.

Copland, Aaron. "Jazz Structure and Influence." *Modern Music* 4 (January-February 1927): 9–14.

———. *Our New Music*. New York: McGraw-Hill, 1941.

Cowell, Henry. "Bericht aus Amerika." *Melos* 9 (1930): 362–64, 417–20, 526–29.

———. "Bericht aus Amerika." *Melos* 10 (1931): 275–77.

cummings, e. e. "Vive la Folie!: An Analysis of the 'Revue' in General and the Parisian Revue in Particular." *Vanity Fair* 27 (September 1926): 55, 116.

Cunard, Nancy. *Negro: An Anthology*. Reprint. New York: Frederick Ungar, 1970.

Dos Passos, John. *Orient Express*. New York: Jonathan Cape and Harrison South, 1930.

DuPree, Mary Herron. "'Jazz,' the Critics, and American Art Music in the 1920s." *American Music* 4 (Fall 1986): 287–301.

Erenberg, Lewis A. *Steppin' Out: New York Nightlife and the Transformation of American Culture, 1890–1930*. Chicago: University of Chicago Press, 1981.

Flanner, Janet. *Paris Was Yesterday, 1925–1939*. Ed. by Irving Drutman. New York: The Viking Press, 1972.

Frueh, Alfred. "The Jazz Debut." *Modern Music* 1 (June 1924): 9.

Fünf Jahre Berliner Rundfunk: Ein Rückblick 1923–28. Berlin: Funk-Stunde, 1928.

Gilbert, Henry F. "Concerning the Jazz Question." *Etude* 53 (February 1935): 74.

Goffin, Robert. *Jazz: From the Congo to the Metropolitan*. New York: Da Capo Press, 1975.

Hamm, Charles. *Yesterdays*. New York: W. W. Norton, 1979.

Handy, W. C. *Father of the Blues*. New York: Macmillan, 1944.

Haney, Lynn. *Naked at the Feast: A Biography of Josephine Baker*. New York: Dodd, Mead, 1981.

Harding, James. *The Ox on the Roof*. London: MacDonald, 1972.

Hasse, John, ed. *Ragtime: Its History, Composers, and Music*. New York: Schirmer, 1985.

Heyman, Barbara B. "Stravinsky and Ragtime." *Musical Quarterly* 68 (October 1972): 543–62.

Honegger, Artur. *I Am a Composer*. Trans. by Wilson O. Clough. New York: St. Martin's Press, 1966.

Hustwitt, Mark. "'Caught in a whirlpool of aching sound': The Production of Dance Music in Britain in the 1920s." *Popular Music* 3 (1983): 7–31.

Kramer, A. Walter. "American Composers III: Louis Gruenberg." *Modern Music* 8 (November–December 1930): 3–9.

Laglenne, Jean-Francis. "Boxeurs." *L'Esprit nouveau* 14 (November 1923): 1673–74.

Lange, Horst H. *Die Geschichte des Jazz in Deutschland*. Lübeck: Uhle and Kleimann, 1960.

Lanoux, Armand. *Paris in the 20s*. Trans. by E. S. Seldon. New York: Golden Griffin, 1960.

Laubenstein, Paul Fitz. "Jazz—Debit and Credit." *Musical Quarterly* 15 (1929): 606–24.

Lewis, David Levering. *When Harlem Was in Vogue*. New York: Vintage, 1982.

Little, Arthur W. *From Harlem to the Rhine: The Story of New York's Colored Volunteers*. New York: Covici-Friede, 1936.

Locke, Alain, ed. *The New Negro*. New York: Arno Press, 1968.

Lopatnikoff, Nikolai. "America in Berlin." *Modern Music* 9 (January–February 1932): 90–92.

Lotz, Ranier E. "Black Diamonds Are Forever: A Glimpse of the Prehistory of Jazz in Europe." *The Black Perspective in Music* 12 (Fall 1984): 216–34.

––––––. "The 'Louisiana Troupes' in Europe." *The Black Perspective in Music* 11 (Fall 1983): 133–42.

McCarthy, Albert. *Big Band Jazz*. New York: G. P. Putnam's Sons, 1974.

––––––. *The Dance Band Era*. Philadelphia: Chilton, 1971.

Mendelsohn, Erich. *Amerika: Bilderbuch eines Architekten*. Berlin: Rudolf Mosse, 1926.

"A Negro Explains 'Jazz'." *Literary Digest*, 26 April 1919.

Nisbett, Robert F. "Louis Gruenberg: A Forgotten Figure of American Music." *Current Musicology*, no. 18 (1974): 90–95.

Ornstein, Arbie. *Ravel: Man and Music*. New York: Columbia, 1975.

Osgood, Henry O. "The Blues." *Modern Music* 4 (November–December 1926): 25–28.

Perloff, Nancy L. "Art and the Everyday: The Impact of Parisian Popular Entertainment on Satie, Milhaud, Poulenc and Auric." Ph.D. Dissertation. The University of Michigan, 1986.

Pound, Ezra. "On the Swings and Roundabouts." *Vanity Fair* 18 (August 1922): 49.

Rigby, Ida Katherine. *Karl Hofer*. New York: Garland, 1976.

Rust, Brian, comp. *Jazz Records 1897–1942*. 2 Vols. London: Storyville, 1969.

Sauvage, Marcel, ed. *Les Mémoires de Josephine Baker*. Paris: Kra, 1927.

Schaeffner, André. "Georges Auric—Peasant of Paris." *Modern Music* 6 (November–December 1929): 11–16.

Schuller, Gunther. *Early Jazz*. New York: Oxford, 1968.

Scott, Emmett J. *Scott's Official History of the American Negro in the World War*. Washington D.C.: 1919.

Seldes, Gilbert. "Jazz Opera or Ballet?" *Modern Music* 3 (January–February 1926): 10–16.

Shapiro, Nat, and Nat Hentoff, eds. *Hear Me Talkin' to Ya: The Story of Jazz by the Men Who Made It*. New York: Rinehart, 1955.

Silvester, Victor, and Philip J. S. Richardson. *The Art of the Ballroom*. London: Herbert Jenkins, 1936.

Southern, Eileen. *The Music of Black Americans*. New York: W. W. Norton, 1971.

Starr, S. Frederick. *Red and Hot: The Fate of Jazz in the Soviet Union 1917–1980*. New York: Oxford University Press, 1983.

Stearns, Marshall, and Jean Stearns. *Jazz Dance: The Story of American Vernacular Dance.* New York: Macmillan, 1968.

Steegmuller, Francis. *Cocteau: A Biography.* Boston: Little, Brown, 1970.

Steinhard, Erich. "Modemusiker Erwin Schulhoff." *Auftakt* 9 (1929): 80–81.

Stringham, Edwin J. "Jazz—An Educational Problem." *Musical Quarterly* 12 (1926): 190–95.

Stuckenschmidt, H. H. "Jean Cocteau." *Blätter der Staatsoper* (February 1928): 17–19.

———. *Musik am Bauhaus.* Berlin: Bauhaus-Archiv, 1976.

———. "Der neue Klaviervirtuose." *Auftakt* 6 (1926): 79–82.

Tschechoslowakischen Akademie der Wissenschaften, ed. *Bibliographisches Verzeichnis der Kompositionen von Erwin Schulhoff.* Berlin: 1967.

Thomson, Virgil. "The Cult of Jazz." *Vanity Fair* 24 (June 1925): 54, 118.

———. *A Virgil Thomson Reader.* Boston: Houghton Mifflin, 1981.

van Vechten, Carl. "The Black Blues." *Vanity Fair* 24 (August 1925): 57, 86, 92.

West, Mae. *Goodness Had Nothing to Do with It.* Englewood Cliffs, N.J.: Prentice-Hall, 1959.

Whiteman, Paul, and Mary Margaret McBride. *Jazz.* New York: J. H. Sears, 1926.

———. "The Progress of Jazz: Problems Which Confront the American Composer in His Search for a Musical Medium." *Vanity Fair* 25 (January 1926): 52, 98.

Widmaier, Wolfgang. "Jazz: ein wilder Sturm über Europa." *Melos* 33 (1966): 12–17.

Wiéner, Jean. *Allegro Appassionato.* Paris: Pièrre Belford, 1978.

Wilson, Edmund, Jr. "The Aesthetic Upheaval in France: The Influence of Jazz in Paris and Americanization of French Literature and Art." *Vanity Fair* (February 1922): 49, 100.

Zwerin, Mike. *La Tristesse de Saint Louis: Swing under the Nazis.* New York: W. Morrow, 1987.

Scores and Recordings

"American" Piano Music by European Composers. Musical Heritage Society, MHS 7035F, 1984.

Auric, Georges. *Adieu! New York.* Paris: Editions Sirène, 1921.

An Experiment in Modern Music: Paul Whiteman at Aeolian Hall. The Smithsonian Collection, RCA RO28 /DMM2–0518, 1981.

Gershwin Plays Gershwin. Victrola American AVMI-1749, 1976.

A History of Jazz: The New York Scene. RBF RF3.

The King of Jazz, Paul Whiteman. Caliban 6025.

Milhaud, Darius. *La Création du monde.* Paris: M. Eschig, 1929.

Paul Whiteman and His Orchestra. Columbia Hall of Fame CL 2830.

Ravel, Maurice. *L'Enfant et les sortilèges.* Piano-vocal score. Paris: Durand, 1925.

Steppin' on the Gas: Rags to Jazz, 1913–1927. Recorded Anthology of American Music, Inc. New World Records NW 269, 1977.

Wiéner, Jean. *Cadences pour deux pianos.* Paris: Salabert, 1930.

———. *Sonatine syncopée.* Paris: M. Eschig, 1923.

———. *Trois blues chantes.* Paris: M. Eschig, 1924.

———. *Trois rag-caprices.* Vienna: Universal Edition, 1923.

———, and Clement Doucet. *Album Wiéner-Doucet.* Vienna: Universal Edition, 1929.

Jazz in France: Coverage from the Time

Ansermet, Ernst. *Ecrits sur la musique.* Ed. by J-Claude Piquet. Neuchâtel: Baconnière, 1983.

Bauer, Marion. "L'Influence du 'Jazz-Band.'" *La Revue musicale* 5 (1924): 31–36.

Bizet, René. "Dialogue sur l'esthetique du music-hall." *L'Esprit nouveau,* no.6 [n.d.]: 675–78.

———. "Le Music-Hall: Les Revues à grand spectacle." *L'Esprit nouveau,* no.3 [n.d.]: 352–54.

Coeuroy, André. *Panorama de la musique contemporaine.* Paris: Kra, 1928.

————, and André Schaeffner. *Le Jazz*. Paris: Claude Aveline, 1926.

Delage, Maurice. "La Musique de jazz." *Revue Pleyel* (April 1926): 18–20.

Jeanneret, Albert. "Les Concerts Wiéner." *L'Esprit nouveau*, no.14 (1923): 1664–65.

Milhaud, Darius. "The Day after Tomorrow." *Modern Music* 3 (November–December 1925): 22–24.

————. "Die Entwicklung der Jazz-Band und die Nordamerikansche Negermusik." *Anbruch* 7 (April 1925): 200–5.

————. "The Jazz Band and Negro Music." *Littell's Living Age*, 18 October 1924.

————. *Notes without Music*. New York: Alfred Knopf, 1953. Reprint. New York: Da Capo Press, 1970.

————. "Les Resources nouvelles de la musique." *L'Esprit nouveau*, no. 25 [n.d.]: [n.p.].

Panassie, Hughes. "La Vraie Physionomie de la musique de jazz." *La Revue musicale* 15 (1934): 359.

Pesquinne, Blaise. "Le Blues." *La Revue musicale* 15 (1934): 177–88.

————. "De l'improvisation dans le jazz." *La Revue musicale* 15 (1934): 273–82.

Rogers, M. Robert. "Jazz Influence on French Music." *Modern Music* 21 (January 1935): 53–68.

Schloezer, Boris van. "Junge Franzosen." *Die Musik* 18 (April 1926): 502–9.

Vuillermoz, Emile. "Rag-Time et jazz-band." In *Musiques d'aujourd'hui*. Paris: Cres, 1923.

Jazz in Germany: Coverage from the Time

Adorno, Theodor W. "Frankfurt a. M. Die Jazzklasse des Hochschen Konservatorium." *Die Musik* 21 (May 1929): 625–26.

Apold, Felix. "Die Jazzmusik." *Signale für die musikalische Welt* 87 (1929): 428–30.

Baresel, Alfred. "Jazz als Rettung." *Auftakt* 6 (1926): 213–16.

————. "Formeln des Jazz" *Die Musik* 22 (February 1930): 354–55.

————. *Instruktive Jazz-Etüden für Klavier*. Leipzig: Wilhelm Zimmerman, 1929.

————. "Kunst-Jazz." *Melos* 7 (1928): 354–57.

————. *Das neue Jazzbuch*. Leipzig: Zimmerman, 1929.

————. "Und dennoch: Jazz." *Rheinische Musik- und Theater-Zeitung* 27 (1926): 182, 184, 186.

————, and N. Federow. *Schule für Saxophon*. Leipzig: Zimmerman, 1926.

————, and Rio Gebhardt. *Jazz-Klavier-Schule*. Leipzig: Zimmerman, 1932.

Bernhard, Paul. *Jazz: Eine musikalische Zeitfrage*. Munich: Delphin, 1927.

Besten, Walter. "Der Jazz." *Rheinische Musik- und Theater-Zeitung* 28 (1927): 218–19.

Bukofzer, Manfred. "Soziologie der Jazz." *Melos* 8 (1929): 387–91.

Burian, Emil. Review of *Jazz-Requiem*. *Auftakt* 8 (1928): 20–21.

Chop, Max. "Jazz als Lehrfach." *Signale für die musikalische Welt* 86 (1928): 43–44.

Connor, Herbert. "Die 'Zukunftsmusik' des Mister Whiteman." *Signale für die musikalische Welt* 84 (1926): 1060–61.

David, Hans T. "Abschied vom Jazz." *Melos* 9 (1930): 413–17.

Felber, Erwin. "Erotismus und Primitivismus in der neueren Musik." *Die Musik* 21 (July 1925): 724–31.

————. Review of "Der Soldat u. die Tänzerin." *Anbruch* 9 (June 1927): 220.

Funkstunde (Berlin). 1924–30.

Grainger, Percy. "Jazz." *Anbruch* 7 (April 1925): 210–12.

Gräner, Georg. "Ein Buch von Jazz." *Allgemeine Musikzeitung* 55 (1928): 141–43.

————. "Jazz-Glosse." *Allgemeine Musikzeitung* 53 (1926): 121–22.

Gruenberg, Louis. "Der Jazz als Ausgangspunkt." *Anbruch* 7 (April 1925): 196–99.

————. "Vom Jazz und anderen Dingen." In *25 Jahre neue Musik*. Vienna: Universal Edition, 1925.

Gutman, Hans. "Mechanisierung und Jazz." *Anbruch* 8 (October–November 1926): 407–8.

Heiniss, William. "Irrationale Prophezeihungen dem Jazz." *Das neue Frankfurt* 6 (1926/27): 142–44.

Heuss, Alfred. "Der Foxtrott im Konzertsaal." *Zeitschrift für Musik* 90 (1923): 54.

Holde, Artur. "Der Sommer der Musik in Frankfurt a. Main." *Allgemeine Musikzeitung* 54 (1927): 918–19.

Holl, Karl. "Jazz im Konservatorium." *Frankfurter Zeitung*, 25 November 1927.

———. "Jazz im Konservatorium." *Melos* 7 (1928): 30–32.

Hornbostel, Erich M. v. "Ethnologisches zu Jazz." *Melos* 6 (1927): 510–12.

Iger, Artur. "Jazz-Industrie." *Auftakt* 6 (1926): 222–25.

"Der Jazz." *Allgemeine Musikzeitung* 55 (1928): 91.

"Jazz Bitterly Opposed in Germany." *The New York Times*, 11 March 1928.

"Jazz-Klasse an Dr. Hochs Konservatorium." *Zeitschrift für Musik* 94 (1927): 706–7."Jazz: Sonderheft." *Anbruch* 7 (April 1925).

"Jazz: Sonderheft." *Auftakt* 6, no. 10 (1926).

Jezek, J. "E. F. Burian." *Auftakt* 8 (1928): 197–98.

"Kampf um das Frankfurter Jazz-Konservatorium." *Neue Musik-Zeitung* 49 (1928): 266–68.

Korngold, Julius. "Jazzkultur." *Allgemeine Musikzeitung* 53 (1926): 225–26.

Kristl, Wilhelm. "Moderne Tanzmusik." *Auftakt* 5 (1925): 19–20.

Lyle, Watson. "Negermusik." *Auftakt* 5 (1925): 15–16.

Mauck, E. "Die Musik im Kabarett." *Berliner Tageblatt*, 22 February 1925.

Melichar, Alois. "Walzer und Jazz." *Die Musik* 20 (February 1928): 345–49.

Müller, E. J. "Jazz als Karikatur." *Auftakt* 6 (1926): 216–18.

Pelegrini, Alfred. "Jazz-Unfug." *Rheinische Musik- und Theater-Zeitung* 29 (1928): 317–18.

Rathaus, Karol. "Jazzdämmerung?" *Die Musik* 19 (February 1927): 333–36.

Riesenfeld, Paul. "Der Amerikanismus in der heutigen Musik." *Rheinische Musik- und Theater-Zeitung* 29 (1928): 303–5.

Schickele, René. *Symphonie für Jazz*. Berlin: Fischer, 1929.

Schildberger-Gleiwitz, Hermann. "Jazz-Musik." *Die Musik* 17 (September 1925): 914–23.

Schoen, Ernst. "Jazz und Kunstmusik." *Melos* 6 (1927): 512–19.

———. "Mátyás Seiber: Schule für Jazz Schlagzeug." *Melos* 8 (1929): 322–23.

———. "Musik und Rundfunk." *Das neue Frankfurt* 2 (1928): 29–31.

———. "Paul Bernhard 'Jazz, eine musikalische Zeitfrage'." *Melos* 6 (1927): 537–38.

Schück, Karl. "Jazz in Amerika." *Melos* 8 (1929): 391–93.

Schulhoff, Erwin. "Eine Jazz-Affaire." *Auftakt* 5 (1925): 220–22.

———. "Der Mondäne Tanz." *Auftakt* 4 (1924): 73–77.

———. "Zeitkunst: Saxophon und Jazzband." *Auftakt* 5 (1925): 179–83.

Schwers, Paul. "Die Frankfurter Jazz-Akademie im Spiegel der Kritik." *Allgemeine Musikzeitung* 54 (1927): 1246–48.

———. "Jazz als akademisches Lehrfach." *Allgemeine Musikzeitung* 54 (1927): 1194–95.

Seiber, Mátyás. "Jazz als Erziehungsmittel." *Melos* 7 (1928): 281–86.

———. "Jazz-Instrumente, Jazz-Klang und neue Musik." *Melos* 9 (1930): 122–26.

———. "Rhythmic Freedom in Jazz?" *Music Review* 6 (1945): 30–41, 89–94, 160–71.

———. *Schule für Schlagzeug*. Mainz: Schott, 1929.

Simon, Alicia. "Frau Musica in Amerika." *Signale für die musikalische Welt* 84 (1926): 1609–14.

———. "Jazz." *Auftakt* 6 (1926): 211–13.

Sonner, Rudolf. "Caféhausmusik." *Die Musik* 21 (March 1929): 440–43.

Steinhard, Erich. "Erwin Schulhoffs Musik zum 'Bürger als Edelmann'." *Auftakt* 7 (1927): 50–51.

———. "Erwin Schulhoffs 'Bürger als Edelmann'." *Allgemeine Musikzeitung* 53 (1926): 1012.

———. Review of *Flammen* by Erwin Schulhoff. *Auftakt* 12 (1932): 78–80.

———. "Whitemans Jazzorchester in Paris." *Auftakt* 6 (1926): 221–22.

Strobel, Heinrich. "Unzeitgemässe Proteste." *Anbruch* 10 (January 1928): 25.

Stuckenschmidt, H. H. "Blues: Anthologie von Negergesängen." *Melos* 6 (1927): 88.
———. "Die heutige Musik." *Das Kunstblatt* 8 (1924): 189.
Weber, Wolfgang. "Negermusik—Eine Urform der Unsrigen?" *Die Musik* 19 (June 1927): 697–702.
Weissmann, Adolph. *Die Entgötterung der Musik.* Trans. by Eric Blom as *Music Come to Earth.* London: J. M. Dent, 1930.
"Weiteres vom Jazz-Konservatorium." *Zeitschrift für Musik* 95 (1928): 32–33.
Westermeyer, Karl. Review of Paul Bernhard: *Jazz. Signale für die musikalische Welt* 85 (1927): 116.
Westphal, Kurt. "Negermusik und ihre Apostel." *Allgemeine Musikzeitung* 54 (1927): 421–22.

Busoni and Bekker

Bekker, Paul. *Briefe an zeitgenössische Musiker.* Berlin: Max Hesse, 1932.
———. *The Changing Opera.* Trans. by Arthur Mendel. London: J. M. Dent, 1936.
———. *Das deutsche Musikleben.* Berlin: Schuster and Loeffler, 1916.
———. "Dream at Twilight." *Modern Music* 12 (November–December 1934): 8–11.
———. "Impotenz oder Potenz?" *Frankfurter Zeitung,* 15 June 1920.
———. *Kritische Zeitbilder.* Berlin: Schuster and Loeffler, 1921.
———. "Die neue Oper." *Anbruch* 7 (January 1925): 8–13.
———. "The Opera Walks New Paths." *Musical Quarterly* 21 (1935): 266–78.
———. "Oper und Operntheater in der Gegenwart." *Die Musik* 22 (February 1930): 333–46.
———. *Das Operntheater.* Musikpädagogische Bibliothek 9. Quelle and Meyer, 1931.
———. *Richard Wagner: His Life in His Work.* Trans. by M. M. Bozman. Freeport, N.Y.: Books for Libraries, 1931.
———. "Was ist 'neue' Musik?" *Die Musik* 20 (December 1927): 161–74.
———. *Wesenformen der Musik.* Berlin: Selbstverlag der Novembergruppe, 1925.
Busoni, Ferruccio. *The Essence of Music and Other Papers.* Trans. by Rosamund Ley. London: Rockliff, 1957.
———. "Neue Klassizität?" *Frankfurter Zeitung,* 9 February 1920.
Dent, Edward J. "Busoni's Doctor Faust." *Music and Letters* 7 (1926): 196–208.
———. *Ferruccio Busoni: A Biography.* London: Oxford University Press, 1933.
Gatti, Guido. "Busoni the Musician." *Modern Music* 2 (April 1925): 21–23.
———. "The Stage-Works of Ferruccio Busoni." *Musical Quarterly* 20 (1934): 267–77.
Krenek, Ernst. "Busoni—Then and Now." *Modern Music* 19 (January–February 1942): 88–91.
Messing, Scott. *Neoclassicism in Music: From the Genesis of the Concept through the Schoenberg/Stravinsky Polemic.* Ann Arbor: UMI Research Press, 1988.
Pfitzner, Hans. *Reden, Schriften, Briefe.* Berlin: Hermann Luchterhand, 1955.
Saminsky, Lazare. "More about Faustus." *Modern Music* 5 (November–December 1927): 38–39.
Scherchen, Hermann. "Neue Klassizität?" *Melos* 1 (July 1920): 242–43.
Schubert, Giselher. "Aspekte der Bekkerschen Musiksoziologie." *The International Review of Music Aesthetics and Sociology* 1 (1970): 179–85.
Stuckenschmidt, H. H. *Ferruccio Busoni: Chronicle of a European.* Trans. by Sandra Morris. London: Calder and Boyars, 1970.

Paul Hindemith

Writings by Hindemith

Briefe. Ed. by Dieter Rexroth. Frankfurt: Fischer, 1982.
A Composer's World: Horizons and Limitations. Cambridge, Mass.: Harvard University Press, 1952.

"Über Musikkritik." *Melos* 8 (1929): 106–8.
"Zur mechanischen Musik." *Die Musikantengilde* 5 (1927): 155–59.

General Bibliography of Hindemith and His Work

Bekker, Paul. "An Paul Hindemith." In *Briefe an zeitgenössische Musiker*. Berlin: Max Hesse, 1932.
Benninghoren, Erich. "Der Geist im Werke Hindemiths." *Die Musik* 21 (July 1929): 718–23.
"Das Bild als Scheidungsgrund." *Berliner Börsen-Courier*, 7 June 1929.
Briner, Andres. *Paul Hindemith*. Mainz: Schott, 1971.
Browne, Arthur G. "Paul Hindemith and the Neo-Classic Music." *Music and Letters* 13 (1932): 42–58.
Die Deutsche Jugendmusikbewegung in Dokumenten ihrer Zeit von Anfängen bis 1933. Hamburg: Archiv der Jugendmusikbewegung, 1980.
Einstein, Alfred. "Paul Hindemith." *Modern Music* 3 (March–April 1926): 21–26.
Fraser, Andrew A. "Paul Hindemith." *Music and Letters* 10 (1929): 167–76.
Hindemith-Jahrbuch. ed. and publ. by the Paul-Hindemith-Institut, Frankfurt am Main.
Kemp, Ian. *Hindemith*. London: Oxford University Press, 1970.
Lippl, Alois Johannes. "Jugendmusik und Musik." In *Deutsche Musikpflege*. Ed. by Josef Fischer. Frankfurt: Bühnenvolksbund, 1925.
de la Motte-Haber, Helga, and Hans Emons. *Filmmusik: Eine systematische Beschreibung*. Munich: Carl Hanser, 1980.
Neumeyer, David. *The Music of Paul Hindemith*. New Haven, Conn.: Yale University Press, 1986.
Reich, Willi. "Paul Hindemith." *Musical Quarterly* 17 (1931): 486–96.
Rexroth, Dieter, ed. *Erprobungen und Erfahrungen zu Paul Hindemiths Schaffen in den zwanziger Jahren*. Mainz: Schott, 1978.
Schubert, Giselher. *Paul Hindemith in Selbstzeugnissen und Bilddokumenten*. Hamburg: Rowohlt, 1981.
Skelton, Geoffrey. *Paul Hindemith: The Man behind the Music*. London: Victor Gollancz, 1976.
Strauss, Richard. *Intermezzo*. London: Boosey and Hawkes, 1952.
Strobel. "Hindemith." *Auftakt* 7 (1927): 145–49.
––––––. *Paul Hindemith*. Mainz: Melos, 1931.
Stuckenschmidt, H. H. "Blick auf Paul Hindemith." *Frankfurter Allgemeine Zeitung*, 24 January 1964.
––––––. "Wandlungen bei Hindemith?" *Die neue Rundschau* 45 (1934): 590–91.
"Im Studio bei Hindemith." *Filmkurier* 10 (20 March 1930).
Weissmann, Adolf. "La Jeune Musique allemande et Paul Hindemith." *L'Esprit nouveau*, nos. 20, 22 (1925): [n.p.]
Westphal, Elizabeth. *Paul Hindemith: Eine Bibliographie des In- und Auslandes seit 1922 über ihn und sein Werk*. Cologne: Greven, 1957.
Willms, Franz. "Paul Hindemith: Ein Versuch." In *Von neuer Musik*. Cologne: F. J. Marcan, 1925.

Neues vom Tage

Altmann, Wilhelm. "Hindemiths *Neues vom Tage*." *Sackbut* 9 (1929): 399–400.
Bie, Oskar. "Festspiele." *Die neue Rundschau* 40 (1929): 264–66.
––––––. "*Neues vom Tage*." *München-Augsburger Zeitung*, 13 June 1929.
––––––. "Organisation der Festspiele? Fünf Premieren in 24 Stunden: *Neues vom Tage*." *Berliner Börsen-Courier*, 10 June 1929.
Blätter der Staatsoper 9 (June 1929).
Einstein, Alfred. "*Neues vom Tage*." *Berliner Tageblatt*, 10 June 1929.

Gutman, Hans. "Tabloid Hindemith." *Modern Music* 7 (December–January 1929–30): 34–37.

Hirschberg, Walther. "Paul Hindemiths *Neues vom Tage.*" *Signale für die musikalische Welt* 87 (1929): 758–60.

Holl, Karl. "*Neues vom Tage* in Darmstadt." *Melos* 8 (1929): 502.

Huth, Arno. "*Neues vom Tage.*" *Frankfurter Nachrichten,* 11 June 1929.

Joachim, Hans. "*Neues vom Tage.*" *B. Z. am Mittag,* 11 June 1929.

Kaiser, Hermann. "Oper: Darmstadt." *Die Musik* 22 (January 1930): 302–3.

Kastner, Rudolf. "*Neues vom Tage.*" *Berliner Morgenpost,* 7 June 1929.

Leichtentritt, Hugo. "Oper: Berlin." *Die Musik* 21 (April 1929): 848–50.

Lindlar, Heinrich. *77 Premieren.* Rodenkirchen: P. J. Tonger, [n.d.].

Marschalk, Max. "Hindemiths lustige Oper." *Vossische Zeitung,* 10 June 1929.

Mersmann, Hans, H. Schultze-Ritter, and H. Strobel. "Paul Hindemith: *Neues vom Tage.*" *Melos* 8 (1929): 369–71.

"Neue Opern. Paul Hindemith: *Neues vom Tage.*" *Rheinische Musik- und Theater-Zeitung* 30 (1929): 244–45.

"*Neues vom Tage.*" *Das Illustrierte Blatt* (Frankfurt), 22 June 1929.

Prunières, Henry. "Allemagne: *Neues vom Tage.*" *La Revue musicale* 10 (1929): 170–72.

Schrenk, Walther. "Berliner Festspiele: *Neues vom Tage* von Hindemith." *Deutsche-Allgemeine Zeitung,* 11 June 1929.

Schwers, Paul. "Hindemith: *Neues vom Tage.*" *Allgemeine Musikzeitung* 56 (1929): 637–38.

Steinhard, Erich. "Paul Hindemith: *Neues vom Tage.*" *Auftakt* 9 (1929): 181–84.

Strobel, Heinrich. "Hindemiths *Neues vom Tage.*" *Melos* 8 (1929): 257–59.

Stuckenschmidt, H. H. "Bühne und Kunst: Hindemiths *Neues vom Tage.*" *Bohemia* [Prague], 9 June 1929.

Wiegard, Heinrich. "*Neues vom Tage.*" *Leipziger Volkszeitung,* 10 June 1929.

Other Hindemith Works

Blitzstein, Marc. "*Hin und Zurück* in Philadelphia." *Modern Music* 5 (May-June 1928): 34–36.

Doflein, Erich. "Kammeroper." *Melos* 7 (1928): 337.

Einstein, Alfred. "Festvorstellung für den Tennis-Club Rot-Weiss." *Berliner Tageblatt,* 1 December 1930.

"Hin und zurück." *Das Illustrierte Blatt* [Frankfurt], 30 July 1927.

"Kleine Oper." *Neue Badische Landeszeitung,* 13 February 1928.

Leifs, Jon. "Deutsche Kammermusik." *Signale für die musikalische Welt* 85 (1927): 1129–32.

"Moderner Opern-Einakter-Abend." *National-Zeitung* [Basel], 15 May 1928.

"Neue Oper in Baden-Baden." *Das Illustrierte Blatt [Frankfurt],* 30 July 1927.

"Neue Opern im Landestheater." *Braunschweiger neuste Nachrichten,* 18 December 1928.

Steinhard, Erich. "Die Miniaturopern von Toch, Hindemith, Krenek." *Auftakt* 9 (1929): 309–12.

Tischer, Gerhard. "Deutsche Kammermusik Baden-Baden 1927." *Rheinische Musik- und Theater-Zeitung* 28 (1927): 320–22.

Scores and Recordings

Hin und zurück. Piano-vocal score. English translation by Marion Farquhar. Mainz: Schott, 1927.

Hin und zurück. On *Theatre Music in Berlin (1920s),* Candide CE 31044.

Kammermusik No. 1. Mainz: Schott, 1922.

Minimax. MHS 4573, 1982.

Neues vom Tage. Piano-vocal score. Mainz: Schott, 1929.

"Ouverture '*Neues vom Tage*'" in *Musik zwischen Kriegen.* Thorofon ETHK 341/4, 1987.

Die 7 Kammermusiken. Telefunken SLT 43110/12-B.
Suite 1922. Mainz: Schott, 1922.
Tanz der Holzpuppen: Foxtrot aus der Musik zu 'Tuttifäntchen.' Mainz: Schott, 1922.
Tuttifäntchen. Piano-vocal score. Mainz: Schott, 1922.

Ernst Krenek

Writings by Krenek

"Autobiographische Skizze." *Blätter der Staatsoper* 9 (December 1928): 1–3.
"Darius Milhaud." *Anbruch* 12 (April-May 1930): 135–40.
"Ernst Krenek über sich und sein Werk." *Blätter der Staatsoper* 8 (October 1927): 2–4.
Exploring Music. Trans. by Margaret Shenfield and Geoffrey Skelton. New York: October House, 1966.
"Forderung auch an diese Zeit: Freiheit des menschlichen Geistes!" *Anbruch* 14 (January 1932): 1–4
"Französisches und deutsches Musikempfinden." *Anbruch* 11 (February 1929): 53–57.
Horizons Circled: Reflections on My Music. Berkeley: University of California Press, 1974.
"Jonny erinnert sich." *Österreichische Musik-Zeitung* 4/5 (1980): 187.
"'Jonny spielt auf' und die Ausführenden." *Literarische Beilage*, 1 October 1927.
"Leben des Orest." *Anbruch* 12 (January 1930): 1–4.
"'Materialbestimmtheit' der Oper." *Anbruch* 9 (January–February 1927): 48–52.
"Mechanisierung der Künste." *i 10* 1 (1927): 376–80.
"Meine Drei Einakter." *Anbruch* 10 (May 1928): 158–61.
Music Here and Now. Trans. by Barthold Fles. New York: W. W. Norton, 1939.
"Musik in der Gegenwart." In *25 Jahre neue Musik*. Vienna: Universal Edition, 1925.
"Neue Humanität und alte Sachlichkeit." *Neue Schweizer Rundschau* 24 (April 1931): 43–60.
"'Neue Sachlichkeit' in der Musik." *i 10* 1 (1927): 216–18.
"The New Music and Today's Theatre." *Modern Music* 14 (May–June 1937): 200–203.
"Notwendige Entscheidungen." *Musica* 25 (1971): 557–61.
"Opera between the Wars." *Modern Music* 20 (January–February 1943): 102–11.
"Operette und Revue, Diagnose ihres Zustandes." *Anbruch* 11 (March 1929): 102–8.
"Opernerfahrung." *Anbruch* 11 (June 1929): 233–37.
Prosa, Dramen, Verse. Munich: Langen-Müller, 1965.
"Selbstportrait." *Melos* 37 (1970): 340–46.
"Self-Analysis." *New Mexico Quarterly* 23 (Spring 1953): 5–57.
"Über Sinn und Zweck des Theaters." *Anbruch* 9 (August–September 1927): 281–82.
"Zum Problem der Oper." In *Von neuer Musik*. Cologne: F. J. Marcan, 1925. Reprint in *Österreichische Musikzeitschrift* 5 (September 1950): 178–81.
"Zur Situation der Oper." *Auftakt* 12 (1932): 131–37.

General Bibliography on Krenek and His Work

Adorno, Theodor W. "Zur Deutung Kreneks." *Anbruch* 14 (February 1932): 42–44.
Austin, William. *"Susanna," "Jeannie," and "The Old Folks at Home."* New York: Macmillan, 1975.
Baresel, Alfred. "Walther Brügmann als Regisseur der Neuen Oper." *Anbruch* 9 (August–September 1927): 297–98.
Bekker, Paul. "An Ernst Krenek." In *Briefe an zeitgenössische Musiker*. Berlin: Max Hesse, 1932.
Bitter, Christof, and Manfred Schlösser, eds. *Begegnungen mit Eduard Erdmann*. Darmstadt: Erato, 1968.

Brecher, Gustav. "Opern-Übersetzung." Foreword by Stephan Stompor. *Jahrbuch der Komischen Oper Berlin* 2 (1962): 46–83

Deford, Frank. "The Ghost of Berlin [Leni Riefenstahl]." *Sports Illustrated,* 4 August 1986: 48–64.

Erdmann, Eduard. *Fox-trot in C-dur für Klavier.* Stockholm: Nordiska Musikförlaget, 1924.

Green, Marcia S. "Ravel and Krenek: Cosmic Music Makers." *College Music Symposium* 24 (Fall 1984): 96–104.

Hilmar, Ernst, ed. *Ernst Krenek: Katalog zur Ausstellung.* Vienna: Universal Edition, 1982.

Knessel, Lothar. "Das dunkle Wasser: Krenek zwischen 'Jonny' und Zeitfragen." *Neue Zeitschrift für Musik* 125 (1964): 553–54.

———— . *Ernst Krenek.* Vienna: Elisabeth Lafite, 1967.

Kolleritsch, Otto, ed. *Ernst Krenek.* Studien zur Wertungsforschung. Vol. 15. Vienna: Universal Edition, 1982.

The Krenek Festival. Program. Santa Barbara, Calif., April 5–8, 1979.

Ogdon, Will. "Conversation with Ernst Krenek." *Perspectives of New Music* 10 (Spring–Summer 1972): 102–10.

Preussner, Eberhard. "Ernst Krenek." *Anbruch* 11 (April 1929): 154–59.

Redlich, Hans F. "Heimat und Freiheit: Zur Ideologie der jüngsten Werke Ernst Kreneks." *Anbruch* 12 (February 1930): 54–58.

Rogge, Wolfgang. *Ernst Kreneks Opern.* Wolfenbüttel: Möseler, 1970.

Rossiter, Frank. *Charles Ives and His America.* New York: Liveright, 1975.

Saylor, Bruce. *The Writings of Henry Cowell.* New York: ISAM, 1977.

Schebera, Jürgen. "Herr Brecht, machen Sie doch weiter: Die Ära Brecher/Brügmann." *Theater der Zeit* 1 (1986): 49–52.

Schnabel, Artur. *My Life and Music.* New York: St. Martin's Press, 1963.

Schoenberg, Arnold. *Drei Satiren.* Vienna: Universal Edition, 1926.

———— . *Style and Idea.* Ed. by Leonard Stein. Trans. by Leo Black. New York: St. Martin's Press, 1975.

Stuckenschmidt, H. H. "Ernst Kreneks Opern." *Melos* 5 (1926): 365–68.

Sturm, George. "Encounters: Ernst Krenek." *EAM Accents* 2 (Spring 1979): 7–11.

Weissmann, Adolf. "Ernst Krenek." *Auftakt* 9 (1929): 268–73.

———— . "Ernst Krenek." *Modern Music* 6 (November–December 1928): 17–23.

Willner, Artur. "Eduard Erdmann." *Die Musik* 19 (May 1927): 582–86.

Zenck, Claudia Maurer. *Ernst Krenek: Ein Komponist im Exil.* Vienna: Elisabeth Lafite, 1980.

Jonny spielt auf

Note: Newspaper reviews are representative.

Aber, Adolf. "Le Dernier Opéra de Krenek." *La Revue musicale* 8 (1927): 305.

———— . "Ernst Krenek: *Jonny spielt auf.*" *Leipziger Neuste Nachrichten,* 11 February 1927.

———— . "Ernst Krenek: *Jonny spielt auf.*" *Signale für die musikalische Welt* 85 (1927): 286–88.

———— . "Ernst Krenek: *Jonny spielt auf* Uraufführung im Neuen Theater." *Leipziger Neuste Nachrichten,* 12 February 1927.

———— . "Ernst Krenek's Latest Opera a Modern Masterpiece." *Musical Courier,* 10 March 1927.

———— . "Ernst Krenek: *Jonny spielt auf.*"*Anbruch* 9 (March 1927): 127–32.

———— . "Oper: Leipzig." *Die Musik* 19 (April 1927): 523–24.

Adler, Lawrence. "'Jonny' and 'Manon'." *The Nation,* 27 February 1929.

"Al Jolson Greets 'Jonny'." *The New York Times,* 20 January 1929.

"American Premiere of *Jonny Spielt Auf* Finds Audience Pleased but Puzzled." *Musical Courier,* 24 January 1929.

Baresel, Alfred. *"Jonny spielt auf.* Leipziger Uraufführung der neuen Krenek-Oper." *Neue Musik-Zeitung* 48 (1927): 293–94.

———. *"Jonny spielt auf:* Leipziger Uraufführung der neuen Krenek-Oper." *Auftakt* 7 (1927).

Belitz, H. "Rostock." *Allgemeine Musikzeitung* 55 (1928): 818–19.

Bie, Oskar. *"Ernst Krenek:* Jonny spielt auf." Berliner *Börsen-Courier,* 9 October 1927.

———. *"Jonny spielt auf."* Berliner *Börsen-Courier,* 12 February 1927.

Blätter der Staatsoper 8 (October 1927).

Bonner, Eugene. "Jazz Operatics in Paris." *Outlook,* 1 August 1928.

Chop, Max. "Ernst Krenek: *Jonny spielt auf."* Signale für die musikalische Welt 85 (1927): 1477–80.

"Deutschland nun auch in Amerika durch *Jonny spielt auf* blossgestellt." *Zeitschrift für Musik* 96 (1929): 160–62.

Downes, Olin. "The Generation of Krenek." *The New York Times,* 13 January 1929.

———. *"Jonny spielt auf* Again." *The New York Times,* 29 January 1929.

———. *"Jonny spielt auf* Opera of this Age." *The New York Times,* 20 January 1929.

———. "Metropolitan Repertory of Next Season Exchanges New Operas for Old." *The New York Times,* 31 March 1929.

———. "Tibbett as Jazz Leader." *The New York Times,* 28 February 1929.

Einstein, Alfred. "Ernst Krenek: *Jonny spielt auf."* Berliner *Tageblatt,* 10 October 1927.

"Ernst Kreneks Jazz-Oper: *Jonny spielt auf."* Zeitschrift für Musik 94 (1927): 168–69.

Ernst Krenek: Jonny spielt auf. Der Sensations-Erfolg am *Leipziger Stadttheater.* Vienna: Universal Edition, 1927.

Fleischmann, Hugo R. "The First Jazz Opera and Operetta." *The Chesterian* (March 1928).

Frankenstein, Alfred V. "Jazz Arrives at the Opera." *Review of Reviews* 79 (1929): 138–40.

"G. F. Baker at Rehearsal." *The New York Times,* 18 January 1929.

Gräner, Georg. "Bruckner und der Geist des 'Jonny'." *Allgemeine Musikzeitung* 54 (1927): 1215–17.

Harry, Walter. "Zeitliches und Überzeitliches in *Jonny spielt auf."* Anbruch 10 (January 1928): 14–17.

Hartmann, Rudolf. "Operndramaturgische Glossen über Kreneks *Jonny spielt auf."* Neue Musik-Zeitung 48 (1927): 382–84.

Helder, Paul. "Florence Magpie and Jazz." *Opera News* 30 (1965): 22–23.

Hellmers, Gerhard. "Oper: Bremen." *Die Musik* 20 (February 1928): 377–78.

Heuss, Alfred. *"Ernst Krenek Jazz-Oper:* Jonny spielt auf." *Zeitschrift für Musik* 94 (1927): 168–69.

"In Aid of Babies' Hospital." *The New York Times,* 8 February 1929.

Jacob, Walter. "Über den Realismus in Kreneks *Jonny spielt auf."* Die Musik 20 (December 1927): 182–85.

"Jazz Opera for Benefit." *The New York Times,* 9 February 1929.

"'Jazz' Opera in Vienna." *The London Times,* 4 January 1928.

"Jonny spielt auf." A. Z. am Abend [Munich], 18 June 1928.

"Jonny spielt auf." Berliner *Börsen-Courier,* 8 October 1927.

"Jonny spielt auf." Blätter des Hamburger Stadttheaters 15 (1926/27).

"Jonny spielt auf." Living Age, 1 March 1929.

"Jonny spielt auf Again." *The New York Times,* 16 February 1929.

"Jonny spielt auf Again." *The New York Times,* 10 March 1929.

"Jonny spielt auf Excites Interest." *The New York Times,* 11 January 1929.

"Jonny Strikes Up the Band." *The Literary Digest* 100 (1929): 20–21.

Kleefeld, Wilhelm. "Drei Berliner Opernaufführungen." *Westermanns Monatshefte* 143 (1928): 675–76.

"Der Krawall im Gärtnerplatztheater." *A. Z. am Abend* [Munich], 18 June 1928.

"Kreneks Jonny-Dichtung im geistesgeschichtlichen Zusammenhang des Weltschmerzes und des Rousseauismus," Rudolf Majut, *Germanisch-Romanische Monatsschrift* 16. Abstract. *Die Musik* 21 (March 1929): 457.

Kutschera, Hans. "Kreneks *Jonny spielt auf* im Salzburger Landestheater." *Österreichische Musik Zeitschrift* 23 (1968): 286–87.

Laszlo, A. "Zürcher Stadttheater: *Jonny spielt auf* von Ernst Krenek." *Signale für die musikalische Welt* 86 (1928): 932–34.

Lohnmüller, Helmut. "Jonny spielt in Regensburg auf." *Melos* 35 (1968): 255.

Marschalk, Max. "Jazz-Oper und Mysterium." *Vossische Zeitung,* 11 October 1927.

Mersmann, Hans. "Ernst Krenek: *Jonny spielt auf.*" *Melos* 7 (1928): 24.

Mittag, Erwin. "Italienische Erstaufführung von Kreneks *Jonny spielt auf.*" *Österreichische Musik Zeitschrift* 18 (1963): 305–6.

"Modern Mechanism in *Jonny spielt auf.*" *The New York Times,* 17 January 1929.

Munk, Alois. "Jonny spielt auf." *Berliner Lokalanzeiger,* 9 October 1928.

Peyser, Herbert. "Jonny over There." *Modern Music* 6 (January–February 1929): 32–35.

Pisk, Paul. "Neue Musik in Wien." *Anbruch* 10 (January 1928): 27.

"Das Raritätenkabinett—Eine Rubrik zur Aufbewahrung von Kuriositäten." *Auftakt* 8 (1928): 21–22.

Raskin, Adolf. "Saarbrücken." *Die Musik* 20 (April 1928): 545–46.

Schaub, Hans F. "Kreneks 'Jonny' im Hamburger Stadttheater." *Allgemeine Musikzeitung* 54 (1927): 731–32.

Schwab, Heinrich W. "The Violinist on the Globe." *RIdIM/RCMI Newsletter* 7 (1983): 10.

Schwers, Paul. "*Jonny spielt auf.*" *Allgemeine Musikzeitung* 54 (1927): 151–52.

Strobel, Heinrich. "Ernst Krenek: *Jonny spielt auf.*" *Melos* 6 (1927): 130–31.

Stuckenschmidt, H. H. "Jazz auf der Opernbühne." *Vossische Zeitung,* 8 October 1927.

Thompson, Oscar. "Heard in New York." *Modern Music* 6 (May–June 1929): 20–24.

Tischer, Gerhard. "*Ernst Krenek:* Jonny spielt auf." *Rheinische Musik- und Theater-Zeitung* 28 (1927): 60.

"Die Universal-Edition im Jahre 1927." *Anbruch* 9 (October–November 1927): 405–6.

Vassenhove, L. Van. "'Jonny' ou le triomphe du jazz." *Courrier musical et théatrel* 30 (1928): 142–43.

Vernon, Grenville. "*Jonny spielt auf.*" *The Commonweal* 9 (1929): 429–30.

Weissmann, Adolf. "Jazz Opera at Leipsic [*sic*] and Berlin." *The Musical Times* 68 (1927): 367.

———. "Oper: Berlin." *Die Musik* 10 (December 1928): 219–20.

———. "Was ist eine Jazzoper?" *B. Z. am Mittag* [Berlin], 5 October 1927.

"Wie es Jonny in München, Budapest und Paris erging." *Zeitschrift für Musik* 95 (1928): 440.

Other Krenek Operas

Aber, Adolf. "Uraufführungen—Zwei Neue Krenek-Werke." *Die Musik* 22 (March 1930): 441–44.

Blätter der Staatsoper. 10 (March 1930). [*Leben des Orest.*]

Einstein, Alfred. "D'Alberts 'Schwarze Orchidee' und das 'Triptychon' von Krenek." *Berliner Tageblatt,* 3 December 1928.

Hiller, Paul. "Aus den westdeutschen Musikleben: Köln." *Allgemeine Musikzeitung* 54 (1927): 1226.

Hirschberg, Walter. "*Ernst Krenek: Leben des Orest,*" *Signale für die musikalische Welt* 88 (1930): 298–300.

Krienitz, Willy. "Oper: München." *Die Musik* 21 (January 1929): 301.

"Das 'Leben des Orest' und der Tod der 'neuen Sachlichkeit'." *Hamburg Mittagsblatt,* 17 April 1930.

List, Kurt. "Political Art: Notes on Krenek's *Karl V.*" *Modern Music* 15 (May-June 1938): 233–35.

Lopatnikoff, Nikolai. "New Life in Berlin." *Modern Music* 6 (May–June 1929): 25–28.

Meisterbernd, Max. "*Der Sprung über den Schatten.*" *Frankfurter Nachrichten,* 10 June 1924.

Mersmann, Hans. "Kurzopern." *Melos* 7 (1928): 347–49.

Pisk, Paul A. "Krenek: *Leben des Orest.*" *Auftakt* 10 (1930): 56–57.

Redlich, Hans F. "Kreneks 'Leben des Orest'." *Anbruch* 12 (February 1930): 75–76.

Rubardt, Paul. "Zwei Krenek-Uraufführungen in Leipzig." *Signale für die musikalische Welt* 88 (1920): 144–46.

Schwers, Paul. "Aus den Berliner Konzertsälen." *Allgemeine Musikzeitung* 50 (1923): 221.

————. "Das Frankfurter Tonkünstlerfest des Allgemeinen deutschen Musikvereins: Die Bühnenwerke." *Allgemeine Musikzeitung* 51 (1924): 526–28.

Musikzeitung 57 (1930): 103–4.

————. "Kreneks drei Einakter in der Berliner Staatsoper." *Allgemeine Musikzeitung* 55 (1928): 1334.

————. "Kreneks *Leben des Orest*. Vorbericht." *Allgemeine Musikzeitung* 57 (1930): 79–80.

————. "Kreneks 'Orestie' in der Krolloper." *Allgemeine Musikzeitung* 57 (1930): 255–56.

————. "*Leben des Orest*—Uraufführung." *Allgemeine* Steinhard, Erich. "Die Miniaturenopern von Toch, Hindemith, Krenek: Premiere in Prague." *Auftakt* 9 (1929): 309–12.

Strobel, Heinrich. "Kreneks 'Orest' in Leipzig." *Melos* 9 (1930): 98–99.

Stuckenschmidt, H. H. "Hellenic Jazz." *Modern Music* 7 (April–May 1930): 22–24.

"Tonkünstlerfest des Allgemeinen deutschen Musikvereins." *Frankfurter General-Anzeiger,* 10 June 1928.

Uhl, E. "Die Mai-Festwoche in Wiesbaden: Kreneks neue Einakter." *Allgemeine Musikzeitung* 55 (1928): 629–31.

Weissmann, Adolf. "Oper: Berlin." *Die Musik* 21 (January 1929): 296.

"Wiesbaden Hears New Krenek Operas." *The New York Times,* 10 June 1928.

Scores and Recordings

Blues aus der Oper, Jonny spielt auf. Gabriel Formiggini mit seinem Orchester. Electro-Vox 08610.

Blues aus Jonny spielt auf. Piano solo. Vienna: Universal Edition, 1927.

Der Diktator. Piano-vocal score. Vienna: Universal Edition, 1928.

Das geheime Königreich. Piano-vocal score. Vienna: Universal Edition, 1928.

Hymne des Jonny: "Nun ist die Geige mein"; "Leb wohl, mein Schatz" Blues und Song. Ludwig Hoffman mit Orchesterbegleitung. Odeon 0–6565.

Jonny spielt auf [excerpts]. Amadeo AVRS 5038.

Jonny spielt auf [excerpts]. Mace MXX 9094.

Jonny spielt auf. Full score. Vienna: Universal Edition, 1927.

Jonny spielt auf. Piano-vocal score. Vienna: Universal Edition, 1926.

Jonny spielt auf: *Libretto.* English version by Frederick H. Martens. New York: Frederick Rullman, 1928.

Kleine Suite für Klarinette und Kavier. Cassel: Bärenreiter, 1969.

'Leb wohl, mein Schatz' Blues aus der Oper Jonny spielt auf. Diez Weismann and Joh. de Leur. Elektrola E. G. 690.

'Leb wohl, mein Schatz' (Blues). Arr. by Gustav Blassner for violin and piano. Vienna: Universal Edition, 1927.

Potpourri aus der Oper Jonny spielt auf. Arr. by Jenö Takacs for piano solo. Vienna: Universal Edition, 1927.

Schwergewicht, oder Die Ehre der Nation. Piano-vocal score. Vienna: Universal Edition, 1928.

Der Sprung über den Schatten. Piano-vocal score. Vienna: Universal Edition, 1923.

"Tanzstudie." In *Grotesken Album.* Ed. by Charles Seelig. Vienna: Universal Edition, 1922.

"Three Merry Marches." On *Music for Winds, Brass and Percussion.* Louisville Orchestra LS-756.

Three Songs (Emile Verhaeren). Orion 79348.

Toccata und Chaconne über den Choral 'Ja, ich glaub an Jesum Christum.' Vienna: Universal Edition, 1923.

Kurt Weill

Essays by Weill

"Aktuelles Theater." *Melos* 8 (1929): 524–27.
"Albert Lortzing: *Zar und Zimmermann;* Jacques Offenbach: *Orpheus in der Unterwelt.*" *Der deutsche Rundfunk* 3 (1925): 1069.
"Albert Lortzing: Zu seinem 125. Geburtstag." *Der deutsche Rundfunk* 4 (1926): 2953.
Ausgewählte Schriften. Edited by David Drew. Frankfurt: Suhrkamp, 1975.
"Bekenntnis zur Oper." In *25 Jahre neue Musik.* Vienna: Universal Edition, 1926.
"Busonis *Faust* und die Erneuerung der Opernform." *Anbruch* 9 (January–February 1927): 53–56.
"Busoni und die neue Musik." *Der neue Weg* 54 (October 1925): 282–83.
"Ewigskeitswert?" *Berliner Tageblatt,* 30 December 1931.
"Ferruccio Busoni: Zu seinem 60. Geburtstag." *Der deutsche Rundfunk* 4 (1926): 872.
"Das Formproblem der modernen Oper." *Der Scheinwerfer,* February 1932.
"The Future of Opera in America." *Modern Music* (May–June 1937): 183–88.
"Gesellschaftsbildende Oper." *Berliner Börsen-Courier,* 19 February 1929.
"Igor Stravinsky: *Oedipus Rex.*" *Der deutsche Rundfunk* 6 (1928): 3177.
"Die neue Oper." *Der neue Weg* 55 (1926): 24–25.
"Notiz zum Jazz." *Anbruch* 11 (March 1929): 138.
"Die Oper—Wohin?" *Berliner Tageblatt,* 31 October 1929.
"Situation der Oper." *Melos* 10 (1931): 43–45.
"Tanzmusik." *Der deutsche Rundfunk* 4 (1926): 732–33.
"Verschiebungen in der musikalischen Produktion." *Berliner Tageblatt,* 1 October 1927.
"Wirklich eine Opernkrise?" *Deutsche Allgemeine Zeitung,* 8 July 1932.
"Zeitoper." *Melos* 7 (1928): 106–8.

General Bibliography on Weill and His Work

Aber, Adolf. "Kurt Weill und sein Schaffen." *Leipziger Bühnenblätter* 14 (1927/28): 116–18.
Bekker, Paul. "An Kurt Weill." In *Briefe an zeitgenössische Musiker.* Berlin: Max Hesse, 1932.
Belaiev, Victor. "Stravinsky, Weill, and Jazz." *Christian Science Monitor,* 18 May 1929.
Brecht, Bertolt. *Brecht on Theatre.* Ed. by John Willett. New York: Hill and Wang, 1964.
Curjel, Hans. "Erinnerungen um Kurt Weill." *Melos* 37 (March 1970): 81–85.
Drew, David. *Kurt Weill: A Handbook.* Berkeley: University of California Press, 1987.
———. *"Kurt Weill and His Critics." Times Literary Supplement,* 3 October 1975: 1142–44 and 10 October 1975: 1198–1200.
———. "Topicality and the Universal: The Strange Case of Weill's *Die Bürgschaft. Music and Letters* 39 (1958): 242–55.
———, ed. *Über Kurt Weill.* Frankfurt: Suhrkamp, 1975.
Fleischer, Herbert. "Kurt Weill: Versuch einer einheitlichen Stilbetrachtung." *Anbruch* 14 (September 1932): 135–37.
Goll, Yvan. *Oeuvres.* Ed. by Claire Goll and François Xavier. 2 Vols. Paris: Emile and Paul, 1968–70.
Jarman, Douglas. *Kurt Weill: An Illustrated Biography.* Bloomington: Indiana University Press, 1982.
Jolles, Heinz. "Paraphrase über Kurt Weill." *Neue Musik-Zeitung* 49 (1928): 541–44.
Kaiser, George. *Werke.* Ed. by Walther Huder. Frankfurt: Propyläen, 1972.
Kastner, Rudolf. "Kurt Weill: Eine Skizze." *Anbruch* 7 (October 1925): 453–56.
Koenigsgarten, Hugo F. "Georg Kaiser, the Leading Playwright of Expressionism." *German Life and Letters* 3 (1938–39): 195–205.

Kotschenreuther, Hellmut. *Kurt Weill.* Berlin: Max Hesse, 1962.

Kowalke, Kim H. *Kurt Weill in Europe.* Ann Arbor: UMI Research Press, 1979.

_____ , ed. *A New Orpheus: Essays on Kurt Weill.* New Haven, Conn.: Yale University Press, 1986.

Krojanker, E. T. "Kurt Weill über seine Oper." *Leipzig Neuste Nachrichten,* 18 February 1928.

"Kurt Weill Has Secured Niche of His Own at 35." *New York World Telegram,* 21 December 1935.

Lenya, Lotte. "Kurt Weill's Universal Appeal." *Music Journal* 17 (1959): 48, 77–78.

Machabey, A. "Kurt Weill et le drame lyrique allemand." *Revue d'allemagne* 7 (1933): 632–38.

Mitchell, Donald. "Kurt Weill's *Dreigroschenoper* and German Cabaret Opera in the 1920s." *The Chesterian* 25 (1950): 1–6.

Padmore, Elaine. "Kurt Weill." *Music and Musicians* 21 (1972): 34–40.

Parmée, Margaret. *Ivan Goll: The Development of his Poetic Themes and Their Images.* Bonn: Bouvier, 1981.

Prigsheim, Klaus. "Kurt Weill." *Blätter der Staatsoper* 9 (October 1928): 1–4.

Sanders, Ronald. *The Days Grow Short.* New York: Holt, Rinehart, and Winston, 1980.

Strobel, Heinrich. "Erinnerung an Kurt Weill." *Melos* 17 (1950): 133–36.

_____ . "Kurt Weill." *Anbruch* 10 (1928): 57–59.

_____ . "Kurt Weill." *Melos* 6 (1927): 427–33.

Toller, Ernst. *Prosa, Briefe, Dramen, Gedichte.* Reinbek bei Hamburg: Rowohlt, 1961.

Waterhouse, John C. G. "Weill's Debt to Busoni." *Musical Times* 105 (1964): 897–99.

Der Zar lässt sich photographieren

Aber, Adolf. "Neuheiten in der Oper." *Leipzig Neuste Nachrichten,* 19 February 1928.

_____ . "Oper: Leipzig." *Die Musik* 20 (April 1928): 542–43.

_____ . "Weill und Spinelli." *Leipzig Neuste Nachrichten,* 20 February 1928.

Adorno, Theodor W. "Frankfurt a. M." *Die Musik* 20 (September 1928): 923–34.

_____ . "Protagonist und Zar." *Die Musik* 20 (September 1928): 923–24.

Baresel, Alfred. "Der neue Kurt Weill." *Neue Musik-Zeitung* 49 (1928): 383–84.

Blätter der Staatsoper 9 (October 1928).

Einstein, Alfred. "Gay German Opera: Reich Provinces Hear Lighter Novelties by Dressel, Weill and Wellesz." *The New York Times,* 22 April 1928.

_____ . "Unproblematische und problematische Oper." *Berliner Tageblatt,* 15 October 1928.

Gail, H. R. "Altenburg: Weill-Doppelpremiere." *Anbruch* 10 (May 1928): 179.

Hamann, Ernst. "Dessau." *Die Musik* 20 (June 1928): 620.

Heinzen, Carl. "Düsseldorf: Oedipus and Zar." *Anbruch* 10 (May 1928): 179.

_____ . "Oper: Düsseldorf." *Die Musik* 20 (May 1928): 613.

Holde, Arthur. "Kurt Weills Operneinakter im Frankfurter Opernhaus." *Allgemeine Musikzeitung* 5 (1928): 856.

Holl, Karl. "*Der Protagonist, Der Zar lässt sich photographieren.*" *Frankfurter Zeitung,* 21 June 1928.

Kastner, Rudolf. "Lustspiel und Opernpremieren." *Berliner Morgenpost,* 16 October 1928.

Müller, Ernst. "*Der Zar lässt sich photographieren.*" *Allgemeine Musikzeitung* 55 (1928): 191–92.

Ohrmann, Fritz. "Kurt Weill in der Berliner Städtischen Oper." *Signale für die musikalische Welt* 86 (1928): 1279–82.

Stefan, Paul. "Antinomie der neuen Oper: Kurt Weill und Stravinsky." *Anbruch* 10 (March–April 1928): 119–22.

Steinhard, Erich. "Praguer Tagebuch." *Auftakt* 8 (1928): 295.

Stier, Ernst. "Der Zar von Kurt Weill." *Braunschweiger Allgemeiner Anzeiger,* 18 December 1928.

Strobel, Heinrich. "Kurt Weill: *Der Zar lässt sich photographieren.*" *Melos* 7 (1928): 137–38.

Stuckenschmidt, H. H. "Kurt Weill: *Der Zar lässt sich photographieren*." In *Oper in dieser Zeit*. Hannover: Friedrich, 1964.

Weissmann, Adolf. "Kurt Weill's New Opera." *Christian Science Monitor*, 24 March 1928.

"*Der Zar lässt sich photographieren*." *Südwestdeutsche Rundfunk Zeitung*, 24 June 1928.

Other Weill Operas

Baresel, Alfred. "*Royal Palace*." *Neue Musik-Zeitung* 48 (1927): 316–17.

"Berlin Opera Mingles Auto Horn, Films, Jazz." *The New York Times*, 3 March 1927.

Bie, Oskar. "*Royal Palace*." *Berliner Börsen-Courier*, 3 March 1927.

Blätter der Staatsoper 7 (February 1927). [*Royal Palace*.]

Gutman, Hans. "Kurt Weill: *Royal Palace*." *Auftakt* 7 (1927): 74–76.

Kastner, Rudolf. "Revue in der Staatsoper." *Berliner Morgenpost*, 4 March 1927.

Leichtentritt, Hugo. "Berlin, Too Has Its Jazz Opera." *Musical Courier*, 24 March 1927.

Marschalk, Max. "Varieté in der Staatsoper." *Vossische Zeitung*, 4 March 1927.

Mersmann, Hans. "*Royal Palace*." *Melos* 6 (1927): 132–33.

"Neue Oper in Baden-Baden." *Das Illustrierte Blatt [Frankfurt]*, 30 July 1927.

Reissig, Elizabeth. "Die moderne Idee in der Opern-Regie: Franz Ludwig Hörth." In *Erlebte Opernkunst*. Berlin: Österheld, 1928.

Schrenk, Walther. "Operndämmerung: *Royal Palace* in der Staatsoper." *Deutsche Allgemeine Zeitung*, 4 March 1927.

Schwers, Paul. "Kurt Weill in der Berliner Staatsoper." *Allgemeine Musikzeitung* 54 (1927): 240–41.

Stefan, Paul. "Berlin: Weill, *Royal Palace*." *Anbruch* 9 (March 1927): 133–34.

Weissmann, Adolf. "Germany's Latest Music Dramas." *Modern Music* 4 (May–June 1927): 24–25.

———. "Oper: Berlin." *Die Musik* 19 (April 1927): 518.

Westermeyer, Karl. "Berlin: Kurt Weill: *Royal Palace*." *Rheinische Musik- und Theater-Zeitung* 28 (1927): 108–110.

———. "*Royal Palace*." *Signale für die musikalische Welt* 8 (1927): 330–32.

Scores and Recordings

Brecht, Bert, and Kurt Weill. *Mahagonny-Songspiel: Das kleine Mahagonny*. Ed. by David Drew. Piano-vocal score. Vienna: Universal Edition, 1963.

Der neue Orpheus. Piano-vocal score. Vienna: Universal Edition, 1926.

Royal Palace. Piano-vocal score. Vienna: Universal-Edition, 1926.

The Unknown Kurt Weill. Nonesuch D-79019, 1981.

Der Zar lässt sich photographieren. Piano-vocal score. Vienna: Universal Edition, 1927.

Sam Wooding

Beaton, Josephine, and Howard Rye. "Sam Wooding in England and France." *Storyville* 74 (December 1977–January 1978): 47–49.

Behncke, Bernard H. "Sam Wooding and the Chocolate Kiddies at the Thalia-Theater in Hamburg 28th July 1925 to 24th August 1925." *Storyville* 60 (August–September 1975): 214–21.

Bergmeier, Horst J. P. "Sam Wooding Recapitulated." *Storyville* 74 (December 1977–January 1978): 44–47.

Englund, Björn. "Chocolate Kiddies: The Show That Brought Jazz to Europe and Russia in 1925." *Storyville* 62 (December 1975–January 1976): 44–50.

———. "Redan för 40 Ar Sedan [Sam Wooding]. *Orkester Journalen* (December 1964): 16–17.

Bibliography 275

Fleming, Herb. "Old Sam: The Man Who Brought Jazz to Europe." *Jazz Journal* (May 1968): 8–10.

Larsen, John, and Hans Larsen. "The Chocolate Kiddies in Copenhagen." *Record Research* (April 1965): 3, 14.

Napoleon, Art. "A Pioneer Looks Back: Sam Wooding 1967." *Storyville* (February-March and April-May 1967): 3–8, 37–39, 4–8.

Olausson, Rune. "Wooding—verklig veteran." *Orkester Journalen* (April 1963): 11.

Sam Wooding and His Chocolate Dandies. Biograph BLP-12025

Wooding, Samuel. "Eight Years Abroad with a Jazz Band." *Etude* 57 (April 1938): 233–34, 282.

D'Albert, Antheil, Brand, Grosz, Rathaus, Schoenberg, Schreker, and Toch

Aber, Adolf. "Oper: Leipzig [*Die schwarze Orchidee*]. *Die Musik* 21 (January 1929): 299–300.

Adorno, Theodor W. "Arnold Schoenberg: *Von Heute auf Morgen.*" *Anbruch* 12 (February 1930): 72–74.

———. "Arnold Schoenberg: *Von Heute auf Morgen.*" *Die Musik* 22 (March 1930): 445–46.

———. "Georg Antheil: *Transatlantik.*" *Die Musik* 22 (July 1930): 754–56.

———. "Oper: Frankfurt a.M. [*Von Heute auf Morgen*]." *Die Musik* 22 (January 1930): 304.

———. "*Transatlantic.*" *Modern Music* 7 (June-July 1930): 38–41.

Antheil, George. *Bad Boy of Music.* Garden City, N.J.: Doubleday, 1945.

———. "The Negro on the Spiral." In *Negro: An Anthology.* Ed. by Nancy Cunard. New York: Frederick Ungar, 1970.

———. "Opera: A Way Out." *Modern Music* 11 (January-February 1934): 89–94.

———. "Voraussetzungen für meine Oper Transatlantic." *Anbruch* 12 (January 1930): 8–10.

———. "Wanted: Opera by and for Americans." *Modern Music* 7 (June–July 1930): 11–16.

"Arnold Schoenberg: *Von Heute auf Morgen.*" *Rheinische Musik- und Theater-Zeitung* 31 (1930): 39.

Baresel, Alfred. "Berichte: D'Albert, *Die schwarze Orchidee.*" *Anbruch* 10 (November–December 1928): 437–38.

Bechert, Paul. "59th German Tonkünstlerfest a Tryout for New Operas." *Musical Courier,* 3 August 1929.

Blätter der Staatsoper 9 (June 1929). [*Die schwarze Orchidee.*]

Blätter der Staatsoper 10 (March 1930). [*Maschinst Hopkins.*]

Blätter der Staatsoper 10 (December 1930). [*Fremde Erde.*]

Eckhardt, Karl Egon. "Bemerkungen zu Max Brands *Maschinist Hopkins.*" *Das Prisma: Blätter der Vereinigten Stadttheater Duisburg-Bochum* 5 (1929–30): 294–96.

Ford, Hugh. *Four Lives in Paris.* San Francisco: North Point Press, 1986.

Gutman, Hans. "Eine Amerika-Oper." *Melos* 9 (1930): 260–62.

Hába, Alois. "Arnold Schoenberg: *Von Heute auf Morgen.*" *Auftakt* 10 (1930): 54–55.

Hailey, Christopher. "Zur Entstehungsgeschichte der Oper 'Christophorus'." In *Franz-Schreker-Symposium.* Ed. by Elmar Budde and Rudolph Stephan. Berlin: Schriftenreihe der Hochschule der Künste, 1980.

Hirschberg, Walther. "Eugen d'Alberts *Die schwarze Orchidee.*" *Signale für die musikalische Welt* 87 (1929): 760.

———. "Fremde Erde." *Signale für die musikalische Welt* 88 (1930): 1494–96.

Holde, Artur. "Achtung, Aufnahme!" *Allgemeine Musikzeitung* 57 (1930): 403–4.

———. "*Transatlantic.*" *Allgemeine Musikzeitung* 57 (1930): 598.

———. "*Von Heute auf Morgen.*" *Allgemeine Musikzeitung* 57 (1930): 133–34.

Holl, Karl. "Es wird gedreht [*Achtung! Aufname!*]." *Melos* 9 (1930): 193–94.

Keller, Hans. "Schoenberg's Comic Opera." *The Score* (July 1958): 27–36.

Kroll, Erwin. "Ernst Tochs Operncapriccio: *Der Fächer.*" *Die Musik* 22 (July 1930): 757–58.

Latzco, Ernst. "Eugen d'Albert: *Die schwarze Orchidee.*" *Rheinische Musik- und Theater-Zeitung* 29 (1928): 543.

"Max Brand: *Maschinist Hopkins.*" *Rheinische Musik- und Theater-Zeitung* 30 (1929): 158–59.

Müller, Ernst. "*Die schwarze Orchidee.*" *Allgemeine Musikzeitung* 55 (1928): 1335.

Ohrmann, Fritz. "Max Brands Oper *Maschinist Hopkins.*" *Signale für die musikalische Welt* 88 (1930): 395–99.

Petzet, Walter. "*Maschinist Hopkins.*" *Signale für die musikalische Welt* 87 (1929): 1363–65.

Pisk, Paul A. "Ernst Toch." *Musical Quarterly* 24 (1938): 438–50.

————. "Schoenberg's Twelve-Tone Opera." *Modern Music* 7 (April–May 1930): 18–21.

Preussner, Eberhard. "Schoenberg: *Von Heute auf Morgen.*" *Melos* 9 (1930): 138–39.

Pringsheim, Heinz. "*Die schwarze Orchidee.*" *Allgemeine Musikzeitung* 56 (1929): 666.

Rasch, Hugo. "*Fremde Erde.*" *Allgemeine Musikzeitung* 57 (1930): 1170–71.

Rathaus, Karol. "Meine Oper, *Fremde Erde.*" *Anbruch* 7 (January 1930): 13.

Redlich, Hans F. "George Antheil: *Transatlantic.*" *Anbruch* 12 (June 1930): 216–17.

Reger, Erik. "Musikfestwoche der 'jungen Generation' [*Maschinist Hopkins*]." *Die Musik* 21 (September 1929): 890–95.

Riesenfeld, Paul. "Die Romantik der neuen Sachlichkeit [*Maschinist Hopkins*]." *Signale für die musikalische Welt* 87 (1929): 1075–78.

Schliepe, Ernst. "*Fremde Erde.*" *Deutsche Musik Zeitung* 32 (1931): 5–6.

Schott, Georg. "Achtung! Aufname!" *Signale für die musikalische Welt* 88 (1930): 394–95.

————. "George Antheil *Transatlantic.*" *Signale für die musikalische Welt* 88 (1930): 263–64.

————. "Schoenbergs *Von Heute auf Morgen.*" *Signale für die musikalische Welt* 88 (1930): 179–80.

Schreker-Bures, Haidy, and H. H. Stuckenschmidt. *Franz Schreker.* Vienna: Elisabeth Lafite, 1970.

Schwers, Paul. "*Maschinist Hopkins.*" *Allgemeine Musikzeitung* 56 (1929): 455.

Shirley, Wayne D. "Another American in Paris: George Antheil's Correspondence with Mary Curtis Bok." *The Quarterly Journal of the Library of Congress* (January 1977): 2–22.

Steinhard, Erich. "*Maschinist Hopkins.*" *Auftakt* 10 (1930): 293–94.

Stuckenschmidt, H. H. "Aereoplansonate." *Auftakt* 6 (1926): 178–81.

————. "Antheil." *Kunstblatt* 9 (1925): 181–83.

————. "Schoenbergs neue Oper in Frankfurt a.M." *Melos* 9 (1930): 96–98.

Thompson, Oscar. "Fly-wheel Opera." *Modern Music* 7 (December–January 1929): 39–42.

————. "*Transatlantic* Brings Novel Variation on the American Theme." *Musical America* 50 (July 1950): 6.

Thompson, Randall. "American Composers V: George Antheil." *Modern Music* 8 (May–June 1931): 17–27.

Weber, Waldemar. "Uraufführung in Duisburg [*Maschinist Hopkins*]." *Anbruch* 11 (May 1929): 223–25.

Whitesitt, Linda. *The Life and Music of George Antheil (1900–1959).* Ann Arbor: UMI Research Press, 1983.

"Zwei Opern-Uraufführungen in Leipzig [*Die schwarze Orchidee*]." *Zeitschrift für Musik* 96 (1929): 36–37.

Scores

Albert, Eugen d'. *Foxtrot der Bessie.* Arr. for voice and piano. Vienna: Universal Edition, 1929.

————. *Phantasie.* Based on music from *Die schwarze Orchidee.* Arr. for piano solo by Otto Singer. Vienna: Universal Edition, 1929.

————. *Die schwarze Orchidee.* Piano-vocal score. Vienna: Universal Edition, 1928.

————. *Walzer de Grace.* Arr. for voice and piano. Vienna: Universal Edition, 1929.

Antheil, George. *Tango aus der Oper* Transatlantic. Vienna: Universal Edition, 1930.

―――― . *Transatlantic*. Piano-vocal score. Vienna: Universal Edition, 1929.

Brand, Max. *'Ma-Bram-Hob-Han' Foxtrot aus der Oper Maschinist Hopkins*. Arr. for voice and piano. Vienna: Universal Edition, 1929.

―――― . *Maschinist Hopkins*. Piano-vocal score. Vienna: Universal Edition, 1928.

Grosz, Wilhelm. *Achtung! Aufname!* Vienna: Universal Edition, 1930.

Rathaus, Karol. *Fremde Erde*. Vienna: Universal Edition, 1930.

Schoenberg, Arnold. *Von Heute auf Morgen*. Sämtliche Werke Abteilung III, vol. 7. Mainz: Schott, 1970.

Schreker, Franz. *Christophorus, oder Die Vision einer Oper*. Piano-vocal score. Berlin: Adler, 1931.

Toch, Ernst. *Der Fächer*. Piano-vocal score. Mainz: Schott, 1930.

Index